PAST AND PRESENT

Jack O'Connell
Portland
1st April 1996

THE GOTHAM LIBRARY
OF THE NEW YORK UNIVERSITY PRESS

The Gotham Library is a series of original works and critical studies, published in paperback primarily for student use and also as the Gotham hardcover edition primarily for use by libraries and the general reader. Devoted to significant works and major authors and to literary topics of enduring importance, Gotham Library texts offer the best in literature and criticism.

Comparative Literature & Foreign Language Literature: Robert J. Clements, Editor

Comparative & English Language Literature: James W. Tuttleton, Editor

Past and Present

BY

THOMAS CARLYLE

EDITED WITH AN INTRODUCTION AND NOTES BY

RICHARD D. ALTICK

NEW YORK · NEW YORK UNIVERSITY PRESS · 1977

Thomas Carlyle: 1795–1881

Past and Present was first published in 1843.

First published by Houghton Mifflin Company as a Riverside Edition. Copyright © 1965 by Richard Altick. Reprinted by special arrangement with Houghton Mifflin Company. All rights reserved.

Library of Congress Catalog Card Number: 77-70381
ISBN: 0-8147-0561-8 cloth
0-8147-0562-6 paper

Manufactured in the United States of America

INTRODUCTION

By Richard D. Altick

I

Like a number of other noteworthy works of English literature, *Past and Present* had its origin in a specific historical circumstance. The "condition of England question" which Carlyle discusses in his impassioned prose had been thrust into the forefront of the English consciousness by the ominous events of the summer of 1842, climaxing developments that had begun six years earlier. Since 1836 England had been suffering from severe economic depression. There was a series of bad harvests, the price of bread was cruelly high, wages were falling, and unemployment was reducing hundreds of thousands of workers to pauperism. For these and other reasons, the anger of the laboring class, already vented over the past several years in sporadic mass meetings and disturbances, exploded in a series of strikes and riots during July and August, 1842. Although centering in the industrial Midlands, and more specifically in the factory city of Manchester, they reached also into Scotland and the Welsh collieries. Military assistance was needed before they could be quelled, and hundreds of demonstrators were arrested, tried, and in many cases given stiff sentences. These outbreaks produced a fresh and alarming recrudescence of the dread under which the country had first lived when the volatile "Jacobin" spirit of the French Revolution filled the English air, and which had periodically been revived in the ensuing half-century as the working class had new cause for disaffection. In the latter months of this year, Carlyle was only one of many who read the latest outbursts of violence as the handwriting on the wall. Unless something were done swiftly and effectively, the country might well see the bitter friction between social classes flame into revolution.

Although the sources of resentment were numerous, in *Past and Present* Carlyle concentrates upon the Corn Laws, which were a dominant political issue in 1842. Enacted in 1815 as a measure to ease the country's passage from a wartime economy to that of peace, they were designed to protect home agriculture. A sliding scale introduced in 1828, and modified in 1842, supported the price of corn (wheat and other cereal grains) by imposing a graduated tariff on foreign corn; the lower the domestic price, the higher the tariff. Only when the domestic price rose to 73 shillings a quarter (eight bushels) was the tariff allowed to fall to a nominal figure. Thus relieved of competition from imported grain, English farmers could charge all the protected market would bear. In 1841–42 bread cost from 10*d.* to 1*s.* 2*d.* — an average of a shilling — a loaf. At that moment, agricultural laborers commonly earned nine or ten shillings a week, miners fifteen, and artisans in the building trades eighteen shillings for a (64-hour) week.

Tight though the squeeze was on the employed, it was even tighter on the jobless, whose numbers were growing every month. In 1842 one person in every eleven was a pauper; in Manchester, where 116 mills were closed, 12,000 families were being supported, in a manner of speaking, by charity, and in Birmingham a fifth of the population was on poor relief. The progress of the industrial revolution, which had made Britain "the workshop of the world," had also drastically altered her economy. The spread of machinery was depriving multitudes of handloom weavers and hosiers of their livelihood; they were, understandably, conspicuous among the crowds who surged through the streets and cheered inflammatory orators in the course of the "Manchester insurrection." At the same time, Britain had also become more sensitive to the fluctuations of foreign trade. She prospered, of course, when other nations were in a position to buy. But countries that constituted markets for her manufactured exports needed to sell grain to her in turn; and this source of foreign exchange the Corn Laws dried up. In retaliation, some European nations erected high tariff barriers against British goods, and in this very summer of 1842, the American tariff also was raised. Hence the country was burdened by serious overproduction; the products of its mills and factories were a glut on the market, finding buyers neither abroad nor at home. This starving-in-the-midst-of-plenty, a condition by no means unknown in our own age, occasioned some of the most bitterly ironic passages in Carlyle's "tract for the times."

The desperation of the masses was intensified by the Poor Law Amendment Act of 1834, which was intended to wipe out the centuries-old abuses and corruption associated with poor relief by taking it out of the hands of the local (parish) authorities and vesting it in a centralized national office, with strict and uniform rules. The most hated feature of the new system was the proposed total abolition of outdoor relief — the dole — and the substitution of workhouses where the conditions of life and labor were deliberately made so wretched as to deter every man and woman, whether able-bodied or unemployable, from being poor. Although the plan made considerable headway, the increase of paupers in these years of the locust outran the building of workhouses, so that, as the figures Carlyle cites on page 7 reveal, more than five times as many persons were on the dole as were in the "Poor Law Bastilles." But the bitterness engendered by this callous institutionalized method of dealing with human misery was not mitigated by the mere fact that its progress had been slowed by events.

These, then, were the chief circumstances leading to the combustible atmosphere of England at the time *Past and Present* was written. The book's *dramatis personae*, drawn directly from the historical situation, consist of three groups, whose conflict forms Carlyle's indignant, indeed tragic, theme. First, the workers. "Chartist," the name applied to their rebellious forces at the time and in subsequent histories, is convenient, but it is inaccurately used in the case of the men who, far from belonging to any special faction or party or subscribing to any formal set of principles, were simply hungry and hopeless. The Chartists, properly speaking, were the organized part of the movement, the people with a program: the famous "six points" (Carlyle insists on saying "five") of universal manhood suffrage, the secret ballot, payment for members of Parliament, abolition of the property qualification for members, annual elections, and equal electoral districts. Thus their propaganda centered upon one of the chief grievances the working people as a whole had against the ruling powers: the betrayal of the hopes they had been encouraged to place in the Reform Bill of 1832, which their demonstrations, and the threat of worse, had played no small part in ramming through a frightened Parliament. In the decade that had since elapsed, it had become amply clear that the electoral reforms achieved had been for the benefit of the middle class alone; the workers had received not a crumb from the table of the enlarged franchise and the abolition of some of the worst political abuses that had characterized the old system.

Chartism, as such, had begun in 1838, as an outgrowth of the London Working Men's Association, founded two years earlier. The organization meeting at Newhall Hill, near Birmingham, had, on fairly good authority, attracted some 200,000 persons. Swiftly the movement spread to the Midlands and the North, enlisting great numbers of miners and technologically displaced handicraftsmen. In 1839 a petition delivered to Parliament, asking for enactment of the "six points," bore some 1,283,000 signatures, a figure far surpassed in the spring of 1842, when a second petition, six miles long and wound on a huge frame that could not be got inside the House of Commons, contained 3,317,000 names. On both occasions the petition was rejected with alacrity mixed with laughter, a combination of reactions that did not noticeably conciliate the protesting crowds.

To the workers generally, however, the Chartist concern for matters relating to the ballot was of less moment than their concern for their bellies. One cannot, after all, eat paper. It was hunger — with its natural concomitant, fury against the ruling elements of the nation whose policies, they were convinced, brought it on — that united their gaunt and motley multitude. The source of their misery lay in the Corn Laws and in Sir Robert Peel's Tory party, which was determined to preserve them. If the workers were a trifle less hostile toward the Whigs, it was only because the party in power customarily endures the brunt of public resentment, and the Whigs (who had done nothing to win the affection of the masses during their years in office) had been ousted by the Tories in 1841.

Behind the Corn Laws, and Peel, stood the "agricultural interests," the landowning aristocracy and superior gentry whose proclivity for idleness alternating with partridge-shooting called forth Carlyle's most vituperative language. As a class, they are the most constantly denounced of all the knaves and fools who populate the chapters of *Past and Present*. Their jealous defense of the institution of game preserving was, to Carlyle, typical of the whole self-regarding spirit of the class. By keeping it illegal for any but themselves to kill game (night-poaching was a felony punishable by transportation) they deprived necessitous tenants not only of food for their own tables but of a commodity they could take to market. Whether living on the land itself or, as absentees, in the unproductive luxury of Mayfair, the "idle dilettantes" maintained an ignorance of, or disregard for, the desperate plight of the masses which enraged Carlyle as, in a little while, it was to inspire Benjamin Disraeli to his remark that England had become divided into two separate, isolated nations — the rich and the poor. Carlyle's assault on them is all the more violent because they had a long tradition of selfless public service: in earlier times, they had been the solid backbone of the nation. But with the coming of the industrial age, these products and mainstays of the older agrarian society had failed to adapt themselves to new conditions; and controlling Parliament as they did, they managed to keep the economy geared for their special benefit at a time when the sources of the nation's wealth had drastically altered. Their anachronism was not merely regrettable. In a period so packed with social dynamite as the early 1840's, their domination of political life and their determination to protect their class interests at all costs were a looming danger to the nation's peace.

The wealthy landowners' anachronism was not lost upon their rivals, the third force in the troubled social situation: the industrialists. These new-style capitalists, whose interest lay in the widespread, indeed worldwide, sale of the products of their mines and mills, rather than in the largely domestic sale of the produce of the land, were as much hurt by the Corn Laws as were the working people, but for different reasons. It was not the price of bread that aroused them, but the stagnation of trade. In 1838 they formed the powerful Anti-Corn Law League, which spent large sums of money in propaganda and political maneuvering in behalf of free trade. Thus, by one of those familiar ironies by which fate assigns bedfellows, the wealthy middle-class factory-owners, outnumbered in Parliament, found common cause with the workers who had no representation whatsoever. Both forces opposed the Tory, agrarian, and Church of England-dominated "establishment." But it was, because fortuitous, an uneasy and incongruous alliance, marked by scanty cooperation and much rivalry and suspicion. To the workers, free trade was a policy which, so far as their own interests went, would prove as much of a snare and delusion as the Reform Act had been. In practice, it would swell their employers' profits and shrink their own wages still further. They also suspected the Anti-Corn Law League, perhaps not without reason, of a kind of Manchester Machiavellianism. According to some Chartist leaders and later sympathetic historians, the employers encouraged the riots of 1842 by announcing impending wage-cuts or by closing more factories because of (alleged) lack of orders, correctly assuming that such measures would, by intensifying the workers' discontent, increase the pressure on the government at no cost to themselves. In time, the separate campaigns of the Anti-Corn Law League and the bread-less proletariat were successful. Thanks to the flow of economic events and political accidents — the most dramatic of which was Peel's reversal of position — the Corn Laws were repealed in 1846 and free trade reigned triumphant. The idle, game-preserving dilettantes gave way to the Mammonistic, bustling Plugsons of Undershot.

Like every other book of permanent literary interest that had its inception in a particular moment of history, however, *Past and Present* is much more than a piece of ephemeral journalism. The crisis of 1842 simply dramatized a set of tendencies that underlay the spirit, the hopes and fears, of the whole early Victorian era. Britain was experiencing both the affluence and the misery generated by the industrial revolution. The affluence, which was channeled to a relatively small class of investors and managers, was evident to anyone who beheld the tasteless but imposing mansions they built in London and the manufacturing towns and the life of equally tasteless luxury they lived. The misery, which was visited upon more people than had ever suffered in England before, was brought home to the public in the days of *Past and Present* by several reports ("blue books") of parliamentary investigating committees and royal commissions which probed into the conditions of working and living among the masses. The statistics and, more vivid, the evidence given by thousands of eyewitnesses, officials, and actual victims revealed a state of affairs that shocked even the most indifferent. Long hours of back-breaking, regimented toil in the mines and factories; a hand-to-mouth existence in foul slums, lacking even the most rudimentary amenities or sanitary arrangements; the absence of education, of recreation, of the very vestiges of justice or hope — these made the lot of the industrialized masses brutal beyond anything ever before experienced in England, and unmatched anywhere in the western world. In 1842 the most appalling blue book was the freshly issued report on the conditions under which women and small children were forced to work in mine tunnels and in the midst of the unguarded flywheels and belts of the factories. The details were so horrifying that this report had the extraordinary effect, for the time, of stirring Parliament to the immediate passage of restrictive legislation.

With two exceptions — the episode in the Stockport cellars alluded to in Book I, Chapter i, and the memorable demonstration of the "brotherhood of man" through the typhoid death of the Irish widow (Book III, Chapter ii) — Carlyle speaks of this side of English life only incidentally, and in general terms. Greater attention to it would have added even more force to his jeremiad; but Carlyle's anger was fed, for the most part, from other sources. It was not he but the future colleague of Marx, Friedrich Engels, who was to write the classic, all too dreadfully documented protest against the exploitation of the industrial proletariat in *The Condition of the Working Class in England in 1844*.

The intellectual rationalization of the get-rich-quick, dog-eat-dog, and devil-take-the-hindmost spirit that dominated British economic life in the age of *Past and Present* was supplied by Benthamite utilitarianism, which receives from Carlyle's pen a spatter of invective equaled only by that addressed against the do-nothing aristocracy. To an increasingly influential portion of the population, not least the middle-class industrialists and traders who followed the banners of Richard Cobden, John Bright, and the Anti-Corn Law League, the materialistic, hedonistic, self-regarding values implied in the term "profit and loss philosophy" were ethical creed as unchallengeable as the ten commandments, and the doctrine of laissez-faire as sacred and incontrovertible as the gospels. The highest social good was freedom: freedom, that is, to make as much money as possible, without limitations imposed by government (regulation only interfered with the operation of immutable "natural" economic law) or by conscience (a merciful heaven would provide for the diseased, mutilated, and worn-out victims of the factory system). It is the frightful price society pays for this so-called freedom on the part of a few that Carlyle inveighs against in one of the most famous chapters of the book, "Democracy" (Book III, Chapter xiii). But his revilement of the various other manifestations of Benthamism and classical economics, couched in a variety of Carlylean tags — "happiness" (with heavily ironic intonation), "the pleasures of virtue," "supply-and-demand" — permeates the whole volume.

Everywhere he looked, Carlyle detected what he had called, in an essay of 1829, "the signs of the times": hypocrisy, the worship of false gods and the pursuit of wrong ends, complacency, dependence upon slogans and legislative contrivance and expediency — all to be summed up by the two words he uses with typical iteration, *quackery* and *cant,* terms that embrace a multitude of deceptions, pretensions, clichés, and platitudes. The contemporary English world was to him a hubbub of talk without substance, action without wholesome result. The democratic electoral process and the fruit it bore in Parliament, the nation's proudest political achievement, were a sham and mockery. Religious institutions, most notably the Established Church but also all others, from "introspective" Methodism to the communion headed by a rheumatic old man who arranged to be assisted on public occasions by a stuffed rump, were empty shells from which true spiritual meaning and value had long since vanished. Commercial life was governed not by the honest old intention of making good merchandise for a reasonable price but by the new zeal for collecting as much as the market would bear for a shoddy product.

But most terrible of all the diseases that gathered in the "social gangrene," Carlyle felt, was the "cash-payment nexus" and all it implied. Under the convenient Benthamite philosophy, the sole obligatory relationship man bore to fellow-man was the exchange of money in payment for labor or goods. Pounds, shillings, and pence were the only cement that pretended to hold society together. Occurring simultaneously with the decline of genuine religious faith with its cohesive force, the ascendancy of industrialism and utilitarianism had fragmented the "brotherhood of man" into millions of atoms, each person a faceless, nameless nullity in the view of all the rest, his value reckoned solely by the contribution he could make toward the nation's material wealth. The necessary dealings of man and man were conducted in an atmosphere of anonymity, heartlessness, mechanical coldness.

Although *Past and Present* is an occasional piece, it is part of the major fabric of Carlyle's thought and writing. His social message, as set forth here, is the logical (if the word is ever permissible in connection with him!) derivation from his transcendental metaphysics and Calvinist heritage. In these pages we witness, in fact, the convergence for the purposes of social criticism of the ideas developed in the most notable works he had written in the preceding decade: *Sartor Resartus* (serialized 1833–34; first edition in book form, 1836), with its mystical "philosophy of clothes," a discourse on the universal confusion of appearance and reality, including some applications of its metaphysics to the immediate social situation; *The French Revolution* (1837) with its interpretation of history as the working-out of the divine will, and its reflection of the contemporary Englishman's lurking dread of indigenous working-class rebellion; and *On Heroes, Hero-Worship, and the Heroic in History* (1841), an elaborate preview of the recipe for society's salvation which Carlyle would offer in the closing chapters of the present book. In addition, his pamphlet *Chartism* (1839) contained many of the salient points, and indeed some of the very allusions and tags, that would shortly be repeated in this most comprehensive statement of his social views. While, thanks to Carlyle's habit of repetition-with-variations which enables the initially hazy eventually to become clear, *Past and Present* is quite understandable without outside aid, its full implications, and the philosophical assumptions underlying it, can be realized only when one has read those preceding works, which in effect serve as compendious commentaries.

Unlike them, however, this book can hardly be said to have been planned; it grew spontaneously out of Carlyle's experiences in the late summer of 1842. Wishing to do some field work in connection with the book on Oliver Cromwell on which he was then engaged, he visited the East Anglian region associated with the Lord Protector — Suffolk, Cambridgeshire, Huntingdonshire. His travels happened to take him to two places, quite unrelated to Cromwell, whose contrasting significances, brought into juxtaposition in his troubled mind, formed the motif of the book he was about to write. One (the "past") was the ruined abbey at Bury St. Edmunds, once the habitation of a prosperous and peaceful community of men. The other (the "present") was the workhouse at St. Ives, where Carlyle saw able-bodied men sitting helplessly idle, as paupers, because they could find no employment. These institutions and their symbolic meaning were given additional point by his memories of a visit in May to Manchester, its unwontedly smokeless air attesting to the closed-down factories, and the newspaper reports of the subsequent turmoil in those very streets. This, Carlyle concluded, was no time to pore over the records of a civil war that had been fought two full centuries before; it was the country's immediate peril, his anxiety over which had been steadily growing for the past two or three years, that demanded his pen. Putting aside the *Cromwell,* he began writing — seemingly in October or early November. He finished the book on the following March 8, and it was published early in April.

II

When Carlyle returned to London after the tour that had taken him to Bury St. Edmunds, he read a book that now held extra interest for him: the *Chronicle* of Jocelin of Brakelond, a narrative of life at the abbey of St. Edmund during the late twelfth-century abbacy of the astute, vigorous monk Samson.[1] This prime document of medieval history had been printed for the first time only two years earlier, under the auspices of the recently founded Camden Society for antiquarian research and publication. Carlyle found it both delightful and, in more than one sense, inspiring. In *Past and Present* he several times pays tribute to the charms of both author and book, calling the monk Jocelin "Bozzy" or Boswell because he is, to quote the latest editor of the *Chronicle,* "a shrewd observer of his fellows, humorous and wise, interested in every detail of the life not merely of Abbot Samson, but of the community in which the greater part of his life was spent."

The greater importance of Jocelin's book, however, resides, as Carlyle understood and the same modern editor repeats, in the fact that "his chronicle, besides being a delight to read, is a mine of information, not merely about the life of a great monastery, but also concerning the management and organization of a vast feudal estate, and something more than that" — for Samson was not only an ecclesiastical dignitary but a secular authority of considerable importance. His influence over the affairs of East Anglian society was in no way limited, symbolically or actually, by the walls of the abbey, a circumstance which made it all the easier for Carlyle to apply the lessons of his career to an England that not only had no monasteries but had neither the capability nor the inclination to submit itself, in any foreseeable future, to theocratic government. That Jocelin's hero was a monk was, for Carlyle's purposes, irrelevant; that he was also a good businessman and a wise leader of his people was much more to the point. Out of the stuff of medieval Abbot Samsons, Carlyle was persuaded, enlightened Plugsons

---

[1] A precious relic of Samson's abbacy, perhaps ordered by him when he was sub-sacristan, was acquired in 1963 by The Cloisters, New York City. It is an intricately carved walrus-ivory cross, a masterpiece of English Romanesque art. See the illustrated article in the *Metropolitan Museum of Art Bulletin* for June, 1964.

of Undershot could be fashioned, with results as happy to Victorian society as — so he was led to believe — Samson's ministrations had been to that of Henry II. In Jocelin's record of the firm but beneficent rule of Samson and the contented obedience of the ruled, he found assurance that the English nation had once proved itself capable of producing the kind of leader and the social organization which alone could bring it out of its present desperate strait.

At the same time that Jocelin's *Chronicle* fed Carlyle's thought and reinforced convictions he had long held, it supplied the guiding principle of art for the book he felt compelled to write. The literary effectiveness of social criticism depends, in part, upon its author's achieving a perspective appropriate to his temperament, his subject, and his purpose. Carlyle sought to avoid the narrow temporality, the parochialism, that is the usual stigma of a tract written for a time. He wished, instead, to comment on the burning issues of the day *sub specie aeternitatis*. The truth he struggled to impress upon his readers was that England's Chartist-Corn Law crisis was not a mere ephemeral situation, recent in origin and likely to be resolved by the normal flow of events, aided perhaps by a change of party in office and the passing of a few laws. On the contrary, to him the condition of England in 1842 was a microcosm of the whole condition of man in the modern world. His aim therefore was to reveal the year in and of which he wrote as the result of a long historical process, of which the building of factories in Manchester and the erection of barricades in the Paris streets had been but the most recent major symbolic events. Jocelin's *Chronicle* was peculiarly, almost uniquely, suited for this purpose, for it enabled Carlyle to survey this moment of contemporary history in the perspective of six and a half centuries.

Thus the very title of *Past and Present* is the key to its rhetorical art. The volume contrasts two societies, one of which had for its characteristic product monastic chronicles, the other, parliamentary blue books. In Books I and II these societies, so widely separated in time and spirit, are viewed in sequence. The "condition of England question" is posed and given a preliminary canvass in "Proem," and in "The Ancient Monk," notwithstanding the frequent side-glances Carlyle cannot resist making at the modern situation, the subject is Abbot Samson's world and deeds. In Books III and IV, past and present are viewed together, the one in effect superimposed upon the other. Once introduced, the materials from the *Chronicle* permeate the remaining pages; its characters, events, and the morals to be drawn from them are constantly turning up side by side with the characters, events, and issues of the age of the Chartists. Life in the abbey of St. Edmund offers a running symbol of the fulfillment of Christian society's purpose, just as Carlyle's description of the current state of England represents its frustration.

In this respect, Carlyle's method is akin to that of many satirists. Candid, ruthless re-examination of society's values and practices is the requisite first step toward rejection of the outmoded and refurbishing of the still useful. By the use of dramatic, often ironic, contrasts, Carlyle forces his readers to consider afresh matters they had been habituated to taking for granted, as part of the immutable system of the universe. The customs and assumptions of the 1840's appear in a strange new light when suddenly confronted with those that attended life in the Middle Ages. Familiar routines, institutions, and shibboleths of religion, politics, economics, and social relations lose their comfortable commonplaceness and, by a kind of contagion, suddenly seem as curious as the fragments of the distant past that are produced alongside them.

In addition, the strength of the contrasts helps emphasize the necessarily drastic nature of Carlyle's remedy for the ills of his age. Nothing short of society's ethical and religious regeneration, a return to the serene faith, obedience, and values of Abbot Samson's time — not identical with them in form or content, to be sure, but harmonious in spirit — will offer any promise of genuine cure. The good society of the future, if it is ever attained, will be as unlike the bad society of 1842 as the latter is unlike the good society of the Middle Ages.

The abbey and its diversified company of brothers constitute the crowning body of allusion that presides over the book's complex pattern of interwoven and repeated quotation, catchword, reference, and metaphor — the symbolic shorthand by which Carlyle casts abstract ideas into striking concretions. The very scope of these references, with their mingling of the topical and the timeless, the commonplace and the cosmic, assists in expanding the relevance of the case of England in 1842 beyond a single year, a single decade, even a single century. One basic set of allusions, of course — the one which identifies *Past and Present* as belonging to the literary mode of the pamphlet — is strictly contemporary, as close to its readers as the contents of their newspaper. The political issues of the day supply some of the references: investigations of electoral bribery, factory bills, the sliding scale of the Corn Laws, church extension, the secret ballot. So do the still vividly remembered continental upheavals of the past decade, the three-day Paris revolution of 1830, the Lyons silkworkers' insurrection, the Poles' doomed revolt against Russian tyranny. We read, too, of such landmarks in man's progress toward the age of the hard sell as Morison's extravagantly publicized patent medicine and the horse-drawn seven-foot hat. Even allusions to such places as the London

Tavern, Palace Yard, and Howell and James's furniture store, familiar to every early-Victorian Londoner, make their modest contributions to effect; and the several mentions of heavy-wet beer help convey Carlyle's scorn of the democratic electoral processes which it lubricated.

Behind the present of the topical references Carlyle paints in the long perspective of the past. Although the world of Jocelin of Brakelond supplies the most extensive historical background, there are also frequent allusions to Cromwell and the Puritan Revolution, whose particular pertinence as analogies and lessons for the earlier nineteenth century probably would have recommended their use here, as in much other argumentative literature of the time, even if they had not occurred naturally to a mind long preoccupied by the study of Cromwell. More remote episodes of English history, Becket at Canterbury, William the Conqueror at Hastings with his minstrel Taillefer, Anglo-Saxon invasions and heptarchies — these, too, help enlarge the chronological dimension of the frame in which the England of 1842 is set. If they are not always really germane, it is not for lack of Carlyle's conviction that they are; and in any case the constant reminders they offer of the long sweep of history and the analogical links that connect events in different ages, lend force to Carlyle's insistence that the particular social phenomena which so alarm him are neither new nor evanescent nor superficial, but are deeply embedded in the historical process.

Beyond these allusions to history and widening the perspective in another way, from a small England to the whole vast globe, lie a host of other references, from the Choctaw Indians to the Calmucks of central Asia with their rotatory calabash, from the chattering Dead Sea apes to the gods and divine events of the world's religions, Norse, Greek, Egyptian, and most of all, Judeo-Christian. In view of Carlyle's belief that man's predicament was due to his loss of true religion and that only his finding his soul again would save him, it was no doubt inevitable that, with over two decades of practice behind him, he should once again borrow the accents of the pulpit, interlarding his sermon with scores of Biblical quotations and allusions which, more than any other single element, lend to the book its memorable atmosphere of prophetic authority and terrible urgency.

These multiple criss-crossing strands of motif make up a strong and capacious netting by which the bulky mass of Carlyle's denunciation and advocacy is held together. In the midst of a disorderliness which is, alas, more real than apparent, there remains a certain order; and this order — both pattern and progress — is supplied by Carlyle's adroit use of his iterated references. The iteration is not, however, mere mechanical repetition, for the tags and allusions themselves acquire new forms and additional meaning in the course of their reappearances. Often, as is true of Gurth's brass collar and the soul-salt fancy from Ben Jonson, they are cast free from their source and become, in effect, newly created independent symbols. Carlyle, in addition to being a skillful rhetorician, was a thrifty one. A considerable portion of his art, once he has set each individual element — symbol, phrase, or reference — afloat in the stream of his discourse, is devoted to extracting as much, and as varied, use from it as its nature and his ingenuity allow. Sometimes, as we read on, his apocalyptic fervor strikes us as overdone and his leading ideas too few and too often repeated. On such occasions it is instructive to note how he seeks to enlist his reader's attention afresh by inventing new variations on his familiar illustrative themes, often with a touch of grotesque humor.

History does not record that *Past and Present* was responsible for any quick improvement in English society, but its long-range effects were impressive. It succeeded in arousing a social conscience which, except in a few honorably remembered contemporaries of Carlyle such as Lord Ashley, John Fielden, the humanitarian factory-owner, and Edwin Chadwick, who devoted his long life to the cause of public health, had been slumbering too long. It lighted the fires of indignation and the passion for reform in the minds of many men who, in the next generation, were successfully to fight for the eradication of at least the worst evils bred by the factory system, the city, and predatory capitalism. In literature, its echoes are found in *Sybil* (1845), by the young Disraeli who was striving to inject the spirit of social responsibility into the Conservative party; in Ruskin's *The Stones of Venice* (1851–53) and *Unto This Last* (1862), as well as in his whole later career as scourge and prophet of Victorian culture; in Dickens' *Bleak House* (1852–53) and *Hard Times* (1854), the latter being dedicated to Carlyle; and in Charles Kingsley's *Alton Locke* (1850).

Only a limited number of readers today sympathize either with the terms of Carlyle's diagnosis or with the nature of his proposed cure. The diagnosis is too heavily derived from German transcendentalism and Scottish Calvinism to command much assent in a scientific and secular age; the cure, for its part, strikes one as being a substitution, for the justly maligned Morison's pill, of something uncomfortably like Prussian authoritarianism. But if Carlyle's remedy fails to satisfy us, the acuteness with which he recognized the symptoms of a diseased society compels our admiration. How much of ourselves, we may well ask, is reflected by anticipation in Carlyle's mirror? His was not the last age to persist in mistaking shadow for substance, scorning calm thought, and spending its energy in frantic but futile motion and words full of sound, fury, and equivocation. If the dignity of the human individual was effaced by the "cash-payment nexus," it can hardly be said to have been restored by batteries of identification numbers and patterns of holes in punch cards. In our day as in Carlyle's, cant and quackery exist, and on occasion actually prevail, in legislatures and churches and public forums, and the voice of Sir Jabesh Windbag, the values of Bobus Higgins the sausage-maker, the editorial punditry of the *Houndsditch Indicator,* and the strong silent labors of Plugson of Undershot are taken to stand for the ultimate in human wisdom and achievement. The seven-foot hat is with us, monstrously multiplied everywhere that the vanity fair of advertising sets up its booths, still promoting the sale of goods whose most dependable quality is their built-in obsolescence. Poverty continues to be endured in a land overflowing with gross national product . . . So long as we live this side of the social millennium, *Past and Present* will continue to speak to us — in a language we can understand.

TEXTUAL AND BIBLIOGRAPHICAL NOTE

This edition reprints the text of the first London edition, from a copy in the Harvard College Library. Two or three obvious misprints have been silently corrected. Carlyle's footnotes are designated by "(C.)". His frequent footnote references to pages in Rokewood's edition of Jocelin's *Chronicle*, however, have been omitted as no longer serving any useful purpose.

Two manuscripts of *Past and Present*, neither of them complete, have been preserved: the first draft, now in the British Museum, and the printer's copy, now in the Yale University Library. These manuscripts, which provide valuable evidence concerning Carlyle's creative use of source material and his habits of original composition and revision, have been studied in Grace J. Calder's *The Writing of "Past and Present"* (New Haven, 1949).

The most fully annotated modern edition of the book, with a long introduction, is that of A. M. D. Hughes (Oxford, 1918). Of Jocelin's *Chronicle*, the most recent edition, with an English translation, is by H. E. Butler (London, 1949).

Probably the most helpful general discussions of *Past and Present* are those found in Louis Cazamian, *Carlyle* (New York, 1932), pp. 193–209, and Emery Neff, *Carlyle* (New York, 1932), pp. 196–209. On some aspects of Carlyle's rhetoric, see John Holloway, *The Victorian Sage* (London, 1953), Chapters ii and iii.

Past and Present

BY

THOMAS CARLYLE

Ernst ist das Leben.
— Schiller

CONTENTS

BOOK I

PROEM

BOOK II

THE ANCIENT MONK

4 CONTENTS

BOOK III

THE MODERN WORKER

CHAP.

PAGE

BOOK IV

HOROSCOPE

BOOK I

Proem

CHAPTER I

THE CONDITION of England, on which many pamphlets are now in the course of publication, and many thoughts unpublished are going on in every reflective head, is justly regarded as one of the most ominous, and withal one of the strangest, ever seen in this world. England is full of wealth, of multifarious produce, supply for human want in every kind; yet England is dying of inanition. With unabated bounty the land of England blooms and grows; waving with yellow harvests; thick-studded with work-shops, industrial implements, with fifteen millions of workers, understood to be the strongest, the cunningest and the willingest our Earth ever had; these men are here; the work they have done, the fruit they have realised is here, abundant, exuberant on every hand of us: and behold, some baleful fiat as of Enchantment has gone forth, saying, "Touch it not, ye workers, ye master-workers, ye master-idlers; none of you can touch it, no man of you shall be the better for it; this is enchanted fruit!" On the poor workers such fiat falls first, in its rudest shape; but on the rich master-workers too it falls; neither can the rich master-idlers, nor any richest or highest man escape, but all are like to be brought low with it, and made 'poor' enough, in the money-sense or a far fataller one.

Of these successful skilful workers some two millions, it is now counted, sit in Workhouses, Poor-law Prisons; or have 'out-door relief' flung over the wall to them, — the workhouse Bastille being filled to bursting, and the strong Poor-law broken asunder by a stronger.[1] They sit there, these many months now; their hope of deliverance as yet small. In workhouses, pleasantly so named, because work cannot be done in them. Twelve hundred thousand workers in England alone; their cunning right-hand lamed, lying idle in their sorrowful bosom; their hopes, outlooks, share of this

---

[1] The Return of Paupers for England and Wales, at Ladyday, 1842, is, "In-door 221,687, Out-door 1,207,402, Total 1,429,089." — (*Official Report.*) (C.)

fair world, shut in by narrow walls. They sit there, pent up, as in a kind of horrid enchantment; glad to be imprisoned and enchanted, that they may not perish starved. The picturesque Tourist,[2] in a sunny autumn day, through this bounteous realm of England, describes the Union Workhouse on his path. 'Passing by the Workhouse of St. Ives in Huntingdonshire, on a bright day last autumn,' says the picturesque Tourist, 'I saw sitting on wooden benches, in front of their Bastille and within their ring-wall and its railings, some half-hundred or more of these men. Tall robust figures, young mostly or of middle age; of honest countenance, many of them thoughtful and even intelligent-looking men. They sat there, near by one another; but in a kind of torpor, especially in a silence, which was very striking. In silence: for, alas, what word was to be said? An Earth all lying round, crying, Come and till me, come and reap me; — yet we here sit enchanted! In the eyes and brows of these men hung the gloomiest expression, not of anger, but of grief and shame and manifold inarticulate distress and weariness; they returned my glance with a glance that seemed to say, "Do not look at us. We sit enchanted here, we know not why. The Sun shines and the Earth calls; and, by the governing Powers and Impotences of this England, we are forbidden to obey. It is impossible, they tell us!" There was something that reminded me of Dante's Hell in the look of all this; and I rode swiftly away.'

So many hundred thousands sit in workhouses: and other hundred thousands have not yet got even workhouses; and in thrifty Scotland itself, in Glasgow or Edinburgh City, in their dark lanes, hidden from all but the eye of God, and of rare Benevolence the minister of God, there are scenes of woe and destitution and desolation, such as, one may hope, the Sun never saw before in the most barbarous regions where men dwelt. Competent witnesses, the brave and humane Dr. Alison,[3] who speaks what he knows, whose noble Healing Art in his charitable hands becomes once more a truly sacred one, report these things for us: these things are not of this year, or of last year, have no reference to our present state of commercial stagnation, but only to the common state. Not in sharp fever-fits, but in chronic gangrene of this kind is Scotland suffering. A Poor-law, any and every Poor-law, it may be observed, is but a temporary measure; an anodyne, not a

---

[2] Carlyle himself.
[3] William P. Alison, philanthropic physician. See below, p. 150.

remedy: Rich and Poor, when once the naked facts of their condition have come into collision, cannot long subsist together on a mere Poor-law. True enough: — and yet, human beings cannot be left to die! Scotland too, till something better come, must have a Poor-law, if Scotland is not to be a byword among the nations.[4] O, what a waste is there; of noble and thrice-noble national virtues; peasant Stoicisms, Heroisms; valiant manful habits, soul of a Nation's worth, — which all the metal of Potosi[5] cannot purchase back; to which the metal of Potosi, and all you can buy with *it*, is dross and dust!

Why dwell on this aspect of the matter? It is too indisputable, not doubtful now to any one. Descend where you will into the lower class, in Town or Country, by what avenue you will, by Factory Inquiries, Agricultural Inquiries, by Revenue Returns, by Mining-Labourer Committees, by opening your own eyes and looking, the same sorrowful result discloses itself: you have to admit that the working body of this rich English Nation has sunk or is fast sinking into a state, to which, all sides of it considered, there was literally never any parallel. At Stockport Assizes,[6] — and this too has no reference to the present state of trade, being of date prior to that, — a Mother and a Father are arraigned and found guilty of poisoning three of their children, to defraud a 'burial-society' of some *3l. 8s.* due on the death of each child: they are arraigned, found guilty; and the official authorities, it is whispered, hint that perhaps the case is not solitary, that perhaps you had better not probe farther into that department of things. This is in the autumn of 1841; the crime itself is of the previous year or season. "Brutal savages, degraded Irish," mutters the idle reader of Newspapers; hardly lingering on this incident. Yet it is an incident worth lingering on; the depravity, savagery and degraded Irishism being never so well admitted. In the British land, a human Mother and Father, of white skin and professing the Christian religion, had done this thing; they, with their Irishism and necessity and savagery, had been driven to do it. Such instances are like the highest mountain apex emerged into view; under which lies a whole mountain region and land, not yet emerged. A human Mother and Father had said to themselves,

---

[4] 1 Kings 9:7.

[5] A silver-rich district of Bolivia.

[6] Court sessions in a town near Manchester. The trial was reported in *The Times*, August 4–6, 1841.

What shall we do to escape starvation? We are deep sunk here, in our dark cellar; and help is far. — Yes, in the Ugolino Hunger-tower stern things happen; best-loved little Gaddo fallen dead on his Father's knees![7] — The Stockport Mother and Father think and hint: Our poor little starveling Tom, who cries all day for victuals, who will see only evil and not good in this world: if he were out of misery at once; he well dead, and the rest of us perhaps kept alive? It is thought, and hinted; at last it is done. And now Tom being killed, and all spent and eaten, Is it poor little starveling Jack that must go, or poor little starveling Will? — What an inquiry of ways and means!

In starved sieged cities, in the uttermost doomed ruin of old Jerusalem fallen under the wrath of God, it was prophesied and said, 'The hands of the pitiful women have sodden their own children.'[8] The stern Hebrew imagination could conceive no blacker gulf of wretchedness; that was the ultimatum of degraded god-punished man. And we here, in modern England, exuberant with supply of all kinds, besieged by nothing if it be not by invisible Enchantments, are we reaching that? — — How come these things? Wherefore are they, wherefore should they be?

Nor are they of the St. Ives workhouses, of the Glasgow lanes, and Stockport cellars, the only unblessed among us. This successful industry of England, with its plethoric wealth, has as yet made nobody rich; it is an enchanted wealth, and belongs yet to nobody. We might ask, Which of us has it enriched? We can spend thousands where we once spent hundreds; but can purchase nothing good with them. In Poor and Rich, instead of noble thrift and plenty, there is idle luxury alternating with mean scarcity and inability. We have sumptuous garnitures for our Life, but have forgotten to *live* in the middle of them. It is an enchanted wealth; no man of us can yet touch it. The class of men who feel that they are truly better off by means of it, let them give us their name!

Many men eat finer cookery, drink dearer liquors, — with what advantage they can report, and their Doctors can: but in the heart of them, if we go out of the dyspeptic stomach, what increase of blessedness is there? Are they better, beautifuller, stronger,

[7] Along with his sons, Count Ugolino was imprisoned and starved to death at Pisa, 1288. See Dante, *Inferno*, XXXIII.
[8] Lamentations 4:10.

braver? Are they even what they call 'happier?' Do they look
with satisfaction on more things and human faces in this God's-
Earth; do more things and human faces look with satisfaction on
them? Not so. Human faces gloom discordantly, disloyally on
one another. Things, if it be not mere cotton and iron things,
are growing disobedient to man. The Master Worker is enchanted, for the present, like his Workhouse Workman; clamours,
in vain hitherto, for a very simple sort of 'Liberty:' the liberty 'to
buy where he finds it cheapest, to sell where he finds it dearest.'[9]
With guineas jingling in every pocket, he was no whit richer; but
now, the very guineas threatening to vanish, he feels that he is
poor indeed. Poor Master Worker! And the Master Unworker, is
not he in a still fataller situation? Pausing amid his game-preserves, with awful eye, — as he well may! Coercing fifty-pound
tenants;[10] coercing, bribing, cajoling; doing what he likes with his
own.[11] His mouth full of loud futilities, and arguments to prove
the excellence of his Corn-law; and in his heart the blackest misgiving, a desperate half-consciousness that his excellent Corn-law
is indefensible, that his loud arguments for it are of a kind to
strike men too literally *dumb*.

To whom, then, is this wealth of England wealth? Who is it
that it blesses; makes happier, wiser, beautifuller, in any way
better? Who has got hold of it, to make it fetch and carry for
him, like a true servant, not like a false mock-servant; to do him
any real service whatsoever? As yet no one. We have more riches
than any Nation ever had before; we have less good of them than
any Nation ever had before. Our successful industry is hitherto
unsuccessful; a strange success, if we stop here! In the midst of
plethoric plenty, the people perish;[12] with gold walls, and full
barns, no man feels himself safe or satisfied. Workers, Master
Workers, Unworkers, all men, come to a pause; stand fixed, and
cannot farther. Fatal paralysis spreading inwards, from the ex-
tremities, in St. Ives workhouses, in Stockport cellars, through all

---

[9] A paraphrase of Adam Smith's doctrine in *The Wealth of Nations*
(1776), bible of laissez-faire economy.

[10] Tenants paying annual rent of £50 were given the vote by the Reform
Act of 1832.

[11] The Duke of Newcastle in 1829 evicted every one of his tenants who
failed to vote for his parliamentary candidate. "Is it not lawful for me to
do what I please with mine own?" he demanded when criticized in the
House of Lords.

[12] Proverbs 29:18.

limbs, as if towards the heart itself. Have we actually got enchanted, then; accursed by some god? —

Midas longed for gold, and insulted the Olympians. He got
gold, so that whatsoever he touched became gold, — and he, with
his long ears, was little the better for it. Midas had misjudged the
celestial music-tones; Midas had insulted Apollo and the gods:
the gods gave him his wish, and a pair of long ears, which also
were a good appendage to it.[13] What a truth in these old Fables!

---

[13] Carlyle here fuses two separate stories about the unlucky king of
Phrygia. His numerous later references are to one or the other of them.
One has it that Dionysus, to repay Midas' kindness to the god's drunken
companion Silenus, promised to grant him whatever request he would make.
Midas asked that all he touched be turned to gold; but when even his
food was so transformed, he begged Dionysus to take back his favor. The
other tells how Midas, refereeing a musical contest between Pan and
Apollo, ill-advisedly decided in favor of Pan. Apollo thereupon changed his
ears into those of an ass.

CHAPTER II

THE SPHINX

How TRUE, for example, is that other old Fable of the Sphinx, who sat by the wayside, propounding her riddle to the passengers, which if they could not answer she destroyed them! Such a Sphinx is this Life of ours, to all men and societies of men. Nature, like the Sphinx, is of womanly celestial loveliness and tenderness; the face and bosom of a goddess, but ending in claws and the body of a lioness. There is in her a celestial beauty, — which means celestial order, pliancy to wisdom; but there is also a darkness, a ferocity, fatality, which are infernal. She is a goddess, but one not yet disimprisoned; one still half-imprisoned, — the inarticulate, lovely still encased in the inarticulate, chaotic. How true! And does she not propound her riddles to us? Of each man she asks daily, in mild voice, yet with a terrible significance, "Knowest thou the meaning of this Day? What thou canst do Today; wisely attempt to do?" Nature, Universe, Destiny, Existence, howsoever we name this grand unnameable Fact in the midst of which we live and struggle, is as a heavenly bride and conquest to the wise and brave, to them who can discern her behests and do them; a destroying fiend to them who cannot. Answer her riddle, it is well with thee. Answer it not, pass on regarding it not, it will answer itself; the solution for thee is a thing of teeth and claws; Nature is a dumb lioness, deaf to thy pleadings, fiercely devouring. Thou art not now her victorious bridegroom; thou art her mangled victim, scattered on the precipices, as a slave found treacherous, recreant, ought to be and must.

With Nations it is as with individuals: Can they rede the riddle of Destiny? This English Nation, will it get to know the meaning of *its* strange new Today? Is there sense enough extant, discoverable anywhere or anyhow, in our united twenty-seven million heads to discern the same; valour enough in our twenty-seven million hearts to dare and do the bidding thereof? It will be seen! —

The secret of gold Midas, which he with his long ears never could discover, was, That he had offended the Supreme Powers; — that he had parted company with the eternal inner Facts of this Universe, and followed the transient outer Appearances thereof; and so was arrived *here*. Properly it is the secret of all unhappy men and unhappy nations. Had they known Nature's right truth, Nature's right truth would have made them free. They have become enchanted; stagger spell-bound, reeling on the brink of huge peril, because they were not wise enough. They have forgotten the right Inner True, and taken up with the Outer Sham-true. They answer the Sphinx's question *wrong*. Foolish men cannot answer it aright! Foolish men mistake transitory semblance for eternal fact, and go astray more and more.

Foolish men imagine that because judgment for an evil thing is delayed, there is no justice, but an accidental one, here below. Judgment for an evil thing is many times delayed some day or two, some century or two, but it is sure as life, it is sure as death! In the centre of the world-whirlwind, verily now as in the oldest days, dwells and speaks a God.[1] The great soul of the world is *just*. O brother, can it be needful now, at this late epoch of experience, after eighteen centuries of Christian preaching for one thing, to remind thee of such a fact; which all manner of Mahometans, old Pagan Romans, Jews, Scythians[2] and heathen Greeks, and indeed more or less all men that God made, have managed at one time to see into; nay which thou thyself, till 'redtape' strangled the inner life of thee, hadst once some inkling of: That there *is* justice here below; and even, at bottom, that there is nothing else but justice! Forget that, thou hast forgotten all. Success will never more attend thee: how can it now? Thou hast the whole Universe against thee. No more success: mere shamsuccess, for a day and days; rising ever higher, — towards its Tarpeian Rock.[3] Alas, how, in thy soft-hung Longacre[4] vehicle, of polished leather to the bodily eye, of redtape philosophy, of expediencies, clubroom moralities, Parliamentary majorities to the mind's eye, thou beautifully rollest: but knowest thou whitherward? It is towards the *road's end*. Old use-and-wont; established methods, habitudes, *once* true and wise; man's noblest

---

[1] Job 38:1; Ezekiel 1:4.
[2] Nomads living, in classical times, north of the Black Sea.
[3] Roman precipice from which state criminals and traitors were thrown.
[4] London district, headquarters of the carriage-building trade.

tendency, his perseverance, and man's ignoblest, his inertia; whatsoever of noble and ignoble Conservatism[5] there is in men and Nations, strongest always in the strongest men and Nations: all this is as a road to thee, paved smooth through the abyss,[6] — till all this *end*. Till men's bitter necessities can endure thee no more. Till Nature's patience with thee is done; and there is no road or footing any farther, and the abyss yawns sheer! —

Parliament and the Courts of Westminster are venerable to me; how venerable; grey with a thousand years of honourable age! For a thousand years and more, Wisdom and faithful Valour, struggling amid much Folly and greedy Baseness, not without most sad distortions in the struggle, have built them up; and they are as we see. For a thousand years, this English Nation has found them useful or supportable; they have served this English Nation's want; *been* a road to it through the abyss of Time. They are venerable, they are great and strong. And yet it is good to remember always that they are not the venerablest, nor the greatest, nor the strongest! Acts of Parliament are venerable; but if they correspond not with the writing on the 'Adamant Tablet,'[7] what are they? Properly their one element of venerableness, of strength or greatness, is, that they at all times correspond therewith as near as by human possibility they can. They are cherishing destruction in their bosom every hour that they continue otherwise.

Alas, how many causes that can plead well for themselves in the Courts of Westminster; and yet in the general Court of the Universe, and free Soul of Man, have no word to utter! Honourable Gentlemen may find this worth considering, in times like ours. And truly, the din of triumphant Law-logic, and all shaking of horse-hair wigs and learned-sergeant[8] gowns having comfortably ended, we shall do well to ask ourselves withal, What says that high and highest Court to the verdict? For it is the Court of Courts, that same; where the universal soul of Fact and very Truth sits President; — and thitherward, more and more swiftly, with a really terrible increase of swiftness, all causes do in these days crowd for revisal, — for confirmation, for modification, for

[5] At this point Carlyle employs the term in its older, more general sense. Later he uses it as a synonym for partisan Toryism, an application still quite novel in 1842.

[6] The lower regions, chaos (see p. 21, n. 5).

[7] Bronze plate upon which ancient laws were inscribed.

[8] A superior rank of lawyers, abolished in the later nineteenth century.

reversal with costs. Dost thou know that Court; hast thou had any Law-practice there? What, didst thou never enter; never file any petition of redress, reclaimer, disclaimer or demurrer, written as in thy heart's blood, for thy own behoof or another's; and silently await the issue? Thou knowest not such a Court? Hast merely heard of it by faint tradition as a thing that was or had been? Of thee, I think, we shall get little benefit.

For the gowns of learned-sergeants are good: parchment records, fixed forms, and poor terrestrial Justice, with or without horse-hair, what sane man will not reverence these? And yet, behold, the man is not sane but insane, who considers these alone as venerable. Oceans of horse-hair, continents of parchment, and learned-sergeant eloquence, were it continued till the learned tongue wore itself small in the indefatigable learned mouth, cannot make unjust just. The grand question still remains, Was the judgment just? If unjust, it will not and cannot get harbour for itself, or continue to have footing in this Universe, which was made by other than One Unjust. Enforce it by never such statuting, three readings, royal assents; blow it to the four winds with all manner of quilted trumpeters and pursuivants, in the rear of them never so many gibbets and hangmen, it will not stand, it cannot stand. From all souls of men, from all ends of Nature, from the Throne of God above, there are voices bidding it: Away, away! Does it take no warning; does it stand, strong in its three readings, in its gibbets and artillery-parks? The more woe is to it, the frightfuller woe. It will continue standing, for its day, for its year, for its century, doing evil all the while; but it has One enemy who is Almighty: dissolution, explosion, and the everlasting Laws of Nature incessantly advance towards it; and the deeper its rooting, more obstinate its continuing, the deeper also and huger will its ruin and overturn be.

In this God's-world, with its wild-whirling eddies and mad foam-oceans, where men and nations perish as if without law, and judgment for an unjust thing is sternly delayed, dost thou think that there is therefore no justice? It is what the fool hath said in his heart.[9] It is what the wise, in all times, were wise because they denied, and knew forever not to be. I tell thee again, there is nothing else but justice. One strong thing I find here below: the just thing, the true thing. My friend, if thou hadst all the artillery of Woolwich[10] trundling at thy back in support of an unjust thing;

---

[9] Psalms 14:1.
[10] Government arsenal on the Thames below London.

and infinite bonfires visibly waiting ahead of thee, to blaze centuries long for thy victory on behalf of it, — I would advise thee to
call halt, to fling down thy baton, and say, "In God's name, No!"
Thy 'success?' Poor devil, what will thy success amount to? If
the thing is unjust, thou hast not succeeded; no, not though bonfires blazed from North to South, and bells rang, and editors wrote
leading-articles, and the just thing lay trampled out of sight, to
all mortal eyes an abolished and annihilated thing. Success? In
few years, thou wilt be dead and dark, — all cold, eyeless, deaf;
no blaze of bonfires, ding-dong of bells or leading-articles visible
or audible to thee again at all forever: What kind of success is
that! —

It is true all goes by approximation in this world; with any not
insupportable approximation we must be patient. There is a noble
Conservatism as well as an ignoble. Would to Heaven, for the
sake of Conservatism itself, the noble alone were left, and the
ignoble, by some kind severe hand, were ruthlessly lopped away,
forbidden ever more to shew itself! For it is the right and noble
alone that will have victory in this struggle; the rest is wholly an
obstruction, a postponement and fearful imperilment of the victory. Towards an eternal centre of right and nobleness, and of
that only, is all this confusion tending. We already know whither
it is all tending; what will have victory, what will have none! The
Heaviest will reach the centre. The Heaviest, sinking through
complex fluctuating media and vortices, has its deflexions, its
obstructions, nay at times its resiliences, its reboundings; whereupon some blockhead shall be heard jubilating, "See, your Heaviest ascends!" — but at all moments it is moving centreward, fast
as is convenient for it; sinking, sinking; and, by laws older than
the World, old as the Maker's first Plan of the World, it has to
arrive there.

Await the issue. In all battles, if you await the issue, each
fighter has prospered according to his right. His right and his
might, at the close of the account, were one and the same. He has
fought with all his might, and in exact proportion to all his right
he has prevailed. His very death is no victory over him. He dies
indeed; but his work lives, very truly lives. A heroic Wallace,[11]
quartered on the scaffold, cannot hinder that his Scotland become, one day, a part of England: but he does hinder that it
become, on tyrannous unfair terms, a part of it; commands still,

[11] Sir William Wallace, Scottish patriot, executed in 1305.

as with a god's voice, from his old Valhalla[12] and Temple of the
Brave, that there be a just real union as of brother and brother,
not a false and merely semblant one as of slave and master. If
the union with England be in fact one of Scotland's chief blessings, we thank Wallace withal that it was not the chief curse.
Scotland is not Ireland: no, because brave men rose there, and
said, "Behold, ye must not tread us down like slaves; and ye shall
not, — and cannot!" Fight on, thou brave true heart, and falter
not, through dark fortune and through bright. The cause thou
fightest for, so far as it is true, no farther, yet precisely so far, is
very sure of victory. The falsehood alone of it will be conquered,
will be abolished, as it ought to be: but the truth of it is part of
Nature's own Laws, cooperates with the World's eternal Tendencies, and cannot be conquered.

The *dust* of controversy, what is it but the *falsehood* flying
off from all manner of conflicting true forces, and making such a
loud dust-whirlwind, — that so the truths alone may remain, and
embrace brother-like in some true resulting-force! It is ever so.
Savage fighting Heptarchies:[13] their fighting is an ascertainment,
who has the right to rule over whom; that out of such waste-
bickering Saxondom a peacefully cooperating England may arise.
Seek through this Universe; if with other than owl's eyes, thou
wilt find nothing nourished there, nothing kept in life, but what
has right to nourishment and life. The rest, look at it with other
than owl's eyes, is not living; is all dying, all as good as dead!
Justice was ordained from the foundations of the world; and will
last with the world and longer.

From which I infer that the inner sphere of Fact, in this present
England as elsewhere, differs infinitely from the outer sphere and
spheres of Semblance. That the Temporary, here as elsewhere,
is too apt to carry it over the Eternal. That he who dwells in the
temporary Semblances, and does not penetrate into the eternal
Substance, will *not* answer the Sphinx-riddle of Today, or of any
Day. For the substance alone is substantial; that *is* the law of
Fact: if you discover not that, Fact, who already knows it, will
let you also know it by and by!

What is Justice? that, on the whole, is the question of the

---

[12] The Norse "hall of the slain" — heroes fallen in battle.
[13] The kingdoms into which Anglo-Saxon England was divided before the
West Saxons achieved supremacy in the ninth century.

Sphinx to us. The law of Fact is, that Justice must and will be done. The sooner the better; for the Time grows stringent, frightfully pressing! "What is Justice?" ask many, to whom cruel Fact alone will be able to prove responsive. It is like jesting Pilate asking, What is Truth?[14] Jesting Pilate had not the smallest chance to ascertain what was Truth. He could not have known it, had a god shewn it to him. Thick serene opacity, thicker than amaurosis,[15] veiled those smiling eyes of his to Truth; the inner *retina* of them was gone paralytic, dead. He looked at Truth; and discerned her not, there where she stood. "What is Justice?" The clothed embodied Justice that sits in Westminster Hall,[16] with penalties, parchments, tipstaves,[17] is very visible. But the *un*embodied Justice, whereof that other is either an emblem, or else is a fearful indescribability, is not so visible! For the unembodied Justice is of Heaven; a Spirit, and Divinity of Heaven, — *in*visible to all but the noble and pure of soul. The impure ignoble gaze with eyes, and she is not there. They will prove it to you by logic, by endless Hansard Debatings,[18] by bursts of Parliamentary eloquence. It is not consolatory to behold! For properly, as many men as there are in a Nation who *can* withal see Heaven's invisible Justice, and know it to be on Earth also omnipotent, so many men are there who stand between a Nation and perdition. So many, and no more. Heavy-laden England, how many hast thou in this hour? The Supreme Power sends new and ever new, all *born* at least with hearts of flesh and not of stone; — and heavy Misery itself, once heavy enough, will prove didactic! —

[14] John 18:38.

[15] Loss of sight caused by a disease of the optic nerve.

[16] The chief surviving portion (built 1097–99) of the palace of Westminster. The highest law courts sat here until 1825, when they moved to buildings immediately adjoining.

[17] Metal-tipped staffs, symbols of the authority of sheriff's officers.

[18] Luke Hansard was the printer, 1774–1828, of the Journals of the House of Commons, which are still called by his name.

CHAPTER III

MANCHESTER INSURRECTION

BLUSTEROWSKI, Colacorde,[1] and other Editorial prophets of the Continental Democratic Movement, have in their leading-articles shewn themselves disposed to vilipend[2] the late Manchester Insurrection, as evincing in the rioters an extreme backwardness to battle; nay as betokening, in the English People itself, perhaps a want of the proper animal-courage indispensable in these ages. A million hungry operative men started up, in utmost paroxysm of desperate protest against their lot; and, ask Colacorde and company, How many shots were fired? Very few in comparison! Certain hundreds of drilled soldiers sufficed to suppress this million-headed hydra,[3] and tread it down, without the smallest appeasement or hope of such, into its subterranean settlements again, there to reconsider itself. Compared with our revolts in Lyons, in Warsaw and elsewhere, to say nothing of incomparable Paris City past or present, what a lamblike Insurrection![4] —

The present Editor is not here, with his readers, to vindicate the character of Insurrections; nor does it matter to us whether Blusterowski and the rest may think the English a courageous people or not courageous. In passing, however, let us mention that, to our view, this was not an unsuccessful Insurrection; that as Insurrections go, we have not heard lately of any that succeeded so well.

A million of hungry operative men, as Blusterowski says, rose all up, came all out into the streets, and — stood there. What other could they do? Their wrongs and griefs were bitter, in-

---

[1] Both names are Carlyle's inventions. It has been suggested that the latter is a coinage from the French *cou* (neck) and *corde* (halter).

[2] Depreciate, disparage.

[3] See below, p. 24, n. 13.

[4] The silk weavers of Lyons had revolted several times in the past decade, most memorably in 1832, when a strike for higher wages threw 30,000 out of work. In 1830–31 Warsaw was the scene of a bloody but unsuccessful rebellion against Russian tyranny. Paris, of course, had witnessed numerous crises since 1789.

supportable, their rage against the same was just: but who are they that cause these wrongs, who that will honestly make effort to redress them? Our enemies are we know not who or what; our friends are we know not where! How shall we attack any one, shoot or be shot by any one? O, if the accursed invisible Nightmare, that is crushing out the life of us and ours, would take a shape; approach us like the Hyrcanian tiger, the Behemoth of Chaos,[5] the Archfiend himself; in any shape that we could see, and fasten on! — A man can have himself shot with cheerfulness; but it needs first that he see clearly for what. Shew him the divine face of Justice, then the diabolic monster which is eclipsing that: he will fly at the throat of such monster, never so monstrous, and need no bidding to do it. Woolwich grapeshot will sweep clear all streets, blast into invisibility so many thousand men: but if your Woolwich grapeshot be but eclipsing Divine Justice, and the God's-radiance itself gleam recognisable athwart such grapeshot, — then, yes then is the time come for fighting and attacking. All artillery-parks have become weak, and are about to dissipate: in the God's-thunder, their poor thunder slackens, ceases; finding that it is, in all senses of the term, a *brute* one! —

That the Manchester Insurrection stood still, on the streets, with an indisposition to fire and bloodshed, was wisdom for it even as an Insurrection. Insurrection, never so necessary, is a most sad necessity; and governors who wait for that to instruct them, are surely getting into the fatallest courses, — proving themselves Sons of Nox and Chaos,[6] of blind Cowardice, not of seeing Valour! How can there be any remedy in insurrection? It is a mere announcement of the disease, — visible now even to Sons of Night. Insurrection usually 'gains' little; usually wastes how much! One of its worst kinds of waste, to say nothing of the rest, is that of irritating and exasperating men against each other, by violence done; which is always sure to be injustice done, for violence does even justice unjustly.

Who shall compute the waste and loss, the obstruction of every sort, that was produced in the Manchester region by Peterloo[7]

[5] *Hyrcanian tiger:* a familiar literary symbol of ferocity; cf. *Hamlet,* II.ii.172. *Behemoth:* a great beast; Job 40:15–24. *Chaos:* the void, or confusion of unformed matter, which existed before creation.

[6] Nox was the Roman goddess of night; Chaos the most ancient of the Greek gods. Cf. *Paradise Lost,* II.960–962.

[7] The famous clash between assembled workingmen and massed cavalry and yeomanry (British equivalent of the American national guard) at St. Peter's Field, Manchester, on August 16, 1819. Some ten people were

alone! Some thirteen unarmed men and women cut down, — the number of the slain and maimed is very countable: but the treasury of rage, burning hidden or visible in all hearts ever since, more or less perverting the effort and aim of all hearts ever since, is of unknown extent. "How ye came among us, in your cruel armed blindness, ye unspeakable County Yeomanry, sabres flourishing, hoofs prancing, and slashed us down at your brute pleasure; deaf, blind to all *our* claims and woes and wrongs; of quick sight and sense to your own claims only! There lie poor sallow workworn weavers, and complain no more now; women themselves are slashed and sabred, howling terror fills the air; and ye ride prosperous, very victorious, — ye unspeakable: give *us* sabres too, and then come-on a little!" Such are Peterloos. In all hearts that witnessed Peterloo, stands written, as in fire-characters, or smoke-characters prompt to become fire again, a legible balance-account of grim vengeance; very unjustly balanced, much exaggerated, as is the way with such accounts; but payable readily at sight, in full with compound interest! Such things should be avoided as the very pestilence. For men's hearts ought not to be set against one another; but set *with* one another, and all against the Evil Thing only. Men's souls ought to be left to see clearly; not jaundiced, blinded, twisted all awry, by revenge, mutual abhorrence, and the like. An Insurrection that can announce the disease, and then retire with no such balance-account opened anywhere, has attained the highest success possible for it.

And this was what these poor Manchester operatives, with all the darkness that was in them and round them, did manage to perform. They put their huge inarticulate question, "What do you mean to do with us?" in a manner audible to every reflective soul in this kingdom; exciting deep pity in all good men, deep anxiety in all men whatever; and no conflagration or outburst of madness came to cloud that feeling anywhere, but everywhere it operates unclouded. All England heard the question: it is the first practical form of *our* Sphinx-riddle. England will answer it; or, on the whole, England will perish; — one does not yet expect the latter result!

For the rest, that the Manchester Insurrection could yet discern no radiance of Heaven on any side of its horizon; but feared that

killed and several hundred injured. For a whole generation Peterloo was the symbol of working-class agitation for parliamentary reform, and of the government's effort to suppress it.

all lights, of the O'Connor[8] or other sorts, hitherto kindled, were but deceptive fish-oil transparencies,[9] or bog will-o'-wisp lights, and no dayspring from on high:[10] for this also we will honour the poor Manchester Insurrection, and augur well of it. A deep unspoken sense lies in these strong men, — inconsiderable, almost stupid, as all they can articulate of it is. Amid all violent stupidity of speech, a right noble instinct of what is doable and what is not doable never forsakes them: the strong inarticulate men and workers, whom *Fact* patronises; of whom, in all difficulty and work whatsoever, there is good augury! This work too is to be done: Governors and Governing Classes that *can* articulate and utter, in any measure, what the law of Fact and Justice is, may calculate that here is a Governed Class who will listen.

And truly this first practical form of the Sphinx-question, inarticulately and so audibly put there, is one of the most impressive ever asked in the world. "Behold us here, so many thousands, millions, and increasing at the rate of fifty every hour. We are right willing and able to work; and on the Planet Earth is plenty of work and wages for a million times as many. We ask, If you mean to lead us towards work; to try to lead us, — by ways new, never yet heard of till this new unheard-of Time? Or if you declare that you cannot lead us? And expect that we are to remain quietly unled, and in a composed manner perish of starvation? What is it you expect of us? What is it you mean to do with us?" This question, I say, has been put in the hearing of all Britain; and will be again put, and ever again, till some answer be given it.

Unhappy Workers, unhappier Idlers, unhappy men and women of this actual England! We are yet very far from an answer, and there will be no existence for us without finding one. "A fair day's-wages for a fair day's-work:"[11] it is as just a demand as Governed men ever made of Governing. It is the everlasting right of man. Indisputable as Gospels, as arithmetical multiplication-tables: it must and will have itself fulfilled; — and yet, in these times of ours, with what enormous difficulty, next-door to impossibility! For the times are really strange; of a complexity intricate with all the new width of the ever-widening world; times here of

---

[8] Feargus O'Connor was a leader of the most radical wing of the Chartists. He was widely feared and abused as a demagogue and inciter to violence.

[9] Pictures painted on cloth and lighted from behind by whale oil lamps.

[10] Luke 1:78.

[11] The slogan of the rebellious workers.

half-frantic velocity of impetus, there of the deadest-looking still-
ness and paralysis; times definable as shewing two qualities, Dilettantism and Mammonism; — most intricate obstructed times!
Nay, if there were not a Heaven's radiance of Justice, prophetic,
clearly of Heaven, discernible behind all these confused world-
wide entanglements, of Landlord interests, Manufacturing interests, Tory-Whig interests, and who knows what other interests,
expediencies, vested interests, established possessions, inveterate
Dilettantisms, Midas-eared Mammonisms, — it would seem to
everyone a flat impossibility, which all wise men might as well at
once abandon. If you do not know eternal Justice from momentary Expediency, and understand in your heart of hearts how Justice, radiant, beneficent, as the all-victorious Light-element, is also
in essence, if need be, an all-victorious *Fire*-element, and melts
all manner of vested interests, and the hardest iron cannon, as if
they were soft wax, and does ever in the long-run rule and reign,
and allows nothing else to rule and reign, — you also would talk
of impossibility! But it is only difficult, it is not impossible. Possible? It is, with whatever difficulty, very clearly inevitable.

Fair day's-wages for fair-day's-work! exclaims a sarcastic man;
alas, in what corner of this Planet, since Adam first awoke on it,
was that ever realised? The day's-wages of John Milton's day's-
work, named *Paradise Lost* and *Milton's Works,* were Ten Pounds
paid by instalments, and a rather close escape from death on the
gallows.[12] Consider that: it is no rhetorical flourish; it is an authentic, altogether quiet fact, — emblematic, quietly documentary
of a whole world of such, ever since human history began. Oliver
Cromwell quitted his farming; undertook a Hercules' Labour and
lifelong wrestle with that Lernean Hydracoil,[13] wide as England,
hissing heaven-high through its thousand crowned, coroneted,
shovel-hatted[14] quackheads; and he did wrestle with it, the truest
and terriblest wrestle I have heard of; and he wrestled it, and
mowed and cut it down a good many stages, so that its hissing is
ever since pitiful in comparison, and one can walk abroad in com-

[12] Milton received £10 for *Paradise Lost,* and at the Restoration was arrested as the author of influential Puritan propaganda.
[13] The nine-headed snake, resident in the marsh of Lerna, slain by Hercules as the second of his labors. For every head cut off, two sprang up
in its place.
[14] A broad-brimmed hat, turned up at the sides and projecting in front:
a familiar article of clerical dress.

parative peace from it; — and his wages, as I understand, were burial under the gallows-tree near Tyburn Turnpike,[15] with his head on the gable of Westminster Hall, and two centuries now of mixed cursing and ridicule from all manner of men. His dust lies under the Edgeware Road, near Tyburn Turnpike, at this hour; and his memory is — Nay, what matters what his memory is? His memory, at bottom, is or yet shall be as that of a god: a terror and horror to all quacks and cowards and insincere persons; an ever-lasting encouragement, new memento, battleword, and pledge of victory to all the brave. It is the natural course and history of the Godlike, in every place, in every time. What god ever carried it with the Tenpound Franchisers;[16] in Open Vestry,[17] or with any Sanhedrim[18] of considerable standing? When was a god found 'agreeable' to everybody? The regular way is to hang, kill, crucify your gods, and execrate and trample them under your stupid hoofs for a century or two; till you discover that they are gods, — and then take to braying over them, still in a very long-eared manner! — So speaks the sarcastic man; in his wild way, very mournful truths.

Day's-wages for day's-work? continues he: The Progress of Human Society consists even in this same, The better and better apportioning of wages to work. Give me this, you have given me all. Pay to every man accurately what he has worked for, what he has earned and done and deserved, — to this man broad lands and honours, to that man high gibbets and treadmills: what more have I to ask? Heaven's Kingdom, which we daily pray for, *has* come; God's will is done on Earth even as it is in Heaven! This *is* the radiance of celestial Justice; in the light or in the fire of which all impediments, vested interests, and iron cannon, are more and more melting like wax, and disappearing from the pathways of men. A thing ever struggling forward; irrepressible, advancing inevitable; perfecting itself, all days, more and more, — never to be *perfect* till that general Doomsday, the ultimate Consummation, and Last of earthly Days.

[15] A London place of execution, near the present Marble Arch.

[16] Owners or tenants of property worth £10 a year in rental were entitled to vote in local elections under the Reform Act of 1832.

[17] The assembled taxpayers of a parish, somewhat analogous to a New England town meeting: in Carlyle's time a symbol of democratic local rule.

[18] In ancient Jerusalem, the supreme tribunal: an aristocratic body composed of the priestly nobility and learned men (scribes).

True, as to 'perfection' and so forth, answer we; true enough!
And yet withal we have to remark, that imperfect Human Society
holds itself together, and finds place under the Sun, in virtue
simply of some *approximation* to perfection being actually made
and put in practice. We remark farther, that there are supportable approximations, and then likewise insupportable. With some,
almost with any, supportable approximation men are apt, perhaps
too apt, to rest indolently patient, and say, It will do. Thus these
poor Manchester manual workers mean only, by day's-wages for
day's-work, certain coins of money adequate to keep them living;
— in return for their work, such modicum of food, clothes and
fuel as will enable them to continue their work itself! They as yet
clamour for no more; the rest, still inarticulate, cannot yet shape
itself into a demand at all, and only lies in them as a dumb wish;
perhaps only, still more inarticulate, as a dumb, altogether unconscious want. *This* is the supportable approximation they would
rest patient with, That by their work they might be kept alive to
work more! — *This* once grown unattainable, I think, your approximation may consider itself to have reached the *in*supportable
stage; and may prepare, with whatever difficulty, reluctance and
astonishment, for one of two things, for changing or perishing!
With the millions no longer able to live, how can the units keep
living? It is too clear the Nation itself is on the way to suicidal
death.

Shall we say then, The world has retrograded in its talent of
apportioning wages to work, in late days? The world had always
a talent of that sort, better or worse. Time was when the mere
*hand*worker needed not announce his claim to the world by Manchester Insurrections! — The world, with its Wealth of Nations,[19]
Supply-and-demand and such like, has of late days been terribly
inattentive to that question of work and wages. We will not say,
the poor world has retrograded even here: we will say rather, the
world has been rushing on with such fiery animation to get work
and ever more work done, it has had no time to think of dividing
the wages; and has merely left them to be scrambled for by the
Law of the Stronger, law of Supply-and-demand, law of Laissez-
faire, and other idle Laws and Un-laws, — saying, in its dire haste
to get the work done, That is well enough!

And now the world will have to pause a little, and take up that
other side of the problem, and in right earnest strive for some

[19] See above, p. 11, n. 9.

solution of that. For it has become pressing. What is the use of your spun shirts? They hang there by the million unsaleable; and here, by the million, are diligent bare backs that can get no hold of them. Shirts are useful for covering human backs; useless otherwise, an unbearable mockery otherwise. You have fallen terribly behind with that side of the problem! Manchester Insurrections, French Revolutions, and thousandfold phenomena great and small, announce loudly that you must bring it forward a little again. Never till now, in the history of an Earth which to this hour nowhere refuses to grow corn if you will plough it, to yield shirts if you will spin and weave in it, did the mere manual two-handed worker (however it might fare with other workers) cry in vain for such 'wages' as *he* means by 'fair wages,' namely food and warmth! The Godlike could not and cannot be paid; but the Earthly always could. Gurth, a mere swineherd, born thrall of Cedric the Saxon, tended pigs in the wood, and did get some parings of the pork.[20] Why, the four-footed worker has already *got* all that this two-handed one is clamouring for! How often must I remind you? There is not a horse in England, able and willing to work, but *has* due food and lodging; and goes about sleek-coated, satisfied in heart. And you say, It is impossible. Brothers, I answer, if for you it be impossible, what is to become of you? It is impossible for us to believe it to be impossible. The human brain, looking at these sleek English horses, refuses to believe in such impossibility for English men. Do you depart quickly; clear the ways soon, lest worse befal. We for our share do purpose, with full view of the enormous difficulty, with total disbelief in the impossibility, to endeavour while life is in us, and to die endeavouring, we and our sons, till we attain it or have all died and ended.

Such a Platitude of a World, in which all working horses could be well fed, and innumerable working men should die starved, were it not best to end it; to have done with it, and restore it once for all to the *Jötuns*,[21] Mud-giants, Frost-giants and Chaotic Brute-gods of the Beginning? For the old Anarchic Brute-gods it may be well enough, but it is a Platitude which Men should be above countenancing by their presence in it. We pray you, let the word *impossible* disappear from your vocabulary in this matter. It is of awful omen; to all of us, and to yourselves first of all.

[20] In Scott's *Ivanhoe*.
[21] Norse giants, enemies of the gods

CHAPTER IV

MORRISON'S PILL

WHAT is to be done, what would you have us do? asks many a one, with a tone of impatience, almost of reproach; and then, if you mention some one thing, some two things, twenty things that might be done, turns round with a satirical tehee, and, "These are your remedies!" The state of mind indicated by such question, and such rejoinder, is worth reflecting on.

It seems to be taken for granted, by these interrogative philosophers, that there is some 'thing,' or handful of 'things,' which could be done; some Act of Parliament, 'remedial measure' or the like, which could be passed, whereby the social malady were fairly fronted, conquered, put an end to; so that, with your remedial measure in your pocket, you could then go on triumphant, and be troubled no farther. "You tell us the evil," cry such persons, as if justly aggrieved, "and do not tell us how it is to be cured!"

How it is to be cured? Brothers, I am sorry I have got no Morrison's Pill[1] for curing the maladies of Society. It were infinitely handier if we had a Morrison's Pill, Act of Parliament, or remedial measure, which men could swallow, one good time, and then go on in their old courses, cleared from all miseries and mischiefs! Unluckily we have none such; unluckily the Heavens themselves, in their rich pharmacopœia, contain none such. There will no 'thing' be done that will cure you. There will a radical universal alteration of your regimen and way of life take place; there will a most agonising divorce between you and your chimeras, luxuries and falsities, take place; a most toilsome, all but 'impossible' return to Nature, and her veracities, and her integrities, take place: that so the inner fountains of life may again begin, like eternal Light-fountains,[2] to irradiate and purify your

[1] James Morison, who died in 1840, was a self-described "Hygeist" who compounded a "vegetable universal medicine" that was widely advertised, for example in the monthly parts in which some of Dickens' novels were first issued. Carlyle consistently misspells his name.

[2] Ancestors of modern therapeutic sun lamps.

bloated, swollen, foul existence, drawing nigh, as at present, to nameless death! Either death or else all this will take place. Judge if, with such diagnosis, any Morrison's Pill is like to be discoverable!

But the Life-fountain within you once again set flowing, what innumerable 'things,' whole sets and classes and continents of 'things,' year after year, and decade after decade, and century after century, will then be doable and done! Not Emigration, Education, Corn-Law Abrogation, Sanitary Regulation, Land Property-Tax; not these alone, nor a thousand times as much as these. Good Heavens, there will then be light in the inner heart of here and there a man, to discern what is just, what is commanded by the Most High God, what *must* be done, were it never so 'impossible.' Vain jargon in favour of the palpably unjust will then abridge itself within limits. Vain jargon, on Hustings,[3] in Parliaments or wherever else, when here and there a man has vision for the essential God's-Truth of the things jargoned of, will become very vain indeed. The silence of here and there such a man, how eloquent in answer to such jargon! Such jargon, frightened at its own gaunt echo, will unspeakably abate; nay, for a while, may almost in a manner disappear, — the wise answering it in silence, and even the simple taking cue from them to hoot it down wherever heard. It will be a blessed time; and many 'things' will become doable, — and when the brains are out,[4] an absurdity will die! Not easily again shall a Corn-Law argue ten years for itself; and still talk and argue, when impartial persons have to say with a sigh that, for so long back, they have heard no 'argument' advanced for it but such as might make the angels and almost the very jackasses weep! —

Wholly a blessed time: when jargon might abate, and here and there some genuine speech begin. When to the noble opened heart, as to such heart they alone do, all noble things began to grow visible; and the difference between just and unjust, between true and false, between work and sham-work, between speech and jargon, was once more, what to our happier Fathers it used to be, *infinite*, — as between a Heavenly thing and an Infernal: the one a thing which you were *not* to do, which you were wise not to attempt doing; which it were better for you to have a millstone

---

[3] Platforms from which candidates for Parliament were nominated and from which they delivered their campaign oratory.

[4] *Macbeth*, III.iv.79.

tied round your neck, and be cast into the sea,[5] than concern yourself with doing! — Brothers, it will not be a Morrison's Pill, or
remedial measure, that will bring all this about for us.

And yet, very literally, till, in some shape or other, it be brought
about, we remain cureless; till it begin to be brought about, the
cure does not begin. For Nature and Fact, not Redtape and
Semblance, are to this hour the basis of man's life; and on those,
through never such strata of these, man and his life and all his
interests do, sooner or later, infallibly come to rest, — and to be
supported or be swallowed according as they agree with those.
The question is asked of them, not, How do you agree with
Downing-street[6] and accredited Semblance? but, How do you
agree with God's Universe and the actual Reality of things? This
Universe *has* its Laws. If we walk according to the Law, the
Law-Maker will befriend us; if not, not. Alas, by no Reform Bill,
Ballot-box,[7] Five-point Charter, by no boxes or bills or charters,
can you perform this alchemy: 'Given a world of Knaves to produce an Honesty from their united action!' It is a distillation,
once for all, not possible. You pass it through alembic after
alembic, it comes out still a Dishonesty, with a new dress on it, a
new colour to it. 'While we ourselves continue valets, how *can*
any hero come to govern us?' We are governed, very infallibly,
by the 'sham-hero,' — whose name is Quack, whose work and
governance is Plausibility, and also is Falsity and Fatuity; to
which Nature says, and must say when it comes to *her* to speak,
eternally No! Nations cease to be befriended of the Law-Maker,
when they walk *not* according to the Law. The Sphinx-question
remains unsolved by them, becomes ever more insoluble.

If thou ask again, therefore, on the Morrison's-Pill hypothesis,
What is to be done? allow me to reply: By thee, for the present,
almost nothing. Thou there, the thing for thee to do is, if possible,
to cease to be a hollow sounding-shell of hearsays, egoisms, pur-
blind dilettantisms; and become, were it on the infinitely small
scale, a faithful discerning soul. Thou shalt descend into thy

[5] Matthew 18:6; Mark 9:42; Luke 17:2.
[6] The London *cul de sac* which contains the official residences of the prime
minister and the chancellor of the exchequer, as well as the Foreign Office.
[7] The secret ballot (to replace the old method of open voting) was provided for in a draft, later discarded, of the 1832 Reform Bill, and was one
of the Chartists' six demands. It was not, however, adopted in parliamentary
elections until 1874.

inner man, and see if there be any traces of a *soul* there; till then there can be nothing done! O brother, we must if possible resuscitate some soul and conscience in us, exchange our dilettantisms for sincerities, our dead hearts of stone for living hearts of flesh. Then shall we discern, not one thing, but, in clearer or dimmer sequence, a whole endless host of things that can be done. *Do* the first of these; do it; the second will already have become clearer, doabler; the second, third and three-thousandth will then have begun to be possible for us. Not any universal Morrison's Pill shall we then, either as swallowers or as venders, ask after at all; but a far different sort of remedies: Quacks shall no more have dominion over us, but true Heroes and Healers!

Will not that be a thing worthy of 'doing;' to deliver ourselves from quacks, sham-heroes; to deliver the whole world more and more from such? They are the one bane of the world. Once clear the world of them, it ceases to be a Devil's-world, in all fibres of it wretched, accursed; and begins to be a God's-world, blessed, and working hourly towards blessedness. Thou for one wilt not again vote for any quack, do honour to any edge-gilt vacuity in man's shape: cant shall be known to thee by the sound of it; — thou wilt fly from cant with a shudder never felt before; as from the opened litany of Sorcerers' Sabbaths,[8] the true Devil-worship of this age, more horrible than any other blasphemy, profanity or genuine blackguardism elsewhere audible among men. It is alarming to witness, — in its present completed state! And Quack and Dupe, as we must ever keep in mind, are upper-side and under of the selfsame substance; convertible personages: turn up your dupe into the proper fostering element, and he himself can become a quack; there is in him the due prurient insincerity, open voracity for profit, and closed sense for truth, whereof quacks too, in all their kinds, are made.

Alas, it is not to the hero, it is to the sham-hero that, of right and necessity, the valet-world belongs. 'What is to be done?' The reader sees whether it is like to be the seeking and swallowing of some 'remedial measure!'

[8] Nocturnal, mischief-bent, and blasphemous convocations of witches and demons.

CHAPTER V

WHEN an individual is miserable, what does it most of all behove him to do? To complain of this man or of that, of this thing or of that? To fill the world and the street with lamentation, objurgation? Not so at all; the reverse of so. All moralists advise him not to complain of any person or of any thing, but of himself only. He is to know of a truth that being miserable he has been unwise, he. Had he faithfully followed Nature and her Laws, Nature, ever true to her Laws, would have yielded fruit and increase and felicity to him: but he has followed other than Nature's Laws; and now Nature, her patience with him being ended, leaves him desolate; answers with very emphatic significance to him: No. Not by this road, my son; by another road shalt thou attain well-being: this, thou perceivest is the road to ill-being; quit this! — So do all moralists advise: that the man penitently say to himself first of all, Behold I was not wise enough; I quitted the laws of Fact, which are also called the Laws of God, and mistook for them the laws of Sham and Semblance, which are called the Devil's Laws; therefore am I here!

Neither with Nations that become miserable is it fundamentally otherwise. The ancient guides of Nations, Prophets, Priests, or whatever their name, were well aware of this; and, down to a late epoch, impressively taught and inculcated it. The modern guides of Nations, who also go under a great variety of names, Journalists, Political Economists, Politicians, Pamphleteers, have entirely forgotten this, and are ready to deny this. But it nevertheless remains eternally undeniable: nor is there any doubt but we shall all be taught it yet, and made again to confess it: we shall all be striped and scourged till we do learn it; and shall at last either get to know it, or be striped to death in the process. For it is undeniable! When a Nation is unhappy, the old Prophet was right and not wrong in saying to it: Ye have forgotten God, ye have quitted the ways of God, or ye would not have been unhappy.[1] It is not

[1] Isaiah 17:10; Jeremiah 3:21, 13:25.

according to the laws of Fact that ye have lived and guided your-selves, but according to the laws of Delusion, Imposture, and wilful and unwilful *Mistake* of Fact; behold therefore the Un-veracity is worn out; Nature's long-suffering with you is ex-hausted; and ye are here!

Surely there is nothing very inconceivable in this, even to the Journalist, to the Political Economist, Modern Pamphleteer, or any two-legged animal without feathers![2] If a country finds itself wretched, sure enough that country has been *mis*guided: it is with the wretched Twenty-seven Millions, fallen wretched, as with the Unit fallen wretched: they as he have quitted the course pre-scribed by Nature and the Supreme Powers, and so are fallen into scarcity, disaster, infelicity; and pausing to consider themselves, have to lament and say, Alas, we were not wise enough. We took transient superficial Semblance for everlasting central Substance; we have departed far away from the *Laws* of this Universe, and behold now lawless Chaos and inane Chimera[3] is ready to devour us! — 'Nature in late centuries,' says Sauerteig,[4] 'was universally supposed to be dead; an old eight-day clock, made many thousand years ago, and still ticking, but dead as brass, — which the Maker, at most, sat looking at, in a distant, singular, and indeed incredible manner:[5] but now I am happy to observe, she is everywhere as-serting herself to be not dead and brass at all, but alive and miraculous, celestial-infernal, with an emphasis that will again penetrate the thickest head of this Planet by and by!' — —

Indisputable enough to all mortals now, the guidance of this country has not been sufficiently wise: men too foolish have been set to the guiding and governing of it, and have guided it *hither;* we must find wiser, — wiser, or else we perish! To this length of insight all England has now advanced; but as yet no farther. All England stands wringing its hands, asking itself, nigh desperate, What farther? Reform Bill proves to be a failure; Benthamee Radicalism,[6] the gospel of 'Enlightened Selfishness,' dies out, or

[2] Plato's definition of man, according to Diogenes Laertius.

[3] A monster composed of the head and forepart of a lion, the body of a goat, and the hindquarters of a dragon (Homer), or possessing the heads of those animals (Hesiod).

[4] Like Teufelsdröckh (below, p. 214), one of Carlyle's mouthpieces: an invented German writer ("sour dough," "leaven").

[5] The Creator's absence from the universe he had created was a major premise of the eighteenth-century deistic religion which Carlyle abhorred.

[6] The utilitarian political and economic system ("philosophical radical-ism") of Jeremy Bentham.

dwindles into Five-point Chartism, amid the tears and hootings of
men: what next are we to hope or try? Five-point Charter, Free-
trade; Church-extension,[7] Sliding-scale; what, in Heaven's name,
are we next to attempt, that we sink not in inane Chimera, and be
devoured of Chaos? — The case is pressing, and one of the most
complicated in the world. A God's-message never came to
thicker-skinned people; never had a God's-message to piece
through thicker integuments, into heavier ears. It is Fact, speaking once more, in miraculous thunder-voice, from out of the centre
of the world;[8] — how unknown its language to the deaf and
foolish many; how distinct, undeniable, terrible and yet beneficent, to the hearing few: Behold, ye shall grow wiser, or ye shall
die! Truer to Nature's Fact, or inane Chimera will swallow you;
in whirlwinds of fire, you and your Mammonisms, Dilettantisms,
your Midas-eared philosophies, double-barrelled Aristocracies,
shall disappear! — Such is the God's-message to *us*, once more,
in these modern days.

We must have more Wisdom to govern us, we must be governed by the Wisest, we must have an Aristocracy of Talent! cry
many. True, most true; but how to get it? The following extract
from our young friend of the *Houndsditch Indicator*[9] is worth
perusing: 'At this time,' says he, 'while there is a cry everywhere,
articulate or inarticulate, for an "Aristocracy of Talent," a Governing Class namely which did govern, not merely which took the
wages of governing, and could not with all our industry be kept
from misgoverning, corn-lawing, and playing the very deuce with
us, — it may not be altogether useless to remind some of the
greener-headed sort what a dreadfully difficult affair the getting
of such an Aristocracy is! Do you expect, my friends, that your
indispensable Aristocracy of Talent is to be enlisted straightway,
by some sort of recruitment aforethought, out of the general
population; arranged in supreme regimental order; and set to
rule over us? That it will be got sifted, like wheat out of chaff,

[7] The proposed endowment of additional clergymen from excess ecclesiastical revenues, principally to bring religion to the "spiritually deprived"
industrial areas.

[8] Probably the Sibylline oracle: cf. *Aeneid*, VI.42–44.

[9] Houndsditch, a district in the East End of London, was then populated
by Jewish second-hand clothes dealers. Carlyle's choice of *Indicator* for the
name of his fictitious paper may have been influenced by the fact that the
Western Vindicator, published in Wales, was an inflammatory Chartist paper.

from the Twenty-seven Million British subjects; that any Ballot-box, Reform Bill, or other Political Machine, with Force of Public Opinion never so active on it, is likely to perform said process of sifting? Would to Heaven that we had a sieve; that we could so much as fancy any kind of sieve, wind-fanners, or ne-plus-ultra of machinery, devisable by man, that would do it!

'Done nevertheless, sure enough, it must be; it shall and will be. We are rushing swiftly on the road to destruction; every hour bringing us nearer, until it be, in some measure, done. The doing of it is not doubtful; only the method and the costs! Nay I will even mention to you an infallible sifting-process whereby he that has ability will be sifted out to rule among us, and that same blessed Aristocracy of Talent be verily, in an approximate degree, vouchsafed us by and by: an infallible sifting-process; to which, however, no soul can help his neighbour, but each must, with devout prayer to Heaven, endeavour to help himself. It is, O friends, that all of us, that many of us, should acquire the true *eye* for talent, which is dreadfully wanting at present! The true eye for talent presupposes the true reverence for it, — O Heavens, presupposes so many things!

'For example, you Bobus Higgins, Sausage-maker on the great scale, who are raising such a clamour for this Aristocracy of Talent, what is it that you do, in that big heart of yours, chiefly in very fact pay reverence to? Is it to talent, intrinsic manly worth of any kind, you unfortunate Bobus? The manliest man that you saw going in a ragged coat, did you ever reverence him; did you so much as know that he was a manly man at all, till his coat grew better? Talent! I understand you to be able to worship the fame of talent, the power, cash, celebrity or other success of talent; but the talent itself is a thing you never saw with eyes. Nay what is it in yourself that you are proudest of, that you take most pleasure in surveying meditatively in thoughtful moments? Speak now, is it the bare Bobus stript of his very name and shirt, and turned loose upon society, that you admire and thank Heaven for; or Bobus with his cash-accounts and larders dropping fatness,[10] with his respectabilities, warm garnitures, and pony-chaise, admirable in some measure to certain of the flunkey species? Your own degree of worth and talent, is it of *infinite* value to you; or only of finite, — measurable by the degree of currency, and conquest of praise or pudding, it has brought you to? Bobus, you

[10] Psalms 65:11.

are in a vicious circle, rounder than one of your own sausages; and will never vote for or promote any talent, except what talent or sham-talent has already *got* itself voted for!' — We here cut short the *Indicator;* all readers perceiving whither he now tends.

'More Wisdom' indeed: but where to find more Wisdom? We have already a Collective Wisdom,[11] after its kind, — though 'class-legislation,' and another thing or two, affect it somewhat! On the whole, as they say, Like people like priest;[12] so we may say, Like people like king. The man gets himself appointed and elected who is ablest — to be appointed and elected. What can the incorruptiblest *Bobuses* elect, if it be not some *Bobissimus,* should they find such?

Or, again, perhaps there is not, in the whole Nation, Wisdom enough, 'collect' it as we may, to make an adequate Collective! That too is a case which may befal: a ruined man staggers down to ruin because there was not wisdom enough in him; so, clearly also, may Twenty-seven Million collective men! — But indeed one of the infalliblest fruits of Unwisdom in a Nation is that it cannot get the use of what Wisdom is actually in it: that it is not governed by the wisest it has, who alone have a divine right to govern in all Nations; but by the sham-wisest, or even by the openly not-so-wise if they are handiest otherwise! This is the infalliblest result of Unwisdom; and also the balefullest, immeasurablest, — not so much what we can call a poison-*fruit,* as a universal death-disease, and poisoning of the whole tree. For hereby are fostered, fed into gigantic bulk, all manner of Unwisdoms, poison-fruits; till, as we say, the life-tree everywhere is made a upas-tree,[13] deadly Unwisdom overshadowing all things; and there is done what lies in human skill to stifle all Wisdom everywhere in the birth, to smite our poor world barren of Wisdom, — and make your utmost Collective Wisdom, were it collected and elected by Rhadamanthus, Æacus and Minos,[14] not to speak of drunken Tenpound Franchisers with their ballot-boxes, an inadequate Collective! The Wisdom is not now there: how will you 'collect' it? As well wash Thames mud, by improved methods, to find more gold in it.

[11] Parliament.   [12] Hosea 4:9.
[13] Javanese tree whose bark contains a poisonous juice. It was said (mistakenly) to kill those who slept in its shade.
[14] Judges of the dead in Hades.

Truly, the first condition is indispensable, That Wisdom be there: but the second is like unto it, is properly one with it: these two conditions act and react through every fibre of them, and go inseparably together. If you have much Wisdom in your Nation, you will get it faithfully collected; for the wise love Wisdom, and will search for it as for life and salvation. If you have little Wisdom, you will get even that little ill-collected, trampled under foot, reduced as near as possible to annihilation; for fools do not love Wisdom; they are foolish, first of all, because they have never loved Wisdom, — but have loved their own appetites, ambitions, their coroneted coaches, tankards of heavy-wet.[15] Thus is your candle lighted at both ends, and the progress towards consummation is swift. Thus is fulfilled that saying in the Gospel: To him that hath shall be given; and from him that hath not shall be taken away even that which he hath.[16] Very literally, in a very fatal manner, that saying is here fulfilled.

Our 'Aristocracy of Talent' seems at a considerable distance yet; does it not, O Bobus?

[15] Strong ale or stout.
[16] Mark 4:25.

CHAPTER VI

HERO-WORSHIP

To the present Editor, not less than to Bobus, a Government of the Wisest, what Bobus calls an Aristocracy of Talent, seems the one healing remedy: but he is not so sanguine as Bobus with respect to the means of realising it. He thinks that we have at once missed realising it, and come to need it so pressingly, by departing far from the inner eternal Laws and taking up with the temporary outer semblances of Laws. He thinks that 'enlightened Egoism,' never so luminous, is not the rule by which man's life can be led. That 'Laissez-faire,' 'Supply-and-demand,' 'Cash-payment for the sole nexus,' and so forth, were not, are not, and will never be, a practicable Law of Union for a Society of Men. That Poor and Rich, that Governed and Governing, cannot long live together on any such Law of Union. Alas, he thinks that man has a soul in him, *different* from the stomach in any sense of this word; that if said soul be asphyxied, and lie quietly forgotten, the man and his affairs are in a bad way. He thinks that said soul will have to be resuscitated from its asphyxia; that if it prove irresuscitable, the man is not long for this world. In brief, that Midas-eared Mammonism, double-barrelled Dilettantism, and their thousand adjuncts and corollaries, are *not* the Law by which God Almighty has appointed this his Universe to go. That, once for all, these are not the Law: and then farther that we shall have to return to what *is* the Law, — not by smooth flowery paths, it is like, and with 'tremendous cheers' in our throat; but over steep untrodden places, through stormclad chasms, waste oceans, and the bosom of tornadoes; thank Heaven, if not through very Chaos and the Abyss! The resuscitating of a soul that has gone to asphyxia is no momentary or pleasant process, but a long and terrible one.

To the present Editor, 'Hero-worship,' as he has elsewhere named it, means much more than an elected Parliament, or stated Aristocracy, of the Wisest; for, in his dialect, it is the summary, ultimate essence, and supreme practical perfection of all manner of 'worship,' and true worships and noblenesses whatsoever. Such blessed Parliament and, were it once in perfection, blessed Aristocracy of the Wisest, god-honoured and man-honoured, he does look for, more and more perfected, — as the topmost blessed practical apex of a whole world reformed from sham-worship, informed anew with worship, with truth and blessedness! He thinks that Hero-worship, done differently in every different epoch of the world, is the soul of all social business among men; that the doing of it well, or the doing of it ill, measures accurately what degree of well-being or of ill-being there is in the world's affairs. He thinks that we, on the whole, do our Hero-worship worse than any Nation in this world ever did it before: that the Burns an Exciseman, the Byron a Literary Lion, are intrinsically, all things considered, a baser and falser phenomenon than the Odin a God, the Mahomet a Prophet of God.[1] It is this Editor's clear opinion, accordingly, that we must learn to do our Hero-worship better; that to do it better and better, means the awakening of the Nation's soul from its asphyxia, and the return of blessed life to us, — Heaven's blessed life, not Mammon's galvanic[2] accursed one. To resuscitate the Asphyxied, apparently now moribund, and in the last agony if not resuscitated: such and no other seems the consummation.

'Hero-worship,' if you will, — yes, friends; but, first of all, by being ourselves of heroic mind. A whole world of Heroes; a world not of Flunkeys, where no Hero-King *can* reign: that is what we aim at! We, for our share, will put away all Flunkeyism, Baseness, Unveracity from us; we shall then hope to have Noblenesses and Veracities set over us; never till then. Let Bobus and Company sneer, "That is your Reform!" Yes, Bobus, that is our Reform; and except in that, and what will follow out of that, we have no hope at all. Reform, like Charity, O Bobus, must begin at home. Once well at home, how will it radiate outwards, irrepressible, into all that we touch and handle, speak and work; kindling ever new light, by incalculable contagion, spreading in geometric ratio, far and wide, — doing good only, wheresoever it spreads, and not evil.

By Reform Bills, Anti-Corn-Law Bills, and thousand other bills

---

[1] Odin is Wotan, king of the Norse gods. For the significance of Burns, Odin, and Mahomet in Carlyle's thought, see *Heroes and Hero-Worship*, Lectures I, II, V.

[2] Stimulating by electric shock.

and methods, we will demand of our Governors, with emphasis, and for the first time not without effect, that they cease to be quacks, or else depart; that they set no quackeries and blockhead-isms anywhere to rule over us, that they utter or act no cant to us, — that it will be better if they do not. For we shall now know quacks when we see them; cant, when we hear it, shall be horrible to us! We will say, with the poor Frenchman at the Bar of the Convention, though in wiser style than he, and 'for the space' not 'of an hour' but of a lifetime: *"Je demande l'arrestation des coquins et des lâches."*[3] 'Arrestment of the knaves and dastards:' ah, we know what a work that is; how long it will be before *they* are all or mostly got 'arrested:'— but here is one; arrest him, in God's name; it is one fewer! We will, in all practicable ways, by word and silence, by act and refusal to act, energetically demand that arrestment, — *"je demande cette arrestation-là!"* — and by degrees infallibly attain it. Infallibly: for light spreads; all human souls, never so bedarkened, love light; light once kindled spreads, till all is luminous; — till the cry, *"Arrest* your knaves and dastards" rises imperative from millions of hearts, and rings and reigns from sea to sea. Nay, how many of them may we not 'arrest' with our own hands, even now; we! Do not countenance them, thou there: turn away from their lackered sumptuosities, their belauded sophistries, their serpent graciosities, their spoken and acted cant, with a sacred horror, with an *Apage Satanas*.[4] — Bobus and Company, and all men will gradually join us. We demand arrestment of the knaves and dastards, and begin by arresting our own poor selves out of that fraternity. There is no other reform conceivable. Thou and I, my friend, can, in the most flunkey world, make, each of us, *one* non-flunkey, one hero, if we like: that will be two heroes to begin with: — Courage! even that is a whole world of heroes to end with, or what we poor Two can do in furtherance thereof!

Yes, friends: Hero-kings and a whole world not unheroic, — there lies the port and happy haven, towards which, through all these stormtost seas, French Revolutions, Chartisms, Manchester Insurrections, that make the heart sick in these bad days, the Supreme Powers are driving us. On the whole, blessed be the Supreme Powers, stern as they are! Towards that haven will we, O friends; let all true men, with what of faculty is in them, bend valiantly, incessantly, with thousandfold endeavour, thither,

[3] Cf. *The French Revolution*, XX.v.
[4] "Get thee hence, Satan": Matthew 4:10.

thither! There, or else in the Ocean-abysses, it is very clear to me, we shall arrive.

Well; here truly is no answer to the Sphinx-question; not the answer a disconsolate Public, inquiring at the College of Health,[5] was in hopes of! A total change of regimen, change of constitution and existence from the very centre of it; a new body to be got, with resuscitated soul, — not without convulsive travail-throes; as all birth and new-birth presupposes travail! This is sad news to a disconsolate discerning Public, hoping to have got off by some Morrison's Pill, some Saint-John's corrosive mixture[6] and perhaps a little blistery friction on the back! — We were prepared to part with our Corn-Law, with various Laws and Unlaws: but this, what is this?

Nor has the Editor forgotten how it fares with your ill-boding Cassandras[7] in Sieges of Troy. Imminent perdition is not usually driven away by words of warning. Didactic Destiny has other methods in store; or these would fail always. Such words should, nevertheless, be uttered, when they dwell truly in the soul of any man. Words are hard, are importunate; but how much harder the importunate events they foreshadow! Here and there a human soul may listen to the words, — who knows how many human souls? whereby the importunate events, if not diverted and prevented, will be rendered *less* hard. The present Editor's purpose is to himself full of hope.

For though fierce travails, though wide seas and roaring gulfs lie before us, is it not something if a Loadstar, in the eternal sky, do once more disclose itself; an everlasting light, shining through all cloud-tempests and roaring billows, ever as we emerge from the trough of the sea: the blessed beacon, far off on the edge of far horizons, towards which we are to steer incessantly for life? Is it not something; O Heavens, is it not all? There lies the Heroic Promised Land; under that Heaven's-light, my brethren, bloom the Happy Isles, — there, O there! Thither will we;

There dwells the great Achilles whom we knew.[8]

[5] The name with which Morison dignified his pill dispensary.

[6] A concoction of St. John Long, quack physician to the carriage trade. Reputed to contain oil of turpentine and mineral acid, it was used to treat consumption, rheumatism, gout, abscesses of the lungs and liver, and insanity. Long was convicted of manslaughter in 1830.

[7] Daughter of Priam whose prophecy of the fall of Troy was disregarded.

[8] Tennyson's *Poems* (Ulysses). (C.)

There dwell all Heroes, and will dwell: thither, all ye heroic-minded! — The Heaven's Loadstar once clearly in our eye, how will each true man stand truly to *his* work in the ship; how, with undying hope, will all things be fronted, all be conquered. Nay, with the ship's prow once turned in that direction, is not all, as it were, already well? Sick wasting misery has become noble manful effort with a goal in our eye. 'The choking Nightmare chokes us no longer; for we *stir* under it; the Nightmare has already fled.'[9] —

Certainly, could the present Editor instruct men how to know Wisdom, Heroism, when they see it, that they might do reverence to *it* only, and loyally make it ruler over them, — yes, he were the living epitome of all Editors, Teachers, Prophets, that now teach and prophesy; he were an *Apollo*-Morrison, a Trismegistus[10] and *effective* Cassandra! Let no Able Editor hope such things. It is to be expected the present laws of copyright, rate of reward per sheet, and other considerations, will save him from that peril. Let no Editor hope such things: no; — and yet let all Editors aim towards such things, and even towards such alone! One knows not what the meaning of editing and writing is, if even this be not it.

Enough, to the present Editor it has seemed possible some glimmering of light, for here and there a human soul, might lie in these confused Paper-Masses now intrusted to him; wherefore he determines to edit the same. Out of old Books, new Writings, and much Meditation not of yesterday, he will endeavour to select a thing or two; and from the Past, in a circuitous way, illustrate the Present and the Future. The Past is a dim indubitable fact: the Future too is one, only dimmer; nay properly it is the *same* fact in new dress and development. For the Present holds in it both the whole Past and the whole Future; — as the LIFE-TREE IGDRASIL,[11] wide-waving, many-toned, has its roots down deep in the Death-kingdoms, among the oldest dead dust of men, and with its boughs reaches always beyond the stars; and in all times and places is one and the same Life-tree!

[9] Jean Paul Richter, quoted in Carlyle's essay "On Richter Again."
[10] Greek name for the Egyptian god Thoth, who patronized learning.
[11] In Norse mythology, the cosmic ash tree.

BOOK II

The Ancient Monk

CHAPTER I

W E WILL, in this Second Portion of our Work, strive to penetrate a little, by means of certain confused Papers, printed and other, into a somewhat remote Century; and to look face to face on it, in hope of perhaps illustrating our own poor Century thereby. It seems a circuitous way; but it may prove a way nevertheless. For man has ever been a striving, struggling, and, in spite of wide-spread calumnies to the contrary, a veracious creature: the Centuries too are all lineal children of one another; and often, in the portrait of early grandfathers, this and the other enigmatic feature of the newest grandson shall disclose itself, to mutual elucidation. This Editor will venture on such a thing.

Besides, in Editors' Books, and indeed everywhere else in the world of Today, a certain latitude of movement grows more and more becoming for the practical man. Salvation lies not in tight lacing, in these times; — how far from that, in any province whatsoever! Readers and men generally are getting into strange habits of asking all persons and things, from poor Editors' Books up to Church Bishops and State Potentates, not, By what designation are thou called; in what wig and black triangle[1] dost thou walk abroad? Heavens, I know thy designation and black triangle well enough! But, in God's name, what *art* thou? Not Nothing, sayest thou! Then if not, How much and what? This is the thing I would know; and even *must* soon know, such a pass am I come to! — — What weather-symptoms, — not for the poor Editor of Books alone! The Editor of Books may understand withal that if, as is said, 'many kinds are permissible,' there is one kind not permissible, 'the kind that has nothing in it, *le genre ennuyeux;*'[2] and go on his way accordingly.

---

[1] Gown of ecclesiastical or state dignitaries?
[2] Voltaire, preface to *L'Enfant Prodigue.*

A certain Jocelinus de Brakelonda, a natural-born Englishman, has left us an extremely foreign Book,[3] which the labours of the Camden Society have brought to light in these days. Jocelin's Book, the 'Chronicle,' or private Boswellean Notebook, of Jocelin, a certain old St. Edmundsbury Monk and Boswell, now seven centuries old, how remote is it from us; exotic, extraneous; in all ways, coming from far abroad! The language of it is not foreign only but dead: Monk-Latin lies across not the British Channel, but the ninefold Stygian Marshes, Stream of Lethe,[4] and one knows not where! Roman Latin itself, still alive for us in the Elysian Fields of Memory, is domestic in comparison. And then the ideas, life-furniture, whole workings and ways of this worthy Jocelin; covered deeper than Pompeii with the lava-ashes and inarticulate wreck of seven hundred years!

Jocelin of Brakelond cannot be called a conspicuous literary character; indeed few mortals that have left so visible a work, or footmark, behind them can be more obscure. One other of those vanished Existences, whose work has not yet vanished; — almost a pathetic phenomenon, were not the whole world full of such! The builders of Stonehenge,[5] for example: — or alas, what say we, Stonehenge and builders? The writers of the *Universal Review*[6] and *Homer's Iliad;* the paviers of London streets; — sooner or later, the entire Posterity of Adam! It is a pathetic phenomenon; but an irremediable, nay, if well meditated, a consoling one.

By his dialect of Monk-Latin, and indeed by his name, this Jocelin seems to have been a Norman Englishman; the surname *de Brakelonda* indicates a native of St. Edmundsbury itself, *Brakelond* being the known old name of a street or quarter in that venerable Town. Then farther, sure enough, our Jocelin was a Monk of St. Edmundsbury Convent; held some '*obedientia,*' subaltern officiality there, or rather, in succession several; was, for one thing, 'chaplain to my Lord Abbot, living beside him night and day for the space of six years;' — which last, indeed, is the grand fact of Jocelin's existence, and properly the origin of this present Book, and of the chief meaning it has for us now. He was,

---

[3] *Chronica* JOCELINI DE BRAKELONDA, *de rebus gestis Samsonis Abbatis Monasterii Sancti Edmundi: nunc primum typis mandata, curante* JOHANNE GAGE ROKEWOOD. (Camden Society, London, 1840.) (C.)

[4] Parts of the landscape of Hades. The Elysian Fields (just following) are the abode of the happy dead.

[5] The mysterious prehistoric arrangement of monoliths near Salisbury.

[6] Perhaps a reference to the *Universal Review, or Chronicle of the Literature of All Nations,* a periodical published in 1824–25.

as we have hinted, a kind of born *Boswell*, though an infinites-
imally small one; neither did he altogether want his *Johnson* even
there and then. Johnsons are rare; yet, as has been asserted,
Boswells perhaps still rarer, — the more is the pity on both sides!
This Jocelin, as we can discern well, was an ingenious and in-
genuous, a cheery-hearted, innocent, yet withal shrewd, noticing,
quick-witted man; and from under his monk's cowl has looked
out on that narrow section of the world in a really *human* manner;
not in any *simial*, canine, ovine, or otherwise *in*human manner, —
afflictive to all that have humanity! The man is of patient, peaceable, loving, clear-smiling nature; open for this and that. A wise
simplicity is in him; much natural sense; a *veracity* that goes
deeper than words. Veracity: it is the basis of all; and, some say,
means genius itself; the prime essence of all genius whatsoever.
Our Jocelin, for the rest, has read his classical manuscripts, his
Virgilius, his Flaccus,[7] Ovidius Naso; of course still more, his
Homilies and Breviaries, and if not the Bible, considerable ex-
tracts of the Bible. Then also he has a pleasant wit; and loves a
timely joke, though in mild subdued manner: very amiable to see.
A learned grown man, yet with the heart of a good child;
whose whole life indeed has been that of a child, — St. Edmundsbury Monastery a larger kind of cradle for him, in which
his whole prescribed duty was to *sleep* kindly, and love his
mother well! This is the Biography of Jocelin; 'a man of excellent
religion,' says one of his contemporary Brother Monks, *'eximiæ
religionis, potens sermone et opere.'*[8]

For one thing, he had learned to write a kind of Monk or Dog-
Latin, still readable to mankind; and, by good luck for us, had
bethought him of noting down thereby what things seemed notablest to him. Hence gradually resulted a *Chronica Jocelini;* new
Manuscript in the *Liber Albus*[9] of St. Edmundsbury. Which
Chronicle, once written in its childlike transparency, in its innocent good-humour, not without touches of ready pleasant wit and
many kinds of worth, other men liked naturally to read: whereby
it failed not to be copied, to be multiplied, to be inserted in the
Liber Albus; and so surviving Henry the Eighth, Putney Cromwell,[10] the Dissolution of Monasteries, and all accidents of malice

[7] Horace.
[8] *potens . . . opere:* "powerful in word and deed."
[9] The collection of manuscripts which includes the *Chronicle* of Jocelin.
[10] Thomas Cromwell, Henry VIII's agent in the dissolution of the monasteries. Carlyle calls him "Putney" (his birthplace) to distinguish him
from the later Oliver Cromwell.

and neglect for six centuries or so, it got into the *Harleian Collection*,[11] — and has now therefrom, by Mr. Rokewood of the Camden Society, been deciphered into clear print; and lies before us, a dainty thin quarto, to interest for a few minutes whomsoever it can.

Here too it will behove a just Historian gratefully to say that Mr. Rokewood, Jocelin's Editor, has done his editorial function well. Not only has he deciphered his crabbed Manuscript into clear print; but he has attended, what his fellow editors are not always in the habit of doing, to the important truth that the Manuscript so deciphered ought to have a meaning for the reader. Standing faithfully by his text, and printing its very errors in spelling, in grammar or otherwise, he has taken care by some note to indicate that they are errors, and what the correction of them ought to be. Jocelin's Monk-Latin is generally transparent, as shallow limpid water. But at any stop that may occur, of which there are a few, and only a very few, we have the comfortable assurance that a meaning does lie in the passage, and may by industry be got at; that a faithful editor's industry had already got at it before passing on. A compendious useful Glossary is given; nearly adequate to help the uninitiated through: sometimes one wishes it had been a trifle larger; but, with a Spelman and Ducange[12] at your elbow, how easy to have made it far too large! Notes are added, generally brief; sufficiently explanatory of most points. Lastly, a copious correct Index; which no such Book should want, and which unluckily very few possess. And so, in a word, the *Chronicle of Jocelin* is, as it professes to be, unwrapped from its thick cerements, and fairly brought forth into the common daylight, so that he who runs, and has a smattering of grammar, may read.

We have heard so much of Monks; everywhere, in real and fictitious History, from Muratori Annals[13] to Radcliffe Romances,[14]

---

[11] An important collection of manuscripts relating to English history, in the library of the British Museum.

[12] Sir Henry Spelman's glossary of Latin and Anglo-Saxon terms appeared in 1616–24; Charles Du Fresne, Sieur Du Cange, compiled important Latin and Greek dictionaries (1678, 1688).

[13] Lodovico Antonio Muratori, eighteenth-century antiquary and historian, edited many documents relating to medieval Italian history.

[14] Ann Radcliffe was among the late eighteenth- and early nineteenth-century writers of Gothic novels whose pictures of medieval life were wildly unhistorical.

these singular two-legged animals, with their rosaries and breviaries, with their shaven crowns, hair-cilices,[15] and vows of
poverty, masquerade so strangely through our fancy; and they are
in fact so very strange an extinct species of the human family, —
a veritable Monk of Bury St. Edmunds is worth attending to,
if by chance made visible and audible. Here he is; and in his
hand a magical speculum, much gone to rust indeed, yet in fragments still clear; wherein the marvellous image of his existence
does still shadow itself, though fitfully, and as with an intermittent
light! Will not the reader peep with us into this singular *camera
lucida*,[16] where an extinct species, though fitfully, can still be seen
alive? Extinct species, we say; for the live specimens which still
go about under that character are too evidently to be classed as
spurious in Natural History: the Gospel of Richard Arkwright[17]
once promulgated, no Monk of the old sort is any longer possible
in this world. But fancy a deep-buried Mastodon, some fossil
Megatherion, Ichthyosaurus, were to begin to *speak* from amid
its rock-swathings, never so indistinctly! The most extinct fossil
species of Men or Monks can do, and does, this miracle, — thanks
to the Letters of the Alphabet, good for so many things.

Jocelin, we said, was somewhat of a Boswell; but unfortunately,
by Nature, he is none of the largest, and distance has now
dwarfed him to an extreme degree. His light is most feeble,
intermittent, and requires the intensest kindest inspection; otherwise it will disclose mere vacant haze. It must be owned, the
good Jocelin, spite of his beautiful childlike character, is but an
altogether imperfect 'mirror' of these old-world things! The good
man, he looks on us so clear and cheery, and in his neighbourly
soft-smiling eyes we see so well our *own* shadow, — we have a
longing always to cross-question him, to force from him an explanation of much. But no; Jocelin, though he talks with such
clear familiarity, like a next-door neighbour, will not answer any
question: that is the peculiarity of him, dead these six hundred
and fifty years, and quite deaf to us, though still so audible! The
good man, he cannot help it, nor can we.

But truly it is a strange consideration this simple one, as we go
on with him, or indeed with any lucid simple-hearted soul like

15 Hair shirts.
16 An optical instrument (soon to be made obsolete by photography)
which projected upon a plane surface the image of an object to be copied.
17 Arkwright invented machines which revolutionized the cloth industry;
hence he was a father of industrialism.

him: Behold therefore, this England of the Year 1200 was no chimerical vacuity or dreamland, peopled with mere vaporous Fantasms, Rymer's Fœdera,[18] and Doctrines of the Constitution,[19] but a green solid place, that grew corn and several other things. The Sun shone on it; the vicissitude of seasons and human fortunes. Cloth was woven and worn; ditches were dug, furrow-fields ploughed, and houses built. Day by day all men and cattle rose to labour, and night by night returned home weary to their several lairs. In wondrous Dualism, then as now, lived nations of breathing men; alternating, in all ways, between Light and Dark; between joy and sorrow, between rest and toil, — between hope, hope reaching high as Heaven, and fear deep as very Hell. Not vapour Fantasms, Rymer's Fœdera at all! Cœur-de-Lion[20] was not a theatrical popinjay with greaves and steel-cap on it, but a man living upon victuals, — *not* imported by Peel's Tariff. Cœur-de-Lion came palpably athwart this Jocelin at St. Edmundsbury; and had almost peeled the sacred gold '*Feretrum*,' or St. Edmund Shrine itself, to ransom him out of the Danube Jail.

These clear eyes of neighbour Jocelin looked on the bodily presence of King John; the very John *Sansterre*, or Lackland, who signed *Magna Charta* afterwards in Runnymead. Lackland, with a great retinue, boarded once, for the matter of a fortnight, in St. Edmundsbury Convent; daily in the very eyesight, palpable to the very fingers of our Jocelin: O Jocelin, what did he say, what did he do; how looked he, lived he; — at the very lowest, what coat or breeches had he on? Jocelin is obstinately silent. Jocelin marks down what interests *him;* entirely deaf to *us.* With Jocelin's eyes we discern almost nothing of John Lackland. As through a glass darkly, we with our own eyes and appliances, intensely looking, discern at most: A blustering, dissipated, human figure, with a kind of blackguard quality air, in cramoisy[21] velvet, or other uncertain texture, uncertain cut, with much plumage and fringing; amid numerous other human figures of the like; riding abroad with hawks; talking noisy nonsense; — tearing out the bowels of

[18] A fifteen-volume collection of historical materials on Britain's foreign relations, published 1704–13.

[19] Possibly a reference to various treatises on constitutional law, such as George Bowyer's *The English Constitution* (1842).

[20] Richard I of England ("the Lion-Hearted"). He was imprisoned in Austria while returning from the third crusade.

[21] Crimson.

St. Edmundsbury Convent (its larders namely and cellars) in the most ruinous way, by living at rack and manger there. Jocelin notes only, with a slight subacidity of manner, that the King's Majesty, *Dominus Rex,* did leave, as gift for our St. Edmund Shrine, a handsome enough silk cloak, — or rather pretended to leave, for one of his retinue borrowed it of us, and *we* never got sight of it again; and, on the whole, that the *Dominus Rex,* at departing, gave us 'thirteen *sterlingii,*' one shilling and one penny, to say a mass for him; and so departed, — like a shabby Lackland as he was! 'Thirteen pence sterling,' this was what the Convent got from Lackland, for all the victuals he and his had made away with. We of course said our mass for him, having covenanted to do it, — but let impartial posterity judge with what degree of fervour!

And in this manner vanishes King Lackland; traverses swiftly our strange intermittent magic-mirror, jingling the shabby thirteen pence merely; and rides with his hawks into Egyptian night again. It is Jocelin's manner with all things; and it is men's manner and men's necessity. How intermittent is our good Jocelin; marking down, without eye to *us,* what *he* finds interesting! How much in Jocelin, as in all History, and indeed in all Nature, is at once inscrutable and certain; so dim, yet so indubitable; exciting us to endless considerations. For King Lackland *was* there, verily he; and did leave these *tredecim sterlingii* if nothing more, and did live and look in one way or the other, and a whole world was living and looking along with him! There, we say, is the grand peculiarity; the immeasurable one; distinguishing, to a really infinite degree, the poorest historical Fact from all Fiction whatsoever. Fiction, 'Imagination,' 'Imaginative Poetry,' &c. &c., except as the vehicle for truth, or *fact* of some sort, — which surely a man should first try various other ways of vehiculating, and conveying safe, — what is it? Let the Minerva[22] and other Presses respond! —

But it is time we were in St. Edmundsbury Monastery, and Seven good Centuries off. If indeed it be possible, by any aid of Jocelin, by any human art, to get thither, with a reader or two still following us?

[22] A London publishing house, famous (or notorious) for its sentimental and sensational fiction.

CHAPTER II

THE *Burg*, Bury, or 'Berry' as they call it, of St. Edmund is still a prosperous brisk Town; beautifully diversifying, with its clear brick houses, ancient clean streets, and twenty or fifteen thousand busy souls, the general grassy face of Suffolk; looking out right pleasantly, from its hill-slope, towards the rising Sun: and on the eastern edge of it, still runs, long, black and massive, a range of monastic ruins; into the wide internal spaces of which the stranger is admitted on payment of one shilling. Internal spaces laid out, at present, as a botanic garden. Here stranger or townsman, sauntering at his leisure amid these vast grim venerable ruins, may persuade himself that an Abbey of St. Edmundsbury did once exist; nay there is no doubt of it: see here the ancient massive Gateway, of architecture interesting to the eye of Dilettantism; and farther on, that other ancient Gateway, now about to tumble, unless Dilettantism, in these very months, can subscribe money to cramp it and prop it![1]

Here, sure enough, is an Abbey; beautiful in the eye of Dilettantism. Giant Pedantry also will step in, with its huge *Dugdale*[2] and other enormous *Monasticons* under its arm, and cheerfully apprise you, That this was a very great Abbey, owner and indeed creator of St. Edmund's Town itself, owner of wide lands and revenues; nay that its lands were once a county of themselves; that indeed King Canute or Knut was very kind to it; and gave St. Edmund his own gold crown off his head, on one occasion: for the rest, that the Monks were of such and such a genus, such and such a number; that they had so many carucates of land in this hundred,[3] and so many in that; and then farther that the large

---

[1] At the time Carlyle wrote, the gate tower of the ruined abbey was in danger of collapse and funds were being sought to preserve it.

[2] The *Monasticon Anglicanum* (1655–73) of Sir William Dugdale; a prime source book for the history of the English monasteries.

[3] *Carucate:* an area that could be plowed in a year by an eight-ox plow. *Hundred:* a subdivision of an English county in late Saxon and Norman times.

Tower or Belfry was built by such a one, and the smaller Belfry was built by &c. &c. — Till human nature can stand no more of it; till human nature desperately take refuge in forgetfulness, almost in flat disbelief of the whole business, Monks, Monastery, Belfries, Carucates and all! Alas, what mountains of dead ashes, wreck and burnt bones, does assiduous Pedantry dig up from the Past Time, and name it History, and Philosophy of History; till, as we say, the human soul sinks wearied and bewildered; till the Past Time seems all one infinite incredible grey void, without sun, stars, hearth-fires, or candle-light; dim offensive dust-whirlwinds filling universal Nature; and over your Historical Library, it is as if all the Titans[4] had written for themselves: DRY RUBBISH SHOT[5] HERE!

And yet these grim old walls are not a dilettantism and dubiety; they are an earnest fact. It was a most real and serious purpose they were built for! Yes, another world it was, when these black ruins, white in their new mortar and fresh chiselling, first saw the sun as walls, long ago. Gauge not, with thy dilettante compasses, with that placid dilettante simper, the Heaven's-Watchtower of our Fathers, the fallen God's-Houses, the Golgotha[6] of true Souls departed!

Their architecture, belfries, land-carucates? Yes, — and that is but a small item of the matter. Does it never give thee pause, this other strange item of it, that men then had a *soul*, — not by hearsay alone, and as a figure of speech; but as a truth that they *knew*, and practically went upon! Verily it was another world then. Their Missals have become incredible, a sheer platitude, sayest thou? Yes, a most poor platitude; and even, if thou wilt, an idolatry and blasphemy, should any one persuade *thee* to believe them, to pretend praying by them. But yet it is pity we had lost tidings of our souls: — actually we shall have to go in quest of them again, or worse in all ways will befal! A certain degree of soul, as Ben Jonson reminds us, is indispensable to keep the very body from destruction of the frightfullest sort; to 'save us,' says he, 'the expense of *salt*.'[7] Ben has known men who had soul enough to keep their body and five senses from becoming carrion,

---

[4] Giants of Greek mythology.   [5] Dumped.
[6] Burial place.
[7] The reference is either to *The Divell is an Asse*, I.vi.89–90, or to *Bartholomew Fair*, IV.ii.54–56.

and save salt: — men, and also Nations. You may look in Manchester Hunger-mobs and Corn-law Commons Houses, and various other quarters, and say whether either soul or else salt is not
somewhat wanted at present! —

Another world, truly: and this present poor distressed world
might get some profit by looking wisely into it, instead of foolishly. But at lowest, O dilettante friend, let us know always that
it *was* a world, and not a void infinite of grey haze with fantasms
swimming in it. These old St. Edmundsbury walls, I say, were
not peopled with fantasms; but with men of flesh and blood, made
altogether as we are. Had thou and I then been, who knows but
we ourselves had taken refuge from an evil Time, and fled to
dwell here, and meditate on an Eternity, in such fashion as we
could? Alas, how like an old osseous fragment, a broken black-
ened shin-bone of the old dead Ages, this black ruin looks out,
not yet covered by the soil; still indicating what a once gigantic
Life lies buried there! It is dead now, and dumb; but was alive
once, and spake. For twenty generations, here was the earthly
arena where painful living men worked out their life-wrestle, —
looked at by Earth, by Heaven and Hell. Bells tolled to prayers;
and men, of many humours, various thoughts, chanted vespers,
matins; — and round the little islet of their life rolled forever (as
round ours still rolls, though we are blind and deaf) the illimita-
ble Ocean, tinting all things with *its* eternal hues and reflexes;
making strange prophetic music! How silent now; all departed,
clean gone. The World-Dramaturgist has written: *Exeunt.* The
devouring Time-Demons have made away with it all: and in its
stead, there is either nothing; or what is worse, offensive universal
dustclouds, and grey eclipse of Earth and Heaven, from 'dry
rubbish shot here!' —

Truly, it is no easy matter to get across the chasm of Seven
Centuries, filled with such material. But here, of all helps, is not
a Boswell the welcomest; even a small Boswell? Veracity, true
simplicity of heart, how valuable are these always! He that speaks
what *is* really in him, will find men to listen, though under never
such impediments. Even gossip, springing free and cheery from a
human heart, this too is a kind of veracity and *speech;* — much
preferable to pedantry and inane grey haze! Jocelin is weak and
garrulous, but he is human. Through the thin watery gossip of
our Jocelin, we do get some glimpses of that deep-buried Time;

discern veritably, though in a fitful intermittent manner, these antique figures and their life-method, face to face! Beautifully, in our earnest loving glance, the old centuries melt from opaque to partially translucent, transparent here and there; and the void black Night, one finds, is but the summing up of innumerable peopled luminous *Days*. Not parchment Chartularies,[8] Doctrines of the Constitution, O Dryasdust;[9] not altogether, my erudite friend! —

Readers who please to go along with us into this poor *Jocelini Chronica* shall wander inconveniently enough, as in wintry twilight, through some poor stript hazel-grove, rustling with foolish noises, and perpetually hindering the eyesight; but across which, here and there, some real human figure is seen moving: very strange; whom we could hail if he would answer; — and we look into a pair of eyes deep as our own, *imaging* our own, but all unconscious of us; to whom we for the time are become as spirits and invisible!

[8] Collections of records.

[9] The fictitious pedant to whom Scott addressed the prefaces of some of his novels.

CHAPTER III

S OME three centuries or so had elapsed since *Beodric's-worth*[1] became St. Edmund's *Stow*, St. Edmund's *Town* and Monastery, before Jocelin entered himself a Novice there. 'It was,' says he, 'the year after the Flemings were defeated at Fornham St. Genevieve.'

Much passes away into oblivion: this glorious victory over the Flemings at Fornham has, at the present date, greatly dimmed itself out of the minds of men. A victory and battle nevertheless it was, in its time: some thrice-renowned Earl of Leicester, not of the De Montfort breed, (as may be read in Philosophical and other Histories, could any human memory retain such things,) had quarrelled with his sovereign, Henry Second of the name; had been worsted, it is like, and maltreated, and obliged to fly to foreign parts; but had rallied there into new vigour; and so, in the year 1173, returns across the German Sea with a vengeful army of Flemings. Returns, to the coast of Suffolk; to Framlingham Castle, where he is welcomed; westward towards St. Edmundsbury and Fornham Church, where he is met by the constituted authorities with *posse comitatus;*[2] and swiftly cut in

---

[1] Dryasdust puzzles and pokes for some biography of this Beodric; and repugns to consider him a mere East-Anglian Person of Condition, not in need of a biography, — whose peoᵽð, *weorth* or *worth*, that is to say, *Growth,* Increase, or as we should now name it, *Estate,* that same Hamlet and wood Mansion, now St. Edmund's Bury, originally was. For, adds our erudite Friend, the Saxon peoᵽðan, equivalent to the German *werden,* means to *grow,* to *become;* traces of which old vocable are still found in the North-country dialects, as, 'What is *word* of him?' meaning 'What is *become* of him?' and the like. Nay we in modern English still say, 'Wo *worth* the hour' (Wo *befal* the hour), and speak of the '*Weird* Sisters;' not to mention the innumerable other names of places still ending in *weorth* or *worth*. And indeed, our common noun *worth,* in the sense of *value,* does not this mean simply, What a thing has *grown* to, What a man has *grown* to, How much he amounts to, — by the Threadneedle-street standard or another! (C.) Threadneedle Street is the center of British banking.

[2] In the Middle Ages, a band of citizens assembled by the sheriff to keep the peace.

56

pieces, he and his, or laid by the heels; on the right bank of the obscure river Lark, — as traces still existing will verify.

For the river Lark, though not very discoverably, still runs or stagnates in that country; and the battle-ground is there; serving at present as a pleasure-ground to his Grace of Newcastle. Copper pennies of Henry II. are still found there; — rotted out from the pouches of poor slain soldiers, who had not had *time* to buy liquor with them. In the river Lark itself was fished up, within man's memory, an antique gold ring; which fond Dilettantism can almost believe may have been the very ring Countess Leicester threw away, in her flight, into that same Lark river or ditch.[3] Nay, few years ago, in tearing out an enormous superannuated ash-tree, now grown quite corpulent, bursten, superfluous, but long a fixture in the soil, and not to be dislodged without revolution, — there was laid bare, under its roots, 'a circular mound of skeletons wonderfully complete,' all radiating from a centre, faces upwards, feet inwards; a 'radiation' not of Light, but of the Nether Darkness rather; and evidently the fruit of battle; for 'many of the heads were cleft, or had arrow-holes in them.' The Battle of Fornham, therefore, is a fact, though a forgotten one; no less obscure than undeniable, — like so many other facts.

Like the St. Edmund's Monastery itself! Who can doubt, after what we have said, that there was a Monastery here at one time? No doubt at all there was a Monastery here; no doubt, some three centuries prior to this Fornham Battle, there dwelt a man in these parts, of the name of Edmund, King, Landlord, Duke or whatever his title was, of the Eastern Counties; — and a very singular man and landlord he must have been.

For his tenants, it would appear, did not complain of him in the least; his labourers did not think of burning his wheatstacks, breaking into his game-preserves; very far the reverse of all that. Clear evidence, satisfactory even to my friend Dryasdust, exists that, on the contrary, they honoured, loved, admired this ancient Landlord to a quite astonishing degree, — and indeed at last to an immeasurable and inexpressible degree; for, finding no limits or utterable words for their sense of his worth, they took to beatifying and adoring him! 'Infinite admiration,' we are taught, 'means worship.'

Very singular, — could we discover it! What Edmund's specific

[3] Lyttelton's *History of Henry II.* (2nd Edition), v. 169, &c. (C.)

58 THE ANCIENT MONK

duties were; above all, what his method of discharging them with
such results was, would surely be interesting to know; but are
not very discoverable now. His Life has become a poetic, nay a
religious *Mythus;* though, undeniably enough, it was once a prose
Fact, as our poor lives are; and even a very rugged unmanageable
one. This landlord Edmund did go about in leather shoes, with
femoralia[4] and bodycoat of some sort on him; and daily had his
breakfast to procure; and daily had contradictory speeches, and
most contradictory facts not a few, to reconcile with himself. No
man becomes a Saint in his sleep. Edmund, for instance, instead
of *reconciling* those same contradictory facts and speeches to
himself; which means *subduing,* and, in a manlike and godlike
manner, conquering them to himself, — might have merely
thrown new contention into them, new unwisdom into them, and
so been conquered *by* them; much the commoner case! In that
way he had proved no 'Saint,' or Divine-looking Man, but a mere
Sinner, and unfortunate, blameable, more or less Diabolic-look-
ing man! No landlord Edmund becomes infinitely admirable in
his sleep.

With what degree of wholesome rigour his rents were collected
we hear not. Still less by what methods he preserved his game,
whether by 'bushing'[5] or how, — and if the partridge-seasons
were 'excellent,' or were indifferent. Neither do we ascertain what
kind of Corn-bill he passed, or wisely-adjusted Sliding-scale: —
but indeed there were few spinners in those days; and the nuisance of spinning, and other dusty labour, was not yet so glaring
a one.

How then, it may be asked, did this Edmund rise into favour;
become to such astonishing extent a recognised Farmer's Friend?[6]
Really, except it were by doing justly and loving mercy, to an
unprecedented extent, one does not know. The man, it would
seem, 'had walked,' as they say, 'humbly with God;'[7] humbly and
valiantly with God; struggling to make the Earth heavenly, as
he could: instead of walking sumptuously and pridefully with
Mammon, leaving the Earth to grow hellish as it liked. Not

[4] Breeches.
[5] Planting bushes to prevent poaching by net.
[6] The sobriquet of Richard Plantagenet Temple Nugent Brydges Chandos
Grenville, second Duke of Buckingham and Chandos, a redoubtable sup-
porter of the Corn Laws. He was in the news in May, 1842, when his
admirers presented him with a testimonial.
[7] Micah 6:8.

sumptuously with Mammon? How then could he 'encourage trade,' — cause Howel and James,[8] and many wine-merchants to bless him, and the tailor's heart (though in a very short-sighted manner) to sing for joy? Much in this Edmund's Life is mysterious.

That he could, on occasion, do what he liked with his own is, meanwhile, evident enough. Certain Heathen Physical-Force Ultra-Chartists,[9] 'Danes' as they were then called, coming into his territory with their 'five points,' or rather with their five-and-twenty thousand *points* and edges too, of pikes namely and battle-axes; and proposing mere Heathenism, confiscation, spoliation, and fire and sword, — Edmund answered that he would oppose to the utmost such savagery. They took him prisoner; again required his sanction to said proposals. Edmund again refused. Cannot we kill you? cried they. — Cannot I die? answered he. My life, I think, is my own to do what I like with! And he died, under barbarous tortures, refusing to the last breath; and the Ultra-Chartist Danes *lost* their propositions; — and went with their 'points' and other apparatus, as is supposed, to the Devil, the Father of them. Some say, indeed, these Danes were not Ultra-Chartists, but Ultra-Tories, demanding to reap where they had not sown, and live in this world without working, though all the world should starve for it; which likewise seems a possible hypothesis. Be what they might, they went, as we say, to the Devil; and Edmund doing what he liked with his own, the Earth was got cleared of them.

Another version is, that Edmund on this and the like occasions stood by his order; the oldest, and indeed only true order of Nobility known under the stars, that of Just Men and Sons of God, in opposition to Unjust and Sons of Belial,[10] — which latter indeed are *second*-oldest, but yet a very unvenerable order. This, truly, seems the likeliest hypothesis of all. Names and appearances alter so strangely, in some half-score centuries; and all fluctuates chameleon-like, taking now this hue, now that. Thus much is very plain, and does not change hue: Landlord Edmund was seen and felt by all men to have done verily a man's part in this life-pilgrimage of his; and benedictions, and outflowing love

---

[8] Dealers in furniture and materials for interior decoration.

[9] The Chartist movement had two factions, the moderate or "moral force" and the extremist or "physical force."

[10] Satan.

and admiration from the universal heart, were his meed. Well-done! Well-done! cried the hearts of all men. They raised his slain and martyred body; washed its wounds with fast-flowing universal tears; tears of endless pity, and yet of a sacred joy and triumph. The beautifullest kind of tears, — indeed perhaps the beautifullest kind of thing: like a sky all flashing diamonds and prismatic radiance; all weeping, yet shone on by the everlasting Sun: — and *this* is not a sky, it is a Soul and living Face! Nothing liker the *Temple of the Highest,* bright with some real effulgence of the Highest, is seen in this world.

O, if all Yankee-land follow a small good 'Schnüspel the distinguished Novelist'[11] with blazing torches, dinner-invitations, universal hep-hep-hurrah, feeling that he, though small, *is* something; how might all Angle-land once follow a hero-martyr and great true Son of Heaven! It is the very joy of man's heart to admire, where he can; nothing so lifts him from all his mean imprisonments, were it but for moments, as true admiration. Thus it has been said, 'all men, especially all women, are born worshippers;'[12] and will worship, if it be but possible. Possible to worship a Something, even a small one; not so possible a mere loud-blaring Nothing! What sight is more pathetic than that of poor multitudes of persons met to gaze at King's Progresses,[13] Lord Mayor's Shews,[14] and other gilt-gingerbread phenomena of the worshipful sort, in these times; each so eager to worship; each, with a dim fatal sense of disappointment, finding that he cannot rightly here! These be thy gods, O Israel?[15] And thou art so *willing* to worship, — poor Israel!

In this manner, however, did the men of the Eastern Counties take up the slain body of their Edmund, where it lay cast forth in the village of Hoxne; seek out the severed head, and reverently reunite the same. They embalmed him with myrrh and sweet spices, with love, pity, and all high and awful thoughts; consecrating him with a very storm of melodious adoring admiration,

[11] Dickens made a triumphal tour of America in 1842. "Schnüspel" evidently is a Carlylean invention; in the manuscript it replaced "Pickwick."
[12] Here, as at a number of other places in the book, Carlyle draws from his previous writings. This echoes a passage in his essay on Goethe's *Works* as well as one near the beginning of that on Scott.
[13] Ceremonial tours by the monarch.
[14] Pageantry celebrating the annual installation of the Lord Mayor of the City of London.
[15] Exodus 32:4.

and sun-dyed showers of tears; — joyfully, yet with awe (as all deep joy has something of the awful in it), commemorating his noble deeds and godlike walk and conversation while on Earth. Till, at length, the very Pope and Cardinals at Rome were forced to hear of it; and they, summing up as correctly as they well could, with *Advocatus-Diaboli*[16] pleadings and their other forms of process, the general verdict of mankind, declared: That he had, in very fact, led a hero's life in this world; and being now *gone*, was gone as they conceived to God above, and reaping his reward *there*. Such, they said, was the best judgment they could form of the case; — and truly not a bad judgment. Acquiesced in, zealously adopted, with full assent of 'private judgment,' by all mortals.

The rest of St. Edmund's history, for the reader sees he has now become a *Saint*, is easily conceivable. Pious munificence provided him a *loculus*, [17] a *feretrum* or shrine; built for him a wooden chapel, a stone temple, ever widening and growing by new pious gifts; — such the overflowing heart feels it a blessedness to solace itself by giving. St. Edmund's Shrine glitters now with diamond flowerages, with a plating of wrought gold. The wooden chapel, as we say, has become a stone temple. Stately masonries, long-drawn arches, cloisters, sounding aisles buttress it, begirdle it far and wide. Regimented companies of men, of whom our Jocelin is one, devote themselves, in every generation, to meditate here on man's Nobleness and Awfulness, and celebrate and shew forth the same, as they best can, — thinking they will do it better here, in presence of God the Maker, and of the so Awful and so Noble made by Him. In one word, St. Edmund's Body has raised a Monastery round it. To such length, in such manner, has the Spirit of the Time visibly taken body, and crystallised itself here. New gifts, houses, farms, *katalla*[18] — come ever in. King Knut, whom men call Canute, whom the Ocean-tide would not be forbidden to wet, — we heard already of this wise King, with his crown and gifts; but of many others, Kings, Queens, wise men and noble loyal women, let Dryasdust and divine Silence be the

[16] In the ecclesiastical process leading to the canonization of a saint, the "devil's advocate" has the duty of presenting evidence against the candidate.

[17] Consecrated coffin.

[18] Goods, properties; what we now call *chattels*, and still more singularly *cattle*, says my erudite friend! (C.)

record! Beodric's-Worth has become St. Edmund's *Bury;* — and lasts visible to this hour. All this that thou now seest, and namest Bury Town, is properly the Funeral Monument of Saint or Landlord Edmund. The present respectable Mayor of Bury may be said, like a Fakeer[19] (little as he thinks of it), to have his dwelling in the extensive, many-sculptured Tombstone of St. Edmund; in one of the brick niches thereof dwells the present respectable Mayor of Bury.

Certain Times do crystallise themselves in a magnificent manner; and others, perhaps, are like to do it in rather a shabby one! — But Richard Arkwright too will have his Monument, a thousand years hence: all Lancashire and Yorkshire, and how many other shires and countries, with their machineries and industries, for his monument! A true *py*ramid or '*flame*-mountain,'[20] flaming with steam fires and useful labour over wide continents, usefully towards the Stars, to a certain height; — how much grander than your foolish Cheops Pyramids or Sakhara clay ones![21] Let us withal be hopeful, be content or patient.

[19] Mohammedan or Hindu religious beggar.

[20] Sometimes, as here, Carlyle's word-derivation is more picturesque than accurate.

[21] The Cheops ("Great") Pyramid is built of stone; those of sixth-dynasty kings, at Saqqara, of brick.

CHAPTER IV

It is true, all things have two faces, a light one and a dark. It is true, in three centuries much imperfection accumulates; many an Ideal, monastic or other, shooting forth into practice as it can, grows to a strange enough Reality; and we have to ask with amazement, Is this your Ideal! For, alas, the Ideal always has to grow in the Real, and to seek out its bed and board there, often in a very sorry way. No beautifullest Poet is a Bird-of-Paradise, living on perfumes; sleeping in the æther with outspread wings. The Heroic, *independent* of bed and board, is found in Drury-Lane Theatre only; to avoid disappointments, let us bear this in mind.

By the law of Nature, too, all manner of Ideals have their fatal limits and lot; their appointed periods, of youth, of maturity or perfection, of decline, degradation, and final death and disappearance. There is nothing born but has to die. Ideal monasteries, once grown real, do seek bed and board in this world; do find it more and more successfully; do get at length too intent on finding it, exclusively intent on that. They are then like diseased corpulent bodies fallen idiotic, which merely eat and sleep; *ready* for 'dissolution,' by a Henry the Eighth or some other. Jocelin's St. Edmundsbury is still far from this last dreadful state: but here too the reader will prepare himself to see an Ideal not sleeping in the æther like a bird-of-paradise, but roosting as the common woodfowl do, in an imperfect, uncomfortable, more or less contemptible manner! —

Abbot Hugo, as Jocelin, breaking at once into the heart of the business, apprises us, had in those days grown old, grown rather blind, and his eyes were somewhat darkened, *aliquantulum caligaverunt oculi ejus.* He dwelt apart very much, in his *Talamus* or peculiar Chamber; got into the hands of flatterers, a set of mealy-mouthed persons who strove to make the passing hour easy for him, — for him easy, and for themselves profitable; ac-

cumulating in the distance mere mountains of confusion. Old
Dominus Hugo sat inaccessible in this way, far in the interior,
wrapt in his warm flannels and delusions; inaccessible to all voice
of Fact; and bad grew ever worse with us. Not that our worthy
old *Dominus Abbas* was inattentive to the divine offices, or to the
maintenance of a devout spirit in us or in himself; but the
Account-Books of the Convent fell into the frightfullest state, and
Hugo's annual Budget grew yearly emptier, or filled with futile
expectations, fatal deficit, wind and debts!

His one worldly care was to raise ready money; sufficient for the
day is the evil thereof.[1] And how he raised it: From usurious
insatiable Jews; every fresh Jew sticking on him like a fresh
horseleech, sucking his and our life out; crying continually, Give,
Give![2] Take one example instead of scores. Our *Camera* having
fallen into ruin, William the Sacristan[3] received charge to repair
it; strict charge, but no money; Abbot Hugo would, and indeed
could, give him no fraction of money. The *Camera* in ruins, and
Hugo penniless and inaccessible, Willelmus Sacrista borrowed
Forty Marcs (some Seven-and-twenty Pounds) of Benedict the
Jew, and patched up our Camera again. But the means of re-
paying him? There were no means. Hardly could *Sacrista,
Cellerarius*,[4] or any public officer, get ends to meet, on the indis-
pensablest scale, with their shrunk allowances: ready money had
vanished.

Benedict's Twenty-seven pounds grew rapidly at compound-
interest; and at length, when it had amounted to One hundred
pounds, he, on a day of settlement, presents the account to Hugo
himself. Hugo already owed him another One hundred of his
own; and so here it has become Two hundred! Hugo, in a fine
frenzy, threatens to depose the Sacristan, to do this and do that;
but, in the mean while, How to quiet your insatiable Jew? Hugo,
for this couple of hundreds, grants the Jew his bond for Four
hundred payable at the end of four years. At the end of four
years there is, of course, still no money; and the Jew now gets a
bond for Eight hundred and eighty pounds, to be paid by instal-

[1] Matthew 6:34.
[2] Proverbs 30:15.
[3] The monk in charge of maintaining the abbey's furnishings and buildings, including the storehouse (*camera*).
[4] The monk who served as general business manager of the abbey.

ments, Four-score pounds every year. Here was a way of doing business!

Neither yet is this insatiable Jew satisfied or settled with: he had papers against us of 'small debts fourteen years old;' his modest claim amounts finally to 'Twelve hundred pounds besides interest;' — and one hopes he never got satisfied in this world; one almost hopes he was one of those beleaguered Jews who hanged themselves in York Castle shortly afterwards, and had his usances and quittances and horseleech papers[5] summarily set fire to! For approximate justice will strive to accomplish itself; if not in one way, then in another. Jews, and also Christians and Heathens, who accumulate in this manner, though furnished with never so many parchments, do, at times, 'get their grinder-teeth successively pulled out of their head, each day a new grinder,'[6] till they consent to disgorge again. A sad fact, — worth reflecting on.

Jocelin, we see, is not without secularity: Our *Dominus Abbas* was intent enough on the divine offices; but then his Account-Books — ? — One of the things that strike us most, throughout, in Jocelin's *Chronicle*, and indeed in Eadmer's *Anselm*,[7] and other old monastic Books, written evidently by pious men, is this, That there is almost no mention whatever of 'personal religion' in them; that the whole gist of their thinking and speculation seems to be the 'privileges of our order,' 'strict exaction of our dues,' 'God's honour' (meaning the honour of our Saint), and so forth. Is not this singular? A body of men, set apart for perfecting and purifying their own souls, do not seem disturbed about that in any measure: the 'Ideal' says nothing about its idea; says much about finding bed and board for itself! How is this?

Why, for one thing, bed and board are a matter very apt to come to speech: it is much easier to *speak* of them than of ideas; and they are sometimes much more pressing with some! Nay, for another thing, may not this religious reticence, in these devout

---

[5] Usances, strictly speaking, are spans of time allowed for the payment of foreign exchange bills; here Carlyle uses the word to refer to the documents themselves. Quittances are receipts; horseleech papers are associated with usury — see Proverbs 30:15.

[6] An episode of 1210, recorded in Holinshed's *Chronicles*.

[7] The life of St. Anselm, written by a monk of Canterbury, early twelfth century; an important source book of early medieval English history.

good souls, be perhaps a merit, and sign of health in them? Jocelin, Eadmer, and such religious men, have as yet nothing of 'Methodism;'[8] no Doubt or even root of Doubt. Religion is not a diseased self-introspection, an agonising inquiry: their duties are clear to them, the way of supreme good plain, indisputable, and they are travelling on it. Religion lies over them like an all-embracing heavenly canopy, like an atmosphere and life-element, which is not spoken of, which in all things is presupposed without speech. Is not serene or complete Religion the highest aspect of human nature; as serene Cant, or complete No-religion, is the lowest and miserablest? Between which two, all manner of earnest Methodisms, introspections, agonising inquiries, never so morbid, shall play their respective parts, not without approbation.

But let any reader fancy himself one of the Brethren in St. Edmundsbury Monastery under such circumstances! How can a Lord Abbot, all stuck over with horseleeches of this nature, front the world? He is fast losing his life-blood, and the Convent will be as one of Pharaoh's lean kine.[9] Old monks of experience draw their hoods deeper down; careful what they say: the monk's first duty is obedience. Our Lord the King, hearing of such work, sends down his Almoner to make investigations: but what boots it? Abbot Hugo assembles us in Chapter; asks, "If there is any complaint?" Not a soul of us dare answer, "Yes, thousands!" but we all stand silent, and the Prior even says that things are in a very comfortable condition. Whereupon old Abbot Hugo, turning to the royal messenger, says, "You see!" — and the business terminates in that way. I, as a brisk-eyed, noticing youth and novice, could not help asking of the elders, asking of Magister Samson in particular: Why he, well-instructed and a knowing man, had not spoken out, and brought matters to a bearing? Magister Samson was Teacher of the Novices, appointed to breed us up to the rules, and I loved him well. "*Fili mi,*" answered Samson, "the burnt child shuns the fire. Dost thou not know, our Lord the Abbot sent me once to Acre in Norfolk, to solitary confinement and bread and water, already? The Hinghams, Hugo

---

[8] Carlyle uses the Methodist movement as a symbol of the substitution of over-emotional, inward religion (his "diseased self-introspection") for serenely confident faith and reliance upon authority.
[9] Genesis 41:14–36.

and Robert, have just got home from banishment for speaking. This is the hour of darkness: the hour when flatterers rule and are believed. *Videat Dominus*, let the Lord see, and judge."

In very truth, what could poor old Abbot Hugo do? A frail old man; and the Philistines were upon him, — that is to say, the Hebrews. He had nothing for it but to shrink away from them; get back into his warm flannels, into his warm delusions again. Happily, before it was quite too late, he bethought him of pilgriming to St. Thomas of Canterbury. He set out, with a fit train, in the autumn days of the year 1180; near Rochester City, his mule threw him, dislocated his poor kneepan, raised incurable inflammatory fever; and the poor old man got his dismissal from the whole coil at once. St. Thomas à Becket, though in a circuitous way, had *brought* deliverance! Neither Jew usurers, nor grumbling monks, nor other importunate despicability of men or mud-elements afflicted Abbot Hugo any more; but he dropt his rosaries, closed his account-books, closed his old eyes, and lay down into the long sleep. Heavy-laden hoary old Dominus Hugo, fare thee well.

One thing we cannot mention without a due thrill of horror: namely, that, in the empty exchequer of Dominus Hugo, there was not found one penny to distribute to the Poor that they might pray for his soul! By a kind of godsend, Fifty shillings did, in the very nick of time, fall due, or seem to fall due, from one of his Farmers (the *Firmarius* de Palegrava), and he paid it, and the Poor had it; though, alas, this too only *seemed* to fall due, and we had it to pay again afterwards. Dominus Hugo's apartments were plundered by his servants, to the last portable stool, in a few minutes after the breath was out of his body. Forlorn old Hugo, fare thee well forever.

CHAPTER V

O<small>UR</small> Abbot being dead, the *Dominus Rex*, Henry II., or Ranulf de Glanvill *Justiciarius*[1] of England for him, set Inspectors or Custodiars over us; — not in any breathless haste to appoint a new Abbot, our revenues coming into his own *Scaccarium*, or royal Exchequer, in the meanwhile. They proceeded with some rigour, these Custodiars; took written inventories, clapt-on seals, exacted everywhere strict tale and measure: but wherefore should a living monk complain? The living monk has to do his devotional drill-exercise; consume his allotted *pitantia*, what we call *pittance*, or ration of victual; and possess his soul in patience.

Dim, as through a long vista of Seven Centuries, dim and very strange looks that monk-life to us; the ever-surprising circumstance this, That it is a *fact* and no dream, that we see it there, and gaze into the very eyes of it! Smoke rises daily from those culinary chimney-throats; there are living human beings there, who chant, loud-braying, their matins, nones, vespers; awakening *echoes*, not to the bodily ear alone. St. Edmund's Shrine, perpetually illuminated, glows ruddy through the Night, and through the Night of Centuries withal; St. Edmundsbury Town paying yearly Forty pounds for that express end. Bells clang out; on great occasions, all the bells. We have Processions, Preachings, Festivals, Christmas Plays, *Mysteries* shewn in the Churchyard, at which latter the Townsfolk sometimes quarrel. Time was, Time is, as Friar Bacon's Brass Head remarked; and withal Time will be.[2] There are three Tenses, *Tempora*, or Times; and there is one Eternity; and as for us,

We are such stuff as Dreams are made of![3]

---

[1] Administrator of justice.
[2] A legend associated with Roger Bacon, the medieval "wonder worker," is that he made a brazen head which, while he slept, spoke thrice: "Time was," "Time is," "Time's past." Having uttered these observations, it fell and broke.
[3] *The Tempest*, IV.i.156–157. "On," not "of."

Indisputable, though very dim to modern vision, rests on its hill-slope that same *Bury, Stow,* or Town of St. Edmund; already a considerable place, not without traffic, nay manufactures, would Jocelin only tell us what. Jocelin is totally careless of telling: but, through dim fitful apertures, we can see *Fullones,* 'Fullers,' see cloth-making; looms dimly going, dye-vats, and old women spinning yarn. We have Fairs too, *Nundinæ,* in due course; and the Londoners give us much trouble, pretending that they, as a metropolitan people, are exempt from toll. Besides there is Field-husbandry, with perplexed settlement of Convent rents: corn-ricks pile themselves within burgh, in their season; and cattle depart and enter; and even the poor weaver has his cow, — 'dung-heaps' lying quiet at most doors (*ante foras,* says the incidental Jocelin), for the Town has yet no improved police. Watch and ward nevertheless we do keep, and have Gates, — as what Town must not; thieves so abounding; war, *werra,* such a frequent thing! Our thieves, at the Abbot's judgment bar, deny; claim wager of battle; fight, are beaten, and *then* hanged. 'Ketel, the thief,' took this course; and it did nothing for him, — merely brought us, and indeed himself, new trouble!

Every way a most foreign Time. What difficulty, for example, has our *Cellerarius* to collect the *repselver,* 'reaping silver,' or penny, which each householder is by law bound to pay for cutting down the Convent grain! Richer people pretend that it is commuted, that it is this and the other; that, in short, they will not pay it. Our *Cellerarius* gives up calling on the rich. In the houses of the poor, our *Cellerarius* finding, in like manner, neither penny nor good promise, snatches, without ceremony, what *vadium* (pledge, *wad*) he can come at: a joint-stool, kettle, nay the very house-door, *'hostium;'* and old women, thus exposed to the unfeeling gaze of the public, rush out after him with their distaffs and the angriest shrieks: *'vetulæ exibant cum colis suis,'* says Jocelin, *'minantes et exprobrantes.'*

What a historical picture, glowing visible, as St. Edmund's Shrine by night, after Seven long Centuries or so! *Vetulæ cum colis:* My venerable ancient spinning grandmothers, — ah, and ye too have to shriek, and rush out with your distaffs; and become Female Chartists, and scold all evening with void doorway; — and in old Saxon, as we in modern, would fain demand some Five-point Charter, could it be fallen in with, the Earth being too tyrannous! — Wise Lord Abbots, hearing of such phenomena,

did in time abolish or commute the reap-penny, and one nuisance
was abated. But the image of these justly offended old women,
in their old wool costumes, with their angry features, and spindles
brandished, lives forever in the historical memory. Thanks to
thee, Jocelin Boswell. Jerusalem was taken by the Crusaders, and
again lost by them; and Richard Cœur-de-Lion 'veiled his face'
as he passed in sight of it: but how many other things went on,
the while!

Thus, too, our trouble with the Lakenheath eels is very great.
King Knut, namely, or rather his Queen who also did herself
honour by honouring St. Edmund, decreed by authentic deed
yet extant on parchment, that the Holders of the Town Fields,
once Beodric's, should, for one thing, go yearly and catch us four
thousand eels in the marsh-pools of Lakenheath. Well, they went,
they continued to go; but, in later times, got into the way of
returning with a most short account of eels. Not the due six-
score apiece; no, Here are two-score, Here are twenty, ten, —
sometimes, Here are none at all; Heaven help us, we *could* catch
no more, they were not there! What is a distressed *Cellerarius*
to do? We agree that each Holder of so many acres shall pay
one penny yearly, and let go the eels as too slippery. But alas,
neither is this quite effectual: the Fields, in my time, have got
divided among so many hands, there is no catching of *them*
either; I have known our Cellarer get seven and twenty pence
formerly, and now it is much if he get ten pence farthing (*vix
decem denarios et obolum*). And then their sheep, which they
are bound to fold nightly in our pens, for the manure's sake; and,
I fear, do not always fold: and their *aver-pennies,* and their
avragiums, and their *foder-corns,* and mill-and-market dues![4]
Thus, in its undeniable but dim manner, does old St. Edmundsbury spin and till, and laboriously keep its pot boiling, and St.
Edmund's Shrine lighted, under such conditions and averages as
it can.

How much is still alive in England; how much has not yet come
into life! A Feudal Aristocracy is still alive, in the prime of life;
superintending the cultivation of the land, and less consciously the
distribution of the produce of the land, the adjustment of the
quarrels of the land; judging, soldiering, adjusting; everywhere
governing the people, — so that even a Gurth born thrall of

[4] All these are payments, in money or service, required under feudal law.

Cedric lacks not his due parings of the pigs he tends. Governing; — and, alas, also game-preserving, so that a Robert Hood,[5] a William Scarlet and others have, in these days, put on Lincoln coats, and taken to living, in some universal-suffrage manner, under the greenwood tree!

How silent, on the other hand, lie all Cotton-trades and such like; not a steeple-chimney yet got on end from sea to sea! North of the Humber, a stern Willelmus Conquestor burnt the Country, finding it unruly, into very stern repose. Wild fowl scream in those ancient silences, wild cattle roam in those ancient solitudes; the scanty sulky Norse-bred population all coerced into silence, — feeling that, under these new Norman Governors, their history has probably as good as *ended*. Men and Northumbrian Norse populations know little what has ended, what is but beginning! The Ribble and the Aire roll down, as yet unpolluted by dyers' chemistry; tenanted by merry trouts and piscatory otters; the sunbeam and the vacant wind's-blast alone traversing those moors. Side by side sleep the coal-strata and the iron-strata for so many ages; no Steam-Demon has yet risen smoking into being. Saint Mungo[6] rules in Glasgow; James Watt[7] still slumbering in the deep of Time. *Mancunium,* Manceaster, what we now call Manchester, spins no cotton, — if it be not *wool* 'cottons,' clipped from the backs of mountain sheep. The Creek of the Mersey gurgles, twice in the four-and-twenty hours, with eddying brine, clangorous with sea-fowl; and is a *Lither*-Pool, a *lazy* or sullen Pool, no monstrous pitchy City, and Seahaven of the world! The Centuries are big; and the birth-hour is coming, not yet come. *Tempus ferax, tempus edax rerum.*[8]

[5] Better known as Robin, the name Carlyle substituted in later editions. Will Scarlet was one of his comrades.

[6] Sixth-century saint who converted a portion of Scotland to Christianity and founded the cathedral at Glasgow.

[7] The man most prominently associated with the development of the steam engine; thus, like Arkwright above, a founder of the machine age.

[8] "Time the bearer, Time the devourer of things." The last three words are from Ovid, *Metamorphoses,* XV.234.

CHAPTER VI

MONK SAMSON

WITHIN doors, down at the hill-foot, in our Convent here, we are a peculiar people, — hardly conceivable in the Arkwright Corn-Law ages, of mere Spinning-Mills and Joe-Mantons![1] There is yet no Methodism among us, and we speak much of Secularities: no Methodism; our Religion is not yet a horrible restless Doubt, still less a far horribler composed Cant; but a great heaven-high Unquestionability, encompassing, interpenetrating the whole of Life. Imperfect as we may be, we are here, with our litanies, shaven crowns, vows of poverty, to testify incessantly and indisputably to every heart, That this Earthly Life, and *its* riches and possessions, and good and evil hap, are not intrinsically a reality at all, but *are* a shadow of realities eternal, infinite; that this Time-world, as an air-image, fearfully *emblematic*, plays and flickers in the grand still mirror of Eternity; and man's little Life has Duties that are great, that are alone great, and go up to Heaven and down to Hell. This, with our poor litanies, we testify and struggle to testify.

Which, testified or not, remembered by all men, or forgotten by all men, does verily remain the fact, even in Arkwright Joe-Manton ages! But it is incalculable, when litanies have grown obsolete; when *fodercorns, avragiums,* and all human dues and reciprocities have been fully changed into one great due of *cash payment;* and man's duty to man reduces itself to handing him certain metal coins, or covenanted money-wages, and then shoving him out of doors; and man's duty to God becomes a cant, a doubt, a dim inanity, a 'pleasure of virtue' or such like; and the thing a man does infinitely fear (the real *Hell* of a man) is 'that he do not make money and advance himself,' — I say, it is incalculable what a change has introduced itself everywhere into human affairs! How human affairs shall now circulate everywhere not healthy life-blood in them, but, as it were, a detestable cop-

---

[1] Guns much used by the game-preserving aristocracy; named for their maker.

peras banker's ink; and all is grown acrid, divisive, threatening dissolution; and the huge tumultuous Life of Society is galvanic, devil-ridden, too truly possessed by a devil! For, in short, Mammon *is* not a god at all; but a devil, and even a very despicable devil. Follow the Devil faithfully, you are sure enough to *go* to the Devil: whither else *can* you go? — In such situations, men look back with a kind of mournful recognition even on poor limited Monk-figures, with their poor litanies; and reflect, with Ben Jonson, that soul is indispensable, some degree of soul, even to save you the expense of salt! —

For the rest, it must be owned, we Monks of St. Edmundsbury are but a limited class of creatures, and seem to have a somewhat dull life of it. Much given to idle gossip; having indeed no other work, when our chanting is over. Listless gossip, for most part, and a mitigated slander; the fruit of idleness, not of spleen. We are dull, insipid men, many of us; easy-minded; whom prayer and digestion of food will avail for a life. We have to receive all strangers in our Convent, and lodge them gratis; such and such sorts go by rule to the Lord Abbot and his special revenues; such and such to us and our poor Cellarer, however straitened. Jews themselves send their wives and little ones hither in war-time, into our *Pitanceria*;[2] where they abide safe, with due *pittances*, — for a consideration. We have the fairest chances for collecting news. Some of us have a turn for reading Books; for meditation, silence; at times we even write Books. Some of us can preach, in English-Saxon, in Norman French, and even in Monk-Latin; others cannot in any language or jargon, being stupid.

Failing all else, what gossip about one another! This is a perennial resource. How one hooded head applies itself to the ear of another, and whispers — *tacenda*.[3] Willelmus Sacrista, for instance, what does he nightly, over in that Sacristy of his? Frequent bibations, '*frequentes bibationes et quædam tacenda*,' — eheu! We have '*tempora minutionis*,' stated seasons of blood-letting, when we are all let blood together; and then there is a general free-conference, a sanhedrim of clatter. For all our vow of poverty, we can by rule amass to the extent of 'two shillings;' but it is to be given to our necessitous kindred, or in charity. Poor Monks! Thus too a certain Canterbury Monk was in the habit of 'slipping, *clanculo* from his sleeve,' five shillings into the

[2] Room where the "pittances" of food were distributed.
[3] Things not to be spoken.

hand of his mother, when she came to see him, at the divine offices, every two months. Once, slipping the money clandestinely, just in the act of taking leave, he slipt it not into her hand but on the floor, and another had it; whereupon the poor Monk, coming to know it, looked mere despair for some days; till Lanfranc the noble Archbishop, questioning his secret from him, nobly made the sum *seven* shillings,[4] and said, Never mind!

One Monk of a taciturn nature distinguishes himself among these babbling ones: the name of him Samson; he that answered Jocelin, "*Fili mi,* a burnt child shuns the fire." They call him 'Norfolk *Barrator*,' or litigious person; for indeed, being of grave taciturn ways, he is not universally a favourite; he has been in trouble more than once. The reader is desired to mark this Monk. A personable man of seven-and-forty; stout-made, stands erect as a pillar; with bushy eyebrows, the eyes of him beaming into you in a really strange way; the face massive, grave, with 'a very eminent nose;' his head almost bald, its auburn remnants of hair, and the copious ruddy beard, getting slightly streaked with grey. This is Brother Samson; a man worth looking at.

He is from Norfolk, as the nickname indicates; from Tottington in Norfolk, as we guess; the son of poor parents there. He has told me, Jocelin, for I loved him much, That once in his ninth year he had an alarming dream; — as indeed we are all somewhat given to dreaming here. Little Samson, lying uneasily in his crib at Tottington, dreamed that he saw the Arch Enemy in person, just alighted in front of some grand building, with outspread bat-wings, and stretching forth detestable clawed hands to grip him, little Samson, and fly off with him: whereupon the little dreamer shrieked desperate to St. Edmund for help, shrieked and again shrieked; and St. Edmund, a reverend heavenly figure, did come, — and indeed poor little Samson's mother, awakened by his shrieking, did come; and the Devil and the Dream both fled away fruitless. On the morrow, his mother, pondering such an awful dream, thought it were good to take him over to St. Edmund's own Shrine, and pray with him there. See, said little Samson at sight of the Abbey-Gate; see, mother, this is the building I dreamed of! His poor mother dedicated him to St. Edmund, — left him there with prayers and tears: what better could she do? The exposition of the dream, Brother Samson used to say, was this: *Diabolus* with outspread bat-wings shadowed forth the pleasures of this world, *voluptates hujus sæculi,* which were about to snatch and fly away with me, had not St. Edmund flung his arms round me, that is to say, made me a monk of his. A monk, accordingly, Brother Samson is; and here to this day where his mother left him. A learned man, of devout grave nature; has studied at Paris, has taught in the Town Schools here, and done much else; can preach in three languages, and, like Dr. Caius, 'has had losses' in his time.[5] A thoughtful, firm-standing man; much loved by some, not loved by all; his clear eyes flashing into you, in an almost inconvenient way!

Abbot Hugo, as we said, has his own difficulties with him; Abbot Hugo had him in prison once, to teach him what authority was, and how to dread the fire in future. For Brother Samson, in the time of the Antipopes, had been sent to Rome on business; and, returning successful, was too late, — the business had all misgone in the interim! As tours to Rome are still frequent with us English, perhaps the reader will not grudge to look at the method of travelling thither in those remote ages. We happily have, in small compass, a personal narrative of it. Through the clear eyes and memory of Brother Samson, one peeps direct into the very bosom of that Twelfth Century, and finds it rather curious. The actual *Papa,* Father, or universal President of Christendom, as yet not grown chimerical, sat there; think of that only! Brother Samson went to Rome as to the real Light-fountain of this lower world; we now — ! — But let us hear Brother Samson, as to his mode of travelling:

'You know what trouble I had for that Church of Woolpit; how I was despatched to Rome in the time of the Schism between Pope Alexander and Octavian; and passed through Italy at that season, when all clergy carrying letters for our Lord Pope Alexander were laid hold of, and some were clapt in prison, some hanged; and some, with nose and lips cut off, were sent forward to our Lord the Pope, for the disgrace and confusion of him (*in dedecus et confusionem ejus*). I, however, pretended to be Scotch, and putting on the garb of a Scotchman, and taking the gesture of one, walked along; and when anybody mocked at me, I would brandish my staff in the manner of that weapon they call *gaveloc,*[6] uttering comminatory words after the way of the Scotch. To those that met and questioned me who I was, I made no an-

---

[5] Carlyle's mistake for Dogberry: see *Much Ado About Nothing,* IV.ii.88. Caius is in *The Merry Wives of Windsor.*

[6] Javelin, missile pike. *Gaveloc* is still the Scotch name for *crowbar.* (C.)

swer but: *Ride, ride Rome; turne Cantwereberei.*[7] Thus did I, to conceal myself and my errand, and get safer to Rome under the guise of a Scotchman.

'Having at last obtained a Letter from our Lord the Pope according to my wishes, I turned homewards again. I had to pass through a certain strong town on my road; and lo, the soldiers thereof surrounded me, seizing me, and saying: "This vagabond (*iste solivagus*), who pretends to be Scotch, is either a spy, or has Letters from the false Pope Alexander." And whilst they examined every stitch and rag of me, my leggings (*caligas*), breeches, and even the old shoes that I carried over my shoulder in the way of the Scotch, — I put my hand into the leather scrip I wore, wherein our Lord the Pope's Letter lay, close by a little jug (*ciffus*) I had for drinking out of; and the Lord God so pleasing, and St. Edmund, I got out both the Letter and the jug together; in such a way that, extending my arm aloft, I held the Letter hidden between jug and hand: they saw the jug, but the Letter they saw not. And thus I escaped out of their hands in the name of the Lord. Whatever money I had they took from me; wherefore I had to beg from door to door, without any payment (*sine omni expensa*) till I came to England again. But hearing that the Woolpit Church was already given to Geoffry Ridell, my soul was struck with sorrow because I had laboured in vain. Coming home, therefore, I sat me down secretly under the Shrine of St. Edmund, fearing lest our Lord Abbot should seize and imprison me, though I had done no mischief; nor was there a monk who durst speak to me, nor a laic who durst bring me food except by stealth.'

Such resting and welcoming found Brother Samson, with his worn soles, and strong heart! He sits silent, revolving many thoughts, at the foot of St. Edmund's Shrine. In the wide Earth, if it be not Saint Edmund, what friend or refuge has he? Our Lord Abbot, hearing of him, sent the proper officer to lead him down to prison, clap 'foot-gyves on him' there. Another poor official furtively brought him a cup of wine; bade him "be comforted in the Lord." Samson utters no complaint; obeys in silence. 'Our Lord Abbot, taking counsel of it, banished me to Acre, and there I had to stay long.'

---

[7] Does this mean, "Rome forever; Canterbury *not*" (which claims an unjust Supremacy over us)! Mr. Rokewood is silent. Dryasdust would perhaps explain it, — in the course of a week or two of talking; did one dare to question him! (C.)

Our Lord Abbot next tried Samson with promotions; made him Subsacristan, made him Librarian, which he liked best of all, being passionately fond of Books: Samson, with many thoughts in him, again obeyed in silence; discharged his offices to perfection, but never thanked our Lord Abbot, — seemed rather as if looking into him, with those clear eyes of his. Whereupon Abbot Hugo said, *Se nunquam vidisse,* he had never seen such a man; whom no severity would break to complain, and no kindness soften into smiles or thanks: — a questionable kind of man!

In this way, not without troubles, but still in an erect clear-standing manner, has Brother Samson reached his forty-seventh year; and his ruddy beard is getting slightly grizzled. He is endeavouring, in these days, to have various broken things thatched in; nay perhaps to have the Choir itself completed, for he can bear nothing ruinous. He has gathered 'heaps of lime and sand;' has masons, slaters working, he and *Warinus monachus noster,*[8] who are joint keepers of the Shrine; paying out the money duly, — furnished by charitable burghers of St. Edmundsbury, they say. Charitable burghers of St. Edmundsbury? To me Jocelin it seems rather, Samson and Warinus, whom he leads, have privily hoarded the oblations at the Shrine itself, in these late years of indolent dilapidation, while Abbot Hugo sat wrapt inaccessible; and are struggling, in this prudent way, to have the rain kept out! — Under what conditions, sometimes, has Wisdom to struggle with Folly; get Folly persuaded to so much as thatch out the rain from itself! For, indeed, if the Infant govern the Nurse, what dexterous practice on the Nurse's part will not be necessary!

It is a new regret to us that, in these circumstances, our Lord the King's Custodiars, interfering, prohibited all building or thatching from whatever source; and no Choir shall be completed, and Rain and Time, for the present, shall have their way. Willelmus Sacrista, he of 'the frequent bibations and some things not to be spoken of;' he, with his red nose, I am of opinion, had made complaint to the Custodiars; wishing to do Samson an ill turn: — Samson his *Sub*-sacristan, with those clear eyes, could not be a prime favourite of his! Samson again obeys in silence.

[8] "Warinus, our monk."

CHAPTER VII

THE CANVASSING

Now, however, come great news to St. Edmundsbury: That there is to be an Abbot elected; that our interlunar obscuration is to cease; St. Edmund's Convent no more to be a doleful widow, but joyous and once again a bride! Often in our widowed state had we prayed to the Lord and St. Edmund, singing weekly a matter of 'one-and-twenty penitential Psalms, on our knees in the Choir,' that a fit Pastor might be vouchsafed us. And, says Jocelin, had some known what Abbot we were to get, they had not been so devout, I believe! — Bozzy Jocelin opens to mankind the floodgates of authentic Convent gossip; we listen, as in a Dionysius' Ear,[1] to the inanest hubbub, like the voices at Virgil's Horn-Gate of Dreams.[2] Even gossip, seven centuries off, has significance. List, list, how like men are to one another in all centuries:

'*Dixit quidam de quodam,* A certain person said of a certain person, "He, that *Frater,* is a good monk, *probabilis persona;* knows much of the order and customs of the church; and though not so perfect a philosopher as some others, would make a very good Abbot. Old Abbot Ording, still famed among us, knew little of letters. Besides, as we read in Fables, it is better to choose a log for king, than a serpent, never so wise, that will venomously hiss and bite his subjects." — "Impossible!" answered the other: "How can such a man make a sermon in the chapter, or to the people on festival days, when he is without letters? How can he have the skill to bind and to loose, he who does not understand the Scriptures? How — ?"'

And then 'another said of another, *alius de alio,* "That *Frater* is a *homo literatus,* eloquent, sagacious; vigorous in discipline; loves the Convent much, has suffered much for its sake." To

---

[1] A large ear-shaped excavation at Syracuse, said to have been built as a prison by the tyrant Dionysius the Elder, who could hear every word spoken in it.

[2] Cf. *Aeneid,* VI.893–896.

which a third party answers, "From all your great clerks good
Lord deliver us! From Norfolk barrators, and surly persons, That
it would please thee to preserve us, We beseech thee to hear us,
good Lord!" ' Then 'another *quidam* said of another *quodam*,
"That *Frater* is a good manager (*husebondus*);" but was swiftly
answered, "God forbid that a man who can neither read nor
chant, nor celebrate the divine offices, an unjust person withal,
and grinder of the faces of the poor, should ever be Abbot!" '
One man, it appears, is nice in his victuals. Another is indeed
wise; but apt to slight inferiors; hardly at the pains to answer, if
they argue with him too foolishly. And so each *aliquis* concerning
his *aliquo*, — through whole pages of electioneering babble. 'For,'
says Jocelin, 'So many men, as many minds.' Our Monks at time
of blood-letting, *tempore minutionis,'* holding their sanhedrim of
babble, would talk in this manner: Brother Samson, I remarked,
never said anything; sat silent, sometimes smiling; but he took
good note of what others said, and would bring it up, on occasion,
twenty years after. As for me Jocelin, I was of opinion that 'some
skill in Dialectics, to distinguish true from false,' would be good
in an Abbot. I spake, as a rash Novice in those days, some con-
scientious words of a certain benefactor of mine; 'and behold,
one of those sons of Belial' ran and reported them to him, so that
he never after looked at me with the same face again! Poor
Bozzy! —

Such is the buzz and frothy simmering ferment of the general
mind and no-mind; struggling to 'make itself up,' as the phrase is,
or ascertain what *it* does really want: no easy matter, in most
cases. St. Edmundsbury, in that Candlemas season of the year
1182, is a busily fermenting place. The very clothmakers sit
meditative at their looms; asking, Who shall be Abbot? The
sochemanni[3] speak of it, driving their ox-teams afield; the old
women with their spindles: and none yet knows what the days
will bring forth.

The Prior, however, as our interim chief, must proceed to work;
get ready 'Twelve Monks,' and set off with them to his Majesty at
Waltham, there shall the election be made. An election, whether
managed directly by ballot-box on public hustings, or indirectly
by force of public opinion, or were it even by open alehouses,

[3] The lowest rank of freehold tenants. Carlyle later uses the anglicized
form *sockmen.*

landlords' coercion, popular club-law, or whatever electoral methods, is always an interesting phenomenon. A mountain tumbling in great travail, throwing up dustclouds and absurd noises, is visibly there; uncertain yet what mouse or monster it will give birth to.

Besides it is a most important social act; nay, at bottom, the one important social act. Given the men a People choose, the People itself, in its exact worth and worthlessness, is given. A heroic people chooses heroes, and is happy; a valet or flunkey people chooses sham-heroes, what are called quacks, thinking them heroes, and is not happy. The grand summary of a man's spiritual condition, what brings out all his herohood and insight, or all his flunkeyhood and horn-eyed dimness, is this question put to him, What man dost thou honour? Which is thy ideal of a man; or nearest that? So too of a People: for a People too, every People, *speaks* its choice, — were it only by silently obeying, and not revolting, — in the course of a century or so. Nor are electoral methods, Reform Bills and such like, unimportant. A People's electoral methods are, in the long-run, the express image of its electoral *talent;* tending and gravitating perpetually, irresistibly, to a conformity with that: and are, at all stages, very significant of the People. Judicious readers, of these times, are not disinclined to see how Monks elect their Abbot in the Twelfth Century: how the St. Edmundsbury mountain manages its midwifery; and what mouse or man the outcome is.

CHAPTER VIII

THE ELECTION

ACCORDINGLY our Prior assembles us in Chapter; and, we adjuring him before God to do justly, nominates, not by our selection, yet with our assent, Twelve Monks, moderately satisfactory. Of whom are Hugo Third-Prior, Brother Dennis a venerable man, Walter the *Medicus,* Samson *Subsacrista,* and other esteemed characters, — though Willelmus *Sacrista,* of the red nose, too is one. These shall proceed straightway to Waltham; elect the Abbot as they may and can. Monks are sworn to obedience; must not speak too loud, under penalty of foot-gyves, limbo, and bread and water: yet monks too would know what it is they are obeying. The St. Edmundsbury Community has no hustings, ballot-box, indeed no open voting: yet by various vague manipulations, pulse-feelings, we struggle to ascertain what its virtual aim is, and succeed better or worse.

This question, however, rises; alas, a quite preliminary question: Will the *Dominus Rex* allow us to choose freely? It is to be hoped! Well, if so, we agree to choose one of our own Convent. If not, if the *Dominus Rex* will force a stranger on us, we decide on demurring, the Prior and his Twelve shall demur: we can appeal, plead, remonstrate; appeal even to the Pope, but trust it will not be necessary. Then there is this other question, raised by Brother Samson: What if the Thirteen should not themselves be able to agree? Brother Samson *Subsacrista,* one remarks, is ready oftenest with some question, some suggestion, that has wisdom in it. Though a servant of servants, and saying little, his words all tell, having sense in them; it seems by his light mainly that we steer ourselves in this great dimness.

What if the Thirteen should not themselves be able to agree? Speak, Samson, and advise. — Could not, hints Samson, Six of our venerablest elders be chosen by us, a kind of electoral committee, here and now: of these, 'with their hand on the Gospels, with their eye on the *Sacrosancta,*'[1] we take oath that they will do

[1] Holy objects; here, specifically, the shrine of St. Edmund, which contained his bones. See below, Ch. xvi.

faithfully; let these, in secret and as before God, agree on Three whom they reckon fittest; write their names in a Paper, and deliver the same sealed, forthwith, to the Thirteen: one of those Three the Thirteen shall fix on, if permitted. If not permitted, that is to say, if the *Dominus Rex* force us to demur, — the Paper shall be brought back unopened, and publicly burned, that no man's secret bring him into trouble.

So Samson advises, so we act; wisely, in this and in other crises of the business. Our electoral committee, its eye on the *Sacrosancta,* is soon named, soon sworn; and we striking up the Fifth Psalm, 'Verba mea,

> 'Give ear unto my words, O Lord,
> My meditation weigh,'

march out chanting, and leave the Six to their work in the Chapter here. Their work, before long, they announce as finished: they, with their eye on the Sacrosancta, imprecating the Lord to weigh and witness their meditation, have fixed on Three Names, and written them in this Sealed Paper. Let Samson Subsacrista, general servant of the party, take charge of it. On the morrow morning, our Prior and his Twelve will be ready to get under way.

This then is the ballot-box and electoral winnowing-machine they have at St. Edmundsbury: a mind fixed on the Thrice Holy, an appeal to God on high to witness their meditation: by far the best, and indeed the only good electoral winnowing-machine, — if men have souls in them. Totally worthless, it is true, and even hideous and poisonous, if men have no souls. But without soul, alas what winnowing-machine in human elections, can be of avail? We cannot get along without soul; we stick fast, the mournfullest spectacle; and salt itself will not save us!

On the morrow morning, accordingly, our Thirteen set forth; or rather our Prior and Eleven; for Samson, as general servant of the party, has to linger, settling many things. At length he too gets upon the road; and, 'carrying the sealed Paper in a leather pouch hung round his neck; and *froccum bajulans in ulnis*' (thanks to thee Bozzy Jocelin), 'his frock-skirts looped over his elbow,' shewing substantial stern-works, tramps stoutly along. Away across the Heath, not yet of Newmarket[2] and horse-jockey-

---

[2] A town near Bury St. Edmunds, in Carlyle's time, as now, a center of horse-breeding and racing.

ing; across your Fleam-dike and Devil's-dike, no longer useful as
a Mercian East-Anglian boundary or bulwark: continually towards Waltham, and the Bishop of Winchester's House there, for
his Majesty is in that. Brother Samson, as purse-bearer, has the
reckoning always, when there is one, to pay; 'delays are numerous,' progress none of the swiftest.

But, in the solitude of the Convent, Destiny thus big and in
her birthtime, what gossiping, what babbling, what dreaming
of dreams! The secret of the Three our electoral elders alone
know: some Abbot we shall have to govern us; but which Abbot,
O which! One Monk discerns in a vision of the night-watches,
that we shall get an Abbot of our own body, without needing to
demur: a prophet appeared to him clad all in white, and said,
"Ye shall have one of yours, and he will rage among you like a
wolf, *sæviet ut lupus.*" Verily! — then which of ours? Another
Monk now dreams: he has seen clearly which; a certain Figure
taller by head and shoulders than the other two, dressed in alb
and *pallium,*[3] and with the attitude of one about to fight; — which
tall Figure a wise Editor would rather not name at this stage of
the business! Enough that the vision is true: that Saint Edmund
himself, pale and awful, seemed to rise from his Shrine, with
naked feet, and say audibly, "He, *ille,* shall veil my feet;" which
part of the vision also proves true. Such guessing, visioning, dim
perscrutation of the momentous future: the very clothmakers, old
women, all townsfolk speak of it, 'and more than once it is reported in St. Edmundsbury, This one is elected; and then, This
one and That other.' Who knows?

But now, sure enough, at Waltham 'on the Second Sunday of
Quadragesima,' which Dryasdust declares to mean the 22d day
of February, year 1182, Thirteen St. Edmundsbury Monks are,
at last, seen processioning towards the Winchester Manorhouse;
and in some high Presence-chamber, and Hall of State, get
access to Henry II. in all his glory. What a Hall, — not imaginary in the least, but entirely real and indisputable, though so extremely dim to us; sunk in the deep distances of Night! The
Winchester Manorhouse has fled bodily, like a Dream of the old
Night; not Dryasdust himself can shew a wreck of it. House and
people, royal and episcopal, lords and varlets, where are they?
Why *there,* I say, Seven Centuries off; sunk *so* far in the Night,

---

[3] Surplice and woollen vestment, the latter worn by archbishops.

there they *are;* peep through the blankets of the old Night,[4] and thou wilt see! King Henry himself is visibly there, a vivid, noble-looking man, with grizzled beard, in glittering uncertain costume; with earls round him, and bishops and dignitaries, in the like. The Hall is large, and has for one thing an altar near it, — chapel and altar adjoining it; but what gilt seats, carved tables, carpeting of rush-cloth, what arras-hangings, and a huge fire of logs: — alas, it has Human Life in it; and is not that the grand miracle, in what hangings or costume soever? —

The *Dominus Rex,* benignantly receiving our Thirteen with their obeisance, and graciously declaring that he will strive to act for God's honour, and the Church's good, commands, 'by the Bishop of Winchester and Geoffrey the Chancellor,' — *Galfridus Cancellarius,* Henry's and the Fair Rosamond's authentic Son[5] present here! — commands, "That they, the said Thirteen, do now withdraw, and fix upon Three from their own Monastery." A work soon done; the Three hanging ready round Samson's neck, in that leather pouch of his. Breaking the seal, we find the names, — what think *ye* of it, ye higher dignitaries, thou indolent Prior, thou Willelmus *Sacrista* with the red bottle-nose? — the names, in this order: of Samson *Subsacrista,* of Roger the distressed Cellarer, of Hugo *Tertius-Prior.*

The higher dignitaries, all omitted here, 'flush suddenly red in the face;' but have nothing to say. One curious fact and question certainly is, How Hugo Third-Prior, who was of the electoral committee, came to nominate *himself* as one of the Three? A curious fact, which Hugo Third-Prior has never yet entirely explained, that I know of! — However, we return, and report to the King our Three names; merely altering the order; putting Samson last, as lowest of all. The King, at recitation of our Three, asks us: "Who are they? Were they born in my domain? Totally unknown to me! You must nominate three others." Whereupon Willelmus Sacrista says, "Our Prior must be named, *quia caput nostrum est,* being already our head." And the Prior responds, "Willelmus Sacrista is a fit man, *bonus vir est,*" — for all his red nose. Tickle me Toby, and I'll tickle thee! Venerable Dennis too is named; none in his conscience can say nay. There are now Six on our List. "Well," said the King, "they have done it swiftly,

---

[4] *Macbeth,* I.v.54.
[5] Geoffrey was the reputed son of Henry II and his mistress, Rosamond de Clifford.

they! *Deus est cum eis.*" The Monks withdraw again; and Majesty revolves, for a little, with his *Pares* and *Episcopi,*[6] Lords or 'Law-wards' and Soul-Overseers, the thoughts of the royal breast. The Monks wait silent in an outer room.

In short while, they are next ordered, To add yet another three; but not from their own Convent; from other Convents, "for the honour of my kingdom." Here, — what is to be done here? We will demur, if need be! We do name three, however, for the nonce: the Prior of St. Faith's, a good Monk of St. Neot's, a good Monk of St. Alban's; good men all; all made abbots and dignitaries since, at this hour. There are now Nine upon our List. What the thoughts of the Dominus Rex may be farther? The Dominus Rex, thanking graciously, sends out word that we shall now strike off three. The three strangers are instantly struck off. Willelmus Sacrista adds, that he will of his own accord decline, — a touch of grace and respect for the *Sacrosancta,* even in Willelmus! The King then orders us to strike off a couple more; then yet one more: Hugo Third-Prior goes, and Roger *Cellerarius,* and venerable Monk Dennis; — and now there remain on our List two only, Samson Subsacrista and the Prior.

Which of these two? It were hard to say, — by Monks who may get themselves foot-gyved and thrown into limbo, for speaking! We humbly request that the Bishop of Winchester and Geoffrey the Chancellor may again enter, and help us to decide. "Which do you want?" asks the Bishop. Venerable Dennis made a speech, 'commending the persons of the Prior and Samson; but always in the corner of his discourse, *in angulo sui sermonis,* brought Samson in.' "I see!" said the Bishop: "We are to understand that your Prior is somewhat remiss; that you want to have him you call Samson for Abbot." "Either of them is good," said venerable Dennis, almost trembling; "but we would have the better, if it pleased God." "Which of the two *do* you want?" inquires the Bishop pointedly. "Samson!" answered Dennis; "Samson!" echoed all of the rest that durst speak or echo anything: and Samson is reported to the King accordingly. His Majesty, advising of it for a moment, orders that Samson be brought in with the other Twelve.

The King's Majesty, looking at us somewhat sternly, then says:

[6] Peers and bishops.

"You present to me Samson; I do not know him: had it been your Prior, whom I do know, I should have accepted him: however, I will now do as you wish. But have a care of yourselves. By the true eyes of God, *per veros oculos Dei,* if you manage badly, I will be upon you!" Samson, therefore, steps forward, kisses the King's feet; but swiftly rises erect again, swiftly turns towards the altar, uplifting with the other Twelve, in clear tenor-note, the Fifty-first Psalm, *'Miserere mei Deus,*

> 'After thy loving-kindness, Lord,
> Have mercy upon *me;*'

with firm voice, firm step and head, no change in his countenance whatever. "By God's eyes," said the King, "that one, I think, will govern the Abbey well." By the same oath (charged to your Majesty's account), I too am precisely of that opinion! It is some while since I fell in with a likelier man anywhere than this new Abbot Samson. Long life to him, and may the Lord *have* mercy on him as Abbot!

Thus, then, have the St. Edmundsbury Monks, without express ballot-box or other good winnowing-machine, contrived to accomplish the most important social feat a body of men can do, to winnow out the man that is to govern them: and truly one sees not that, by any winnowing-machine whatever, they could have done it better. O ye kind Heavens, there is in every Nation and Community *a fittest,* a wisest, bravest, best; whom could we find and make King over us, all were in very truth well; — the best that God and Nature had permitted *us* to make it! By what art discover him? Will the Heavens in their pity teach us no art; for our need of him is great!

Ballot-boxes, Reform Bills, winnowing-machines: all these are good, or are not so good; — alas, brethren, how *can* these, I say, be other than inadequate, be other than failures, melancholy to behold? Dim all souls of men to the divine, the high and awful meaning of Human Worth and Truth, we shall never, by all the machinery in Birmingham, discover the True and Worthy. It is written, 'if we are ourselves valets, there shall exist no hero for us; we shall not know the hero when we see him;' — we shall take the quack for a hero; and cry, audibly through all ballot-boxes and machinery whatsoever, Thou art he; be thou King over us!

What boots it? Seek only deceitful Speciosity, money with gilt carriages, 'fame' with newspaper-paragraphs, whatever name it bear, you will find only deceitful Speciosity; godlike Reality will be forever far from you. The Quack shall be legitimate inevitable King of you; no earthly machinery able to exclude the Quack. Ye shall be born thralls of the Quack, and suffer under him, till your hearts are near broken, and no French Revolution or Manchester Insurrection, or partial or universal volcanic combustions and explosions, never so many, can do more than 'change the *figure* of your Quack;' the essence of him remaining, for a time and times. — "How long, O Prophet?" say some, with a rather melancholy sneer. Alas, ye *un*prophetic, ever till this come about: Till deep misery, if nothing softer will, have driven you out of your Speciosites *into* your Sincerities; and you find that there either is a Godlike in the world, or else ye are an unintelligible madness; that there is a God, as well as a Mammon and a Devil, and a Genius of Luxuries and canting Dilettantisms and Vain Shows! How long that will be, compute for yourselves. My unhappy brothers! —

CHAPTER IX

So then the bells of St. Edmundsbury clang out one and all, and in church and chapel the organs go: Convent and Town, and all the west side of Suffolk, are in gala; knights, viscounts, weavers, spinners, the entire population, male and female, young and old, the very sockmen with their chubby infants, — out to have a holiday, and see the Lord Abbot arrive! And there is 'stripping barefoot' of the Lord Abbot at the Gate, and solemn leading of him in to the High Altar and Shrine; with sudden 'silence of all the bells and organs,' as we kneel in deep prayer there; and again with outburst of all the bells and organs, and loud *Te Deum* from the general human windpipe; and speeches by the leading viscount, and giving of the kiss of brotherhood; the whole wound up with popular games, and dinner within doors of more than a thousand strong, *plus quam mille comedentibus in gaudio magno.*

In such manner is the selfsame Samson once again returning to us, welcomed on *this* occasion. He that went away with his frock-skirts looped over his arm, comes back riding high; suddenly made one of the dignitaries of this world. Reflective readers will admit that here was a trial for a man. Yesterday a poor mendicant, allowed to possess not above two shillings of money, and without authority to bid a dog run for him, this man today finds himself a *Dominus Abbas*, mitred Peer of Parliament, Lord of manorhouses, farms, manors, and wide lands; a man with 'Fifty Knights under him,' and dependent swiftly obedient multitudes of men. It is a change greater than Napoleon's; so sudden withal. As if one of the Chandos daydrudges[1] had, on awakening some morning, found that *he* overnight was become Duke! Let Samson with his clear-beaming eyes see into that, and discern it if he can. We shall now get the measure of him by a new scale

[1] Chandos (see above, p. 58, n. 6) was notorious for the low wages he paid his farm workers. A free spender, he eventually ran a million pounds into debt.

of inches, considerably more rigorous than the former was. For if a noble soul is rendered tenfold beautifuller by victory and prosperity, springing now radiant as into his own due element and sunthrone; an ignoble one is rendered tenfold and hundredfold uglier, pitifuller. Whatsoever vices, whatsoever weaknesses were in the man, the parvenu will shew us them enlarged, as in the solar microscope,[2] into frightful distortion. Nay, how many mere seminal principles of vice, hitherto all wholesomely kept latent, may we now see unfolded, as in the solar hothouse, into growth, into huge universally-conspicuous luxuriance and development!

But is not this, at any rate, a singular aspect of what political and social capabilities, nay let us say what depth and opulence of true social vitality, lay in those old barbarous ages, That the fit Governor could be met with under such disguises, could be recognised and laid hold of under such? Here he is discovered with a maximum of two shillings in his pocket, and a leather scrip round his neck; trudging along the highway, his frock-skirts looped over his arm. They think this is he nevertheless, the true Governor; and he proves to be so. Brethren, have we no need of discovering true Governors, but will sham ones forever do for us? These were absurd superstitious blockheads of Monks; and we are enlightened Tenpound Franchisers, without taxes on knowledge![3] Where, I say, are our superior, are our similar or at all comparable discoveries? We also have eyes, or ought to have; we have hustings, telescopes; we have lights, link-lights and rushlights of an enlightened free Press, burning and dancing everywhere, as in a universal torch-dance; singeing your whiskers as you traverse the public thoroughfares in town and country. Great souls, true Governors, go about under all manner of disguises now as then. Such telescopes, such enlightenment, — and such discovery! How comes it, I say; how comes it? Is it not lamentable; is it not even, in some sense, amazing?

Alas, the defect, as we must often urge and again urge, is less a defect of telescopes than of some eyesight. Those superstitious

[2] An optical device, employing the concentrated rays of the sun, which projected magnified images of minute objects on a screen. (*Solar hothouse*, just following, is, of course, a greenhouse.)

[3] Taxes on paper, individual copies of newspapers, and advertisements. Their abolition was much agitated by the liberal-radical politicians of the time. "Without" presumably is ironical.

blockheads of the Twelfth Century had no telescopes, but they had still an eye: not ballot-boxes; only reverence for Worth, abhorrence of Unworth. It is the way with all barbarians. Thus Mr. Sale[4] informs me, the old Arab Tribes would gather in liveliest *gaudeamus*,[5] and sing, and kindle bonfires, and wreathe crowns of honour, and solemnly thank the gods that, in their Tribe too, a Poet had shewn himself. As indeed they well might; for what usefuller, I say not nobler and heavenlier thing could the gods, doing their very kindest, send to any Tribe or Nation, in any time or circumstances? I declare to thee, my afflicted quack-ridden brother, in spite of thy astonishment, it is very lamentable! We English find a Poet, as brave a man as has been made for a hundred years or so anywhere under the Sun; and do we kindle bonfires, thank the gods? Not at all. We, taking due counsel of it, set the man to gauge ale-barrels in the Burgh of Dumfries; and pique ourselves on our 'patronage of genius.'

Genius, Poet: do we know what these words mean? An inspired Soul once more vouchsafed us, direct from Nature's own great fire-heart, to see the Truth, and speak it, and do it; Nature's own sacred voice heard once more athwart the dreary boundless element of hearsaying and canting, of twaddle and poltroonery, in which the bewildered Earth, nigh perishing, has *lost its way*. Hear once more, ye bewildered benighted mortals; listen once again to a voice from the inner Light-sea and Flame-sea, Nature's and Truth's own heart; know the Fact of your Existence what it is, put away the Cant of it which it is *not;* and knowing, do, and let it be well with you! —

George the Third is Defender of something we call 'the Faith' in those years; George the Third is head charioteer of the Destinies of England, to guide them through the gulf of French Revolutions, American Independences; and Robert Burns is Gauger of ale in Dumfries. It is an Iliad in a nutshell. The physiognomy of a world now verging towards dissolution, reduced now to spasms and death-throes, lies pictured in that one fact, — which astonishes nobody, except at me for being astonished at it. The fruit of long ages of confirmed Valethood, entirely confirmed as into a Law of Nature; cloth-worship and quack-worship: entirely *confirmed* Valethood, — which will have to *un*confirm itself again; God knows, with difficulty enough! —

[4] George Sale, early eighteenth-century Orientalist and translator of the Koran.
[5] Funmaking.

Abbot Samson had found a Convent all in dilapidation; rain beating through it, material rain and metaphorical, from all quarters of the compass. Willelmus Sacrista sits drinking nightly, and doing mere *tacenda*. Our larders are reduced to leanness, Jew Harpies[6] and unclean creatures our purveyors; in our basket is no bread. Old women with their distaffs rush out on a distressed Cellarer in shrill Chartism. 'You cannot stir abroad but Jews and Christians pounce upon you with unsettled bonds;' debts boundless seemingly as the National Debt of England. For four years our new Lord Abbot never went abroad but Jew creditors and Christian, and all manner of creditors, were about him; driving him to very despair. Our Prior is remiss; our Cellarers, officials are remiss, our monks are remiss: what man is not remiss? Front this, Samson, thou alone art there to front it; it is thy task to front and fight this, and to die or kill it. May the Lord have mercy on thee!

To our antiquarian interest in poor Jocelin and his Convent, where the whole aspect of existence, the whole dialect, of thought, of speech, of activity, is so obsolete, strange, long-vanished, there now superadds itself a mild glow of human interest for Abbot Samson; a real pleasure, as at sight of man's work, especially of governing, which is man's highest work, done *well*. Abbot Samson had no experience in governing; had served no apprenticeship to the trade of governing, — alas, only the hardest apprenticeship to that of obeying. He had never in any court given *vadium* or *plegium*,[7] says Jocelin; hardly ever seen a court, when he was set to preside in one. But it is astonishing, continues Jocelin, how soon he learned the ways of business; and, in all sort of affairs, became expert beyond others. Of the many persons offering him their service 'he retained one Knight skilled in taking *vadia* and *plegia*;' and within the year was himself well skilled. Nay, by and by, the Pope appoints him Justiciary in certain causes; the King one of his new Circuit Judges: official Osbert is heard saying, "That Abbot is one of your shrewd ones, *disputator est*; if he go on as he begins, he will cut out every lawyer of us!"

Why not? What is to hinder this Samson from governing? There is in him what far transcends all apprenticeships; in the

[6] Rapacious monsters, half women, half birds.

[7] A formula guaranteeing one's appearance in court. The terms mean, respectively, security in the form of property or money and the person who stands security for another.

man himself there exists a model of governing, something to govern by! There exists in him a heart-abhorrence of whatever is incoherent, pusillanimous, unveracious, — that is to say, chaotic, *ungoverned*; of the Devil, not of God. A man of this kind cannot help governing! He has the living ideal of a governor in him; and the incessant necessity of struggling to unfold the same out of him. Not the Devil or Chaos, for any wages, will he serve; no, this man is the born servant of Another than them. Alas, how little avail all apprenticeships, when there is in your governor himself what we may well call *nothing* to govern by: nothing; — a general grey twilight, looming with shapes of expediencies, parliamentary traditions, division-lists,[8] election-funds, leading-articles; this, with what of vulpine alertness and adroitness soever, is not much!

But indeed what say we, apprenticeship? Had not this Samson served, in his way, a right good apprenticeship to governing; namely, the harshest slave-apprenticeship to obeying! Walk this world with no friend in it but God and St. Edmund, you will either fall into the ditch, or learn a good many things. To learn obeying is the fundamental art of governing. How much would many a Serene Highness have learned, had he travelled through the world with water-jug and empty wallet, *sine omni expensa;* and, at his victorious return, sat down not to newspaper-paragraphs and city-illuminations, but at the foot of St. Edmund's Shrine to shackles and bread and water! He that cannot be servant of many, will never be master, true guide and deliverer of many; — that is the meaning of true mastership. Had not the Monk-life extraordinary 'political capabilities' in it; if not imitable by us, yet enviable? Heavens, had a Duke of Logwood,[9] now rolling sumptuously to his place in the Collective Wisdom, but himself happened to plough daily, at one time, on seven-and-sixpence a week, with no out-door relief, — what a light, unquenchable by logic and statistic and arithmetic, would it have thrown on several things for him!

In all cases, therefore, we will agree with the judicious Mrs. Glass: 'First catch your hare!'[10] First get your man; all is got: he

---

[8] Voting records.

[9] A peer on his way to his seat in the House of Lords.

[10] A phrase traditionally said to begin a recipe in *The Art of Cookery Made Plain and Easy* (1747) by "Hannah Glasse" (Dr. John Hill?). It is not there; but it was a proverbial expression long before the book was printed.

can learn to do all things, from making boots, to decreeing judgments, governing communities; and will do them like a man. Catch your no-man, — alas, have you not caught the terriblest Tartar in the world! Perhaps all the terribler, the quieter and gentler he looks. For the mischief that one blockhead, that every blockhead does, in a world so feracious, teeming with endless results as ours, no ciphering will sum up. The quack bootmaker is considerable; as corn-cutters can testify, and desperate men reduced to buckskin and list-shoes. But the quack priest, quack high-priest, the quack king! Why do not all just citizens rush, half-frantic, to stop him, as they would a conflagration? Surely a just citizen *is* admonished by God and his own Soul, by all silent and articulate voices of this Universe, to do what in *him* lies towards relief of this poor blockhead-quack, and of a world that groans under him. Runs swiftly; relieve him, — were it even by extinguishing him! For all things have grown so old, tinder-dry, combustible; and he is more ruinous than conflagration. Sweep him *down*, at least; keep him strictly within the hearth: he will then cease to be conflagration; he will then become useful, more or less, as culinary fire. Fire is the best of servants; but what a master! This poor blockhead too is born for uses: why, elevating him to mastership, will you make a conflagration, a parish-curse or world-curse of him?

CHAPTER X

How Abbot Samson, giving his new subjects seriatim the kiss of fatherhood in the St. Edmundsbury chapterhouse, proceeded with cautious energy to set about reforming their disjointed distracted way of life; how he managed with his Fifty rough *Milites* (Feudal Knights), with his lazy Farmers, remiss refractory Monks, with Pope's Legates, Viscounts, Bishops, Kings; how on all sides he laid about him like a man, and putting consequence on premiss, and everywhere the saddle on the right horse, struggled incessantly to educe organic method out of lazily fermenting wreck, — the careful reader will discern, not without true interest, in these pages of Jocelin Boswell. In most antiquarian quaint costume, not of garments alone, but of thought, word, action, outlook and position, the substantial figure of a man with eminent nose, bushy brows and clear-flashing eyes, his russet beard growing daily greyer, is visible, engaged in true governing of men. It is beautiful how the chrysalis governing-soul, shaking off its dusty slough and prison, starts forth winged, a true royal soul! Our new Abbot has a right honest unconscious feeling, without insolence as without fear or flutter, of what he is and what others are. A courage to quell the proudest, an honest pity to encourage the humblest. Withal there is a noble reticence in this Lord Abbot: much vain unreason he hears; lays up without response. He is not there to expect reason and nobleness of others; he is there to give them of his own reason and nobleness. Is he not their servant, as we said, who can suffer from them, and for them; bear the burden their poor spindle-limbs totter and stagger under; and in virtue *thereof* govern them, lead them out of weakness into strength, out of defeat into victory!

One of the first Herculean Labours Abbot Samson undertook, or the very first, was to institute a strenuous review and radical reform of his economics. It is the first labour of every governing man, from *Paterfamilias* to *Dominus Rex*. To get the rain thatched out from you is the preliminary of whatever farther, in the way of speculation or of action, you may mean to do. Old Abbot Hugo's budget, as we saw, had become empty, filled with deficit and wind. To see his account-books clear, be delivered from those ravening flights of Jew and Christian creditors, pouncing on him like obscene harpies[1] wherever he shewed face, was a necessity for Abbot Samson.

On the morrow after his instalment, he brings in a load of money-bonds, all duly stamped, sealed with this or the other Convent Seal: frightful, unmanageable, a bottomless confusion of Convent finance. There they are; — but there at least they all are; all that shall be of them. Our Lord Abbot demands that all the official seals in use among us be now produced and delivered to him. Three-and-thirty seals turn up; are straightway broken, and shall seal no more: the Abbot only, and those duly author-ised by him shall seal any bond. There are but two ways of paying debt: increase of industry in raising income, increase of thrift in laying it out. With iron energy, in slow but steady un-deviating perseverance, Abbot Samson sets to work in both direc-tions. His troubles are manifold: cunning *milites,* unjust bailiffs, lazy sockmen, he an inexperienced Abbot; relaxed lazy monks, not disinclined to mutiny in mass: but continued vigilance, rigorous method, what we call 'the eye of the master,' work won-ders. The clear-beaming eyesight of Abbot Samson, steadfast, severe, all-penetrating, — it is like *Fiat lux*[2] in that inorganic waste whirlpool; penetrates gradually to all nooks, and of the chaos makes a *kosmos* or ordered world!

He arranges everywhere, struggles unweariedly to arrange, and place on some intelligible footing, the 'affairs and dues, *res ac redditus,*' of his dominion. The Lakenheath eels cease to breed squabbles between human beings; the penny of *reap-silver* to ex-plode into the streets the Female Chartism of St. Edmundsbury. These and innumerable greater things. Wheresoever Disorder may stand or lie, let it have a care; here is the man that has declared war with it, that never will make peace with it. Man is the Missionary of Order; he is the servant not of the Devil and Chaos, but of God and the Universe! Let all sluggards and cowards, remiss, false-spoken, unjust, and otherwise diabolic persons have a care: this is a dangerous man for them. He has a

[1] Cf. *Aeneid,* III.241.
[2] "Let there be light": Genesis 1:3.

mild grave face; a thoughtful sternness, a sorrowful pity: but there is a terrible flash of anger in him too; lazy monks often have to murmur, "*Sævit ut lupus,* He rages like a wolf; was not our Dream true!" 'To repress and hold-in such sudden anger he was continually careful,' and succeeded well: — right, Samson; that it may become in thee as noble central heat, fruitful, strong, beneficent; not blaze out, or the seldomest possible blaze out, as wasteful volcanoism to scorch and consume!

"We must first creep, and gradually learn to walk," had Abbot Samson said of himself, at starting. In four years he has become a great walker; striding prosperously along; driving much before him. In less than four years, says Jocelin, the Convent Debts were all liquidated: the harpy Jews not only settled with, but banished, bag and baggage, out of the *Bannaleuca* (Liberties, *Banlieue*) of St. Edmundsbury, — so has the King's Majesty been persuaded to permit. Farewell to *you,* at any rate; let us, in no extremity, apply again to you! Armed men march them over the borders, dismiss them under stern penalties, — sentence of excommunication on all that shall again harbour them here: there were many dry eyes at their departure.

New life enters everywhere, springs up beneficent, the Incubus of Debt once rolled away. Samson hastes not; but neither does he pause to rest. This of the Finance is a life-long business with him; — Jocelin's anecdotes are filled to weariness with it. As indeed to Jocelin it was of very primary interest.

But we have to record also, with a lively satisfaction, that spiritual rubbish is as little tolerated in Samson's Monastery as material. With due rigour, Willelmus Sacrista, and his bibations and *tacenda* are, at the earliest opportunity, softly, yet irrevocably put an end to. The bibations, namely, had to end; even the building where they used to be carried on was razed from the soil of St. Edmundsbury, and 'on its place grow rows of beams:' Willelmus himself, deposed from the Sacristry and all offices, retires into obscurity, into absolute taciturnity unbroken thenceforth to this hour. Whether the poor Willelmus did not still, by secret channels, occasionally get some slight wetting of vinous or alcoholic liquor, — now grown, in a manner, indispensable to the poor man? Jocelin hints not; one knows not how to hope, what to hope! But if he did, it was in silence and darkness; with an ever-present feeling that teetotalism was his only true course.

Drunken dissolute Monks are a class of persons who had better keep out of Abbot Samson's way. *Sævit ut lupus;* was not the Dream true! murmured many a Monk. Nay Ranulf de Glanville, Justiciary in Chief, took umbrage at him, seeing these strict ways; and watched farther with suspicion: but discerned gradually that there was nothing wrong, that there was much the opposite of wrong.

CHAPTER XI

THE ABBOT'S WAYS

ABBOT SAMSON shewed no extraordinary favour to the Monks who had been his familiars of old; did not promote them to offices, — *nisi essent idonei,* unless they chanced to be fit men! Whence great discontent among certain of these, who had contributed to make him Abbot: reproaches, open and secret, of his being 'ungrateful, hard-tempered, unsocial, a Norfolk *barrator* and *paltenerius.*'[1]

Indeed, except it were for *idonei,* 'fit men,' in all kinds, it was hard to say for whom Abbot Samson had much favour. He loved his kindred well, and tenderly enough acknowledged the poor part of them; with the rich part, who in old days had never acknowledged him, he totally refused to have any business. But even the former he did not promote into offices; finding none of them *idonei.* 'Some whom he thought suitable he put into situations in his own household, or made keepers of his country places: if they behaved ill, he dismissed them without hope of return.' In his promotions, nay almost in his benefits, you would have said there was a certain impartiality. 'The official person who had, by Abbot Hugo's order, put the fetters on him at his return from Italy, was now supported with food and clothes to the end of his days at Abbot Samson's expense.'

Yet he did not forget benefits; far the reverse, when an opportunity occurred of paying them at his own cost. How pay them at the public cost; — how, above all, by *setting fire* to the public, as we said; clapping 'conflagrations' on the public, which the services of blockheads, *non-idonei,* intrinsically are! He was right willing to remember friends, when it could be done. Take these instances: 'A certain chaplain who had maintained him at the Schools of Paris by the sale of holy water, *quæstu aquæ benedictæ;* — to this good chaplain he did give a vicarage, adequate to the comfortable sustenance of him.' 'The Son of Elias, too,

---

[1] A man with the qualities just enumerated. (For *barrator,* see text above, p. 74.

that is, of old Abbot Hugo's Cupbearer, coming to do homage for his Father's land, our Lord Abbot said to him in full court: "I have, for these seven years, put off taking thy homage for the land which Abbot Hugo gave thy Father, because that gift was to the damage of Elmswell, and a questionable one: but now I must profess myself overcome; mindful of the kindness thy Father did me when I was in bonds; because he sent me a cup of the very wine his master had been drinking, and bade me be comforted in God." '

'To Magister Walter, son of Magister William de Dice, who wanted the vicarage of Chevington, he answered: "Thy Father was Master of the Schools; and when I was an indigent *clericus,* he granted me freely and in charity an entrance to his School, and opportunity of learning; wherefore I now, for the sake of God, grant to thee what thou askest." ' Or lastly, take this good instance, — and a glimpse, along with it, into long-obsolete times: 'Two *Milites* of Risby, Willelm and Norman, being adjudged in Court to come under his mercy, *in misericordia ejus,*' for a certain very considerable fine of twenty shillings, 'he thus addressed them publicly on the spot: "When I was a Cloister-monk, I was once sent to Durham on business of our Church; and coming home again, the dark night caught me at Risby, and I had to beg a lodging there. I went to Dominus Norman's, and he gave me a flat refusal. Going then to Dominus Willelm's, and begging hospitality, I was by him honourably received. The twenty shillings therefore of *mercy,* I, without mercy, will exact from Dominus Norman; to Dominus Willelm, on the other hand, I, with thanks, will wholly remit the said sum." ' Men know not always to whom they refuse lodgings; men have lodged Angels unawares![2] —

It is clear Abbot Samson had a talent; he had learned to judge better than Lawyers, to manage better than bred Bailiffs: — a talent shining out indisputable, on whatever side you took him. 'An eloquent man he was,' says Jocelin, 'both in French and Latin; but intent more on the substance and method of what was to be said, than on the ornamental way of saying it. He could read English Manuscripts very elegantly, *elegantissime:* he was wont to preach to the people in the English tongue, though according to the dialect of Norfolk, where he had been brought up; wherefore indeed he had caused a Pulpit to be erected in our Church

[2] Hebrews 13:2.

both for ornament of the same, and for the use of his audiences.'
There preached he, according to the dialect of Norfolk: a man
worth going to hear.

That he was a just clear-hearted man, this, as the basis of all
true talent, is presupposed. How can a man, without clear vision
in his heart first of all, have any clear vision in the head? It is
impossible! Abbot Samson was one of the justest of judges; in-
sisted on understanding the case to the bottom, and then swiftly
decided without feud or favour. For which reason, indeed, the
Dominus Rex, searching for such men, as for hidden treasure and
healing to his distressed realm, had made him one of the new
Itinerant Judges, — such as continue to this day. "My curse on
that Abbot's court," a suitor was heard imprecating, "*Maledicta sit
curia istius Abbatis,* where neither gold nor silver can help me
to confound my enemy!" And old friendships and all connexions
forgotten, when you go to seek an office from him! "A kinless
loon," as the Scotch said of Cromwell's new judges, — intent on
mere indifferent fair-play!

Eloquence in three languages is good; but it is not the best.
To us, as already hinted, the Lord Abbot's eloquence is less
admirable than his *in*eloquence, his great invaluable 'talent of
silence!' '"*Deus, Deus,*" said the Lord Abbot to me once, when
he heard the Convent were murmuring at some act of his, "I have
much need to remember that Dream they had of me, that I was
to rage among them like a wolf. Above all earthly things I dread
their driving me to do it. How much do I hold in, and wink at;
raging and shuddering in my own secret mind, and not out-
wardly at all!" He would boast to me at other times: "This and
that I have seen, this and that I have heard; yet patiently stood
it." He had this way, too, which I have never seen in any other
man, that he affectionately loved many persons to whom he never
or hardly ever shewed a countenance of love. Once on my ven-
turing to expostulate with him on the subject, he reminded me
of Solomon: "Many sons I have; it is not fit that I should smile
on them."[3] He would suffer faults, damage from his servants, and
know what he suffered, and not speak of it; but I think the reason
was, he waited a good time for speaking of it, and in a wise way
amending it. He intimated, openly in chapter to us all, that he
would have no eavesdropping: "Let none," said he, "come to me
secretly accusing another, unless he will publicly stand to the

[3] Untraced.

same; if he come otherwise, I will openly proclaim the name of him. I wish, too, that every Monk of you have free access to me, to speak of your needs or grievances when you will." '

The kinds of people Abbot Samson liked worst were these three: 'Mendaces, ebriosi, verbosi, Liars, drunkards, and wordy or windy persons;' — not good kinds, any of them! He also much condemned 'persons given to murmur at their meat or drink, especially Monks of that disposition.' We remark, from the very first, his strict anxious order to his servants to provide handsomely for hospitality, to guard 'above all things that there be no shabbiness in the matter of meat and drink; no look of mean parsimony, *in novitate mea*, at the beginning of my Abbotship;' and to the last he maintains a due opulence of table and equipment for others: but he is himself in the highest degree indifferent to all such things.

'Sweet milk, honey, and other naturally sweet kinds of food, were what he preferred to eat: but he had this virtue,' says Jocelin, 'he never changed the dish (*ferculum*) you set before him, be what it might. Once when I, still a novice, happened to be waiting table in the refectory, it came into my head' (rogue that I was!) 'to try if this were true; and I thought I would place before him a *ferculum* that would have displeased any other person, the very platter being black and broken. But he, seeing it, was as one that saw it not: and now some little delay taking place, my heart smote me that I had done this; and so, snatching up the platter (*discus*), I changed both it and its contents for a better, and put down that instead; which emendation he was angry at, and rebuked me for,' — the stoical monastic man! 'For the first seven years he had commonly four sorts of dishes on his table; afterwards only three, except it might be presents, or venison from his own parks, or fishes' from his ponds. And if, at any time, he had guests living in his house at the request of some great person, or of some friend, or had public messengers, or had harpers (*citharœdos*), or any one of that sort, he took the first opportunity of shifting to another of his Manor-houses, and so got rid of such superfluous individuals,' — very prudently, I think.

As to his parks, of these, in the general repair of buildings, general improvement and adornment of the St. Edmund Domains, 'he had laid out several, and stocked them with animals, retaining a proper huntsman with hounds: and, if any guest of great quality were there, our Lord Abbot with his Monks would sit in some opening of the woods, and see the dogs run; but he himself never meddled with hunting, that I saw.'

'In an opening of the woods;' — for the country was still dark with wood in those days; and Scotland itself still rustled shaggy and leafy, like a damp black American Forest, with cleared spots and spaces here and there. Dryasdust advances several absurd hypotheses as to the insensible but almost total disappearance of these woods; the thick wreck of which now lies as *peat,* sometimes with huge heart-of-oak timber logs imbedded in it, on many a height and hollow. The simplest reason doubtless is, that by increase of husbandry, there was increase of cattle; increase of hunger for green spring food; and so, more and more, the new seedlings got yearly eaten out in April; and the old trees, having only a certain length of life in them, died gradually, no man heeding it, and disappeared into *peat.*

A sorrowful waste of noble wood and umbrage! Yes, — but a very common one; the course of most things in this world. Monachism itself, so rich and fruitful once, is now all rotted into *peat;* lies sleek and buried, — and a most feeble bog-grass of Dilettantism all the crop we reap from it! That also was frightful waste; perhaps among the saddest our England ever saw. Why will men destroy noble Forests, even when in part a nuisance, in such reckless manner; turning loose four-footed cattle and Henry-the-Eighths into them! The fifth part of our English soil, Dryasdust computes, lay consecrated to 'spiritual uses,' better or worse; solemnly set apart to foster spiritual growth and culture of the soul, by the methods then known: and now — it too, like the four-fifths, fosters what? Gentle shepherd, tell me what![4]

[4] Echo of a song by an eighteenth-century composer, Dr. Samuel Howard.

CHAPTER XII

THE ABBOT'S TROUBLES

THE troubles of Abbot Samson, as he went along in this ab-
stemious, reticent, rigorous way, were more than tongue can
tell. The Abbot's mitre once set on his head, he knew rest no
more. Double, double, toil and trouble;[1] that is the life of all
governors that really govern: not the spoil of victory, only the
glorious toil of battle can be theirs. Abbot Samson found all men
more or less headstrong, irrational, prone to disorder; continually
threatening to prove *un*governable.

His lazy Monks gave him most trouble. 'My heart is tortured,'
said he, 'till we get out of debt, *cor meum cruciatum est.*' Your
heart, indeed; — but not altogether ours! By no devisable
method, or none of three or four that he devised, could Abbot
Samson get these Monks of his to keep their accounts straight;
but always, do as he might, the Cellerarius at the end of the term
is in a coil, in a flat deficit, — verging again towards debt and
Jews. The Lord Abbot at last declares sternly he will keep our
accounts too himself; will appoint an officer of his own to see
our Cellerarius keep them. Murmurs thereupon among us: Was
the like ever heard? Our Cellerarius a cipher; the very Townsfolk
know it: *subsannatio et derisio sumus,* we have become a laugh-
ingstock to mankind. The Norfolk barrator and paltener!

And consider, if the Abbot found such difficulty in the mere
economic department, how much in more complex ones, in
spiritual ones perhaps! He wears a stern calm face; raging and
gnashing teeth, *fremens* and *frendens,* many times, in the secret
of his mind. Withal, however, there is noble slow perseverance
in him; a strength of 'subdued rage' calculated to subdue most
things: always, in the long-run, he contrives to gain his point.

Murmurs from the Monks, meanwhile, cannot fail; ever deeper
murmurs, new grudges accumulating. At one time, on slight
cause, some drop making the cup run over, they burst into open

[1] *Macbeth,* IV.i.20.

mutiny: the Cellarer will not obey, prefers arrest on bread and water to obeying; the Monks thereupon strike work; refuse to do the regular chanting of the day, at least the younger part of them with loud clamour and uproar refuse: — Abbot Samson has withdrawn to another residence, acting only by messengers: the awful report circulates through St. Edmundsbury that the Abbot is in danger of being murdered by the Monks with their knives! How wilt thou appease this, Abbot Samson? Return; for the Monastery seems near catching fire!

Abbot Samson returns; sits in his *Thalamus* or inner room, hurls out a bolt or two of excommunication: lo, one disobedient Monk sits in limbo, excommunicated, with foot-shackles on him, all day; and three more our Abbot has gyved 'with the lesser sentence, to strike fear into the others!' Let the others think with whom they have to do. The others think; and fear enters into them. 'On the morrow morning we decide on humbling ourselves before the Abbot, by word and gesture, in order to mitigate his mind. And so accordingly was done. He, on the other side, replying with much humility, yet always alleging his own justice and turning the blame on us, when he saw that we were conquered, became himself conquered. And bursting into tears, *perfusus lachrymis,* he swore that he had never grieved so much for anything in the world as for this, first on his own account, and then secondly and chiefly for the public scandal which had gone abroad, that St. Edmund's Monks were going to kill their Abbot. And when he had narrated how he went away on purpose till his anger should cool, repeating this word of the philosopher, "I would have taken vengeance on thee, had not I been angry,"[2] he arose weeping, and embraced each and all of us with the kiss of peace. He wept; we all wept:' — what a picture! Behave better, ye remiss Monks, and thank Heaven for such an Abbot; or know at least that ye must and shall obey him.

Worn down in this manner, with incessant toil and tribulation, Abbot Samson had a sore time of it; his grizzled hair and beard grew daily greyer. Those Jews, in the first four years, had 'visibly emaciated him:' Time, Jews, and the task of Governing, will make a man's beard very grey! 'In twelve years,' says Jocelin, 'our Lord Abbot had grown wholly white as snow, *totus efficitur*

[2] Seneca, *De Ira,* I.15.3. Seneca's attribution of the remark to Socrates is without foundation.

albus sicut nix.' White, atop, like the granite mountains: — but his clear-beaming eyes still look out, in their stern clearness, in their sorrow and pity; the heart within him remains unconquered.

Nay sometimes there are gleams of hilarity too; little snatches of encouragement granted even to a Governor. 'Once my Lord Abbot and I, coming down from London through the Forest, I inquired of an old woman whom we came up to, Whose wood this was, and of what manor; who the master, who the keeper?' — All this I knew very well beforehand, and my Lord Abbot too, Bozzy that I was! But 'the old woman answered, The wood belonged to the new Abbot of St. Edmund's, was of the manor of Harlow, and the keeper of it was one Arnald. How did he behave to the people of the manor? I asked farther. She answered that he used to be a devil incarnate, *dæmon vivus,* an enemy of God, and flayer of the peasants' skins,' — skinning them like live eels, as the manner of some is: 'but that now he dreads the new Abbot, knowing him to be a wise and sharp man, and so treats the people reasonably, *tractat homines pacifice.*' Whereat the Lord Abbot *factus est hilaris,* — could not but take a triumphant laugh for himself; and determines to leave that Harlow manor yet unmeddled with, for a while.

A brave man, strenuously fighting, fails not of a little triumph, now and then, to keep him in heart. Everywhere we try at least to give the adversary as good as he brings; and, with swift force or slow watchful manœuvre, extinguish this and the other solecism, leave one solecism less in God's Creation; and so *proceed* with our battle, not slacken or surrender in it! The Fifty feudal Knights, for example, were of unjust greedy temper, and cheated us, in the Installation-day, of ten knights'-fees; — but they know now whether that has profited them aught, and I Jocelin know. Our Lord Abbot for the moment had to endure it, and say nothing; but he watched his time.

Look also how my Lord of Clare, coming to claim his *undue* 'debt' in the Court at Witham, with barons and apparatus, gets a Rowland for his Oliver![3] Jocelin shall report: 'The Earl, crowded round (*constipatus*) with many barons and men at arms, Earl Alberic and others standing by him, said, "That his bailiffs had given him to understand they were wont annually to receive for his behoof, from the Hundred of Risebridge and the bailiffs thereof, a sum of five shillings, which sum was now unjustly held

[3] Tit for tat.

back;" and he alleged farther that his predecessors had been infeft,[4] at the Conquest, in the lands of Alfric son of Wisgar, who was Lord of that Hundred, as may be read in Domesday Book by all persons. — The Abbot, reflecting for a moment, without stirring from his place, made answer: "A wonderful deficit, my Lord Earl, this that thou mentionest! King Edward gave to St. Edmund that entire Hundred, and confirmed the same with his Charter; nor is there any mention there of those five shillings. It will behove thee to say, for what service, or on what ground, thou exactest those five shillings." Whereupon the Earl, consulting with his followers, replied, That he had to carry the Banner of St. Edmund in war-time, and for this duty the five shillings were his. To which the Abbot: "Certainly, it seems inglorious, if so great a man, Earl of Clare no less, receive so small a gift for such a service. To the Abbot of St. Edmund's it is no unbearable burden to give five shillings. But Roger Earl Bigot holds himself duly seised,[5] and asserts that he by such seisin has the office of carrying St. Edmund's Banner; and he did carry it when the Earl of Leicester and his Flemings were beaten at Fornham. Then again Thomas de Mendham says that the right is his. When you have made out with one another, that this right is thine, come then and claim the five shillings, and I will promptly pay them!" Whereupon the Earl said, He would speak with Earl Roger his relative; and so the matter *cepit dilationem,*' and lies undecided to the end of the world. Abbot Samson answers by word or act, in this or the like pregnant manner, having justice on his side, innumerable persons: Pope's Legates, King's Viscounts, Canterbury Archbishops, Cellarers, *Sochemanni;* — and leaves many a solecism extinguished.

On the whole, however, it is and remains sore work. 'One time, during my chaplaincy, I ventured to say to him: "*Domine,* I heard thee, this night after matins, wakeful, and sighing deeply, *valde suspirantem,* contrary to thy usual wont." He answered: "No wonder. Thou, son Jocelin, sharest in my good things, in food and drink, in riding and such like; but thou little thinkest concerning the management of House and Family, the various and arduous businesses of the Pastoral Care, which harass me, and make my soul to sigh and be anxious." Whereto I, lifting up my hands to Heaven: "From such anxiety, Omnipotent Merciful Lord de-

---

[4] Possessed of inheritable property.
[5] Put into legal possession.

liver me!" — I have heard the Abbot say, If he had been as he was before he became a Monk, and could have anywhere got five or six marcs of income,' some three pound ten of yearly revenue, 'whereby to support himself in the schools, he would never have been Monk nor Abbot. Another time he said with an oath, If he had known what a business it was to govern the Abbey, he would rather have been Almoner, how much rather Keeper of the Books, than Abbot and Lord. That latter office he said he had always longed for, beyond any other. *Quis talia crederet,*' concludes Jocelin, 'Who can believe such things?'

Three pound ten, and a life of Literature, especially of quiet Literature, without copyright, or world-celebrity of literary-gazettes, — yes, thou brave Abbot Samson, for thyself it had been better, easier, perhaps also nobler! But then, for thy disobedient Monks, unjust Viscounts; for a Domain of St. Edmund overgrown with Solecisms, human and other, it had not been so well. Nay neither could *thy* Literature, never so quiet, have been easy Literature, when noble, is not easy; but only when ignoble. Literature too is a quarrel, and internecine duel, with the whole World of Darkness that lies without one and within one; — rather a hard fight at times, even with the three pound ten secure. Thou, there where thou art, wrestle and duel along, cheerfully to the end; and make no remarks!

CHAPTER XIII

O F Abbot Samson's public business we say little, though that also was great. He had to judge the people as Justice Errant, to decide in weighty arbitrations and public controversies; to equip his *milites,* send them duly in war-time to the King; — strive every way that the Commonweal, in his quarter of it, take no damage.

Once, in the confused days of Lackland's usurpation, while Cœur-de-Lion was away, our brave Abbot took helmet himself, having first excommunicated all that should favour Lackland; and led his men in person to the siege of *Windleshora,* what we now call Windsor; where Lackland had entrenched himself, the centre of infinite confusions; some Reform Bill, then as now, being greatly needed. There did Abbot Samson 'fight the battle of reform,' — with other ammunition, one hopes, than 'tremendous cheering' and such like! For these things he was called 'the magnanimous Abbot.'

He also attended duly in his place in Parliament *de arduis regni;*[1] attended especially, as in *arduissimo,* when 'the news reached London that King Richard was a captive in Germany.' Here 'while all the barons sat to consult,' and many of them looked blank enough, 'the Abbot started forth, *prosiliit coram omnibus,* in his place in Parliament, and said, That *he* was ready to go and seek his Lord the King, either clandestinely by subterfuge (*in tapinagio*), or by any other method; and search till he found him, and got certain notice of him; he for one! By which word,' says Jocelin, 'he acquired great praise for himself,' — unfeigned commendation from the Able Editors of that age.

By which word; — and also by which *deed:* for the Abbot actually went 'with rich gifts to the King in Germany;' Usurper Lackland being first rooted out from Windsor, and the King's peace somewhat settled.

[1] "To deal with the kingdom's troubles."

As to these 'rich gifts,' however, we have to note one thing: In all England, as appeared to the Collective Wisdom, there was not like to be treasure enough for ransoming King Richard; in which extremity certain Lords of the Treasury, *Justiciarii ad Scaccarium,* suggested that St. Edmund's Shrine, covered with thick gold, was still untouched. Could not it, in this extremity, be peeled off, at least in part; under condition, of course, of its being replaced, when times mended? The Abbot, starting plumb up, *se erigens,* answered: "Know ye for certain, that I will in no wise do this thing; nor is there any man who could force me to consent thereto. But I will open the doors of the Church: Let him that likes enter; let him that dares come forward!" Emphatic words, which created a sensation round the woolsack. For the Justiciaries of the *Scaccarium* answered, 'with oaths, each for himself: "I won't come forward, for my share; nor will I, nor I! The distant and absent who offended him, Saint Edmund has been known to punish fearfully; much more will he those close by, who lay violent hands on his coat, and would strip it off!" These things being said, the Shrine was not meddled with, nor any ransom levied for it.'

For Lords of the Treasury have in all times their impassable limits, be it by 'force of public opinion' or otherwise; and in those days a Heavenly Awe overshadowed and encompassed, as it still ought and must, all earthly Business whatsoever.

CHAPTER XIV

O F St. Edmund's fearful avengements have they not the remarkablest instance still before their eyes? He that will go to
Reading Monastery may find there, now tonsured into a mournful
penitent Monk, the once proud Henry Earl of Essex; and discern
how St. Edmund punishes terribly, yet with mercy! This Narrative is too significant to be omitted as a document of the Time.
Our Lord Abbot, once on a visit at Reading, heard the particulars
from Henry's own mouth; and thereupon charged one of his
monks to write it down; — as accordingly the Monk has done, in
ambitious rhetorical Latin; inserting the same, as episode, among
Jocelin's garrulous leaves. Read it here; with ancient yet with
modern eyes.

Henry Earl of Essex, standard-bearer of England, had high
places and emoluments; had a haughty high soul, yet with various
flaws, or rather with one many-branched flaw and crack, running
through the texture of it. For example, did he not treat Gilbert
de Cereville in the most shocking manner? He cast Gilbert into
prison; and, with chains and slow torments, wore the life out of
him there. And Gilbert's crime was understood to be only that
of innocent Joseph: the Lady Essex was a Potiphar's Wife,[1] and
had accused poor Gilbert! Other cracks, and branches of that
widespread flaw in the Standard-bearer's soul we could point out:
but indeed the main stem and trunk of all is too visible in this,
That he had no right reverence for the Heavenly in Man, — that
far from shewing due reverence to St. Edmund, he did not even
shew him common justice. While others in the Eastern Counties
were adorning and enlarging with rich gifts St. Edmund's resting-
place, which had become a city of refuge for many things, this
Earl of Essex flatly defrauded him, by violence or quirk of law,
of five shillings yearly, and converted said sum to his own poor
uses! Nay, in another case of litigation, the unjust Standard-

Genesis 39:7–20.

bearer, for his own profit, asserting that the cause belonged not to St. Edmund's Court, but to *his* in Lailand Hundred, 'involved us in travellings and innumerable expenses, vexing the servants of St. Edmund for a long tract of time.' In short, he is without reverence for the Heavenly, this Standard-bearer; reveres only the Earthly, Gold-coined; and has a most morbid lamentable flaw in the texture of him. It cannot come to good.

Accordingly, the same flaw, or St.-Vitus' *tic*, manifests itself ere long in another way. In the year 1157, he went with his Standard to attend King Henry, our blessed Sovereign (whom *we* saw afterwards at Waltham), in his War with the Welsh. A somewhat disastrous War; in which while King Henry and his force were struggling to retreat Parthian-like,[2] endless clouds of exasperated Welshmen hemming them in, and now we had come to the 'difficult pass of Coleshill,' and as it were to the nick of destruction, — Henry Earl of Essex shrieks out on a sudden (blinded doubtless by his inner flaw, or 'evil genius' as some name it), That King Henry is killed, That all is lost, — and flings down his Standard to shift for itself there! And, certainly enough, all *had* been lost, had all men been as he; — had not brave men, without such miserable jerking *tic-douloureux* in the souls of them, come dashing up, with blazing swords and looks, and asserted That nothing was lost yet, that all must be regained yet. In this manner King Henry and his force got safely retreated, Parthian-like, from the pass of Coleshill and the Welsh War.[3] But, once home again, Earl Robert de Montfort, a kinsman of this Standard-bearer's, rises up in the King's Assembly to declare openly that such a man is unfit for bearing English Standards, being in fact either a special traitor, or something almost worse, a coward namely, or universal traitor. Wager of Battle in consequence; solemn Duel, by the King's appointment, 'in a certain Island of the Thames-stream at Reading, *apud Radingas*, short way from the Abbey there.' King, Peers, and an immense multitude of people, on such scaffoldings and heights as they can come at, are gathered round, to see what issue the business will take. The business takes this bad issue, in our Monk's own words faithfully rendered:

'And it came to pass, while Robert de Montfort thundered on him manfully (*viriliter intonâsset*) with hard and frequent

---

[2] The Parthians were noted for the vigor of their rear-guard actions.
[3] See Lyttelton's *Henry II.*, ii. 384. (C.)

strokes, and a valiant beginning promised the fruit of victory, Henry of Essex, rather giving way, glanced round on all sides; and lo, at the rim of the horizon, on the confines of the River and land, he discerned the glorious King and Martyr Edmund, in shining armour, and as if hovering in the air; looking towards him with severe countenance, nodding his head with a mien and motion of austere anger. At St. Edmund's hand there stood also another Knight, Gilbert de Cereville, whose armour was not so splendid, whose stature was less gigantic; casting vengeful looks at him. This he seeing with his eyes, remembered that old crime brings new shame. And now wholly desperate, and changing reason into violence, he took the part of one blindly attacking, not skilfully defending. Who while he struck fiercely was more fiercely struck; and so, in short, fell down vanquished, and it was thought, slain. As he lay there for dead, his kinsmen, Magnates of England, besought the King, that the Monks of Reading might have leave to bury him. However, he proved not to be dead, but got well again among them; and now, with recovered health, assuming the Regular Habit, he strove to wipe out the stain of his former life, to cleanse the long week of his dissolute history by at least a purifying sabbath, and cultivate the studies of Virtue into fruits of eternal Felicity.'

Thus does the Conscience of man project itself athwart whatsoever of knowledge or surmise, of imagination, understanding, faculty, acquirement, or natural disposition he has in him; and, like light through coloured glass, paint strange pictures 'on the rim of the horizon' and elsewhere! Truly, this same 'sense of the Infinite nature of Duty' is the central part of all with us; a ray as of Eternity and Immortality, immured in dusky many-coloured Time, and its deaths and births. Your 'coloured glass' varies so much from century to century; — and, in certain money-making, game-preserving centuries, it gets so terribly opaque! Not a Heaven with cherubim surrounds you then, but a kind of vacant leaden-coloured Hell. One day it will again cease to be *opaque,* this 'coloured glass.' Nay, may it not become at once translucent and *un*coloured? Painting no Pictures more for us, but only the everlasting Azure itself? That will be a right glorious consummation! —

Saint Edmund from the horizon's edge, in shining armour, threatening the misdoer in his hour of extreme need: it is beautiful, it is great and true. So old, yet so modern, actual; true yet for every one of us, as for Henry the Earl and Monk! A glimpse as of the Deepest in Man's Destiny, which is the same for all times and ages. Yes, Henry my brother, there in thy extreme need, thy soul is *lamed;* and behold thou canst not so much as fight! For Justice and Reverence *are* the everlasting central Law of this Universe; and to forget them, and have all the Universe against one, God and one's own Self for enemies, and only the Devil and the Dragons for friends, is not that a 'lameness' like few? That some shining armed St. Edmund hang minatory on thy horizon, that infinite sulphur-lakes hang minatory, or do not now hang, — this alters no whit the eternal fact of the thing. I say, thy soul is lamed, and the God and all Godlike in it marred: lamed, paralytic, tending towards baleful eternal death, whether thou know it or not; — nay hadst thou never known it, that surely had been worst of all! —

Thus, at any rate, by the heavenly Awe that overshadows earthly Business, does Samson, readily in those days, save St. Edmund's Shrine, and innumerable still more precious things.

CHAPTER XV

HERE indeed, perhaps, by rule of antagonisms, may be the place to mention that, after King Richard's return, there was a liberty of tourneying given to the fighting men of England: that a Tournament was proclaimed in the Abbot's domain, 'between Thetford and St. Edmundsbury,' — perhaps in the Euston region, on Fakenham Heights, midway between these two localities: that it was publicly prohibited by our Lord Abbot; and nevertheless was held in spite of him, — and by the parties, as would seem, considered 'a gentle and free passage of arms.'

Nay, next year, there came to the same spot four-and-twenty young men, sons of Nobles, for another passage of arms; who, having completed the same, all rode into St. Edmundsbury to lodge for the night. Here is modesty! Our Lord Abbot, being instructed of it, ordered the Gates to be closed; the whole party shut in. The morrow was the Vigil of the Apostles Peter and Paul; no outgate on the morrow. Giving their promise not to depart without permission, those four-and-twenty young bloods dieted all that day (*manducaverunt*) with the Lord Abbot, waiting for trial on the morrow. 'But after dinner,' — mark it, posterity! — 'the Lord Abbot retiring into his *Thalamus*, they all started up, and began carolling and singing (*carolare et cantare*); sending into the Town for wine; drinking, and afterwards howling (*ululantes*); — totally depriving the Abbot and Convent of their afternoon's nap; doing all this in derision of the Lord Abbot, and spending in such fashion the whole day till evening, nor would they desist at the Lord Abbot's order! Night coming on, they broke the bolts of the Town-Gates, and went off by violence!' Was the like ever heard of? The roysterous young dogs; carolling, howling, breaking the Lord Abbot's sleep, — after that sinful chivalry cock-fight of theirs! They too are a feature of distant centuries, as of near ones. St. Edmund on the edge of your horizon, or whatever else there, young scamps, in the dandy state, whether cased in iron or in whalebone, begin to caper and carol on the green Earth! Our Lord Abbot excommunicated most of them; and they gradually came in for repentance.

Excommunication is a great recipe with our Lord Abbot; the prevailing purifier in those ages. Thus when the Townsfolk and Monks-menials quarrelled once at the Christmas Mysteries in St. Edmund's Churchyard, and 'from words it came to cuffs, and from cuffs to cuttings and the effusion of blood,' — our Lord Abbot excommunicates sixty of the rioters, with bell, book and candle (*accensis candelis*),[1] at one stroke. Whereupon they all come suppliant, indeed nearly naked, 'nothing on but their breeches, *omnino nudi præter femoralia*, and prostrate themselves at the Church-door.' Figure that!

In fact, by excommunication or persuasion, by impetuosity of driving or adroitness in leading, this Abbot, it is now becoming plain everywhere, is a man that generally remains master at last. He tempers his medicine to the malady, now hot, now cool; prudent though fiery, an eminently practical man. Nay sometimes in his adroit practice there are swift turns almost of a surprising nature! Once, for example, it chanced that Geoffrey Riddell Bishop of Ely, a Prelate rather troublesome to our Abbot, made a request of him for timber from his woods towards certain edifices going on at Glemsford. The Abbot, a great builder himself, disliked the request; could not however give it a negative. While he lay, therefore, at his Manorhouse of Melford not long after, there comes to him one of the Lord Bishop's men or monks, with a message from his Lordship, "That he now begged permission to cut down the requisite trees in Elmswell Wood," — so said the monk: Elms*well*, where there are no trees but scrubs and shrubs, instead of Elms*et*, our true *nemus*,[2] and high-towering oak-wood, here on Melford Manor! Elmswell? The Lord Abbot, in surprise, inquires privily of Richard his Forester; Richard answers that my Lord of Ely has already had his *carpentarii* in Elms*et*, and marked out for his own use all the best trees in the compass of it. Abbot Samson thereupon answers the monk: "Elmswell? Yes surely, be it as my Lord Bishop wishes." The successful monk, on the morrow morning, hastens home to Ely; but, on the morrow morning, 'directly after mass,' Abbot Samson

[1] After the sentence of excommunication was read, a bell was rung, a book closed, and a candle extinguished — acts symbolic of exclusion from the sacraments and divine worship.
[2] Forest.

too was busy! The successful monk, arriving at Ely, is rated for a goose and an owl; is ordered back to say that Elmset was the place meant. Alas, on arriving at Elmset, he finds the Bishop's trees, they 'and a hundred more,' all felled and piled, and the stamp of St. Edmund's Monastery burnt into them, — for roofing of the great tower we are building there! Your importunate Bishop must seek wood for Glemsford edifices in some other *nemus* than this. A practical Abbot!

We said withal there was a terrible flash of anger in him: witness his address to old Herbert the Dean, who in a too thrifty manner has erected a wind-mill for himself on his glebe-lands at Haberdon. On the morrow, after mass, our Lord Abbot orders the Cellerarius to send off his carpenters to demolish the said structure *brevi manu*,[3] and lay up the wood in safe keeping. Old Dean Herbert, hearing what was toward, comes tottering along hither, to plead humbly for himself and his mill. The Abbot answers: "I am obliged to thee as if thou hadst cut off both my feet! By God's face, *per os Dei*, I will not eat bread till that fabric be torn in pieces. Thou art an old man, and shouldst have known that neither the King nor his Justiciary dare change aught within the Liberties, without consent of Abbot and Convent: and thou hast presumed on such a thing? I tell thee, it will *not* be without damage to my mills; for the Townsfolk will go to thy mill, and grind their corn (*bladum suum*) at their own good pleasure; nor can I hinder them, since they are free men. I will allow no new mills on such principle. Away, away; before thou gettest home again, thou wilt see what thy mill has grown to!" — The very reverend, the old Dean totters home again, in all haste; tears the mill in pieces by his own *carpentarii*, to save at least the timber; and Abbot Samson's workmen, coming up, find the ground already clear of it.

Easy to bully down poor old rural Deans, and blow their wind-mills away: but who is the man that dare abide King Richard's anger; cross the Lion in his path, and take him by the whiskers! Abbot Samson too; he is that man, with justice on his side. The case was this. Adam de Cokefield, one of the chief feudatories[4] of St. Edmund, and a principal man in the Eastern Counties, died, leaving large possessions, and for heiress a daughter of three

---

[3] At once.   [4] Feudal vassals.

months; who by clear law, as all men know, became thus Abbot Samson's ward; whom accordingly he proceeded to dispose of to such person as seemed fittest. But now King Richard has another person in view, to whom the little ward and her great possessions were a suitable thing. He, by letter, requests that Abbot Samson will have the goodness to give her to this person. Abbot Samson, with deep humility, replies that she is already given. New letters from Richard, of severer tenor; answered with new deep humilities, with gifts and entreaties, with no promise of obedience. King Richard's ire is kindled; messengers arrive at St. Edmundsbury, with emphatic message to obey or tremble! Abbot Samson, wisely silent as to the King's threats, makes answer: "The King can send if he will, and seize the ward: force and power he has to do his pleasure, and abolish the whole Abbey. I never can be bent to wish this that he seeks, nor shall it by me be ever done. For there is danger lest such things be made a precedent of, to the prejudice of my successors. *Videat Altissimus,* Let the Most High look on it. Whatsoever thing shall befall I will patiently endure."

Such was Abbot Samson's deliberate decision. Why not? Cœur-de-Lion is very dreadful, but not the dreadfulest. *Videat Altissimus.* I reverence Cœur-de-Lion to the marrow of my bones, and will in all right things be *homo suus;* but it is not, properly speaking, with terror, with any fear at all. On the whole, have I not looked on the face of 'Satan with outspread wings;[5] steadily into Hellfire these seven-and-forty years; — and was not melted into terror even at that, such the Lord's goodness to me? Cœur-de-Lion!

Richard swore tornado oaths, worse than our armies in Flanders,[6] To be revenged on that proud Priest. But in the end he discovered that the Priest was right; and forgave him, and even loved him. 'King Richard wrote, soon after, to Abbot Samson, That he wanted one or two of the St. Edmundsbury dogs, which he heard were good.' Abbot Samson sent him dogs of the best; Richard replied by the present of a ring, which Pope Innocent the Third had given him. Thou brave Richard, thou brave Samson! Richard too, I suppose, 'loved a man,' and knew one when he saw him.

[5] *Paradise Lost,* I.20.
[6] Cf. Sterne, *Tristram Shandy,* III.xi.

No one will accuse our Lord Abbot of wanting worldly wisdom, due interest in worldly things. A skilful man; full of cunning insight, lively interests; always discerning the road to his object, be it circuit, be it short-cut, and victoriously travelling forward thereon. Nay rather it might seem, from Jocelin's Narrative, as if he had his eye all but exclusively directed on terrestrial matters, and was much too secular for a devout man. But this too, if we examine it, was right. For it is *in* the world that a man, devout or other, has his life to lead, his work waiting to be done. The basis of Abbot Samson's, we shall discover, was truly religion, after all. Returning from his dusty pilgrimage, with such welcome as we saw, 'he sat down at the foot of St. Edmund's Shrine.' Not a talking theory that; no, a silent practice: Thou St. Edmund with what lies in thee, thou now must help me, or none will!

This also is a significant fact: the zealous interest our Abbot took in the Crusades. To all noble Christian hearts of that era, what earthly enterprise so noble? 'When Henry II., having taken the cross, came to St. Edmund's, to pay his devotions before setting out, the Abbot secretly made for himself a cross of linen cloth: and, holding this in one hand and a threaded needle in the other, asked leave of the King to assume it!' The King could not spare Samson out of England; — the King himself indeed never went. But the Abbot's eye was set on the Holy Sepulchre, as on the spot of this Earth where the true cause of Heaven was deciding itself. 'At the retaking of Jerusalem by the Pagans, Abbot Samson put on a cilice and hair-shirt, and wore under-garments of hair-cloth ever after; he abstained also from flesh and flesh-meats (*carne et carneis*) thenceforth to the end of his life.' Like a dark cloud eclipsing the hopes of Christendom, those tidings cast their shadow over St. Edmundsbury too: Shall Samson Abbas take pleasure while Christ's Tomb is in the hands of the Infidel? Samson, in pain of body, shall daily be reminded of it, admonished to grieve for it.

The great antique heart: how like a child's in its simplicity, like a man's in its earnest solemnity and depth! Heaven lies over him wheresoever he goes or stands on the Earth; making all the Earth a mystic Temple to him, the Earth's business all a kind of worship. Glimpses of bright creatures flash in the common sunlight; angels yet hover doing God's messages among men: that rainbow was set in the clouds by the hand of God! Wonder, miracle encompass the man; he lives in an element of miracle;

Heaven's splendour over his head, Hell's darkness under his feet. A great Law of Duty, high as these two Infinitudes, dwarfing all else, annihilating all else, — making royal Richard as small as peasant Samson, smaller if need be! — The 'imaginative faculties?' 'Rude poetic ages?' The 'primeval poetic element?' O for God's sake, good reader, talk no more of all that! It was not a Dilettantism this of Abbot Samson. It was a Reality, and it is one. The garment only of it is dead; the essence of it lives through all Time and all Eternity! —

And truly, as we said above, is not this comparative silence of Abbot Samson as to his religion, precisely the healthiest sign of him and of it? 'The Unconscious is the alone Complete.' Abbot Samson all along a busy working man, as all men are bound to be, his religion, his worship was like his daily bread to him; — which he did not take the trouble to talk much about; which he merely ate at stated intervals, and lived and did his work upon! This is Abbot Samson's Catholicism of the Twelfth Century; — something like the *Ism* of all true men in all true centuries, I fancy! Alas, compared with any of the *Isms* current in these poor days, what a thing! Compared with the respectablest, morbid, struggling Methodism, never so earnest; with the respectablest, ghastly, dead or galvanised Dilettantism, never so spasmodic!

Methodism with its eye forever turned on its own navel; asking itself with torturing anxiety of Hope and Fear, "Am I right, am I wrong? Shall I be saved, shall I not be damned?" — what is this, at bottom, but a new phasis of *Egoism,* stretched out into the Infinite; not always the heavenlier for its infinitude! Brother, so soon as possible, endeavour to rise above all that. "Thou *art* wrong; thou art like to be damned:" consider that as the fact, reconcile thyself even to that, if thou be a man; — then first is the devouring Universe subdued under thee, and from the black murk of midnight and noise of greedy Acheron;[7] dawn as of an everlasting morning, how far above all Hope and all Fear, springs for thee, enlightening thy steep path, awakening in thy heart celestial Memnon's[8] music!

But of our Dilettantisms, and galvanised Dilettantisms; of Puseyism — O Heavens, what shall we say of Puseyism, in com-

[7] Hades.
[8] A statue in Thebes (not actually of Memnon) which emitted a musical sound when lighted by the first rays of the sunrise.

parison to Twelfth-Century Catholicism? Little or nothing; for indeed it is a matter to strike one dumb.

> The Builder of this Universe was wise,
> He plann'd all souls, all systems, planets, particles:
> The Plan He shap'd His Worlds and Æons by
> Was — — Heavens! — Was thy small Nine-and-thirty Articles?[9]

That certain human souls, living on this practical Earth, should think to save themselves and a ruined world by noisy theoretic demonstrations and laudations of *the* Church, instead of some unnoisy, unconscious, but *practical,* total, heart-and-soul demonstration of *a* Church: this, in the circle of revolving ages, this also was a thing we were to see. A kind of penultimate thing, precursor of very strange consummations; last thing but one? If there is no atmosphere, what will it serve a man to demonstrate the excellence of lungs? How much profitabler when you can, like Abbot Samson, breathe; and go along your way!

[9] The authorship of the quatrain seems not to have been established. The passage as a whole probably refers to the furor created by John Henry Newman's *Tract XC* ("Remarks on Certain Passages in the Thirty-Nine Articles"), published early in 1841. This concluding number of *Tracts for the Times* brought to a crisis the Oxford Movement, or Puseyism (from the name of one of its leaders, Edward B. Pusey), which sought to prove the affinity of the Anglican to the Roman Church by, among other things, re-examining the historical origins and intentions of the Thirty-Nine Articles, the basis of Anglican doctrine.

CHAPTER XVI

ST. EDMUND

ABBOT SAMSON built many useful, many pious edifices; human dwellings, churches, church-steeples, barns; — all fallen now and vanished, but useful while they stood. He built and endowed 'the Hospital of Babwell;' built 'fit houses for the St. Edmundsbury Schools.' Many are the roofs once 'thatched with reeds' which he 'caused to be covered with tiles;' or if they were churches, probably 'with lead.' For all ruinous incomplete things, buildings or other, were an eye-sorrow to the man. We saw his 'great tower of St. Edmund's;' or at least the roof-timbers of it, lying cut and stamped in Elmset Wood. To change combustible decaying reed-thatch into tile or lead, and material, still more, moral wreck into rain-tight order, what a comfort to Samson!

One of the things he could not in any wise but rebuild was the great Altar, aloft on which stood the Shrine itself; the great Altar, which had been damaged by fire, by the careless rubbish and careless candle of two somnolent Monks, one night, — the Shrine escaping almost as if by miracle! Abbot Samson read his Monks a severe lecture: "A Dream one of us had, that he saw St. Edmund naked and in lamentable plight. Know ye the interpretation of that Dream? St. Edmund proclaims himself naked, because ye defraud the naked Poor of your old clothes, and give with reluctance what ye are bound to give them of meat and drink: the idleness moreover and negligence of the Sacristan and his people is too evident from the late misfortune by fire. Well might our Holy Martyr seem to lie cast out from his Shrine, and say with groans that he was stript of his garments, and wasted with hunger and thirst!"

This is Abbot Samson's interpretation of the Dream; — diametrically the reverse of that given by the Monks themselves, who scruple not to say privily, "It is *we* that are the naked and famished limbs of the Martyr; we whom the Abbot curtails of all our privileges, setting his own official to control our very Cellarer!"

Abbot Samson adds, that this judgment by fire has fallen upon them for murmuring about their meat and drink.

Clearly enough, meanwhile, the Altar, whatever the burning of it mean or foreshadow, must needs be reedified. Abbot Samson reedifies it, all of polished marble; with the highest stretch of art and sumptuosity, reembellishes the Shrine for which it is to serve as pediment. Nay farther, as had ever been among his prayers, he enjoys, he sinner, a glimpse of the glorious Martyr's very Body in the process; having solemnly opened the *Loculus*, Chest or sacred Coffin, for that purpose. It is the culminating moment of Abbot Samson's life. Bozzy Jocelin himself rises into a kind of Psalmist solemnity on this occasion; the laziest monk 'weeps' warm tears, as *Te Deum* is sung.

Very strange; — how far vanished from us in these unworshipping ages of ours! The Patriot Hampden, best beatified man we have, had lain in like manner some two centuries in his narrow home, when certain dignitaries of us, 'and twelve grave-diggers with pulleys,' raised him also up, under cloud of night; cut off his arm with penknifes, pulled the scalp off his head, — and otherwise worshipped our Hero Saint in the most amazing manner![1] Let the modern eye look earnestly on that old midnight hour in St. Edmundsbury Church, shining yet on us, ruddybright, through the depths of seven hundred years; and consider mournfully what our Hero-worship once was, and what it now is! We translate with all the fidelity we can:

'The Festival of St. Edmund now approaching, the marble blocks are polished, and all things are in readiness for lifting of the Shrine to its new place. A fast of three days was held by all the people, the cause and meaning thereof being publicly set forth to them. The Abbot announces to the Convent that all must prepare themselves for transferring of the Shrine, and appoints time and way for the work. Coming therefore that night to matins, we found the great Shrine (*feretrum magnum*) raised upon the Altar, but empty; covered all over with white doeskin leather, fixed to the wood with silver nails; but one pannel of the Shrine was left down below, and resting thereon, beside its old column of the Church, the Loculus with the Sacred Body yet lay

---

[1] *Annual Register* (year 1828, Chronicle, p. 93), *Gentleman's Magazine*, &c. &c. (C.) — Lord Nugent directed the exhumation, in an Oxfordshire church, to settle whether Hampden, the seventeenth-century anti-royalist, had been killed by a bullet in the shoulder or by the explosion of a pistol he was holding.

where it was wont. Praises being sung, we all proceeded to commence our disciplines (*ad disciplinas suscipiendas*). These finished, the Abbot and certain with him are clothed in their albs; and, approaching reverently, set about uncovering the Loculus. There was an outer cloth of linen, enwrapping the Loculus and all; this we found tied on the upper side with strings of its own: within this was a cloth of silk, and then another linen cloth, and then a third; and so at last the Loculus was uncovered, and seen resting on a little tray of wood, that the bottom of it might not be injured by the stone. Over the breast of the Martyr, there lay, fixed to the surface of the Loculus, a Golden Angel about the length of a human foot; holding in one hand a golden sword, and in the other a banner: under this there was a hole in the lid of the Loculus, on which the ancient servants of the Martyr had been wont to lay their hands for touching the Sacred Body. And over the figure of the Angel was this verse inscribed:

Martiris ecce zoma servat Michaelis agalma.[2]

At the head and foot of the Loculus were iron rings whereby it could be lifted.

'Lifting the Loculus and Body, therefore, they carried it to the Altar; and I put-to my sinful hand to help in carrying, though the Abbot had commanded that none should approach except called. And the Loculus was placed in the Shrine; and the pannel it had stood on was put in its place, and the Shrine for the present closed. We all thought that the Abbot would shew the Loculus to the people; and bring out the Sacred Body again, at a certain period of the Festival. But in this we were wofully mistaken, as the sequel shews.

'For in the fourth holiday of the Festival, while the Convent were all singing *Completorium*, our Lord Abbot spoke privily with the Sacristan and Walter the Medicus; and order was taken that twelve of the Brethren should be appointed against midnight, who were strong for carrying the pannel-planks of the Shrine, and skilful in unfixing them, and putting them together again. The Abbot then said that it was among his prayers to look once upon the Body of his Patron; and that he wished the Sacristan and Walter the Medicus to be with him. The Twelve appointed Brethren were these: The Abbot's two Chaplains, the two Keepers of the Shrine, the two Masters of the Vestry; and six more, namely, the Sacristan Hugo, Walter the Medicus, Augustin,

[2] This is the Martyr's Garment, which Michael's Image guards. (C.)

William of Dice, Robert, and Richard. I, alas, was not of the number.

'The Convent therefore being all asleep, these Twelve, clothed in their albs, with the Abbot, assembled at the Altar; and opening a pannel of the Shrine, they took out the Loculus; laid it on a table, near where the Shrine used to be; and made ready for unfastening the lid, which was joined and fixed to the Loculus with sixteen very long nails. Which when, with difficulty, they had done, all except the two forenamed associates are ordered to draw back. The Abbot and they two were alone privileged to look in. The Loculus was so filled with the Sacred Body that you could scarcely put a needle between the head and the wood, or between the feet and the wood: the head lay united to the body, a little raised with a small pillow. But the Abbot, looking close, found now a silk cloth veiling the whole Body, and then a linen cloth of wondrous whiteness; and upon the head was spread a small linen cloth, and then another small and most fine silk cloth, as if it were the veil of a nun. These coverings being lifted off, they found now the Sacred Body all wrapt in linen; and so at length the lineaments of the same appeared. But here the Abbot stopped; saying he durst not proceed farther, or look at the sacred flesh naked. Taking the head between his hands, he thus spake groaning: "Glorious Martyr, holy Edmund, blessed be the hour when thou wert born. Glorious Martyr, turn it not to my perdition that I have so dared to touch thee, I miserable and sinful; thou knowest my devout love, and the intention of my mind." And proceeding, he touched the eyes; and the nose, which was very massive and prominent (*valde grossum et valde eminentem*); and then he touched the breast and arms; and raising the left arm he touched the fingers, and placed his own fingers between the sacred fingers. And proceeding he found the feet standing stiff up, like the feet of a man dead yesterday; and he touched the toes, and counted them (*tangendo numeravit*).

'And now it was agreed that the other Brethren should be called forward to see the miracles; and accordingly those ten now advanced, and along with them six others who had stolen in without the Abbot's assent, namely, Walter of St. Alban's, Hugh the Infirmirarius, Gilbert brother of the Prior, Richard of Henham, Jocellus our Cellarer, and Turstan the Little; and all these saw the Sacred Body, but Turstan alone of them put forth his hand, and touched the Saint's knees and feet. And that there might be abundance of witnesses, one of our Brethren, John of Dice, sitting on the roof of the Church, with the servants of the Vestry, and looking through, clearly saw all these things.'

What a scene; shining luminous effulgent, as the lamps of St. Edmund do, through the dark Night; John of Dice, with vestry-men, clambering on the roof to look through; the Convent all asleep, and the Earth all asleep, — and since then, Seven Centuries of Time mostly gone to sleep! Yes, there, sure enough, is the martyred Body of Edmund landlord of the Eastern Counties, who, nobly doing what he liked with his own, was slain three hundred years ago: and a noble awe surrounds the memory of him, symbol and promoter of many other right noble things.

Have not we now advanced to strange new stages of Hero-worship, now in the little Church of Hampden, with our pen-knives out, and twelve grave-diggers with pulleys? The manner of men's Hero-worship, verily it is the innermost fact of their existence, and determines all the rest, — at public hustings, in private drawing-rooms, in church, in market, and wherever else. Have true reverence, and what indeed is inseparable therefrom, reverence the right man, all is well; have sham-reverence, and what also follows, greet with it the wrong man, then all is ill, and there is nothing well. Alas, if Hero-worship become Dilettantism, and all except Mammonism be a vain grimace, how much, in this most earnest Earth, has gone and is evermore going to fatal destruction, and lies wasting in quiet lazy ruin, no man regarding it! Till at length no heavenly *Ism* any longer coming down upon us, *Isms* from the other quarter have to mount up. For the Earth, I say, is an earnest place; Life is no grimace, but a most serious fact. And so, under universal Dilettantism much having been stript bare, not the souls of men only, but their very bodies and bread-cupboards having been stript bare, and life now no longer possible, — all is reduced to desperation, to the iron law of Necessity and very Fact again; and to temper Dilettantism, and astonish it, and burn it up with infernal fire, arises Chartism, *Bare-back-ism*, Sansculottism[3] so-called! May the gods, and what of unworshipped heroes still remain among us, avert the omen. —

[3] "Breechlessness": originally applied to the republican fanaticism of lower-class Parisians in the French Revolution, then broadened to designate, as here, any republican or revolutionary movement. Knee-breeches were the garb and symbol of the *ancien régime;* trousers, of democracy.

But however this may be, St. Edmund's Loculus, we find, has the veils of silk and linen reverently replaced, the lid fastened down again with its sixteen ancient nails; is wrapt in a new costly covering of silk, the gift of Hubert Archbishop of Canterbury: and through the sky-window John of Dice sees it lifted to its place in the Shrine, the pannels of this latter duly refixed, fit parchment documents being introduced withal; — and now John and his vestrymen can slide down from the roof, for all is over, and the Convent wholly awakens to matins. 'When we assembled to sing matins,' says Jocelin, 'and understood what had been done, grief took hold of all that had not seen these things, each saying to himself, "Alas, I was deceived." Matins over, the Abbot called the Convent to the great Altar; and briefly recounting the matter, alleged that it had not been in his power, nor was it permissible or fit, to invite us all to the sight of such things. At hearing of which, we all wept, and with tears sang *Te Deum laudamus;* and hastened to toll the bells in the Choir.'

Stupid blockheads, to reverence their St. Edmund's dead Body in this manner? Yes, brother; — and yet, on the whole, who knows how to reverence the Body of a Man? It is the most reverend phenomenon under this Sun. For the Highest God dwells visible in that mystic unfathomable Visibility, which calls itself "I" on the Earth. 'Bending before men,' says Novalis,[4] 'is a reverence done to this Revelation in the Flesh. We touch Heaven when we lay our hand on a human Body.' And the Body of one Dead; — a temple where the Hero-soul once was and now is not: Oh, all mystery, all pity, all mute *awe* and wonder; *Super*naturalism brought home to the very dullest; Eternity laid open, and the nether Darkness and the upper Light-Kingdoms; — do conjoin there, or exist nowhere! Sauerteig used to say to me, in his peculiar way: "A Chancery Lawsuit; justice, nay justice in mere money, denied a man, for all his pleading, till twenty, till forty years of his Life are gone seeking it: and a Cockney Funeral, Death reverenced by hatchments, horsehair, brass-lacker, and unconcerned bipeds carrying long poles and bags of black silk: — are not these two reverences, this reverence for Death and that reverence for Life, a notable pair of reverences among you English?"

[4] Friedrich von Hardenberg, late eighteenth-century German poet and philosopher. Carlyle quotes his own translation of Novalis printed in his essay on the poet.

Abbot Samson, at this culminating point of his existence, may, and indeed must, be left to vanish with his Life-scenery from the eyes of modern men. He had to run into France, to settle with King Richard for the military service there of his St. Edmundsbury Knights; and with great labour got it done. He had to decide on the dilapidated Coventry Monks; and with great labour, and much pleading and journeying, got them reinstated; dined with them all, and with the 'Masters of the Schools of Oxneford,' — the veritable Oxford *Caput* sitting there at dinner, in a dim but undeniable manner, in the City of Peeping Tom! He had, not without labour, to controvert the intrusive Bishop of Ely, the intrusive Abbot of Cluny. Magnanimous Samson, his life is but a labour and a journey; a bustling and a justling, till the still Night come. He is sent for again, over sea, to advise King Richard touching certain Peers of England, who had taken the Cross, but never followed it to Palestine; whom the Pope is inquiring after. The magnanimous Abbot makes preparation for departure; departs, and — — And Jocelin's Boswellean Narrative, suddenly shorn through by the scissors of Destiny, *ends*.[5] There are no words more; but a black line, and leaves of blank paper. Irremediable: the miraculous hand that held all this theatric-machinery suddenly quits hold; impenetrable Time-Curtains rush down; in the mind's eye all is again dark, void; with loud dinning in the mind's ear, our real-phantasmagory of St. Edmundsbury plunges into the bosom of the Twelfth Century again, and all is over. Monks, Abbot, Hero-worship, Government, Obedience, Cœur-de-Lion and St. Edmund's Shrine, vanish like Mirza's Vision;[6] and there is nothing left but a mutilated black Ruin amid green botanic expanses, and oxen, sheep and dilettanti pasturing in their places.

[5] The scissors belonged to Atropos, one of the Fates.
[6] Cf. Addison, *Spectator*, 159.

CHAPTER XVII

THE BEGINNINGS

WHAT a singular shape of a Man, shape of a Time, have we in this Abbot Samson and his history; how strangely do modes, creeds, formularies, and the date and place of a man's birth, modify the figure of the man!

Formulas too, as we call them, have a *reality* in Human Life. They are real as the very *skin* and *muscular tissue* of a Man's Life; and a most blessed indispensable thing, so long as they have *vitality* withal, and are a *living* skin and tissue to him! No man, or man's life, can go abroad and do business in the world without skin and tissues. No; first of all, these have to fashion themselves, — as indeed they spontaneously and inevitably do. Foam itself, and this is worth thinking of, can harden into oyster-shell; all living objects do by necessity form to themselves a skin.

And yet, again, when a man's Formulas become *dead;* as all Formulas, in the progress of living growth, are very sure to do! When the poor man's integuments, no longer nourished from within, become dead skin, mere adscititious[1] leather and callosity, wearing thicker and thicker, uglier and uglier; till no *heart* any longer can be felt beating through them, so thick, callous, calcified are they; and all over it has now grown mere calcified oyster-shell, or were it polished mother-of-pearl, inwards almost to the very heart of the poor man: — yes then, you may say, his usefulness once more is quite obstructed; once more, he cannot go abroad and do business in the world; it is time that *he* take to bed, and prepare for departure, which cannot now be distant!

Ubi homines sunt modi sunt.[2] Habit is the deepest law of human nature. It is our supreme strength; if also, in certain circumstances, our miserablest weakness. — From Stoke to Stowe is as yet a field, all pathless, untrodden: from Stoke where I live, to Stowe where I have to make my merchandises, perform my businesses, consult my heavenly oracles, there is as yet no path or

[1] Superfluous.
[2] "Wherever men are, there are conventions."

human footprint; and I, impelled by such necessities, must nevertheless undertake the journey. Let me go once, scanning my way with any earnestness of outlook, and successfully arriving, my footprints are an invitation to me a second time to go by the same way. It is easier than any other way: the industry of 'scanning' lies already invested in it for me; I can go this time with less of scanning, or without scanning at all. Nay the very sight of my footprints, what a comfort for me; and in a degree, for all my brethren of mankind! The footprints are trodden and retrodden; the path wears ever broader, smoother, into a broad highway, where even wheels can run; and many travel it; — till — till the Town of Stowe disappear from that locality (as towns have been known to do), or no merchandising, heavenly oracle, or real business any longer exist for one there: then why should anybody travel the way? — Habit is our primal, fundamental law; Habit and Imitation, there is nothing more perennial in us than these two. They are the source of all Working and all Apprenticeship, of all Practice and all Learning, in this world.

Yes, the wise man too speaks, and acts, in Formulas; all men do so. In general the more completely cased with Formulas a man may be, the safer, happier is it for him. Thou who, in an All of rotten Formulas, seemest to stand nigh bare, having indignantly shaken off the superannuated rags and unsound callosities of Formulas, — consider how thou too art still clothed! This English Nationality, whatsoever from uncounted ages is genuine and a fact among thy native People, and their words and ways: all this, has it not made for thee a skin or second-skin, adhesive actually as thy natural skin? This thou hast not stript off, this thou wilt never strip off: the humour that thy mother gave thee has to shew itself through this. A common, or it may be an uncommon Englishman thou art: but good Heavens, what sort of Arab, Chinaman, Jew-Clothesman, Turk, Hindoo, African Mandingo,[3] wouldst thou have been, *thou* with those mother-qualities of thine!

It strikes me dumb to look over the long series of faces, such as any full Church, Courthouse, London-Tavern[4] Meeting, or miscellany of men will shew them. Some score or two of years ago, all these were little red-coloured pulpy infants; each of them

[3] Sudanese.
[4] A tavern in Bishopsgate much used for dinners and meetings of companies, lodges, charitable funds, etc. Here, for instance, was organized the United Metropolitan Improved Hot Muffin and Crumpet Baking and Punctual Delivery Company (*Nicholas Nickleby*).

capable of being kneaded, baked into any social form you chose: yet see now how they are fixed and hardened, — into artisans, artists, clergy, gentry, learned sergeants, unlearned dandies, and can and shall now be nothing else henceforth!

Mark on that nose the colour left by too copious port and viands; to which the profuse cravat with exorbitant breastpin, and the fixed, forward, and as it were menacing glance of the eyes correspond. That is a 'Man of Business;' prosperous manufacturer, house-contractor, engineer, law-manager; his eye, nose, cravat have, in such work and fortune, got such a character: deny him not thy praise, thy pity. Pity him too, the Hard-handed, with bony brow, rudely combed hair, eyes looking out as in labour, in difficulty and uncertainty; rude mouth, the lips coarse, loose, as in hard toil and lifelong fatigue they have got the habit of hanging: — hast thou seen aught more touching than the rude intelligence, so cramped, yet energetic, unsubduable, true, which looks out of that marred visage? Alas, and his poor wife, with her own hands, washed that cotton neckcloth for him, buttoned that coarse shirt, sent him forth creditably trimmed as she could. In such imprisonment lives he, for his part; man cannot now deliver him: the red pulpy infant has been baked and fashioned *so*.

Or what kind of baking was it that this other brother-mortal got, which has baked him into the genus Dandy? Elegant Vacuum; serenely looking down upon all Plenums[5] and Entities, as low and poor to his serene Chimeraship and *Non*entity laboriously attained! Heroic Vacuum; inexpugnable, while purse and present condition of society hold out; curable by no hellebore.[6] The doom of Fate was, Be thou a Dandy! Have thy eye-glasses, operaglasses, thy Long-Acre cabs with white-breeched tiger,[7] thy yawning impassivities, pococurantisms;[8] *fix* thyself in Dandyhood, undeliverable; it is thy doom.

And all these, we say, were red-coloured infants; of the same pulp and stuff, few years ago; now irretrievably shaped and kneaded as we see! Formulas? There is no mortal extant, out of the depths of Bedlam, but lives all skinned, thatched, covered over with Formulas; and is, as it were, held in from delirium and the Inane by his Formulas! They are withal the most beneficent, indispensable of human equipments: blessed he who has a skin

---

[5] Completely filled spaces.
[6] Ancient name of various plants supposed to cure madness.
[7] Liveried groom or footman.
[8] Apathies. (Cf. the character of Pococurante in Voltaire's *Candide*.)

and tissues, so it be a living one, and the heart-pulse everywhere discernible through it. Monachism, Feudalism, with a real King Plantagenet, with real Abbots Samson, and their other living realities, how blessed! —

Not without a mournful interest have we surveyed this authentic image of a Time now wholly swallowed. Mournful reflections crowd on us; and yet consolatory. How many brave men have lived before Agamemnon![9] Here is a brave governor Samson, a man fearing God, and fearing nothing else; of whom as First Lord of the Treasury, as King, Chief Editor, High Priest, we could be so glad and proud; of whom nevertheless Fame has altogether forgotten to make mention! The faint image of him, revived in this hour, is found in the gossip of one poor Monk, and in Nature nowhere else. Oblivion had so nigh swallowed him altogether, even to the echo of his ever having existed. What regiments and hosts and generations of such has Oblivion already swallowed! Their crumbled dust makes up the soil our life-fruit grows on. Said I not, as my old Norse Fathers taught me, The Life-tree Igdrasil, which waves round thee in this hour, whereof thou in this hour art portion, has its roots down deep in the oldest Death-Kingdoms; and grows; the Three Nornas,[10] or *Times,* Past, Present, Future, watering it from the Sacred Well!

For example, who taught thee to *speak?* From the day when two hairy-naked or fig-leaved Human Figures began, as uncomfortable dummies, anxious no longer to be dumb, but to impart themselves to one another; and endeavoured, with gaspings, gesturings, with unsyllabled cries, with painful pantomime and interjections, in a very unsuccessful manner, — up to the writing of this present copyright Book, which also is not very successful! Between that day and this, I say, there has been a pretty space of time; a pretty spell of work, which *somebody* has done! Thinkest thou there were no poets till Dan Chaucer? No heart burning with a thought, which it could not hold, and had no word for; and needed to shape and coin a word for, — what thou callest a metaphor, trope, or the like? For every word we have, there was such a man and poet. The coldest word was once a glowing new metaphor, and bold questionable originality. 'Thy very ATTEN-TION, does it not mean an *attentio,* a STRETCHING-TO?' Fancy that act of the mind, which all were conscious of, which none had yet

9 Cf. Horace, *Odes,* IV.ix.25–26.
10 Norse fates.

named, — when this new 'poet' first felt bound and driven to
name it! His questionable originality, and new glowing metaphor, was found adoptable, intelligible; and remains our name
for it to this day.

Literature: — and look at Paul's Cathedral, and the Masonries
and Worships and Quasi-Worships that are there; not to speak
of Westminster Hall and its wigs! Men had not a hammer to
begin with, not a syllabled articulation: they had it all to make;
— and they have made it. What thousand thousand articulate,
semi-articulate, earnest-stammering *Prayers* ascending up to
Heaven, from hut and cell, in many lands, in many centuries,
from the fervent kindled souls of innumerable men, each struggling to pour itself forth incompletely as it might, before the
incompletest *Liturgy* could be compiled! The Liturgy, or adoptable and generally adopted Set of Prayers and Prayer-Method,
was what we can call the Select Adoptabilities, 'Select Beauties'
well-edited (by Œcumenic Councils and other Useful-Knowl-
edge Societies)[11] from that wide waste imbroglio of Prayers already extant and accumulated, good and bad. The good were
found adoptable by men; were gradually got together, well-
edited, accredited: the bad, found inappropriate, unadoptable,
were gradually forgotten, disused and burnt. It is the way with
human things. The first man who, looking with opened soul on
this august Heaven and Earth, this Beautiful and Awful, which
we name Nature, Universe and such like, the essence of which
remains forever UNNAMEABLE; he who first, gazing into this, fell
on his knees awestruck, in silence as is likeliest, — he, driven by
inner necessity, the 'audacious original' that he was, had done a
thing, too, which all thoughtful hearts saw straightway to be an
expressive, altogether adoptable thing! To bow the knee was
ever since the attitude of supplication. Earlier than any spoken
Prayers, *Litanias,* or *Leitourgias;* the beginning of all Worship, —
which needed but a beginning, so rational was it. What a poet
he! Yes, this bold original was a successful one withal. The

---

[11] "Select Beauties" was a title often used for the elegantly printed
anthologies of excerpts from poetry and prose that were favorite gift-books
of the period. *Œcumenic Councils* is possibly a reference to Paragraph 4 of
Tract XC, in which Newman, apropos of Article XXI, discusses the infalli-
bility of the church's ecumenic (universal) councils. The Society for the
Diffusion of Useful Knowledge (founded 1826) sought to educate the
masses through cheap periodicals, encyclopedias, and series of informing
and entertaining books.

wellhead this one, hidden in the primeval dusks and distances, from whom as from a Nile-source all *Forms of Worship* flow: — such a Nile-river (somewhat muddy and malarious now!) of Forms of Worship sprang there, and flowed, and flows, down to Puseyism, Rotatory Calabash,[12] Archbishop Laud at St. Catherine Creed's,[13] and perhaps lower!

Things rise, I say, in that way. The *Iliad* Poem, and indeed most other poetic, especially epic things, have risen as the Liturgy did. The great *Iliad* in Greece, and the small *Robin Hood's Garland*[14] in England, are each, as I understand, the well-edited 'Select Beauties' of an immeasurable waste imbroglio of Heroic Ballads in their respective centuries and countries. Think what strumming of the seven-stringed heroic lyre, torturing of the less heroic fiddle-catgut, in Hellenic Kings' Courts, and English wayside Public Houses; and beating of the studious Poetic brain, and gasping here too in the semi-articulate windpipe of Poetic men, before the Wrath of a Divine Achilles, the Prowess of a Will Scarlet or Wakefield Pinder,[15] could be adequately sung! Honour to you, ye nameless great and greatest ones, ye long-forgotten brave!

Nor was the Statute *De Tallagio non concedendo*,[16] nor any Statute, Law-method, Lawyer's-wig, much less were the Statute-Book and Four Courts,[17] with Coke upon Lyttleton[18] and Three Estates of Parliament[19] in the rear of them, got together without human labour, — mostly forgotten now! From the time of Cain's slaying Abel by swift head-breakage, to this time of killing your man in Chancery[20] by inches, and slow heart-break for forty

[12] A gourd into which the Buddhist Calmucks of central Asia were said to put written prayers; it was then whirled by way of petitioning the deity.

[13] When he consecrated the London church of St. Catherine Cree (not "Creed") in 1631, William Laud, then archbishop of London, indulged in Romish ceremonial gestures which were later charged against him when he was tried before the Long Parliament.

[14] A collection of ballads.

[15] Like Will Scarlet, one of Robin Hood's merry men.

[16] Statute of 1297 concerning taxation.

[17] Exchequer, Common Pleas, King's Bench, and Chancery.

[18] A classic of English law of property.

[19] Lords Spiritual, Lords Temporal, and Commons. (For the "fourth estate," see below, p. 261, n.12.)

[20] The long delays in Chancery were already scandalous, ten years before Dickens made them the subject of *Bleak House*. In 1842 one case, involving an estate of £1,500,000, was forty-four years old; it was still unsettled in 1915, by which time its costs had consumed £250,000.

years, — there too is an interval! Venerable Justice herself began
by Wild-Justice; all Law is as a tamed furrowfield, slowly worked
out, and rendered arable, from the waste jungle of Club-Law.
Valiant Wisdom tilling and draining; escorted by owl-eyed
Pedantry, by owlish and vulturish and many other forms of Folly;
— the valiant husbandman assiduously tilling; the blind greedy
enemy *too* assiduously sowing tares![21] It is because there is yet
in venerable wigged Justice some wisdom, amid such mountains
of wiggeries and folly, that men have not cast her into the River;
that she still sits there, like Dryden's Head in the *Battle of the
Books*,[22] — a huge helmet, a huge mountain of greased parchment, of unclean horsehair, first striking the eye; and then in the
innermost corner, visible at last, in size as a hazelnut, a real fraction of God's Justice, perhaps not yet unattainable to some, surely
still indispensable to all; — and men know not what to do with
her! Lawyers were not all pedants, voluminous voracious persons; Lawyers too were poets, were heroes, — or their Law had
been past the Nore[23] long before this time. Their Owlisms, Vul-
turisms, to an incredible extent, will disappear by and by, their
Heroisms only remaining, and the helmet be reduced to something like the size of the head, we hope! —

It is all work and forgotten work, this peopled, clothed,
articulate-speaking, high-towered, wide-acred World. The hands
of forgotten brave men have made it a World for us; they, —
honour to them; they, in *spite* of the idle and the dastard. This
English Land, here and now, is the summary of what was found
of wise, and noble, and accordant with God's Truth, in all the
generations of English Men. Our English Speech is speakable
because there were Hero-Poets of our blood and lineage; speakable in proportion to the number of these. This Land of England
has its conquerors, possessors, which change from epoch to epoch,
from day to day; but its real conquerors, creators, and eternal
proprietors are these following, and their representatives if you
can find them: All the Heroic Souls that ever were in England,
each in their degree; all the men that ever cut a thistle, drained
a puddle out of England, contrived a wise scheme in England,

[21] Matthew 13:24–30, 36–43.
[22] In a cutting satirical passage, Swift described the helmet as being nine
times too large for the head.
[23] Gone out of existence. (The Nore is a sandbar, marked by a light, at
the mouth of the Thames; hence "to pass it" means to be on the way out.)

did or said a true and valiant thing in England. I tell thee, they
had not a hammer to begin with; and yet Wren built St. Paul's:
not an articulated syllable; and yet there have come English Literatures, Elizabethan Literatures, Satanic-School,[24] Cockney-
School[25] and other Literatures; — once more, as in the old time of
the *Leitourgia,* a most waste imbroglio, and world-wide jungle
and jumble; waiting terribly to be 'well-edited,' and 'well-burnt!'
Arachne[26] started with forefinger and thumb, and had not even a
distaff; yet thou seest Manchester, and Cotton Cloth, which will
shelter naked backs, at two-pence an ell.

Work? The quantity of done and forgotten work that lies
silent under my feet in this world, and escorts and attends me,
and supports and keeps me alive, wheresoever I walk or stand,
whatsoever I think or do, gives rise to reflections! Is it not
enough, at any rate, to strike the thing called 'Fame' into total
silence for a wise man? For fools and unreflective persons, she
is and will be very noisy, this 'Fame,' and talks of her 'immortals'
and so forth: but if you will consider it, what is she? Abbot
Samson was not nothing because nobody *said* anything of him.
Or thinkest thou, the Right Honourable Sir Jabesh Windbag can
be made something by Parliamentary Majorities and Leading
Articles? Her 'immortals!' Scarcely two hundred years back can
Fame recollect articulately at all; and there she but maunders and
mumbles. She manages to recollect a Shakspeare or so; and
prates, considerably like a goose, about him; — and in the rear of
that, onwards to the birth of Theuth,[27] to Hengst's Invasion,[28]
and the bosom of Eternity, it was all blank; and the respectable
Teutonic Languages, Teutonic Practices, Existences all came of
their own accord, as the grass springs, as the trees grow; no Poet,
no work from the inspired heart of a Man needed there; and
Fame has not an articulate word to say about it! Or ask her, What,
with all conceivable appliances and mnemonics, including apoth-
eosis and human sacrifices among the number, she carries in her
head with regard to a Wodan, even a Moses, or other such? She
begins to be uncertain as to what they were, whether spirits or
men of mould, — gods, charlatans; begins sometimes to have a

[24] Southey's name for Byron, Shelley, and their imitators.
[25] Lockhart's contemptuous term for young London writers of the early
nineteenth century — Leigh Hunt, Keats, Hazlitt, et al.
[26] The expert weaver whom a jealous Athene turned into a spider.
[27] Thoth or Trismegistus (see above, p. 42, n. 10).
[28] Hengist, fifth-century founder of the kingdom of Kent.

misgiving that they were mere symbols, ideas of the mind; perhaps nonentities, and Letters of the Alphabet! She is the noisiest, inarticulately babbling, hissing, screaming, foolishest, unmusicalest of fowls that fly; and needs no 'trumpet,' I think, but her own enormous goose-throat, — measuring several degrees of celestial latitude, so to speak. Her 'wings,' in these days, have grown far swifter than ever; but her goose-throat hitherto seems only larger, louder and foolisher than ever. *She* is transitory, futile, a goose-goddess: — if she were not transitory, what would become of us! It is a chief comfort that she forgets us all; all, even to the very Wodans; and grows to consider us, at last, as probably nonentities and Letters of the Alphabet.

Yes, a noble Abbot Samson resigns himself to Oblivion too; feels *it* no hardship, but a comfort; counts it as a still resting-place, from much sick fret and fever and stupidity, which in the night-watches often made his strong heart sigh. Your most sweet voices, making one enormous goose-voice, O Bobus and Company, how can they be a guidance for any Son of Adam? In *silence* of you and the like of you, the 'small still voices'[29] will speak to him better; in which does lie guidance.

My friend, all speech and rumour is shortlived, foolish, untrue. Genuine WORK alone, what thou workest faithfully, that is eternal, as the Almighty Founder and World-Builder himself. Stand thou by that; and let 'Fame' and the rest of it go prating.

> Heard are the Voices,
> Voice of the Sages,
> The Worlds and the Ages:
> "Choose well, your choice is
> Brief and yet endless;
>
> Here eyes do regard you,
> In Eternity's stilness;
> Here is all fulness,
> Ye brave, to reward you;
> Work, and despair not."[30]

[29] 1 Kings 19:12.
[30] Goethe. (C.) ("Symbolum," lines 21–30.)

BOOK III

The Modern Worker

CHAPTER I

PHENOMENA

B ᴜᴛ, it is said, our religion is gone: we no longer believe in St. Edmund, no longer see the figure of him 'on the rim of the sky,' minatory or confirmatory! God's absolute Laws, sanctioned by an eternal Heaven and an eternal Hell, have become Moral Philosophies, sanctioned by able computations of Profit and Loss, by weak considerations of Pleasures of Virtue and the Moral Sublime.

It is even so. To speak in the ancient dialect, we 'have forgotten God;'[1] — in the most modern dialect and very truth of the matter, we have taken up the Fact of this Universe as it *is not*. We have quietly closed our eyes to the eternal Substance of things, and opened them only to the Shews and Shams of things. We quietly believe this Universe to be intrinsically a great unintelligible Pᴇʀʜᴀᴘs; extrinsically, clear enough, it is a great, most extensive Cattlefold and Workhouse, with most extensive Kitchen-ranges, Dining-tables, — whereat he is wise who can find a place! All the Truth of this Universe is uncertain; only the profit and loss of it, the pudding and praise of it, are and remain very visible to the practical man.

There is no longer any God for us! God's Laws are become a Greatest-Happiness Principle,[2] a Parliamentary Expediency: the Heavens overarch us only as an Astronomical Time-keeper; a butt for Herschel-telescopes[3] to shoot science at, to shoot sentimentalities at: — in our and old Jonson's dialect, man has lost the *soul* out of him; and now, after the due period, — begins to find the want of it! This is verily the plague-spot; centre of the universal Social Gangrene, threatening all modern things with frightful death. To him that will consider it, here is the stem, with its

---

[1] See above, p. 32, n.1.

[2] The hedonistic basis of utilitarian social ethics.

[3] The reference is either to Sir William Herschel (d. 1822), leading astronomer of his time and the maker of improved telescopes, or to his son, Sir John (b. 1792), also a noted astronomer.

roots and taproot, with its world-wide upas-boughs and accursed poison-exudations, under which the world lies writhing in atrophy and agony. You touch the focal-centre of all our disease, of our frightful nosology of diseases, when you lay your hand on this. There is no religion; there is no God; man has lost his soul, and vainly seeks antiseptic salt. Vainly: in killing Kings, in passing Reform Bills, in French Revolutions, Manchester Insurrections, is found no remedy. The foul elephantine leprosy, alleviated for an hour, reappears in new force and desperateness next hour.

For actually this is *not* the real fact of the world; the world is not made so, but otherwise! — Truly, any Society setting out from this No-God hypothesis will arrive at a result or two. The *Un*-veracities, escorted, each Unveracity of them by its corresponding Misery and Penalty; the Phantasms, and Fatuities, and ten-years Corn-Law Debatings, that shall walk the Earth at noonday, — must needs be numerous! The Universe *being* intrinsically a Perhaps, being too probably an 'infinite Humbug,' why should any minor Humbug astonish us? It is all according to the order of Nature; and Phantasms riding with huge clatter along the streets, from end to end of our existence, astonish nobody. Enchanted St. Ives' Workhouses and Joe-Manton Aristocracies; giant Working Mammonism near strangled in the partridge-nets of giant-looking Idle Dilettantism, — this, in all its branches, in its thousand thousand modes and figures, is a sight familiar to us.

The Popish Religion, we are told, flourishes extremely in these years; and is the most vivacious-looking religion to be met with at present. *"Elle a trois cents ans dans le ventre,"* counts M. Jouffroy;[4] *"c'est pourquoi je la respecte!"* — The old Pope of Rome, finding it laborious to kneel so long while they cart him through the streets to bless the people on *Corpus-Christi* Day, complains of rheumatism; whereupon his Cardinals consult; — construct him, after some study, a stuffed cloaked figure, of iron and wood, with wool or baked hair; and place it in a kneeling posture. Stuffed figure, or rump of a figure; to this stuffed rump he, sitting at his ease on a lower level, joins, by the aid of cloaks and drapery, his living head and outspread hands: the rump with its cloaks kneels, the Pope looks, and holds his hands spread; and so the

---

[4] A French philosopher who died in 1842. "She has three centuries to go, and that is why I respect her."

two in concert bless the Roman population on *Corpus-Christi* Day, as well as they can.[5]

I have considered this amphibious Pope, with the wool-and iron back, with the flesh head and hands; and endeavoured to calculate his horoscope. I reckon him the remarkablest Pontiff that has darkened God's daylight, or painted himself in the human retina, for these several thousand years. Nay, since Chaos first shivered, and 'sneezed,' as the Arabs say, with the first shaft of sunlight shot through it, what stranger product was there of Nature and Art working together? Here is a Supreme Priest who believes God to be — What in the name of God *does* he believe God to be? — and discerns that all worship of God is a scenic phantasmagory of wax-candles, organ-blasts, Gregorian Chants, mass-brayings, purple monsignori, wool-and-iron rumps, artistically spread out, — to save the ignorant from worse.

O reader, I say not who are Belial's elect. This poor amphibious Pope too gives loaves to the Poor; has in him more good latent than he is himself aware of. His poor Jesuits, in the late Italian Cholera,[6] were, with a few German Doctors, the only creatures whom dastard terror had not driven mad: they descended fearless into all gulfs and bedlams; watched over the pillow of the dying, with help, with counsel and hope; shone as luminous fixed stars, when all else had gone out in chaotic night: honour to them! This poor Pope, — who knows what good is in him? In a Time otherwise too prone to forget, he keeps up the mournfulest ghastly memorial of the Highest, Blessedest, which once was; which, in new fit forms, will again partly have to be. Is he not as a perpetual death's-head and cross-bones, with their *Resurgam,*[7] on the grave of a Universal Heroism, — grave of a Christianity? Such Noblenesses, purchased by the world's best heart's-blood, must not be lost; we cannot afford to lose them, in what confusions soever. To all of us the day will come, to a few of us it has already come, when no mortal, with his heart yearning for a 'Divine Humility,' or other 'Highest form of Valour,' will need to look for it in death's-heads, but will see it round him in here and there a beautiful living head.

[5] This ingenious contrivance was often used in Corpus Christi Day processions in Rome. Henry Crabb Robinson describes it in his *Diary* (Boston, 1869), II, 129–130.

[6] The most recent serious outbreak had been in 1837.

[7] "I shall rise again."

Besides, there is in this poor Pope, and his practice of the Scenic Theory of Worship, a frankness which I rather honour. Not half and half, but with undivided heart does *he* set about worshipping by stage-machinery; as if there were now, and could again be, in Nature no other. He will ask you, What other? Under this my Gregorian Chant, and beautiful wax-light Phantasmagory, kindly hidden from you is an Abyss, of black Doubt, Scepticism, nay Sansculottic Jacobinism;[8] an Orcus[9] that has no bottom. Think of that. 'Groby Pool *is* thatched with pancakes,' — as Jeannie Deans's Innkeeper defied it to be![10] The Bottomless of Scepticism, Atheism, Jacobinism, behold, it is thatched over, hidden from your despair, by stage-properties judiciously arranged. This stuffed rump of mine saves not me only from rheumatism, but you also from what other *isms!* In this your Life-pilgrimage Nowhither, a fine Squallacci[11] marching-music, and Gregorian Chant, accompanies you, and the hollow Night of Orcus is well hid!

Yes truly, few men that worship by the rotatory Calabash of the Calmucks do it in half so great, frank or effectual a way. Drury-lane, it is said, and that is saying much, may learn from him in the dressing of parts, in the arrangement of lights and shadows. He is the greatest Play-actor that at present draws salary in this world. Poor Pope; and I am told he is fast growing bankrupt too; and will, in a measurable term of years (a great way *within* the 'three hundred'), not have a penny to make his pot boil! His old rheumatic back will then get to rest; and himself and his stage-properties sleep well in Chaos forevermore.

Or, alas, why go to Rome for Phantasms walking the streets? Phantasms, ghosts, in this midnight hour, hold jubilee, and screech and jabber; and the question rather were, What high Reality anywhere is yet awake? Aristocracy has become Phantasm-Aristocracy, no longer able to *do* its work, not in the least conscious that it has any work longer to do. Unable, totally careless to *do* its work; careful only to clamour for the *wages* of doing its work, — nay for higher, and *palpably* undue wages, and Corn-Laws and *increase* of rents; the old rate of wages not being adequate

---

[8] Political (left-wing) extremism; originally applied to the principles and spirit of the French Revolution.

[9] Hades.

[10] Cf. Scott's *The Heart of Midlothian*.

[11] Carlyle's invention.

now! In hydra-wrestle, giant '*Millo*cracy' so-called, a real giant, though as yet a blind one and but half-awake, wrestles and wrings in choking nightmare, 'like to be strangled in the partridge-nets of Phantasm-Aristocracy,' as we said, which fancies itself still to be a giant. Wrestles, as under nightmare, till it do awaken; and gasps and struggles thousandfold, we may say, in a truly painful manner, through all fibres of our English Existence, in these hours and years! Is our poor English Existence wholly becoming a Nightmare; full of mere Phantasms? —

The Champion of England, cased in iron or tin, rides into Westminster Hall, 'being lifted into his saddle with little assistance,' and there asks, If in the four quarters of the world, under the cope of Heaven, is any man or demon that dare question the right of this King?[12] Under the cope of Heaven no man makes intelligible answer, — as several men ought already to have done. Does not this Champion too know the world; that it is a huge Imposture, and bottomless Inanity, thatched over with bright cloth and other ingenious tissues? Him let us leave there, questioning all men and demons.

Him we have left to his destiny; but whom else have we found? From this the highest apex of things, downwards through all strata and breadths, how many fully awakened Realities have we fallen in with: — alas, on the contrary, what troops and populations of Phantasms, not God-Veracities but Devil-Falsities, down to the very lowest stratum, — which now, by such superincumbent weight of Unveracities, lies enchanted in St. Ives' Workhouses, broad enough, helpless enough! You will walk in no public thoroughfare or remotest byway of English Existence but you will meet a man, an interest of men, that has given up hope in the Everlasting, True, and placed its hope in the Temporary, half or wholly False. The Honourable Member complains unmusically that there is 'devil's-dust'[13] in Yorkshire cloth. Yorkshire cloth, — why, the very Paper I now write on is made, it seems, partly of plaster-lime well-smoothed, and obstructs my writing! You are lucky if you can find now any good Paper, — any work really *done;* search where you will, from highest Phantasm apex to lowest Enchanted basis!

---

[12] In 1821, the last time this ceremony was performed, the young man who inherited the office was weighed down with seventy pounds of armor and had to be helped onto his horse.

[13] Fibre made from old cloth put through a shredding machine.

Consider, for example, that great Hat seven-feet high, which now perambulates London Streets;[14] which my Friend Sauerteig regarded justly as one of our English notabilities; "the topmost point as yet," said he, "would it were your culminating and returning point, to which English Puffery[15] has been observed to reach!" — The Hatter in the Strand of London, instead of making better felt-hats than another, mounts a huge lath-and-plaster Hat, seven-feet high, upon wheels; sends a man to drive it through the streets; hoping to be saved *thereby*. He has not attempted to *make* better hats, as he was appointed by the Universe to do, and as with this ingenuity of his he could very probably have done; but his whole industry is turned to *persuade* us that he has made such! He too knows that the Quack has become God. Laugh not at him, O reader; or do not laugh only. He has ceased to be comic; he is fast becoming tragic. To me this all-deafening blast of Puffery, of poor Falsehood grown necessitous, of poor Heart-Atheism fallen now into Enchanted Workhouses, sounds too surely like a Doom's-blast! I have to say to myself in old dialect: "God's blessing is not written on all this; His curse is written on all this!" Unless perhaps the Universe *be* a chimera; — some old totally deranged eightday clock, dead as brass; which the Maker, if there ever was any Maker, has long ceased to meddle with? — To my Friend Sauerteig this poor seven-feet Hat-manufacturer, as the topstone of English Puffery, was very notable.

Alas, that we natives note him little, that we view him as a thing of course, is the very burden of the misery.[16] We take it for granted, the most rigorous of us, that all men who have made anything are expected and entitled to make the loudest possible proclamation of it; call on a discerning public to reward them for it. Every man his own trumpeter; that is, to a really alarming extent, the accepted rule. Make loudest possible proclamation of your Hat: true proclamation if that will do; if that will not do, then false proclamation, — to such extent of falsity as will serve your purpose; as will not seem too false to be credible! — I answer, once for all, that the fact is not so. Nature requires no man to make

---

[14] There is a picture of it in John W. Dodds, *The Age of Paradox* (New York, 1952), p. 277.

[15] See below, p. 234, n.26.

[16] Cf. Wordsworth's "Lines Composed a Few Miles Above Tintern Abbey," line 38: "the burthen of the *mystery*."

proclamation of his doings and hat-makings; Nature forbids all men to make such. There is not a man or hat-maker born into the world but feels, at first, that he is degrading himself if he speak of his excellencies and prowesses, and supremacy in his craft: his inmost heart says to him, "Leave thy friends to speak of these; if possible, thy enemies to speak of these; but at all events, thy friends!" He feels that he is already a poor braggart; fast hastening to be a falsity and speaker of the Untruth.

Nature's Laws, I must repeat, are eternal: her small still voice, speaking from the inmost heart of us, shall not, under terrible penalties, be disregarded. No one man can depart from the truth without damage to himself; no one million of men; no Twenty-seven Millions of men. Shew me a Nation fallen everywhere into this course, so that each expects it, permits it to others and himself, I will shew you a Nation travelling with one assent on the broad way.[17] The broad way, however many Banks of England, Cotton-Mills and Duke's Palaces it may have! Not at happy Elysian fields, and everlasting crowns of victory, earned by silent Valour, will this Nation arrive; but at precipices, devouring gulfs, if it pause not. Nature has appointed happy fields, victorious laurel-crowns; but only to the brave and true: Unnature, what we call Chaos, holds nothing in it but vacuities, devouring gulfs. What are Twenty-seven Millions, and their unanimity? Believe them not: the Worlds and the Ages, God and Nature and All Men say otherwise.

'Rhetoric all this?' No, my brother, very singular to say, it is Fact all this. Cocker's Arithmetic[18] is not truer. Forgotten in these days, it is old as the foundations of the Universe, and will endure till the Universe cease. It is forgotten now; and the first mention of it puckers thy sweet countenance into a sneer: but it will be brought to mind again, — unless indeed the Law of Gravitation chance to cease, and men find that they *can* walk on vacancy. Unanimity of the Twenty-seven Millions will do nothing: walk not thou with them; fly from them as for thy life. Twenty-seven Millions travelling on such courses, with gold jingling in every pocket, with vivats[19] heaven-high, are incessantly advancing, let me again remind thee, towards the *firm-*

17 Matthew 7:13.
18 First published in 1678, a textbook that remained in wide use for well over a century.
19 Cries of "Long live the Queen."

land's end, — towards the end and extinction of what Faithfulness, Veracity, real Worth, was in their way of life. Their noble
ancestors have fashioned for them a 'life-road!' — in how many
thousand senses, this! There is not an old wise Proverb on their
tongue, an honest Principle articulated in their hearts into utterance, a wise true method of doing and despatching any work or
commerce of men, but helps yet to carry them forward. Life is
still possible to them, because all is not yet Puffery, Falsity,
Mammon-worship and Unnature; because somewhat is yet Faithfulness, Veracity and Valour. With a certain very considerable
finite quantity of Unveracity and Phantasm, social life is still
possible; not with an infinite quantity! Exceed your certain quantity, the seven-feet Hat, and all things upwards to the very
Champion cased in tin, begin to reel and flounder, — in Manchester Insurrections, Chartisms, Sliding-scales; the Law of Gravitation not forgetting to act. You advance incessantly towards the
land's end; you are, literally enough, 'consuming the way.' Step
after step, Twenty-seven Million unconscious men; — till you are
at the land's end; till there is not Faithfulness enough among you
any more: and the next step now is lifted *not* over land, but into
air, over ocean-deeps and roaring abysses: — unless perhaps the
Law of Gravitation have forgotten to act?

O, it is frightful when a whole Nation, as our Fathers used
to say, has 'forgotten God;' has remembered only Mammon, and
what Mammon leads to! When your self-trumpeting Hatmaker
is the emblem of almost all makers, and workers, and men, that
make anything, — from soul-overseerships, body-overseerships,
epic poems, acts of parliament, to hats and shoe-blacking! Not
one false man but does uncountable mischief: how much, in a
generation or two, will Twenty-seven Millions, mostly false, manage to accumulate? The sum of it, visible in every street, market-
place, senate-house, circulating-library, cathedral, cotton-mill, and
union-workhouse, fills one *not* with a comic feeling!

CHAPTER II

R EADER, even Christian Reader as thy title goes, hast thou any notion of Heaven and Hell? I rather apprehend, not. Often as the words are on our tongue, they have got a fabulous or semi-fabulous character for most of us, and pass on like a kind of transient similitude, like a sound signifying little.

Yet it is well worth while for us to know, once and always, that they are not a similitude, nor a fable nor semi-fable; that they are an everlasting highest fact! "No Lake of Sicilian or other sulphur burns now anywhere in these ages," sayest thou? Well, and if there did not! Believe that there does not; believe it if thou wilt, nay hold by it as a real increase, a rise to higher stages, to wider horizons and empires. All this has vanished, or has not vanished; believe as thou wilt as to all this. But that an Infinite of Practical Importance, speaking with strict arithmetical exactness, an *Infinite,* has vanished or can vanish from the Life of any Man: this thou shalt not believe! O brother, the Infinite of Terror, of Hope, of Pity, did it not at any moment disclose itself to thee, indubitable, unnameable? Came it never, like the gleam of *preter*-natural eternal Oceans, like the voice of old Eternities, far-sounding through thy heart of hearts? Never? Alas, it was not thy Liberalism then; it was thy Animalism! The Infinite is more sure than any other fact. But only men can discern it; mere building beavers, spinning arachnes, much more the predatory vulturous and vulpine species, do not discern it well! —

'The word Hell,' says Sauerteig, 'is still frequently in use among the English People: but I could not without difficulty ascertain what they meant by it. Hell generally signifies the Infinite Terror, the thing a man *is* infinitely afraid of, and shudders and shrinks from, struggling with his whole soul to escape from it. There is a Hell therefore, if you will consider, which accompanies man, in all stages of his history, and religious or other development: but the Hells of men and Peoples differ notably. With Christians it is the infinite terror of being found guilty before the Just Judge.

With old Romans, I conjecture, it was the terror not of Pluto,[1] for whom probably they cared little, but of doing unworthily, doing unvirtuously, which was their word for un*man*fully. And now what is it, if you pierce through his Cants, his oft-repeated Hearsays, what he calls his Worships and so forth, — what is it that the modern English soul does, in very truth, dread infinitely, and contemplate with entire despair? What *is* his Hell; after all these reputable, oft-repeated Hearsays, what is it? With hesitation, with astonishment, I pronounce it to be: The terror of "Not succeeding;" of not making money, fame, or some other figure in the world, — chiefly of not making money! Is not that a somewhat singular Hell?'

Yes, O Sauerteig, it is very singular. If we do not 'succeed,' where is the use of us? We had better never have been born. "Tremble intensely," as our friend the Emperor of China says:[2] *there* is the black Bottomless of Terror; what Sauerteig calls the 'Hell of the English!' — But indeed this Hell belongs naturally to the Gospel of Mammonism, which also has its corresponding Heaven. For there *is* one Reality among so many Phantasms; about one thing we are entirely in earnest: The making of money. Working Mammonism does divide the world with idle game-preserving Dilettantism: — thank Heaven that there is even a Mammonism, *any*thing we are in earnest about! Idleness is worst, Idleness alone is without hope: work earnestly at anything, you will by degrees learn to work at almost all things. There is endless hope in work, were it even work at making money.

True, it must be owned, we for the present, with our Mammon-Gospel, have come to strange conclusions. We call it a Society; and go about professing openly the totalest separation, isolation. Our life is not a mutual helpfulness; but rather, cloaked under due laws-of-war, named 'fair competition' and so forth, it is a mutual hostility. We have profoundly forgotten everywhere that *Cash-payment* is not the sole relation of human beings; we think, nothing doubting, that *it* absolves and liquidates all engagements of man. "My starving workers?" answers the rich Mill-owner: "Did not I hire them fairly in the market? Did I not pay them, to the last sixpence, the sum covenanted for? What have I to do

---

[1] The ruler of the underworld.

[2] Apparently an allusion to a favorite expression of the Emperor's, contained in his proclamations reported in current newspapers. See below, p. 232, n.23.

with them more?" — Verily Mammon-worship is a melancholy creed. When Cain, for his own behoof, had killed Abel, and was questioned, "Where is thy brother" he too made answer, "Am I my brother's keeper?" Did I not pay my brother *his* wages, the thing he had merited from me?

O sumptuous Merchant-Prince, illustrious game-preserving Duke, is there no way of 'killing' thy brother but Cain's rude way! 'A good man by the very look of him, by his very presence with us as a fellow wayfarer in this Life-pilgrimage, *promises* so much:' wo to him if he forget all such promises, if he never know that they were given! To a deadened soul, seared with the brute Idolatry of Sense, to whom going to Hell is equivalent to not making money, all 'promises,' and moral duties, that cannot be pleaded for in Courts of Requests,[3] address themselves in vain. Money he can be ordered to pay, but nothing more. I have not heard in all Past History, and expect not to hear in all Future History, of any Society anywhere under God's Heaven supporting itself on such Philosophy. The Universe is not made so; it is made otherwise than so. The man or nation of men that thinks it is made so, marches forward nothing doubting, step after step; but marches — whither we know! In these last two centuries of Atheistic Government (near two centuries now, since the blessed restoration of his Sacred Majesty, and Defender of the Faith,[4] Charles Second), I reckon that we have pretty well exhausted what of 'firm earth' there was for us to march on; — and are now, very ominously, shuddering, reeling, and let us hope trying to recoil, on the cliff's edge! —

For out of this that we call Atheism come so many other *isms* and falsities, each falsity with its misery at its heels! — A soul is not like wind (*spiritus,* or breath) contained within a capsule; the ALMIGHTY MAKER is not like a Clockmaker that once, in old immemorial ages, having *made* his Horologe of a Universe, sits ever since and sees it go! Not at all. Hence comes Atheism; come, as we say, many other *isms;* and as the sum of all, comes Valetism, the *reverse* of Heroism; sad root of all woes whatsoever. For indeed, as no man ever saw the above-said wind-element enclosed within its capsule, and finds it at bottom more deniable than conceivable; so too he finds, in spite of Bridgewater Be-

---

[3] Small claims courts, abolished in 1846.
[4] A title first bestowed on the English monarch by Pope Leo X in 1521 but only loosely applicable to Charles II.

quests,[5] your Clockmaker Almighty[6] an entirely questionable affair, a deniable affair; — and accordingly denies it, and along with it so much else. Alas, one knows not what and how much else! For the faith in an Invisible, Unnameable, Godlike, present everywhere in all that we see and work and suffer, is the essence of all faith whatsoever; and that once denied, or still worse, asserted with lips only, and out of bound prayerbooks only, what other thing remains believable? That Cant well-ordered is marketable Cant; that Heroism means gas-lighted Histrionism;[7] that seen with 'clear eyes' (as they call Valet-eyes), no man is a Hero, or ever was a Hero, but all men are Valets and Varlets. The accursed practical quintessence of all sorts of Unbelief! For if there be now no Hero, and the Histrio himself begin to be seen into, what hope is there for the seed of Adam here below? We are the doomed everlasting prey of the Quack; who, now in this guise, now in that, is to filch us, to pluck and eat us, by such modes as are convenient for him. For the modes and guises I care little. The Quack once inevitable, let him come swiftly, let him pluck and eat me; — swiftly, that I may at least have done with him; for in his Quack-world I can have no wish to linger. Though he slay me, yet will I despise him.[8] Though he conquer nations, and have all the Flunkeys of the Universe shouting at his heels, yet will I know well that *he* is an Inanity; that for him and his there is no continuance appointed, save only in Gehenna and the Pool.[9] Alas, the Atheist world, from its utmost summits of Heaven and Westminster Hall, downwards through poor seven-feet Hats and 'Unveracities fallen hungry,' down to the lowest cellars and neglected hunger-dens of it, is very wretched.

One of Dr. Alison's Scotch facts struck us much.[10] A poor Irish Widow, her husband having died in one of the Lanes of Edinburgh, went forth with her three children, bare of all resource, to solicit help from the Charitable Establishments of that City. At this Charitable Establishment and then at that she was refused;

---

[5] The eighth Earl of Bridgewater (d. 1829) left £8,000 which was divided as prize-money among eight authors of treatises on "the Power, Wisdom, and Goodness of God, as Manifested in the Creation" (so-called "natural theology").

[6] See above, p. 33.

[7] Play-acting.

[8] Job 13:15: "Though he slay me, yet will I *trust in* him."

[9] Hell.

[10] *Observations on the Management of the Poor in Scotland:* By William Pulteney Alison, M.D. (Edinburgh, 1840.) (C.)

referred from one to the other, helped by none; — till she had exhausted them all; till her strength and heart failed her: she sank down in typhus-fever; died, and infected her Lane with fever, so that 'seventeen other persons' died of fever there in consequence. The humane Physician asks thereupon, as with a heart too full for speaking, Would it not have been *economy* to help this poor Widow? She took typhus-fever, and killed seventeen of you! — Very curious. The forlorn Irish Widow applies to her fellow-creatures, as if saying, "Behold I am sinking, bare of help: ye must help me! I am your sister, bone of your bone; one God made us: ye must help me!" They answer, "No; impossible: thou art no sister of ours." But she proves her sisterhood; her typhus-fever kills *them:* they actually were her brothers, though denying it! Had man ever to go lower for a proof?

For, as indeed was very natural in such case, all government of the Poor by the Rich has long ago been given over to Supply-and-demand, Laissez-faire and such like, and universally declared to be 'impossible.' "You are no sister of ours; what shadow of proof is there? Here are our parchments, our padlocks, proving indisputably our money-safes to be *ours*, and you to have no business with them. Depart! It is impossible!" — Nay, what wouldst thou thyself have us do? cry indignant readers. Nothing, my friends, — till you have got a soul for yourselves again. Till then all things are 'impossible.' Till then I cannot even bid you buy, as the old Spartans would have done, two-pence worth of powder and lead, and compendiously shoot to death this poor Irish Widow: even that is 'impossible' for you. Nothing is left but that she prove her sisterhood by dying, and infecting you with typhus. Seventeen of you lying dead will not deny such proof that she *was* flesh of your flesh; and perhaps some of the living may lay it to heart.

'Impossible:' of a certain two-legged animal with feathers, it is said if you draw a distinct chalk-circle round him, he sits imprisoned, as if girt with the iron ring of Fate; and will die there, though within sight of victuals, — or sit in sick misery there, and be fatted to death. The name of this poor two-legged animal is — Goose; and they make of him, when well fattened, *Pâté de foie gras,* much prized by some!

CHAPTER III

GOSPEL OF DILETTANTISM

B UT after all, the Gospel of Dilettantism, producing a Governing Class who do not govern, nor understand in the least
that they are bound or expected to govern, is still mournfuler than
that of Mammonism. Mammonism, as we said, at least works;
this goes idle. Mammonism has seized some portion of the message of Nature to man; and seizing that, and following it, will
seize and appropriate more and more of Nature's message: but
Dilettantism has missed it wholly. 'Make money:' that will mean
withal, 'Do work in order to make money.' But, 'Go gracefully
idle in Mayfair,'[1] what does or can that mean? An idle, game-
preserving and even corn-lawing Aristocracy, in such an England
as ours: has the world, if we take thought of it, ever seen such a
phenomenon till very lately? Can it long continue to see such?

Accordingly the impotent, insolent Donothingism in Practice,
and Saynothingism in Speech, which we have to witness on that
side of our affairs, is altogether amazing. A Corn-Law demon-
strating itself openly, for ten years or more, with 'arguments' to
make the angels, and some other classes of creatures, weep! For
men are not ashamed to rise in Parliament and elsewhere, and
speak the things they do *not* think. 'Expediency,' 'Necessities of
Party,' &c. &c.! It is not known that the Tongue of Man is a
sacred organ; that Man himself is definable in Philosophy as an
'Incarnate *Word*;' the Word not there, you have no Man there
either, but a Phantasm instead! In this way it is that Absurdities
may live long enough, — still walking, and talking for themselves,
years and decades after the brains are quite out! How are 'the
knaves and dastards' ever to be got 'arrested' at that rate? —

"No man in this fashionable London of yours," friend Sauerteig
would say, "speaks a plain word to me. Every man feels bound
to be something more than plain; to be pungent withal, witty,
ornamental. His poor fraction of sense has to be perked into
some epigrammatic shape, that it may prick into me; — perhaps

---

[1] London's most fashionable quarter.

(this is the commonest) to be topsyturvied, left standing on its head, that I may remember it the better! Such grinning inanity is very sad to the soul of man. Human faces should not grin on one like masks; they should look on one like faces! I love honest laughter, as I do sunlight; but not dishonest: most kinds of dancing too; but the St.-Vitus kind not at all! A fashionable wit, *ach Himmel,* if you ask, Which, he or a Death's-head, will be the cheerier company for me? pray send *not* him!"

Insincere Speech, truly, is the prime material of insincere Action. Action hangs, as it were, *dissolved* in Speech, in Thought whereof Speech is the shadow; and precipitates itself therefrom. The kind of Speech in a man betokens the kind of Action you will get from him. Our Speech, in these modern days, has become amazing. Johnson complained, "Nobody speaks in earnest, Sir; there is no serious conversation."[2] To us all serious speech of men, as that of Seventeenth-Century Puritans, Twelfth-Century Catholics, German Poets of this Century, has become jargon, more or less insane. Cromwell was mad and a quack; Anselm, Becket, Goethe, *ditto ditto.*

Perhaps few narratives in History or Mythology are more significant than that Moslem one, of Moses and the Dwellers by the Dead Sea. A tribe of men dwelt on the shores of that same Asphaltic Lake; and having forgotten, as we are all too prone to do, the inner facts of Nature, and taken up with the falsities and outer semblances of it, were fallen into sad conditions, — verging indeed towards a certain far deeper Lake. Whereupon it pleased kind Heaven to send them the Prophet Moses, with an instructive word of warning, out of which might have sprung 'remedial measures' not a few. But no: the men of the Dead Sea discovered, as the valet-species always does in heroes or prophets, no comeliness in Moses; listened with real tedium to Moses, with light grinning, or with splenetic sniffs and sneers, affecting even to yawn; and signified, in short, that they found him a humbug, and even a bore. Such was the candid theory these men of the Asphalt Lake formed to themselves of Moses, That probably he was a humbug, that certainly he was a bore.

[2] Possibly a reference to Johnson's remark (Boswell's miscellaneous records for 1776) when Boswell "complained of having dined at a splendid table without hearing one sentence of conversation worthy of being remembered": "Sir, there seldom is any such conversation."

Moses withdrew; but Nature and her rigorous veracities did not withdraw. The men of the Dead Sea, when we next went to visit them, were all 'changed into Apes;'[3] sitting on the trees there, grinning now in the most *un*affected manner; gibbering and chattering *complete* nonsense; finding the whole Universe now a most indisputable Humbug! The Universe has *become* a Humbug to these Apes who thought it one! There they sit and chatter, to this hour: only, I think, every Sabbath there returns to them a bewildered half-consciousness, half-reminiscence; and they sit, with their wizened smoke-dried visages, and such an air of supreme tragicality as Apes may; looking out, through those blinking smoke-bleared eyes of theirs, into the wonderfulest universal smoky Twilight and undecipherable disordered Dusk of Things; wholly an Uncertainty, Unintelligibility, they and it; and for commentary thereon, here and there an unmusical chatter or mew: — truest, tragicalest Humbug conceivable by the mind of man or ape! They made no use of their souls; and *so* have lost them. Their worship on the Sabbath now is to roost there, with unmusical screeches, and half-remember that they had souls.

Didst thou never, O Traveller, fall in with parties of this tribe? Meseems they are grown somewhat numerous in our day.

[3] Sale's *Koran* (*Introduction*). (C.)

CHAPTER IV

HAPPY

ALL work, even cotton-spinning, is noble; work is alone noble: be that here said and asserted once more. And in like manner too all dignity is painful; a life of ease is not for any man, nor for any god. The life of all gods figures itself to us as a Sublime Sadness — earnestness of Infinite Battle against Infinite Labour. Our highest religion is named the 'Worship of Sorrow.' For the son of man there is no noble crown, well worn, or even ill worn, but is a crown of thorns! — These things, in spoken words, or still better, in felt instincts alive in every heart, were once well known.

Does not the whole wretchedness, the whole *Atheism* as I call it, of man's ways, in these generations, shadow itself for us in that unspeakable Life-philosophy of his: The pretension to be what he calls 'happy?' Every pitifulest whipster[1] that walks within a skin has his head filled with the notion that he is, shall be, or by all human and divine laws ought to be, 'happy.' His wishes, the pitifulest whipster's, are to be fulfilled for him; his days, the pitifulest whipster's, are to flow on in ever-gentle current of enjoyment, impossible even for the gods. The prophets preach to us, Thou shalt be happy; thou shalt love pleasant things, and find them. The people clamour, Why have we not found pleasant things?

We construct our theory of Human Duties, not on any Greatest-Nobleness Principle, never so mistaken; no, but on a Greatest-Happiness Principle. 'The word *Soul* with us, as in some Slavonic dialects, seems to be synonymous with *Stomach*.' We plead and speak, in our Parliaments and elsewhere, not as from the Soul, but from the Stomach; — wherefore, indeed, our pleadings are so slow to profit. We plead not for God's Justice; we are not ashamed to stand clamouring and pleading for our own 'interests,' our own rents and trade-profits; we say, They are the 'interests' of so many; there is such an intense desire for them in us! We demand Free-Trade, with much just vociferation and benevo-

[1] An all-purpose term of reproach or contempt.

155

lence, That the poorer classes, who are terribly ill-off at present, may have cheaper New-Orleans bacon. Men ask on Free-trade platforms, How can the indomitable spirit of Englishmen be kept up without plenty of bacon? We shall become a ruined Nation! — Surely, my friends, plenty of bacon is good and indispensable: but, I doubt, you will never get even bacon by aiming only at that. You are men, not animals of prey, well-used or ill-used! Your Greatest-Happiness Principle seems to me fast becoming a rather unhappy one. — What if we should cease babbling about 'happiness,' and leave *it* resting on its own basis, as it used to do!

A gifted Byron rises in his wrath; and feeling too surely that he for his part is not 'happy,' declares the same in very violent language, as a piece of news that may be interesting. It evidently has surprised him much. One dislikes to see a man and poet reduced to proclaim on the streets such tidings: but on the whole, as matters go, that is not the most dislikable. Byron speaks the *truth* in this matter. Byron's large audience indicates how true it is felt to be.

'Happy,' my brother? First of all, what difference is it whether thou art happy or not! Today becomes Yesterday so fast, all Tomorrows become Yesterdays; and then there is no question whatever of the 'happiness,' but quite another question. Nay, thou hast such a sacred pity left at least for thyself, thy very pains once gone over into Yesterday become joys to thee. Besides, thou knowest not what heavenly blessedness and indispensable sanative virtue was in them; thou shalt only know it after many days, when thou art wiser! — A benevolent old Surgeon sat once in our company, with a Patient fallen sick by gourmandising, whom he had just, too briefly in the Patient's judgment, been examining. The foolish Patient still at intervals continued to break in on our discourse, which rather promised to take a philosophic turn: "But I have lost my appetite," said he, objurgatively, with a tone of irritated pathos; "I have no appetite; I can't eat!" — "My dear fellow," answered the Doctor in mildest tone, "it isn't of the slightest consequence;" — and continued his philosophical discoursings with us!

Or does the reader not know the history of that Scottish iron Misanthrope? The inmates of some town-mansion, in those Northern parts, were thrown into the fearfulest alarm by indubitable symptoms of a ghost inhabiting the next house, or perhaps even the partition-wall! Ever at a certain hour, with pre-

ternatural gnarring, growling and screeching, which attended as
running bass, there began, in a horrid, semi-articulate, unearthly
voice, this song: "Once I was hap-hap-happy, but now I'm *mees*-
erable! Clack-clack-clack, gnarr-r-r, whuz-z: Once I was hap-hap-
happy, but now I'm *mees*-erable!" — Rest, rest, perturbed spirit;[2]
— or indeed, as the good old Doctor said: My dear fellow, it isn't
of the slightest consequence! But no; the perturbed spirit could
not rest; and to the neighbours, fretted, affrighted, or at least
insufferably bored by him, it *was* of such consequence that they
had to go and examine in his haunted chamber. In his haunted
chamber, they find that the perturbed spirit is an unfortunate —
Imitator of Byron? No, is an unfortunate rusty Meat-jack, gnarring and creaking with rust and work; and this, in Scottish dialect,
is *its* Byronian musical Life-philosophy, sung according to ability!

Truly, I think the man who goes about pothering and uproaring
for his 'happiness,' — pothering, and were it ballot-boxing, poem-
making, or in what way soever fussing and exerting himself, — he
is not the man that will help us to 'get our knaves and dastards
arrested!' No; he rather is on the way to increase the number, —
by at least one unit and *his* tail! Observe, too, that this is all a
modern affair; belongs not to the old heroic times, but to these
dastard new times. 'Happiness our being's end and aim'[3] is at
bottom, if we will count well, not yet two centuries old in the
world.

The only happiness a brave man ever troubled himself with
asking much about was, happiness enough to get his work done.
Not "I can't eat!" but "I can't work!" that was the burden of all
wise complaining among men. It is, after all, the one unhappiness
of a man. That he cannot work; that he cannot get his destiny
as a man fulfilled. Behold, the day is passing swiftly over, our
life is passing swiftly over; and the night cometh, wherein no
man can work.[4] The night once come, our happiness, our unhappiness, — it is all abolished; vanished, clean gone; a thing
that has been: 'not of the slightest consequence' whether we were
happy as eupeptic Curtis,[5] as the fattest pig of Epicurus,[6] or un-

[2] *Hamlet*, I.v.183.
[3] Pope, *Essay on Man*, IV.i.   [4] John 9:4.
[5] Sir William Curtis (d. 1829), London merchant and M.P., was a fat,
vulgar sensualist. "No man of his time," it is said, "was ever the subject of
so much ridicule."
[6] Cf. Horace, *Epistles*, I.iv.15–16.

happy as Job with potsherds,[7] as musical Byron with Giaours[8] and sensibilities of the heart; as the unmusical Meat-jack with hard labour and rust! But our work, — behold that is not abolished, that has not vanished: our work, behold, it remains, or the want of it remains; — for endless Times and Eternities, remains; and that is now the sole question with us forevermore! Brief brawling Day, with its noisy phantasms, its poor paper-crowns tinsel-gilt, is gone; and divine everlasting Night, with her star-diadems, with her silences and her veracities, is come! What hast thou done, and how? Happiness, unhappiness: all that was but the *wages* thou hadst; thou hast spent all that, in sustaining thyself hitherward; not a coin of it remains with thee, it is all spent, eaten: and now thy work, where is thy work? Swift, out with it, let us see thy work!

Of a truth, if man were not a poor hungary dastard, and even much of a blockhead withal, he would cease criticising his victuals to such extent; and criticise himself rather, what he does with his victuals!

[7] Job 2:8.
[8] Byron's poetic romance *The Giaour*.

A<small>ND</small> yet, with all thy theoretic platitudes, what a depth of practical sense in thee, great England! A depth of sense, of justice, and courage; in which, under all emergencies and world-bewilderments, and under this most complex of emergencies we now live in, there is still hope, there is still assurance!

The English are a dumb people. They can do great acts, but not describe them. Like the old Romans, and some few others, *their* Epic Poem is written on the Earth's surface: England her Mark! It is complained that they have no artists: one Shakspeare indeed; but for Raphael only a Reynolds; for Mozart nothing but a Mr. Bishop:[1] not a picture, not a song. And yet they did produce one Shakspeare: consider how the element of Shakspearean melody does lie imprisoned in their nature; reduced to unfold itself in mere Cotton-mills, Constitutional Governments, and such like; — all the more interesting when it does become visible, as even in such unexpected shapes it succeeds in doing! Goethe spoke of the Horse, how impressive, almost affecting it was that an animal of such qualities should stand obstructed so; its speech nothing but an inarticulate neighing, its handiness mere *hoof*iness, the fingers all constricted, tied together, the fingernails coagulated into a mere hoof, shod with iron. The more significant, thinks he, are those eye-flashings of the generous noble quadruped; those prancings, curvings of the neck clothed with thunder.[2]

A Dog of Knowledge[3] has *free* utterance; but the Warhorse is almost mute, very far from free! It is even so. Truly, your freest utterances are not by any means always the best: they are the worst rather; the feeblest, trivialest; their meaning prompt, but small, ephemeral. Commend me to the silent English, to the silent Romans. Nay, the silent Russians too I believe to be worth

---

[1] Sir Henry Bishop, popular contemporary composer.
[2] Job 39:19.
[3] A performing — "educated" — dog.

something: are they not even now drilling, under much obloquy, an immense semi-barbarous half-world from Finland to Kamtschatka,[4] into rule, subordination, civilisation, — really in an old Roman fashion; speaking no word about it; quietly hearing all manner of vituperative Able Editors speak! While your ever-talking, ever-gesticulating French, for example, what are they at this moment drilling? — Nay, of all animals, the freest of utterance, I should judge, is the genus *Simia:* go into the Indian woods, say all Travellers, and look what a brisk, adroit, unresting Ape-population it is!

The spoken Word, the written Poem, is said to be an epitome of the man; how much more the done Work. Whatsoever of morality and of intelligence; what of patience, perseverance, faithfulness, of method, insight, ingenuity, energy; in a word, whatsoever of Strength the man had in him will lie written in the Work he does. To work: why, it is to try himself against Nature, and her everlasting unerring Laws; these will tell a true verdict as to the man. So much of virtue and of faculty did *we* find in him; so much and no more! He had such capacity of harmonising himself with *me* and my unalterable ever-veracious Laws; of cooperating and working as *I* bade him; — and has prospered, and has not prospered, as you see! — Working as great Nature bade him: does not that mean virtue of a kind; nay, of all kinds? Cotton can be spun and sold, Lancashire operatives can be got to spin it, and at length one has the woven webs and sells them, by following Nature's regulations in that matter: by not following Nature's regulations, you have them not. You have them not; — there is no Cotton-web to sell: Nature finds a bill against you; your 'Strength' is not Strength, but Futility! Let faculty be honoured, so far as it is faculty. A man that can succeed in working is to me always a man.

How one loves to see the burly figure of him, this thick-skinned, seemingly opaque, perhaps sulky, almost stupid Man of Practice, pitted against some light adroit Man of Theory, all equipt with clear logic, and able anywhere to give you Why for Wherefore! The adroit Man of Theory, so light of movement, clear of utterance, with his bow full-bent and quiver full of arrow-arguments, — surely he will strike down the game, transfix everywhere the heart of the matter; triumph everywhere, as he proves that he

---

4 Peninsula in northeastern Siberia.

shall and must do? To your astonishment, it turns out oftenest
No. The cloudy-browed, thick-soled, opaque Practicality, with
no logic-utterance, in silence mainly, with here and there a low
grunt or growl, has in him what transcends all logic-utterance: a
Congruity with the Unuttered! The Speakable, which lies atop,
as a superficial film, or outer skin, is his or is not his: but the
Doable, which reaches down to the World's centre, you find him
there!

The rugged Brindley[5] has little to say for himself; the rugged
Brindley, when difficulties accumulate on him, retires silent,
'generally to his bed;' retires 'sometimes for three days together
to his bed, that he may be in perfect privacy there,' and ascertain
in his rough head how the difficulties can be overcome. The
ineloquent Brindley, behold he *has* chained seas together; his
ships do visibly float over valleys, invisibly through the hearts
of mountains; the Mersey and the Thames, the Humber and the
Severn have shaken hands: Nature most audibly answers, Yea!
The man of Theory twangs his full-bent bow: Nature's Fact ought
to fall stricken, but does not: his logic-arrow glances from it
as from a scaly dragon, and the obstinate Fact keeps walking
its way. How singular! At bottom, you will have to grapple
closer with the dragon; take it home to you, by real faculty,
not by seeming faculty; try whether you are stronger or it is
stronger. Close with it, wrestle it: sheer obstinate toughness
of muscle; but much more, what we call toughness of heart,
which will mean persistance hopeful and even desperate, unsubduable patience, composed candid openness, clearness of
mind: all this shall be 'strength' in wrestling your dragon; the
whole man's real strength is in this work, we shall get the measure
of him here.

Of all the Nations in the world at present we English are the
stupidest in speech, the wisest in action. As good as a 'dumb'
Nation, I say, who cannot speak, and have never yet spoken, —
spite of the Shakspeares and Miltons who shew us what possibilities there are! — O Mr. Bull, I look in that surly face of thine
with a mixture of pity and laughter, yet also with wonder and
veneration. Thou complainest not, my illustrious friend; and yet
I believe the heart of thee is full of sorrow, of unspoken sadness,
seriousness, — profound melancholy (as some have said) the

[5] James Brindley, illiterate mid-eighteenth-century builder of canals and
aqueducts.

basis of thy being. Unconsciously, for thou speakest of nothing, this great Universe is great to thee. Not by levity of floating, but by stubborn force of swimming, shalt thou make thy way. The Fates sing of thee that thou shalt many times be thought an ass and a dull ox, and shalt with a god-like indifference believe it. My friend, — and it is all untrue, nothing ever falser in point of fact! Thou art of those great ones whose greatness the small passer-by does not discern. Thy very stupidity is wiser than their wisdom. A grand *vis inertiæ*[6] is in thee; how many grand qualities unknown to small men! Nature alone knows thee, acknowledges the bulk and strength of thee: thy Epic, unsung in words, is written in huge characters on the face of this Planet, — sea-moles, cotton-trades, railways, fleets and cities, Indian Empires, Americas, New-Hollands;[7] legible throughout the Solar System!

But the dumb Russians too, as I said, they, drilling all wild Asia and wild Europe into military rank and file, a terrible yet hitherto a prospering enterprise, are still dumber. The old Romans also could not *speak,* for many centuries: — not till the world was theirs; and so many speaking Greekdoms, their logic-arrows all spent, had been absorbed and abolished. The logic-arrows, how they glanced futile from obdurate thick-skinned Facts; Facts to be wrestled down only by the real vigour of Roman thews! — As for me, I honour, in these loud-babbling days, all the Silent rather. A grand Silence that of Romans; — nay the grandest of all, is it not that of the gods! Even Triviality, Imbecility, that can sit silent, how respectable is it in comparison! The 'talent of silence' is our fundamental one. Great honour to him whose Epic is a melodious hexameter Iliad; not a jingling Sham-Iliad, nothing true in it but the hexameters and forms merely. But still greater honour, if his Epic be a mighty Empire slowly built together, a mighty Series of Heroic Deeds, — a mighty Conquest over Chaos; *which* Epic the 'Eternal Melodies' have, and must have, informed and dwelt in, as *it* sung itself! There is no mistaking that latter Epic. Deeds are greater than Words. Deeds have such a life, mute but undeniable, and grow as living trees and fruit-trees do; they people the vacuity of Time, and make it green and worthy. Why should the oak prove logically that it ought to grow, and will grow? Plant it, try it; what gifts of diligent judicious assimilation and secretion it has,

---

[6] Inert strength.
[7] Australias.

of progress and resistance, of *force* to grow, will then declare themselves. My much-honoured, illustrious, extremely inarticulate Mr. Bull! —

Ask Bull his spoken opinion of any matter, — oftentimes the force of dulness can no farther go. You stand silent, incredulous, as over a platitude that borders on the Infinite. The man's Churchisms, Dissenterisms, Puseyisms, Benthamisms, College Philosophies, Fashionable Literatures, are unexampled in this world. Fate's prophecy is fulfilled; you call the man an ox and an ass. But set him once to work, — respectable man! His spoken sense is next to nothing, nine-tenths of it palpable *non*sense: but his unspoken sense, his inner silent feeling of what is true, what does agree with fact, what is doable and what is not doable, — this seeks its fellow in the world. A terrible worker; irresistible against marshes, mountains, impediments, disorder, in civilisation; everywhere vanquishing disorder, leaving it behind him as method and order. He 'retires to his bed three days,' and considers!

Nay withal, stupid as he is, our dear John, — ever, after infinite tumblings, and spoken platitudes innumerable from barrel-heads and parliament-benches, he does settle down somewhere about the just conclusion; you are certain that his jumblings and tumblings will end, after years or centuries, in the stable equilibrium. Stable equilibrium, I say; centre-of-gravity lowest; — not the unstable, with centre-of-gravity highest, as I have known it done by quicker people! For indeed, do but jumble and tumble sufficiently, you avoid that worst fault, of settling with your centre-of-gravity highest; your centre-of-gravity is certain to come lowest, and to stay there. If slowness, what we in our impatience call 'stupidity,' be the price of stable equilibrium over unstable, shall we grudge a little slowness? Not the least admirable quality of Bull is, after all, that of remaining insensible to logic; holding out for considerable periods, ten years or more, as in this of the Corn-Laws, after all arguments and shadow of arguments have faded away from him, till the very urchins on the street titter at the arguments he brings. Logic, — Λογικὴ, the 'Art of Speech,' — does indeed speak so and so; clear enough: nevertheless Bull still shakes his head; will see whether nothing else *illogical,* not yet 'spoken,' not yet able to be 'spoken,' do not lie in the business, as there so often does! — My firm belief is, that, finding himself now enchanted, hand-shackled, foot-shackled, in Poor-Law Bastilles and elsewhere, he will retire three days to his bed, and *arrive* at a conclusion or two! His three-years 'total stagnation of trade,' alas, is not that a painful enough 'lying in bed to consider himself?' Poor Bull!

Bull is a born Conservative; for this too I inexpressibly honour him. All great Peoples are conservative; slow to believe in novelties; patient of much error in actualities; deeply and forever certain of the greatness that is in LAW, in Custom once solemnly-established, and now long recognised as just and final. — True, O Radical Reformer, there is no Custom that can, properly speaking, be final; none. And yet thou seest *Customs* which, in all civilised countries, are accounted final; nay, under the Old-Roman name of *Mores,* are accounted *Morality,* Virtue, Laws of God Himself. Such, I assure thee, not a few of them are; such almost all of them once were. And greatly do I respect the solid character, — a blockhead, thou wilt say; yes, but a well-conditioned blockhead, and the best-conditioned, — who esteems all 'Customs once solemnly acknowledged' to be ultimate, divine, and the rule for a man to walk by, nothing doubting, not inquiring farther. What a time of it had we, were all men's life and trade still, in all parts of it, a problem, a hypothetic seeking, to be settled by painful Logics and Baconian Inductions! The Clerk in Eastcheap[8] cannot spend the day in verifying his Ready-Reckoner;[9] he must take it as verified, true and indisputable; or his Book-keeping by Double Entry will stand still. "Where is your Posted Ledger?" asks the Master at night. — "Sir," answers the other, "I was verifying my Ready-Reckoner, and find some errors. The Ledger is — !" — Fancy such a thing!

True, all turns on your Ready-Reckoner being moderately correct, — being *not* insupportably incorrect! A Ready-Reckoner which has led to distinct entries in your Ledger such as these: '*Creditor* an English People by fifteen hundred years of good Labour; and *Debtor* to lodging in enchanted Poor-Law Bastilles: *Creditor* by conquering the largest Empire the Sun ever saw; and *Debtor* to Donothingism and "Impossible" written on all departments of the government thereof: *Creditor* by mountains of gold ingots earned; and *Debtor* to No Bread purchasable by them:' — *such* Ready-Reckoner, methinks, is beginning to be suspect; nay is ceasing, and has ceased, to be suspect! Such Ready-Reckoner is a Solecism in Eastcheap; and must, what-

---

[8] A street in London's financial district.
[9] Mathematical tables for commercial use.

ever be the press of business, and will and shall be rectified a little. Business can go on no longer with *it*. The most Conservative English People, thickest-skinned, most patient of Peoples, is driven alike by its Logic and its Unlogic, by things 'spoken,' and by things not yet spoken or very speakable, but only felt and very unendurable, to be wholly a Reforming People. Their Life as it is has ceased to be longer possible for them.

Urge not this noble silent People; rouse not the Berserkir-rage[10] that lies in them! Do you know their Cromwells, Hampdens, their Pyms and Bradshaws?[11] Men very peaceable, but men that can be made very terrible! Men who, like their old Teutsch Fathers in Agrippa's days,[12] 'have a soul that despises death;' to whom 'death,' compared with falsehoods and injustices, is light; — 'in whom there is a range unconquerable by the immortal gods!' Before this, the English People have taken very preternatural-looking Spectres by the beard; saying virtually: "And if thou *wert* 'preternatural?' Thou with thy 'divine-rights' grown diabolic wrongs? Thou, — not even 'natural;' decapitable; totally extinguishable!" — — Yes, just so godlike as this People's patience was, even so godlike will and must its impatience be. Away, ye scandalous Practical Solecisms, children actually of the Prince of Darkness; ye have near broken our hearts; we can and will endure you no longer. Begone, we say; depart, while the play is good! By the Most High God, whose sons and born missionaries true men are, ye shall not continue here! You and we have become incompatible; can inhabit one house no longer. Either you must go, or we. Are ye ambitious to try *which* it shall be?

O my Conservative friends, who still specially name and struggle to approve yourselves 'Conservative,' would to Heaven I could persuade you of this world-old fact, than which Fate is not surer, That Truth and Justice alone are *capable* of being 'conserved' and preserved! The thing which is unjust, which is *not* according to God's Law, will you, in a God's Universe, try to conserve that? It is so old, say you? Yes, and the hotter haste ought *you*, of all others, to be in to let it grow no older! If but the faintest whisper in your hearts intimate to you that it is

[10] A Norse warrior given to frenzy, and thereby rendered invulnerable, in battle.

[11] Like Cromwell and Hampden, leaders of the seventeenth-century English revolution.

[12] Marcus Vipsanius Agrippa campaigned against the Germans in 38 B.C.

not fair, — hasten, for the sake of Conservatism itself, to probe it rigorously, to cast it forth at once and forever if guilty. How will or can you preserve *it*, the thing that is not fair? 'Impossibility' a thousandfold is marked on that. And ye call yourselves Conservatives, Aristocracies: — ought not honour and nobleness of mind, if they had departed from all the Earth elsewhere, to find their last refuge with you? Ye unfortunate!

The bough that is dead shall be cut away, for the sake of the tree itself. Old? Yes, it is too old. Many a weary winter has it swung and creaked there, and gnawed and fretted, with its dead wood, the organic substance and still living fibre of this good tree; many a long summer has its ugly naked brown defaced the fair green umbrage; every day it has done mischief, and that only: off with it, for the tree's sake, if for nothing more; let the Conservatism that would preserve cut *it* away. Did no wood-forester apprise you that a dead bough with its dead root left sticking there is extraneous, poisonous; is as a dead iron spike, some horrid rusty ploughshare driven into the living substance; — nay is far worse; for in every windstorm ('commercial crisis' or the like), it frets and creaks, jolts itself to and fro, and cannot lie quiet as your dead iron spike would!

If I were the Conservative Party of England (which is another bold figure of speech), I would not for a hundred thousand pounds an hour allow those Corn-Laws to continue! Potosi and Golconda[13] put together would not purchase my assent to them. Do you count what treasuries of bitter indignation they are laying up for you in every just English heart? Do you know what questions, not as to Corn-prices and Sliding-scales alone, they are *forcing* every reflective Englishman to ask himself? Questions insoluble, or hitherto unsolved; deeper than any of our Logic-plummets hitherto will sound: questions deep enough, — which it were better that we did not name even in thought! You are forcing us to think of them, to begin uttering them. The utterance of them is begun; and where will it be ended, think you? When two millions of one's brother-men sit in Workhouses, and five millions, as is insolently said, 'rejoice in potatoes,'[14] there are various things that must be begun, let them end where they can.

[13] Ruined city in India famous for its diamonds.
[14] Potatoes were the standard diet of the Irish masses. Failure of the potato crop later in the decade led to national catastrophe.

CHAPTER VI

TWO CENTURIES

THE Settlement effected by our 'Healing Parliament'[1] in the Year of Grace 1660, though accomplished under universal acclamations from the four corners of the British Dominions, turns out to have been one of the mournfulest that ever took place in this land of ours. It called and thought itself a Settlement of brightest hope and fulfilment, bright as the blaze of universal tar-barrels and bonfires could make it: and we find it now, on looking back on it with the insight which trial has yielded, a Settlement as of despair. Considered well, it was a settlement to govern henceforth without God, with only some decent Pretence of God.

Governing by the Christian Law of God had been found a thing of battle, convulsion, confusion, an infinitely difficult thing: wherefore let us now abandon it, and govern only by so much of God's Christian Law as — as may prove quiet and convenient for us. What is the end of Government? To guide men in the way wherein they should go; towards their true good in this life, the portal of infinite good in a life to come? To guide men in such way, and ourselves in such way, as the Maker of men, whose eye is upon us, will sanction at the Great Day? — Or alas, perhaps at bottom *is* there no Great Day, no sure outlook of any life to come; but only this poor life, and what of taxes, felicities, Nell-Gwyns[2] and entertainments, we can manage to muster here? In that case, the end of Government will be, To suppress all noise and disturbance, whether of Puritan preaching, Cameronian[3] psalm-singing, thieves'-riot, murder, arson, or what noise soever, and — be careful that supplies do not fail! A very notable con-

[1] It was hoped that the Parliament which witnessed the restoration of the monarchy would witness also the healing of the nation's wounds caused by the long political and religious strife.

[2] Nell Gwyn was the most famous of Charles II's mistresses.

[3] A fanatical seventeenth-century sect who separated from the Church of Scotland.

clusion, if we will think of it; and not without an abundance of fruits for us. Oliver Cromwell's body hung on the Tyburn-gallows, as the type of Puritanism found futile, inexecutable, execrable, — yes, that gallows-tree has been a fingerpost into very strange country indeed. Let earnest Puritanism die; let decent Formalism,[4] whatsoever cant it be or grow to, live! We have had a pleasant journey in that direction; and are — arriving at our inn?

To support the Four Pleas of the Crown,[5] and keep Taxes coming in: in very sad seriousness, has not this been, ever since, even in the best times, almost the one admitted end and aim of Government? Religion, Christian Church, Moral Duty; the fact that man had a soul at all; that in man's life there was any eternal truth or justice at all, — has been as good as left quietly out of sight. Church indeed, — alas, the endless talk and struggle we have had of High-Church, Low-Church,[6] Church-Extension, Church-in-Danger:[7] we invite the Christian reader to think whether it has not been a too miserable screech-owl phantasm of talk and struggle, as for a 'Church,' — which one had rather not define at present!

But now in these godless two centuries, looking at England and her efforts and doings, if we ask, What of England's doings the Law of Nature had accepted, Nature's King had actually fur-thered and pronounced to have truth in them, — where is our answer? Neither the 'Church' of Hurd and Warburton,[8] nor the Anti-church of Hume and Paine;[9] not in any shape the Spiritual-ism of England: all this is already seen, or beginning to be seen, for what it is; a thing that Nature does *not* own. On the one side is dreary Cant, with a *reminiscence* of things noble and divine; on the other is but acrid Candour, with a *prophecy* of things

[4] The emphasis on ritual characteristic of the Anglican Church, as con-trasted with Puritan emphasis on the spirit.

[5] I.e., to support the administration of justice; the term embraces all criminal, as opposed to civil, proceedings.

[6] The two portions of the Church of England; the former, especially influenced by the Oxford Movement, laid more stress than did the latter on the saving grace of the sacraments, the liturgy, and the authority of bishops and priests.

[7] Alarm over steps, proposed and accomplished, to reduce the power of the Anglican Church, e.g., by the abolition of certain Irish bishoprics.

[8] Two notably orthodox eighteenth-century Anglican bishops.

[9] David Hume, Scottish rationalist philosopher, and Thomas Paine, atheist, symbolized the anti-Christian tendencies of the eighteenth century.

brutal, infernal. Hurd and Warburton are sunk into the sere and yellow leaf;[10] no considerable body of true-seeing men looks thitherward for healing: the Paine-and-Hume Atheistic theory, of 'things well let alone,' with Liberty, Equality and the like, is also in these days declaring itself naught, unable to keep the world from taking fire.

The theories and speculations of both these parties, and, we may say, of all intermediate parties and persons, prove to be things which the Eternal Veracity did not accept; things superficial, ephemeral, which already a near Posterity, finding them already dead and brown-leafed, is about to suppress and forget. The Spiritualism of England, for those godless years, is, as it were, all forgettable. Much has been written: but the perennial Scriptures of Mankind have had small accession: from all English Books, in rhyme or prose, in leather binding or in paper wrappage, how many verses have been added to these? Our most melodious Singers have sung as from the throat outwards: from the inner Heart of Man, from the great Heart of Nature, through no Pope or Philips,[11] has there come any tone. The Oracles have been dumb.[12] In brief, the Spoken Word of England has not been true. The Spoken Word of England turns out to have been trivial; of short endurance; not valuable, not available as a Word, except for the passing day. It has been accordant with transitory Semblance; discordant with eternal Fact. It has been unfortunately not a Word, but a Cant; a helpless involuntary Cant, nay too often a cunning voluntary one: either way, a very mournful Cant; the Voice not of Nature and Fact, but of something other than these.

With all its miserable shortcomings, with its wars, controversies, with its trades-unions, famine-insurrections, — it is her Practical Material Work alone that England has to shew for herself! This, and hitherto almost nothing more; yet actually this. The grim inarticulate veracity of the English People, unable to speak its meaning in words, has turned itself silently on things; and the dark powers of Material Nature have answered: Yes, this at least is true, this is not false! So answers Nature. Waste

---

[10] *Macbeth*, V.iii.23.

[11] The gamut of quality in early eighteenth-century English poetry: Alexander Pope at the top, his rival and victim Ambrose ("Namby-Pamby") Philips at the bottom.

[12] Milton, "On the Morning of Christ's Nativity," line 173.

desert-shrubs of the Tropical swamps have become Cotton-trees; and here, under my furtherance, are verily woven shirts, — hanging unsold, undistributed, but capable to be distributed, capable to cover the bare backs of my children of men. Mountains, old as the Creation, I have permitted to be bored through: bituminous fuel-stores, the wreck of forests that were green a million years ago, — I have opened them from my secret rock-chambers, and they are yours, ye English. Your huge fleets, steamships, do sail the sea: huge Indias do obey you; from huge *New* Englands and Antipodal Australias, comes profit and traffic to this Old England of mine! So answers Nature. The Practical Labour of England is *not* a chimerical Triviality: it is a Fact, acknowledged by all the Worlds; which no man and no demon will contradict. It is, very audibly, though very inarticulately as yet, the one God's Voice we have heard in these two atheistic centuries.

And now to observe with what bewildering obscurations and impediments all this as yet stands entangled, and is yet intelligible to no man! How, with our gross Atheism, we hear it not to be the Voice of God to us, but regard it merely as a Voice of earthly Profit-and-Loss. And have a Hell in England, — the Hell of not making money. And coldly see the all-conquering valiant Sons of Toil sit enchanted, by the million, in their Poor-Law Bastille, as if this were Nature's Law; — mumbling to ourselves some vague janglement of Laissez-faire, Supply-and-demand, Cash-payment the one nexus of man to man: Free-trade, Competition, and Devil take the hindmost, our latest Gospel yet preached!

As if, in truth, there were no God of Labour; as if godlike Labour and brutal Mammonism were convertible terms. A serious, most earnest Mammonism grown Midas-eared; an unserious Dilettantism, earnest about nothing, grinning with inarticulate incredulous incredible jargon about all things, as the *enchanted* Dilettanti do by the Dead Sea! It is mournful enough, for the present hour; were there not an endless hope in it withal. Giant LABOUR, truest emblem there is of God the World-Worker, Demiurgus, and Eternal Maker; noble LABOUR, which is yet to be the King of this Earth, and sit on the highest throne, — staggering hitherto like a blind irrational giant, hardly allowed to have his common place on the street-pavements; idle Dilettantism, Dead-Sea Apism, crying out, "Down with him, he is dangerous!"

Labour must become a seeing rational giant, with a *soul* in the body of him, and take his place on the throne of things, — leaving his Mammonism, and several other adjuncts, on the lower steps of said throne.

CHAPTER VII

BUT what will reflective readers say of a Governing Class, such as ours, addressing its Workers with an indictment of 'Over-production!' Over-production: runs it not so? "Ye miscellaneous, ignoble manufacturing individuals, ye have produced too much! We accuse you of making above two-hundred thousand shirts for the bare backs of mankind. Your trousers too, which you have made, of fustian, of cassimere, of Scotch-plaid, of jane, nankeen and woollen broadcloth, are they not manifold? Of hats for the human head, of shoes for the human foot, of stools to sit on, spoons to eat with — Nay, what say we hats or shoes? You produce gold-watches, jewelleries, silver-forks and epergnes, commodes, chiffoniers, stuffed sofas — Heavens, the Commercial Bazaar[1] and multitudinous Howel-and-Jameses cannot contain you. You have produced, produced; — he that seeks your indictment, let him look around.[2] Millions of shirts, and empty pairs of breeches, hang there in judgment against you. We accuse you of over-producing: you are criminally guilty of producing shirts, breeches, hats, shoes and commodities, in a frightful over-abundance. And now there is a glut, and your operatives cannot be fed!"

Never surely, against an earnest Working Mammonism was there brought, by Game-preserving aristocratic Dilettantism, a stranger accusation, since this world began. My lords and gentlemen, — why, it was *you* that were appointed, by the fact and by the theory of your position on the Earth, to 'make and administer Laws,' — that is to say, in a world such as ours, to guard against 'gluts;' against honest operatives, who had done their work, remaining unfed! I say, *you* were appointed to preside over the Distribution and Apportionment of the Wages of Work done; and to see well that there went no labourer without his hire, were

---

[1] A store in contemporary London.
[2] An adaptation of the epitaph of Sir Christopher Wren in St. Paul's Cathedral, which he designed: "Si monumentum requiris, circumspice."

it of money-coins, were it of hemp gallows-ropes: that function was yours, and from immemorial time has been; yours, and as yet no other's. These poor shirt-spinners have forgotten much, which by the virtual unwritten law of their position they should have remembered: but by any written recognised law of their position, what have they forgotten? They were set to make shirts. The Community with all its voices commanded them, saying, "Make shirts;" — and there the shirts are! Too many shirts? Well, that is a novelty, in this intemperate Earth, with its nine-hundred millions of bare backs! But the Community commanded you, saying, "See that the shirts are well apportioned, that our Human Laws be emblem of God's Laws;" — and where is the apportionment? Two million shirtless or ill-shirted workers sit enchanted in Workhouse Bastilles, five million more (according to some) in Ugolino Hunger-cellars; and for remedy, you say, — what say you? — "Raise *our* rents!" I have not in my time heard any stranger speech, not even on the Shores of the Dead Sea. You continue addressing those poor shirt-spinners and over-producers, in really a *too* triumphant manner:

"Will you bandy accusations, will you accuse *us* of over-production? We take the Heavens and the Earth to witness that we have produced nothing at all. Not from us proceeds this frightful overplus of shirts. In the wide domains of created Nature, circulates no shirt or thing of our producing. Certain fox-brushes nailed upon our stable-door, the fruit of fair audacity at Melton Mowbray;[3] these we have produced, and they are openly nailed up there. He that accuses us of producing, let him shew himself, let him name what and when. We are innocent of producing; — ye ungrateful, what mountains of things have we not, on the contrary, had to 'consume,' and make away with! Mountains of those your heaped manufactures, wheresoever edible or wearable, have they not disappeared before us, as if we had the talent of ostriches, of cormorants, and a kind of divine faculty to eat? Ye ungrateful! — and did you not grow under the shadow of our wings? Are not your filthy mills built on these fields of ours; on this soil of England, which belongs to — whom think you? And we shall not offer you our own wheat at the price that pleases us, but that partly pleases you? A precious notion! What would become of you, if we chose, at any time, to decide on growing no wheat more?"

[3] A Leicestershire market town, headquarters of several famous hunts.

Yes, truly, *here* is the ultimate rock-basis of all Corn-Laws; whereon, at the bottom of much arguing, they rest, as securely as they can: What would become of you, if we decided, some day, on growing no more wheat at all? If we chose to grow only partridges henceforth, and a modicum of wheat for our own uses? Cannot we do what we like with our own? — Yes, indeed! For my share, if I could melt Gneiss Rock,[4] and create Law of Gravitation; if I could stride out to the Doggerbank,[5] some morning, and striking down my trident there into the mudwaves, say, "Be land, be fields, meadows, mountains and fresh-rolling streams!" by Heaven, I should incline to have the letting of *that* land in perpetuity, and sell the wheat of it, or burn the wheat of it, according to my own good judgment! My Corn-Lawing friends, you affright me.

To the 'Millo-cracy' so-called, to the Working Aristocracy, steeped too deep in mere ignoble Mammonism, and as yet all unconscious of its noble destinies, as yet but an irrational or semirational giant, struggling to awake some soul in itself, — the world will have much to say, reproachfully, reprovingly, admonishingly. But to the Idle Aristocracy, what will the world have to say? Things painful and not pleasant!

To the man who *works*, who attempts, in never so ungracious barbarous a way, to get forward with some work, you will hasten out with furtherances, with encouragements, corrections; you will say to him: "Welcome, thou art ours; our care shall be of thee." To the idler, again, never so gracefully going idle, coming forward with never so many parchments, you will not hasten out; you will sit still, and be disinclined to rise. You will say to him: "Not welcome, O complex Anomaly; would thou hadst staid out of doors: for who of mortals knows what to do with thee? Thy parchments: yes, they are old, of venerable yellowness; and we too honour parchment, old-established settlements, and venerable use and wont. Old parchments in very truth: — yet on the whole, if thou wilt remark, they are young to the Granite Rocks, to the Groundplan of God's Universe! We advise thee to put up thy parchments; to go home to thy place, and make no needless noise whatever. Our heart's wish is to save thee: yet there as thou art, hapless Anomaly, with nothing but thy yellow parchments,

---

[4] Slaty granite.
[5] A rich fishing ground in the North Sea.

noisy futilities, and shotbelts[6] and fox-brushes, who of gods or men can avert dark Fate? Be counselled, ascertain if no work exist for thee on God's Earth; if thou find no commanded-duty there but that of going gracefully idle? Ask, inquire earnestly, with a half-frantic earnestness; for the answer means Existence or Annihilation to thee. We apprise thee of the world-old fact, becoming sternly disclosed again in these days, That he who cannot work in this Universe cannot get existed in it: had he parchments to thatch the face of the world, these, combustible fallible sheepskin, cannot avail him. Home, thou unfortunate; and let us have at least no noise from thee!"

Suppose the unfortunate Idle Aristocracy, as the unfortunate Working one has done, were to 'retire three days to *its* bed,' and consider itself there, what o'clock it had become? —

How have we to regret not only that men have 'no religion,' but that they have next to no reflection; and go about with heads full of mere extraneous noises, with eyes wide-open but visionless, — for most part, in the somnambulist state!

[6] Ammunition belts.

CHAPTER VIII

I T is well said, 'Land is the right basis of an Aristocracy;' who- ever possesses the Land, he, more emphatically than any other, is the Governor, Viceking of the people on the Land. It is in these days as it was in those of Henry Plantagenet and Abbot Samson; as it will in all days be. The Land is *Mother* of us all; nourishes, shelters, gladdens, lovingly enriches us all; in how many ways, from our first wakening to our last sleep on her blessed mother-bosom, does she, as with blessed mother-arms, enfold us all!

The Hill I first saw the Sun rise over, when the Sun and I and all things were yet in their auroral hour, who can divorce me from it? Mystic, deep as the world's centre, are the roots I have struck into my Native Soil; no *tree* that grows is rooted so. From noblest Patriotism to humblest industrial Mechanism; from high- est dying for your country, to lowest quarrying and coal-boring for it, a Nation's Life depends upon its Land. Again and again we have to say, there can be no true Aristocracy but must possess the Land.

Men talk of 'selling' Land. Land, it is true, like Epic Poems and even higher things, in such a trading world, has to be pre- sented in the market for what it will bring, and as we say be 'sold:' but the notion of 'selling,' for certain bits of metal, the *Iliad* of Homer, how much more the *Land* of the World-Creator, is a ridiculous impossibility! We buy what is saleable of it; noth- ing more was ever buyable. Who can, or could, sell it to us? Properly speaking, the Land belongs to these two: To the Al- mighty God; and to all His Children of Men that have ever worked well on it, or that shall ever work well on it. No genera- tion of men can or could, with never such solemnity and effort, sell Land on any other principle: it is not the property of any generation, we say, but that of all the past generations that have worked on it, and of all the future ones that shall work on it.

Again, we hear it said, The soil of England, or of any country, is properly worth nothing, except 'the labour bestowed on it.' This, speaking even in the language of Eastcheap, is not correct. The rudest space of country equal in extent to England, could a whole English Nation, with all their habitudes, arrangements, skills, with whatsoever they do carry within the skins of them, and cannot be stript of, suddenly take wing, and alight on it, — would be worth a very considerable thing! Swiftly, within year and day, this English Nation, with its multiplex talents of ploughing, spinning, hammering, mining, road-making and trafficking, would bring a handsome value out of such a space of country. On the other hand, fancy what an English Nation, once 'on the wing,' could have done with itself, had there been simply no soil, not even an inarable one, to alight on? Vain all its talents for ploughing, hammering, and whatever else; there is no Earth-room for this Nation with its talents: this Nation will have to *keep* hovering on the wing, dolefully shrieking to and fro; and perish piecemeal; burying itself, down to the last soul of it, in the waste unfirmamented seas. Ah yes, soil, with or without ploughing, is the gift of God. The soil of all countries belongs evermore, in a very considerable degree, to the Almighty Maker! The last stroke of labour bestowed on it is not the making of its value, but only the increasing thereof.

It is very strange, the degree to which these truisms are forgotten in our days; how, in the ever-whirling chaos of Formulas, we have quietly lost sight of Fact, — which it is so perilous not to keep forever in sight! Fact, if we do not see it, will make us *feel* it by and by! — From much loud controversy and Corn-Law debating there rises, loud though inarticulate, once more in these years, this very question among others, Who made the Land of England? Who made it, this respectable English Land, wheat-growing, metalliferous, carboniferous, which will let readily hand over head for seventy millions or upwards, as it here lies: who did make it? — "We!" answer the much-*consuming* Aristocracy; "We!" as they ride in, moist with the sweat of Melton Mowbray: "It is we that made it; or are the heirs, assigns and representatives of those who did!" — My brothers, You? Everlasting honour to you, then; and Corn-Laws as many as you will, till your own deep stomachs cry Enough, or some voice of human pity for our famine bids you Hold![1] Ye are as gods, that can create soil. Soil-creating gods there is no withstanding. They have the might to sell wheat

[1] An echo of *Macbeth*, V.viii.34.

at what price they list; and the right, to all lengths, and famine-lengths, — if they be pitiless infernal gods! Celestial gods, I think, would stop short of the famine-price; but no infernal nor any kind of god can be bidden stop! — — Infatuated mortals, into what questions are you driving every thinking man in England?

I say, you did *not* make the Land of England; and, by the possession of it, you *are* bound to furnish guidance and governance to England! That is the law of your position on this God's-Earth; an everlasting act of Heaven's Parliament, not repealable in St. Stephen's[2] or elsewhere! True government and guidance; not no-government and Laissez-faire; how much less, *mis*government and Corn-Law! There is not an imprisoned Worker looking out from these Bastilles but appeals, very audibly in Heaven's High Courts, against you, and me, and every one who is not imprisoned, "Why am I here?" His appeal is audible in Heaven; and will become audible enough on Earth too, if it remain unheeded here. His appeal is against you, foremost of all; you stand in the front-rank of the accused; you, by the very place you hold, have first of all to answer him and Heaven!

What looks maddest, miserablest in these mad and miserable Corn-Laws is independent altogether of their 'effect on wages,' their effect on 'increase of trade,' or any other such effect: it is the continual maddening proof they protrude into the faces of all men, that our Governing Class, called by God and Nature and the inflexible law of Fact, either to do something towards governing, or to die and be abolished, — have not yet learned even to sit still, and do no mischief! For no Anti-Corn-Law League yet asks more of them than this; — Nature and Fact, very imperatively, asking so much more of them. Anti-Corn-Law League asks not, Do something; but, Cease your destructive misdoing, Do ye nothing!

Nature's message will have itself obeyed: messages of mere Free-Trade, Anti-Corn-Law League and Laissez-faire, will then need small obeying! — Ye fools, in name of Heaven, work, work, at the Ark of Deliverance[3] for yourselves and us, while hours are

[2] Until it burned in 1834, St. Stephen's Chapel, Westminster, was the seat of the House of Commons. The name continued to be applied to Commons.

[3] Exodus 36–38.

still granted you! No: instead of working at the Ark, they say, "We cannot get our hands kept rightly warm;" and *sit obstinately burning the planks.* No madder spectacle at present exhibits itself under this Sun.

The Working Aristocracy; Mill-owners, Manufacturers, Commanders of Working Men: alas, against them also much shall be brought in accusation; much, — and the freest Trade in Corn, total abolition of Tariffs, and uttermost 'Increase of Manufactures' and 'Prosperity of Commerce,' will permanently mend no jot of it. The Working Aristocracy must strike into a new path; must understand that money alone is *not* the representative either of man's success in the world, or of man's duties to man; and reform their own selves from top to bottom, if they wish England reformed. England will not be habitable long, unreformed.

The Working Aristocracy — Yes, but on the threshold of all this, it is again and again to be asked, What of the Idle Aristocracy? Again and again, what shall we say of the Idle Aristocracy, the Owners of the Soil of England; whose recognised function is that of handsomely consuming the rents of England, shooting the partridges of England, and as an agreeable amusement (if the purchase-money and other conveniences serve), dilettante-ing in Parliament and Quarter-Sessions[4] for England? We will say mournfully, in the presence of Heaven and Earth, — that we stand speechless, stupent, and know not what to say! That a class of men entitled to live sumptuously on the marrow of the earth; permitted simply, nay entreated, and as yet entreated in vain, to do nothing at all in return, was never heretofore seen on the face of this Planet. That such a class is transitory, exceptional, and, unless Nature's Laws fall dead, cannot continue. That it has continued now a moderate while; has, for the last fifty years, been rapidly attaining its state of perfection. That it will have to find its duties and do them; or else that it must and will cease to be seen on the face of this Planet, which is a Working one, not an Idle one.

Alas, alas, the Working Aristocracy, admonished by Trades-unions, Chartist conflagrations, above all by their own shrewd sense kept in perpetual communion with the fact of things, will assuredly reform themselves, and a working world will still be possible: — but the fate of the Idle Aristocracy, as one reads its

[4] General courts held four times a year in every English county.

horoscope hitherto in Corn-Laws and such like, is an abyss that fills one with despair. Yes, my rosy fox-hunting brothers, a terrible *Hippocratic look*[5] reveals itself (God knows, not to my joy) through those fresh buxom countenances of yours. Through your Corn-Law Majorities, Sliding-Scales, Protecting-Duties, Bribery-Elections and triumphant Kentish-fire,[6] a thinking eye discerns ghastly images of ruin, too ghastly for words; a handwriting as of MENE, MENE.[7] Men and brothers, on your Sliding-scale you seem sliding, and to have slid, — you little know whither! Good God! did not a French Donothing Aristocracy, hardly above half a century ago, declare in like manner, and in its featherhead believe in like manner, "We cannot exist, and continue to dress and parade ourselves, on the just rent of the soil of France; but we must have farther payment than rent of the soil, we must be exempted from taxes too," — we must have a Corn-Law to extend our rent? This was in 1789: in four years more — Did you look into the Tanneries of Meudon,[8] and the long-naked making for themselves breeches of human skins! May the merciful Heavens avert the omen; may we be wiser, that so we be less wretched.

A High Class without duties to do is like a tree planted on precipices; from the roots of which all the earth has been crumbling. Nature owns no man who is not a Martyr withal. Is there a man who pretends to live luxuriously housed up; screened from all work, from want, danger, hardship, the victory over which is what we name work; — he himself to sit serene, amid down-bolsters and appliances, and have all his work and battling done by other men? And such man calls himself a *noble*-man? His fathers worked for him, he says; or successfully gambled for him: here *he* sits; professes, not in sorrow but in pride, that he and his have done no work, time out of mind. It is the law of the land, and is thought to be the law of the Universe, that he, alone of recorded men, shall have no task laid on him, except that of eating his cooked victuals, and not flinging himself out of window. Once more I will say, there was no stranger spectacle ever shewn under this Sun. A veritable fact in our England of the Nineteenth

[5] The shrunken appearance of the face when death is imminent (named for the Greek physician who described it).

[6] *Bribery-Elections:* see below, p. 250. *Kentish-fire:* sustained, purposeful applause.

[7] Daniel 5:26.

[8] Cf. *The French Revolution,* XVIII.vii.

Century. His victuals he does eat: but as for keeping in the inside of the window, — have not his friends, like me, enough to do? Truly, looking at his Corn-Laws, Game-Laws, Chandos-Clauses,[9] Bribery-Elections and much else, you do shudder over the tumbling and plunging he makes, held back by the lappelles and coatskirts; only a thin fence of window-glass before him, — and in the street mere horrid iron spikes! My sick brother, as in hospital-maladies men do, thou dreamest of Paradises and Eldorados, which are far from thee. 'Cannot I do what I like with my own?' Gracious Heaven, my brother, this that thou seest with those sick eyes is no firm Eldorado, and Corn-Law Paradise of Donothings, but a dream of thy own fevered brain. It is a glass-window, I tell thee, so many stories from the street; where are iron spikes and the law of gravitation!

What is the meaning of nobleness, if this be 'noble?' In a valiant suffering for others, not in a slothful making others suffer for us, did nobleness ever lie. The chief of men is he who stands in the van of men; fronting the peril which frightens back all others; which, if it be not vanquished, will devour the others. Every noble crown is, and on Earth will forever be, a crown of thorns. The Pagan Hercules, why was he accounted a hero? Because he had slain Nemean Lions, cleansed Augean Stables, undergone Twelve Labours only not too heavy for a god. In modern, as in ancient and all societies, the Aristocracy, they that assume the functions of an Aristocracy, doing them or not, have taken the post of honour; which is the post of difficulty, the post of danger, — of death, if the difficulty be not overcome. *Il faut payer de sa vie.*[10] Why was our life given us, if not that we should manfully give it? Descend, O Donothing Pomp; quit thy down-cushions; expose thyself to learn what wretches feel, and how to cure it! The Czar of Russia became a dusty toiling shipwright; worked with his axe in the Docks of Saardam;[11] and his aim was small to thine. Descend thou: undertake this horrid 'living chaos of Ignorance and Hunger' weltering round thy feet; say, "I will heal it, or behold I will die foremost in it." Such is verily the law. Everywhere and everywhen a man has to '*pay*

---

[9] The Marquess of Chandos (as he then was) moved the amendment to the Reform Bill enfranchising fifty-pound tenants.

[10] "We must pay with our lives."

[11] To learn about shipbuilding, Peter the Great worked incognito in Dutch shipyards, 1697.

with his life;' to do his work, as a soldier does, at the expense of life. In no Piepowder earthly Court[12] can you sue an Aristocracy to do its work, at this moment: but in the Higher Court, which even *it* calls 'Court of Honour,' and which is the Court of Necessity withal, and the eternal Court of the Universe, in which all Fact comes to plead, and every Human Soul is an apparitor, — the Aristocracy is answerable, and even now answering, *there*.

Parchments? Parchments are venerable: but they ought at all times to represent, as near as they by possibility can, the writing of the Adamant Tablets; otherwise they are not so venerable! Benedict the Jew in vain pleaded parchments; his usuries were too many. The King said, "Go to, for all thy parchments, thou shalt pay just debt; down with thy dust, or observe this tooth-forceps!" Nature, a far juster Sovereign, has far terribler forceps. Aristocracies, actual and imaginary, reach a time when parchment pleading does not avail them. "Go to, for all thy parchments, thou shalt pay due debt!" shouts the Universe to them, in an emphatic manner. They refuse to pay, confidently pleading parchment: their best grinder-tooth, with horrible agony, goes out of their jaw. Wilt thou pay now? A second grinder, again in horrible agony, goes: a second, and a third, and if need be, all the teeth and grinders, and the life itself with them; — and *then* there is free payment, and an anatomist-subject into the bargain!

Reform Bills, Corn-Law Abrogation Bills, and then Land-Tax Bill, Property-Tax Bill,[13] and still dimmer list of *etceteras;* grinder after grinder: — my lords and gentlemen, it were better for you to arise, and begin doing your work, than sit there and plead parchments!

We write no Chapter on the Corn-Laws, in this place; the Corn-Laws are too mad to have a Chapter. There is a certain immorality, when there is not a necessity, in speaking about things finished; in chopping into small pieces the already slashed and slain. When the brains are out, why does not a Solecism die! It is at its own peril if it refuse to die; it ought to make all conceivable haste to die, and get itself buried! The trade of Anti-Corn-Law Lecturer in these days, still an indispensable, is a highly tragic one.

[12] A court held to settle disputes between hawkers at fairs.
[13] The last two were part of Peel's 1842 income tax bill.

The Corn-Laws will go, and even soon go: would we were all as sure of the Millennium as they are of going! They go swiftly in these present months; with an increase of velocity, an ever-deepening, ever-widening sweep of momentum, truly notable. It is at the Aristocracy's own damage and peril, still more than at any other's whatsoever, that the Aristocracy maintains them; — at a damage, say only, as above computed, of a 'hundred thousand pounds an hour!' The Corn-Laws keep all the air hot: fostered by their fever-warmth, much that is evil, but much also, how much that is good and indispensable, is rapidly coming to life among us!

CHAPTER IX

A POOR Working Mammonism getting itself 'strangled in the partridge-nets of an Unworking Dilettantism,' and bellowing dreadfully, and already black in the face, is surely a disastrous spectacle! But of a Midas-eared Mammonism, which indeed at bottom all pure Mammonisms are, what better can you expect? No better; — if not this, then something other equally disastrous, if not still more disastrous. Mammonisms, grown asinine, have to become human again, and rational; they have, on the whole, to cease to be Mammonisms, were it even on compulsion, and pressure of the hemp round their neck! — My friends of the Working Aristocracy, there are now a great many things which you also, in your extreme need, will have to consider.

The Continental people, it would seem, are 'exporting our machinery, beginning to spin cotton and manufacture for themselves, to cut us out of this market and then out of that!' Sad news indeed; but irremediable; — by no means the saddest news. The saddest news is, that we should find our National Existence, as I sometimes hear it said, depend on selling manufactured cotton at a farthing an ell cheaper than any other People. A most narrow stand for a great Nation to base itself on! A stand which, with all the Corn-Law Abrogations conceivable, I do not think will be capable of enduring.

My friends, suppose we quitted that stand; suppose we came honestly down from it, and said: "This is our minimum of cotton-prices. We care not, for the present, to make cotton any cheaper. Do you, if it seem so blessed to you, make cotton cheaper. Fill your lungs with cotton-fuz, your hearts with copperas-fumes, with rage and mutiny; become ye the general gnomes of Europe, slaves of the lamp!" — I admire a Nation which fancies it will die if it do not undersell all other Nations, to the end of the world. Brothers, we will cease to *under*sell them; we will be content to *equal*-sell them; to be happy selling equally with them! I do not see the use of underselling them. Cotton-cloth is already two-pence a yard or lower; and yet bare backs were never more numerous among us. Let inventive men cease to spend their existence incessantly contriving how cotton can be made cheaper; and try to invent, a little, how cotton at its present cheapness could be somewhat justlier divided among us! Let inventive men consider, Whether the Secret of this Universe, and of Man's Life there, does, after all, as we rashly fancy it, consist in making money? There is One God, just, supreme, almighty: but is Mammon the name of him? — With a Hell which means 'Failing to make money,' I do not think there is any Heaven possible that would suit one well; nor so much as an Earth that can be habitable long! In brief, all this Mammon-Gospel, of Supply-and-demand, Competition, Laissez-faire, and Devil take the hindmost, begins to be one of the shabbiest Gospels ever preached on Earth; or altogether the shabbiest. Even with Dilettante partridge-nets, and at a horrible expenditure of pain, who shall regret to see the entirely transient, and at best somewhat despicable life strangled out of it? At the best, as we say, a somewhat despicable, unvenerable thing, this same 'Laissez-faire;' and now, at the *worst*, fast growing an altogether detestable one!

"But what is to be done with our manufacturing population, with our agricultural, with our ever-increasing population?" cry many. — Aye, what? Many things can be done with them, a hundred things, and a thousand things, — had we once got a soul, and begun to try. This one thing, of doing for them by underselling all people,' and filling our own bursten pockets and appetites by the road; and turning over all care for any 'population,' or human or divine consideration except cash only, to the winds, with a "Laissez-faire" and the rest of it: this is evidently not the thing. 'Farthing cheaper per yard:' no great Nation can stand on the apex of such a pyramid; screwing itself higher and higher; balancing itself on its great-toe! Can England not subsist without being *above* all people in working? England never deliberately purposed such a thing. If England work better than all people, it shall be well. England, like an honest worker, will work as well as she can; and hope the gods may allow her to live on that basis. Laissez-faire and much else being once well dead, how many 'impossibles' will become possible! They are 'impossible,' as cotton-cloth at two-pence an ell was — till men set about making it. The inventive genius of great England will not forever sit patient with mere wheels and pinions, bobbins, straps and billy-rollers[1] whirring in the head of it. The inventive genius of England is not a Beaver's, or a Spinner's or Spider's genius: it is a *Man's* genius, I hope, with a God over him!

Supply-and-demand? One begins to be weary of such work. Leave all to egoism, to ravenous greed of money, of pleasure, of applause: — it is the Gospel of Despair! Man *is* a Patent-Digester,[2] then: only give him Free Trade, Free digesting-room; and each of us digest what he can come at, leaving the rest to Fate! My unhappy brethren of the Working Mammonism, my unhappier brethren of the Idle Dilettantism, no world was ever held together in that way for long. A world of mere Patent-Digesters will soon have nothing to digest: such world ends, and by Law of Nature must end, in 'over-population;' in howling universal famine, 'impossibility,' and suicidal madness, as of endless dog-kennels run rabid. Supply-and-demand shall do its full part, and Free Trade shall be free as air; — thou of the shotbelts, see thou forbid it not, with those paltry, *worse* than 'Mammonish' swindleries and Sliding-scales of thine, which are seen to be swindleries for all thy canting, which in times like ours are very scandalous to see! And Trade never so well freed, and all Tariffs settled or abolished, and Supply-and-demand in full operation, — let us all know that we have yet done nothing; that we have merely cleared the ground for doing.

Yes, were the Corn-Laws ended tomorrow, there is nothing yet ended; there is only room made for all manner of things beginning. The Corn-Laws gone, and Trade made free, it is as good as certain this paralysis of industry will pass away. We shall have another period of commercial enterprise, of victory and prosperity; during which, it is likely, much money will again be made, and all the people may, by the extant methods, still for a space of years, be kept alive and physically fed. The strangling band of Famine will be loosened from our necks; we shall have room again to breathe; time to bethink ourselves, to repent and consider! A precious and thrice-precious space of years; wherein to struggle as for life in reforming our foul ways; in alleviating, in-

---

[1] Mechanisms associated with textile weaving.

[2] Carlyle's ingenious adaptation of "Papin's digester" (named for the inventor, a seventeenth-century French physicist), a landmark on the way to the steam engine and forerunner of the modern pressure cooker. Carlyle of course uses "digest" in another, more usual, sense.

structing, regulating our people; seeking, as for life, that something like spiritual food be imparted them, some real governance
and guidance be provided them! It will be a priceless time. For
our new period or paroxysm of commercial prosperity will and
can, on the old methods of 'Competition and Devil take the hindmost,' prove but a paroxysm: a new paroxysm, — likely enough,
if we do not use it better, to be our *last*. In this, of itself, is no
salvation. If our Trade in twenty years, 'flourishing' as never
Trade flourished, could double itself; yet then also, by the old
Laissez-faire method, our Population is doubled: we shall then
be as we are, only twice as many of us, twice and ten times as
unmanageable!

All this dire misery, therefore; all this of our poor Workhouse
Workmen, of our Chartisms, Trades-strikes, Corn-Laws, Toryisms,
and the general downbreak of Laissez-faire in these days, — may
we not regard it as a voice from the dumb bosom of Nature, saying to us: Behold! Supply-and-demand is not the one Law of
Nature; Cash-payment is not the sole nexus of man with man, —
how far from it! Deep, far deeper than Supply-and-demand, are
Laws, Obligations sacred as Man's Life itself: these also, if you
will continue to do work, you shall now learn and obey. He that
will learn them, behold Nature is on his side, he shall yet work
and prosper with noble rewards. He that will not learn them,
Nature is against him; he shall not be able to do work in Nature's
empire, — not in hers. Perpetual mutiny, contention, hatred, isolation, execration shall wait on his footsteps, till all men discern
that the thing which he attains, however golden it look or be, is
not success, but the want of success.

Supply-and-demand, — alas! For what noble work was there
ever yet any audible 'demand' in that poor sense? The man of
Macedonia, speaking in vision to an Apostle Paul, "Come over
and help us,"[3] did not specify what rate of wages he would give!
Or was the Christian Religion itself accomplished by Prize-Essays,
Bridgewater Bequests, and a 'minimum of Four thousand five
hundred a year?'[4] No demand that I heard of was made then,
audible in any Labour-market, Manchester Chamber of Com-

[3] Acts 16:9.
[4] In 1835 the Ecclesiastical Commission, deploring the wholesale corrup-
tions that afflicted an over-rich Church of England, suggested that a bishop
could get along on £4500 a year.

merce, or other the like emporium and hiring establishment; silent
were all these from any whisper of such demand; — powerless
were all these to 'supply' it, had the demand been in thunder and
earthquake, with gold Eldorados and Mahometan Paradises for
the reward. Ah me, into what waste latitudes, in this Time-Voy-
age, have we wandered; like adventurous Sindbads; — where the
men go about as if by galvanism, with meaningless glaring eyes,
and have no soul, but only a beaver-faculty and stomach! The
haggard despair of Cotton-factory, Coal-mine operatives, Chandos Farm-labourers, in these days, is painful to behold; but not
so painful, hideous to the inner sense, as the brutish godforgetting
Profit-and-Loss Philosophy, and Life-theory, which we hear
jangled on all hands of us, in senate-houses, spouting-clubs,[5]
leading-articles, pulpits and platforms, everywhere as the Ultimate Gospel and candid Plain-English of Man's Life, from the
throats and pens and thoughts of all but all men! —

Enlightened Philosophies, like Molière Doctors, will tell you:
"Enthusiasms, Self-sacrifice, Heaven, Hell and such like: yes, all
that was true enough for old stupid times; all that used to be true:
but we have changed all that, *nous avons changé tout cela!*"[6]
Well; if the heart be got round now into the right side, and the
liver to the left; if man have no heroism in him deeper than the
wish to eat, and in his soul there dwell now no Infinite of Hope
and Awe, and no divine Silence can become imperative because
it is not Sinai Thunder,[7] and no tie will bind if it be not that of
Tyburn gallows-ropes, — then verily you have changed all that;
and for it, and for you, and for me, behold the Abyss and nameless
Annihilation is ready. So scandalous a beggarly Universe deserves
indeed nothing else; I cannot say I would save it from Annihilation. Vacuum, and the serene Blue, will be much handsomer;
easier too for all of us. I, for one, decline living as a Patent-Digester. Patent-Digester, Spinning-Mule, Mayfair Clothes-Horse:
many thanks, but your Chaosships will have the goodness to ex-
cuse me!

[5] Debating societies.
[6] Cf. *Le Médecin malgré lui*, II.vi.
[7] Exodus 19:16–19.

CHAPTER X

PLUGSON OF UNDERSHOT

ONE thing I do know: Never, on this Earth, was the relation of man to man long carried on by Cash-payment alone. If, at any time, a philosophy of Laissez-faire, Competition and Supply-and-demand, start up as the exponent of human relations, expect that it will soon end.

Such philosophies will arise: for man's philosophies are usually the 'supplement of his practice;' some ornamental Logic-varnish, some outer skin of Articulate Intelligence, with which he strives to render his dumb Instinctive Doings presentable when they are done. Such philosophies will arise; be preached as Mammon-Gospels, the ultimate Evangel of the World; be believed, with what is called belief, with much superficial bluster, and a kind of shallow satisfaction real in its way: — but they are ominous gospels! They are the sure, and even swift, forerunner of great changes. Expect that the old System of Society is done, is dying and fallen into dotage, when it begins to rave in that fashion. Most Systems that I have watched the death of, for the last three thousand years, have gone just so. The Ideal, the True and Noble that was in them having faded out, and nothing now remaining but naked Egoism, vulturous Greediness, they cannot live; they are bound and inexorably ordained by the oldest Destinies, Mothers of the Universe, to die. Curious enough: they thereupon, as I have pretty generally noticed, devise some light comfortable kind of 'wine-and-walnuts philosophy' for themselves, this of Supply-and-demand or another; and keep saying, during hours of mastication and rumination, which they call hours of meditation: "Soul, take thy ease,[1] it is all *well* that thou art a vulture-soul;" — and pangs of dissolution come upon them, oftenest before they are aware!

Cash-payment never was, or could except for a few years be, the union-bond of man to man. Cash never yet paid one man fully his deserts to another; nor could it, nor can it, now or henceforth

[1] Luke 12:19.

to the end of the world. I invite his Grace of Castle-Rackrent[2]
to reflect on this; — does he think that a Land Aristocracy when
it becomes a Land Auctioneership can have long to live? Or
that Sliding-scales will increase the vital stamina of it? The indomitable Plugson too, of the respected Firm of Plugson, Hunks
and Company, in St. Dolly Undershot,[3] is invited to reflect on
this; for to him also it will be new, perhaps even newer. Book-
keeping by double entry is admirable, and records several things
in an exact manner. But the Mother-Destinies also keep their
Tablets; in Heaven's Chancery also there goes on a recording;
and things, as my Moslem friends say, are 'written on the iron
leaf.'

Your Grace and Plugson, it is like, go to Church occasionally:
did you never in vacant moments, with perhaps a dull parson
droning to you, glance into your New Testament, and the cash-
account stated four times over, by a kind of quadruple entry, — in
the Four Gospels there? I consider that a cash-account, and
balance-statement of work done and wages paid, worth attending
to. Precisely *such,* though on a smaller scale, go on at all moments
under this Sun; and the statement and balance of them in the
Plugson Ledgers and on the Tablets of Heaven's Chancery are
discrepant exceedingly; — which ought really to teach, and to
have long since taught, an indomitable common-sense Plugson of
Undershot, much more an unattackable *un*common-sense Grace
of Rackrent, a thing or two! — In brief, we shall have to dismiss
the Cash-Gospel rigorously into its own place: we shall have to
know, on the threshold, that either there is some infinitely deeper
Gospel, subsidiary, explanatory and daily and hourly corrective,
to the Cash one; or else that the Cash one itself and all others
are fast travelling!

For all human things do require to have an Ideal in them; to
have some Soul in them, as we said, were it only to keep the Body
unputrefied. And wonderful it is to see how the Ideal or Soul,

---

[2] *Castle Rackrent* was a novel by Maria Edgeworth (1800). Rackrent
was the practice of letting tenant cottages to the highest bidder.

[3] The names are both topical and symbolic. The disturbances in the summer of 1842 were called the "Plug Plot Riots" because the strikers forced the
closing of factories by pulling the plugs of their boilers. A dolly was a
machine used for cleansing strips of textiles. An undershot wheel, the
source of power in many factories, was one worked by water passing beneath it.

place it in what ugliest Body you may, will irradiate said Body with its own nobleness; will gradually, incessantly, mould, modify, new-form or reform said ugliest Body, and make it at last beautiful, and to a certain degree divine! — O, if you could dethrone that Brute-god Mammon, and put a Spirit-god in his place! One way or other, he must and will have to be dethroned.

Fighting, for example, as I often say to myself, Fighting with steel murder-tools is surely a much uglier operation than Working, take it how you will. Yet even of Fighting, in religious Abbot Samson's days, see what a Feudalism there had grown, — a 'glorious Chivalry,' much besung down to the present day. Was not that one of the 'impossiblest' things? Under the sky is no uglier spectacle than two men with clenched teeth, and hellfire eyes, hacking one another's flesh; converting precious living bodies, and priceless living souls, into nameless masses of putrescence, useful only for turnip-manure. How did a Chivalry ever come out of that; how anything that was not hideous, scandalous, infernal? It will be a question worth considering by and by.

I remark, for the present, only two things: first, that the Fighting itself was not, as we rashly suppose it, a Fighting without cause, but more or less with cause. Man is created to fight; he is perhaps best of all definable as a born soldier; his life 'a battle and a march,' under the right General. It is forever indispensable for a man to fight: now with Necessity, with Barrenness, Scarcity, with Puddles, Bogs, tangled Forests, unkempt Cotton; — now also with the hallucinations of his poor fellow Men. Hallucinatory visions rise in the head of my poor fellow man; make him claim over me rights which are not his. All Fighting, as we noticed long ago, is the dusty conflict of strengths each thinking itself the strongest, or, in other words, the justest; — of Mights which do in the long-run, and forever will in this just Universe in the long-run, mean Rights. In conflict the perishable part of them, beaten sufficiently, flies off into dust: this process ended, appears the imperishable, the true and exact.

And now let us remark a second thing: how, in these baleful operations, a noble devout-hearted Chevalier will comfort himself, and an ignoble godless Bucanier and Chactaw[4] Indian. Victory is the aim of each. But deep in the heart of the noble man it lies forever legible, that, as an Invisible Just God made him, so will and must God's Justice and this only, were it never so

[4] More commonly "Choctaw": a tribe of the Muskhogean family.

invisible, ultimately prosper in all controversies and enterprises
and battles whatsoever. What an Influence; ever-present, — like
a Soul in the rudest Caliban[5] of a body; like a ray of Heaven,
and illuminative creative *Fiat-Lux,* in the wastest terrestrial
Chaos! Blessed divine Influence, traceable even in the horror of
Battlefields and garments rolled in blood:[6] how it ennobles even
the Battlefield; and, in place of a Chactaw Massacre, makes it a
Field of Honour! A Battlefield too is great. Considered well, it is
a kind of Quintessence of Labour; Labour distilled into its utmost
concentration; the significance of years of it compressed into an
hour. Here too thou shalt be strong, and not in muscle only, if
thou wouldst prevail. Here too thou shalt be strong of heart,
noble of soul; thou shalt dread no pain or death, thou shalt not
love ease or life; in rage, thou shalt remember mercy, justice; —
thou shalt be a Knight and not a Chactaw, if thou wouldst prevail!
It is the rule of all battles, against hallucinating fellow Men,
against unkempt Cotton, or whatsoever battles they may be which
a man in this world has to fight.

Howel Davies[7] dyes the West Indian Seas with blood, piles his
decks with plunder; approves himself the expertest Seaman, the
daringest Seafighter: but he gains no lasting victory, lasting victory is not possible for him. Not, had he fleets larger than the
combined British Navy all united with him in bucaniering. He,
once for all, cannot prosper in his duel. He strikes down his man:
yes; but his man, or his man's representative, has no notion to
lie struck down; neither, though slain ten times, will he keep
so lying; — nor has the Universe any notion to keep him so
lying! On the contrary, the Universe and he have, at all moments,
all manner of motives to start up again, and desperately fight
again. Your Napoleon is flung out, at last, to St. Helena; the
latter end of him sternly compensating the beginning. The Bucanier strikes down a man, a hundred or a million men: but what
profits it? He has one enemy never to be struck down; nay two
enemies: Mankind and the Maker of Men. On the great scale
or on the small, in fighting of men or fighting of difficulties, I will
not embark my venture with Howel Davies: it is not the Bucanier,
it is the Hero only that can gain victory, that can do more than
seem to succeed. These things will deserve meditating; for they

[5] The monster in *The Tempest.*
[6] Isaiah 9:5.
[7] Apparently Carlyle means Edward Davis, late seventeenth-century
scourge of the Spanish Main.

apply to all battle and soldiership, all struggle and effort whatsoever in this Fight of Life. It is a poor Gospel, Cash-Gospel or whatever name it have, that does not, with clear tone, uncontradictable, carrying conviction to all hearts, forever keep men in mind of these things.

Unhappily, my indomitable friend Plugson of Undershot has, in a great degree, forgotten them; — as, alas, all the world has; as, alas, our very Dukes and Soul-Overseers have, whose special trade it was to remember them! Hence these tears. — Plugson, who has indomitably spun Cotton merely to gain thousands of pounds, I have to call as yet a Bucanier and Chactaw; till there come something better, still more indomitable from him. His hundred Thousand-pound Notes, if there be nothing other, are to me but as the hundred Scalps in a Chactaw wigwam. The blind Plugson: he was a Captain of Industry, born member of the Ultimate genuine Aristocracy of this Universe, could he have known it! These thousand men that span and toiled round him, they were a regiment whom he had enlisted, man by man; to make war on a very genuine enemy: Bareness of back, and disobedient Cotton-fibre, which will not, unless forced to it, consent to cover bare backs. Here is a most genuine enemy; over whom all creatures will wish him victory. He enlisted his thousand men; said to them, "Come, brothers, let us have a dash at Cotton!" They follow with cheerful shout; they gain such a victory over Cotton as the Earth has to admire and clap hands at: but, alas, it is yet only of the Bucanier or Chactaw sort, — as good as no victory! Foolish Plugson of St. Dolly Undershot: does he hope to become illustrious by hanging up the scalps in his wigwam, the hundred thousands at his banker's, and saying, Behold my scalps? Why, Plugson, even thy own host is all in mutiny: Cotton is conquered; but the 'bare backs' — are worse covered than ever! Indomitable Plugson, thou must cease to be a Chactaw; thou and others; thou thyself, if no other!

Did William the Norman Bastard, or any of his Taillefers,[8] *Ironcutters,* manage so? Ironcutter, at the end of the campaign, did not turn off his thousand fighters, but said to them: "Noble fighters, this is the land we have gained; be I Lord in it, — what we will call *Law-ward,* maintainer and *keeper* of Heaven's *Laws:* be I *Law-ward,* or in brief orthoepy Lord in it, and be ye Loyal Men around me in it; and we will stand by one another, as soldiers

[8] Taillefer was a Norman minstrel who sang of Roland and Charlemagne as he accompanied the troops of William the Conqueror.

round a captain, for again we shall have need of one another!" Plugson, bucanier-like, says to them: "Noble spinners, this is the Hundred Thousand we have gained, wherein I mean to dwell and plant vineyards; the hundred thousand is mine, the three and sixpence daily was yours: adieu, noble spinners; drink my health with this groat each, which I give you over and above!" The entirely unjust Captain of Industry, say I; not Chevalier, but Bucanier! 'Commercial Law' does indeed acquit him; asks, with wide eyes, What else? So too Howel Davies asks, Was it not according to the strictest Bucanier Custom? Did I depart in any jot or tittle from the Laws of the Bucaniers?

After all, money, as they say, is miraculous. Plugson wanted victory; as Chevaliers and Bucaniers, and all men alike do. He found money recognised, by the whole world with one assent, as the true symbol, exact equivalent and synonym of victory; — and here we have him, a grimbrowed, indomitable Bucanier, coming home to us with a 'victory,' which the whole world is *ceasing* to clap hands at! The whole world, taught somewhat impressively, is beginning to recognise that such victory is but half a victory; and that now, if it please the Powers, we must — have the other half!

Money is miraculous. What miraculous facilities has it yielded, will it yield us; but also what never-imagined confusions, obscurations has it brought in; down almost to total extinction of the moral-sense in large masses of mankind! 'Protection of property,' of what is '*mine*,' means with most men protection of money, — the thing which, had I a thousand padlocks over it, is least of all *mine;* is, in a manner, scarcely worth calling mine! The symbol shall be held sacred, defended everywhere with tipstaves, ropes and gibbets; the thing signified shall be composedly cast to the dogs. A human being who has worked with human beings clears all scores with them, cuts himself with triumphant completeness forever loose from them, by paying down certain shillings and pounds. Was it not the wages I promised you? There\they are, to the last sixpence, — according to the Laws of the Bucaniers! — Yes, indeed; — and, at such times, it becomes imperatively necessary to ask all persons, bucaniers and others, Whether these same respectable Laws of the Bucaniers are written on God's eternal Heavens at all, on the inner Heart of Man at all; or on the respectable Bucanier Logbook merely, for the convenience of bucaniering merely? What a question; — whereat Westminster Hall shudders to its driest parchment; and on the dead wigs each particular horsehair stands on end!

The Laws of Laissez-faire, O Westminster, the laws of industrial Captain and industrial Soldier, how much more of idle Captain and industrial Soldier, will need to be remodelled, and modified, and rectified in a hundred and a hundred ways, — and *not* in the Sliding-scale direction, but in the totally opposite one! With two million industrial Soldiers already sitting in Bastilles, and five million pining on potatoes, methinks Westminster cannot begin too soon! — A man has other obligations laid on him, in God's Universe, than the payment of cash: these also Westminster, if it will continue to exist and have board-wages, must contrive to take some charge of: — by Westminster or by another, they must and will be taken charge of; be, with whatever difficulty, got articulated, got enforced, and to a certain approximate extent, put in practice. And, as I say, it cannot be too soon! For Mammonism, left to itself, has become Midas-eared; and with all its gold mountains, sits starving for want of bread: and Dilettantism with its partridge-nets, in this extremely earnest Universe of ours, is playing somewhat too high a game. 'A man by the very look of him promises so much:' yes; and by the rent-roll of him does he promise nothing? —

Alas, what a business will this be, which our Continental friends, groping this long while somewhat absurdly about it and about it, call 'Organisation of Labour;' — which must be taken out of the hands of absurd windy persons, and put into the hands of wise, laborious, modest and valiant men, to begin with it straightway: to proceed with it, and succeed in it more and more, if Europe, at any rate if England, is to continue habitable much longer. Looking at the kind of most noble Corn-Law Dukes or Practical *Duces* we have, and also of right reverend Soul-Overseers, Christian Spiritual *Duces* 'on a minimum of four thousand five hundred,' one's hopes are a little chilled. Courage, nevertheless; there are many brave men in England! My indomitable Plugson, — nay is there not even in thee some hope? Thou art hitherto a Bucanier, as it was written and prescribed for thee by an evil world: but in that grim brow, in that indomitable heart which *can* conquer Cotton, do there not perhaps lie other ten times nobler conquests?

CHAPTER XI

LABOUR[1]

FOR there is a perennial nobleness, and even sacredness, in Work. Were he never so benighted, forgetful of his high calling, there is always hope in a man that actually and earnestly works: in Idleness alone is there perpetual despair. Work, never so Mammonish, mean, *is* in communication with Nature; the real desire to get Work done will itself lead one more and more to truth, to Nature's appointments and regulations, which are truth.

The latest Gospel in this world is, Know thy work and do it. 'Know thyself:'[2] long enough has that poor 'self' of thine tormented thee; thou wilt never get to 'know' it, I believe! Think it not thy business, this of knowing thyself; thou art an unknowable individual: know what thou canst work at; and work at it, like a Hercules! That will be thy better plan.

It has been written, 'an endless significance lies in Work;'[3] a man perfects himself by working. Foul jungles are cleared away, fair seedfields rise instead, and stately cities; and withal the man himself first ceases to be a jungle and foul unwholesome desert thereby. Consider how, even in the meanest sorts of Labour, the whole soul of a man is composed into a kind of real harmony, the instant he sets himself to work! Doubt, Desire, Sorrow, Remorse, Indignation, Despair itself, all these like hell-dogs lie beleaguering the soul of the poor dayworker, as of every man: but he bends himself with free valour against his task, and all these are stilled, all these shrink murmuring far off into their caves. The man is now a man. The blessed glow of Labour in him, is it not as purifying fire, wherein all poison is burnt up, and of sour smoke itself there is made bright blessed flame!

[1] Some aspects of the rhetorical patterns of this chapter and the following one are analyzed in John Holloway, *The Victorian Sage*, pp. 44–46. The process of composition of this chapter is minutely studied, by way of the first draft and the printer's copy, in Grace J. Calder, *The Making of "Past and Present"*, pp. 126–197.

[2] Variously attributed to Solon, Socrates, Thales, etc.

[3] A commonplace in the writings of Goethe and Carlyle.

Destiny, on the whole, has no other way of cultivating us. A formless Chaos, once set it *revolving*, grows round and ever rounder; ranges itself, by mere force of gravity, into strata, spherical courses; is no longer a Chaos, but a round compacted World. What would become of the Earth, did she cease to revolve? In the poor old Earth, so long as she revolves, all inequalities, irregularities disperse themselves; all irregularities are incessantly becoming regular. Hast thou looked on the Potter's wheel, — one of the venerablest objects; old as the Prophet Ezechiel and far older?[4] Rude lumps of clay, how they spin themselves up, by mere quick whirling, into beautiful circular dishes. And fancy the most assiduous Potter, but without his wheel; reduced to make dishes, or rather amorphous botches, by mere kneading and baking! Even such a Potter were Destiny, with a human soul that would rest and lie at ease, that would not work and spin! Of an idle unrevolving man the kindest Destiny, like the most assiduous Potter without wheel, can bake and knead nothing other than a botch; let her spend on him what expensive colouring, what gilding and enamelling she will, he is but a botch. Not a dish; no, a bulging, kneaded, crooked, shambling, squint-cornered, amorphous botch, — a mere enamelled vessel of dishonour! Let the idle think of this.

Blessed is he who has found his work; let him ask no other blessedness. He has a work, a life-purpose; he has found it, and will follow it! How, as a free-flowing channel, dug and torn by noble force through the sour mud-swamp of one's existence, like an ever-deepening river there, it runs and flows; — draining off the sour festering water, gradually from the root of the remotest grass-blade; making, instead of pestilential swamp, a green fruitful meadow with its clear-flowing stream. How blessed for the meadow itself, let the stream and *its* value be great or small! Labour is Life: from the inmost heart of the Worker rises his god-given Force, the sacred celestial Life-essence breathed into him by Almighty God; from his inmost heart awakens him to all nobleness, — to all knowledge, 'self-knowledge' and much else, so soon as Work fitly begins. Knowledge? The knowledge that will hold good in working, cleave thou to that; for Nature herself accredits that, says Yea to that. Properly thou hast no other knowledge but what thou hast got by working: the rest is yet all a hypothesis of knowledge; a thing to be argued of in schools, a

4 Jeremiah 18:2–3.

thing floating in the clouds, in endless logic-vortices, till we try it and fix it. 'Doubt, of whatever kind, can be ended by Action alone.'[5]

And again, hast thou valued Patience, Courage, Perseverance, Openness to light; readiness to own thyself mistaken, to do better next time? All these, all virtues, in wrestling with the dim brute Powers of Fact, in ordering of thy fellows in such wrestle, there and elsewhere not at all, thou wilt continually learn. Set down a brave Sir Christopher[6] in the middle of black ruined Stoneheaps, of foolish unarchitectural Bishops, redtape Officials, idle Nell-Gwyn Defenders of the Faith; and see whether he will ever raise a Paul's Cathedral out of all that, yea or no! Rough, rude, contradictory are all things and persons, from the mutinous masons and Irish hodmen, up to the idle Nell-Gwyn Defenders, to blustering redtape Officials, foolish unarchitectural Bishops. All these things and persons are there not for Christopher's sake and his Cathedral's; they are there for their own sake mainly! Christopher will have to conquer and constrain all these, — if he be able. All these are against him. Equitable Nature herself, who carries her mathematics and architectonics not on the face of her, but deep in the hidden heart of her, — Nature herself is but partially for him; will be wholly against him, if he constrain her not! His very money, where is it to come from? The pious munificence of England lies far-scattered, distant, unable to speak, and say, "I am here;" — must be spoken to before it can speak. Pious munificence, and all help, is so silent, invisible like the gods; impediment, contradictions manifold are so loud and near! O brave Sir Christopher, trust thou in those, notwithstanding, and front all these; understand all these; by valiant patience, noble effort, insight, by man's-strength, vanquish and compel all these, — and, on the whole, strike down victoriously the last topstone of that Paul's Edifice; thy monument for certain centuries, the stamp 'Great Man' impressed very legibly on Portland-stone there! —

Yes, all manner of help, and pious response from Men or Nature, is always what we call silent; cannot speak or come to light, till it be seen, till it be spoken to. Every noble work is at first 'impossible.' In very truth, for every noble work the possibili-

[5] Goethe, *Wilhelm Meister's Apprenticeship*, Book VI.
[6] Sir Christopher Wren, who rebuilt St. Paul's Cathedral after the Great Fire of 1666.

ties will lie diffused through Immensity; inarticulate, undiscoverable except to faith. Like Gideon thou shalt spread out thy fleece at the door of thy tent;[7] see whether under the wide arch of Heaven there be any bounteous moisture, or none. Thy heart and life-purpose shall be as a miraculous Gideon's fleece, spread out in silent appeal to Heaven; and from the kind Immensities, what from the poor unkind Localities and town and country Parishes there never could, blessed dew-moisture to suffice thee shall have fallen!

Work is of a religious nature: — work is of a *brave* nature; which it is the aim of all religion to be. 'All work of man is as the swimmer's:' a waste ocean threatens to devour him; if he front it not bravely, it will keep its word. By incessant wise defiance of it, lusty rebuke and buffet of it, behold how it loyally supports him, bears him as its conqueror along. 'It is so,' says Goethe, 'with all things that man undertakes in this world.'[8]

Brave Sea-captain, Norse Sea-king, — Columbus, my hero, royalest Sea-king of all! it is no friendly environment this of thine, in the waste deep waters; around thee mutinous discouraged souls, behind thee disgrace and ruin, before thee the unpenetrated veil of Night. Brother, these wild water-mountains, bounding from their deep bases (ten miles deep, I am told), are not entirely there on thy behalf! Meseems *they* have other work than floating thee forward: — and the huge Winds, that sweep from Ursa Major[9] to the Tropics and Equators, dancing their giant-waltz through the kingdoms of Chaos and Immensity, they care little about filling rightly or filling wrongly the small shoulder-of-mutton sails in this cockle-skiff of thine! Thou art not among articulate-speaking friends, my brother; thou art among immeasurable dumb monsters, tumbling, howling wide as the world here. Secret, far off, invisible to all hearts but thine, there lies a help in them: see how thou wilt get at that. Patiently thou wilt wait till the mad Southwester spend itself, saving thyself by dexterous science of defence, the while; valiantly, with swift decision, wilt thou strike in, when the favouring East, the Possible, springs up. Mutiny of men thou wilt sternly repress; weakness, despondency, thou wilt cheerily encourage: thou wilt swallow down complaint, unreason, weariness, weakness of others and

[7] Judges 6:36–38.
[8] Goethe, *Wilhelm Meister's Travels*, Ch. XIV.
[9] The constellation Great Bear.

thyself; — how much wilt thou swallow down! There shall be a depth of Silence in thee, deeper than this Sea, which is but ten miles deep: a Silence unsoundable; known to God only. Thou shalt be a Great Man. Yes, my World-Soldier, thou of the World Marine-service, — thou wilt have to be *greater* than this tumultuous unmeasured World here round thee is: thou, in thy strong soul, as with wrestler's arms, shalt embrace it, harness it down; and make it bear thee on, — to new Americas, or whither God wills!

CHAPTER XII

'RELIGION,' I said; for properly speaking, all true Work is Religion: and whatsoever Religion is not Work may go and dwell among the Brahmins, Antinomians, Spinning Dervishes,[1] or where it will; with me it shall have no harbour. Admirable was that of the old Monks, '*Laborare est Orare*, Work is Worship.'

Older than all preached Gospels was this unpreached, inarticulate, but ineradicable, forever-enduring Gospel: Work, and therein have wellbeing. Man, Son of Earth and of Heaven, lies there not, in the innermost heart of thee, a Spirit of active Method, a Force for Work; — and burns like a painfully smouldering fire, giving thee no rest till thou unfold it, till thou write it down in beneficent Facts around thee! What is immethodic, waste, thou shalt make methodic, regulated, arable; obedient and productive to thee. Wheresoever thou findest Disorder, there is thy eternal enemy; attack him swiftly, subdue him; make Order of him, the subject not of Chaos, but of Intelligence, Divinity and Thee! The thistle that grows in thy path, dig it out, that a blade of useful grass, a drop of nourishing milk, may grow there instead. The waste cotton-shrub, gather its waste white down, spin it, weave it; that, in place of idle litter, there may be folded webs, and the naked skin of man be covered.

But above all, where thou findest Ignorance, Stupidity, Brute-mindedness, — yes, there, with or without Church-tithes and Shovel-hat, with or without Talfourd-Mahon Copyrights,[2] or were it with mere dungeons and gibbets and crosses, attack it, I say; smite it wisely, unweariedly, and rest not while thou livest and it lives; but smite, smite, in the name of God! The Highest God, as I understand it, does audibly so command thee; still audibly,

---

[1] Respectively: the highest caste of Hindus; believers in the sixteenth-century Christian heresy that faith alone is necessary for salvation; and members of a Mohammedan religious order whose devotion took the form of frenzied dancing.

[2] Thomas Noon Talfourd and Viscount Mahon sponsored a revised copyright act passed in 1842.

if thou have ears to hear.[3] He, even He, with his *un*spoken voice, awfuler than any Sinai thunders or syllabled speech of Whirlwinds;[4] for the SILENCE of deep Eternities, of Worlds from beyond the morning-stars, does it not speak to thee? The unborn Ages; the old Graves, with their long-mouldering dust, the very tears that wetted it now all dry, — do not these speak to thee, what ear hath not heard? The deep Death-kingdoms, the Stars in their never-resting courses, all Space and all Time, proclaim it to thee in continual silent admonition. Thou too, if ever man should, shalt work while it is called Today. For the Night cometh, wherein no man can work.

All true Work is sacred; in all true Work, were it but true hand-labour, there is something of divineness. Labour, wide as the Earth, has its summit in Heaven. Sweat of the brow; and up from that to sweat of the brain, sweat of the heart; which includes all Kepler calculations,[5] Newton meditations, all Sciences, all spoken Epics, all acted Heroisms, Martyrdoms, — up to that 'Agony of bloody sweat,'[6] which all men have called divine! O brother, if this is not 'worship,' then I say, the more pity for worship; for this is the noblest thing yet discovered under God's sky. Who art thou that complainest of thy life of toil? Complain not. Look up, my wearied brother; see thy fellow Workmen there, in God's Eternity; surviving there, they alone surviving: sacred Band of the Immortals, celestial Bodyguard of the Empire of Mankind. Even in the weak Human Memory they survive so long, as saints, as heroes, as gods; they alone surviving; peopling, they alone, the unmeasured solitudes of Time! To thee Heaven, though severe, is *not* unkind; Heaven is kind, — as a noble Mother; as that Spartan Mother, saying while she gave her son his shield, "With it, my son, or upon it!" Thou too shalt return *home* in honour; to thy far-distant Home, in honour; doubt it not, — if in the battle thou keep thy shield! Thou, in the Eternities and deepest Death-kingdoms, art not an alien; thou everywhere art a denizen! Complain not; the very Spartans did not *complain*.

And who art thou that braggest of thy life of Idleness; com-

---

[3] Mark 4:9 and elsewhere.

[4] Ezekiel 1–2; 1 Kings 19:11–12; Job 34.

[5] Johann Kepler, physicist and astronomer, prepared the way for Newton's discovery of the law of gravitation.

[6] Luke 22:44.

placently shewest thy bright gilt equipages; sumptuous cushions; appliances for folding of the hands to mere sleep?[7] Looking up, looking down, around, behind or before, discernest thou, if it be not in Mayfair alone, any *idle* hero, saint, god, or even devil? Not a vestige of one. In the Heavens, in the Earth, in the Waters under the Earth, is none like unto thee. Thou art an original figure in this Creation; a denizen in Mayfair alone, in this extraordinary Century or Half-Century alone! One monster there is in the world: the idle man. What is his 'Religion?' That Nature is a Phantasm, where cunning, beggary or thievery may sometimes find good victual. That God is a lie; and that Man and his Life are a lie. — Alas, alas, who of us *is* there that can say, I have worked? The faithfulest of us are unprofitable servants;[8] the faithfulest of us know that best. The faithfulest of us may say, with sad and true old Samuel, "Much of my life has been trifled away!"[9] But he that has, and except 'on public occasions' professes to have, no function but that of going idle in a graceful or graceless manner; and of begetting sons to go idle; and to address Chief Spinners and Diggers, who at least *are* spinning and digging, "Ye scandalous persons who produce too much" — My Corn-Law friends, on what imaginary still richer Eldorados, and true iron-spikes with law of gravitation, are ye rushing!

As to the Wages of Work there might innumerable things be said; there will and must yet innumerable things be said and spoken, in St. Stephen's and out of St. Stephen's; and gradually not a few things be ascertained and written, on Law-parchment, concerning this very matter: — 'Fair day's-wages for a fair day's-work' is the most unrefusable demand! Money-wages 'to the extent of keeping your worker alive that he may work more;' these, unless you mean to dismiss him straightway out of this world, are indispensable alike to the noblest Worker and to the least noble!

One thing only I will say here, in special reference to the former class, the noble and noblest; but throwing light on all the other classes and their arrangements of this difficult matter: The 'wages' of every noble Work do yet lie in Heaven or else Nowhere.

[7] Proverbs 6:10, 24:33. [8] Luke 17:10.
[9] Dr. Johnson: "I have been an idle fellow all my life." (Boswell, under date of August 5, 1763).

Not in Bank-of-England bills, in Owen's Labour-bank,[10] or any
the most improved establishment of banking and money-chang-
ing, needest thou, heroic soul, present thy account of earnings.
Human banks and labour-banks know thee not; or know thee
after generations and centuries have passed away, and thou art
clean gone from 'rewarding,' — all manner of bank-drafts, shop-
tills, and Downing-street Exchequers lying very invisible, so far
from thee! Nay, at bottom, dost thou need any reward? Was it
thy aim and life-purpose to be filled with good things for thy
heroism; to have a life of pomp and ease, and be what men call
'happy,' in this world, or in any other world? I answer for thee
deliberately, No. The whole spiritual secret of the new epoch lies
in this, that thou canst answer for thyself, with thy whole clearness of head and heart, deliberately, No!

My brother, the brave man has to give his Life away. Give it,
I advise thee; — thou dost not expect to *sell* thy Life in an
adequate manner? What price, for example, would content thee?
The just price of thy LIFE to thee, — why, God's entire Creation
to thyself, the whole Universe of Space, the whole Eternity of
Time, and what they hold: that is the price which would content
thee; that, and if thou wilt be candid, nothing short of that! It is
thy all; and for it thou wouldst have all. Thou art an unreasonable mortal; — or rather thou art a poor *infinite* mortal, who, in
thy narrow clay-prison here, *seemest* so unreasonable! Thou wilt
never sell thy Life, or any part of thy Life, in a satisfactory manner. Give it, like a royal heart; let the price be Nothing: thou
hast then, in a certain sense, got All for it! The heroic man, —
and is not every man, God be thanked, a potential hero? — has
to do so, in all times and circumstances. In the most heroic age,
as in the most unheroic, he will have to say, as Burns said proudly
and humbly of his little Scottish Songs, little dewdrops of Celestial
Melody in an age when so much was unmelodious: "By Heaven,
they shall either be invaluable or of no value; I do not need your
guineas for them!"[11] It is an element which should, and must,
enter deeply into all settlements of wages here below. They
never will be 'satisfactory' otherwise; they cannot, O Mammon

[10] Among the coöperative projects of the socialist mill-owner Robert Owen
was a goods exchange in which the prices of articles were determined by the
actual value of the raw material and labor that went into their making.

[11] Burns in a letter of September 16, 1792: "You may think my Songs
either *above*, or *below* price; for they shall absolutely be the one or the
other."

Gospel, they never can! Money for my little piece of work 'to
the extent that will allow me to keep working;' yes, this, — unless
you mean that I shall go my ways *before* the work is all taken out
of me: but as to 'wages' — ! —

On the whole, we do entirely agree with those old Monks,
Laborare est Orare. In a thousand senses, from one end of it to
the other, true Work *is* Worship. He that works, whatsoever be
his work, he bodies forth the form of Things Unseen;[12] a small
Poet every Worker is. The idea, were it but of his poor Delf
Platter, how much more of his Epic Poem, is as yet 'seen,' half-
seen, only by himself; to all others it is a thing unseen, impossible;
to Nature herself it is a thing unseen, a thing which never hitherto
was; — very 'impossible,' for it is as yet a No-thing! The Unseen
Powers had need to watch over such a man; he works in and for
the Unseen. Alas, if he look to the Seen Powers only, he may as
well quit the business; his No-thing will never rightly issue as a
Thing, but as a Deceptivity, a Sham-thing, — which it had better
not do!

Thy No-thing of an Intended Poem, O Poet who hast looked
merely to reviewers, copyrights, booksellers, popularities, behold
it has not yet become a Thing; for the truth is not in it! Though
printed, hotpressed, reviewed, celebrated, sold to the twentieth
edition: what is all that? The Thing, in philosophical uncommer-
cial language, is still a No-thing, mostly semblance, and deception
of the sight; — benign Oblivion incessantly gnawing at it, impatient till chaos to which it belongs do reabsorb it! —

He who takes not counsel of the Unseen and Silent, from him
will never come real visibility and speech. Thou must descend to
the *Mothers*,[13] to the *Manes*,[14] and Hercules-like long suffer and
labour there, wouldst thou emerge with victory into the sunlight.
As in battle and the shock of war, — for is not this a battle? —
thou too shalt fear no pain or death, shalt love no ease or life; the
voice of festive Lubberlands,[15] the noise of greedy Acheron shall
alike lie silent under thy victorious feet. Thy work, like Dante's,
shall 'make thee lean for many years.'[16] The world and its wages,
its criticisms, counsels, helps, impediments, shall be as a waste

---

[12] *A Midsummer Night's Dream,* V.i.14–15.
[13] Mater Gloriosa and Mater Dolorosa: cf. *Faust,* II.v, end.
[14] The souls of the departed, worshiped by their Roman descendants.
[15] Lands of luxurious idleness.
[16] *Paradiso,* XXV.1–3.

ocean-flood; the chaos through which thou art to swim and sail. Not the waste waves and their weedy gulf-streams, shalt thou take for guidance: thy star alone, — '*Se tu segui tua stella!*'[17] Thy star alone, now clear-beaming over Chaos, nay now by fits gone out, disastrously eclipsed: this only shalt thou strive to follow. O, it is a business, as I fancy, that of weltering your way through Chaos and the murk of Hell! Green-eyed dragons watching you, three-headed Cerberuses, — not without sympathy of *their* sort! "*Eccovi l'uom ch'è stato all'Inferno.*"[18] For in fine, as Poet Dryden says, you do walk hand in hand with sheer Madness, all the way,[19] — who is by no means pleasant company! You look fixedly into Madness, and *her* undiscovered, boundless, bottomless Night-empire; that you may extort new Wisdom out of it, as an Eurydice from Tartarus.[20] The higher the Wisdom, the closer was its neighbourhood and kindred with mere Insanity; literally so; — and thou wilt, with a speechless feeling, observe how highest Wisdom, struggling up into this world, has oftentimes carried such tinctures and adhesions of Insanity still cleaving to it hither!

All Works, each in their degree, are a making of Madness sane; — truly enough a religious operation; which cannot be carried on without religion. You have not work otherwise; you have eye-service, greedy grasping of wages, swift and ever swifter manufacture of semblances to get hold of wages. Instead of better felt-hats to cover your head, you have bigger lath-and-plaster hats set travelling the streets on wheels. Instead of heavenly and earthly Guidance for the souls of men, you have 'Black or White Surplice' Controversies,[21] stuffed hair-and-leather Popes; — terrestrial *Law-wards,* Lords and Law-bringers, 'organising Labour' in these years, by passing Corn-Laws. With all which, alas, this distracted Earth is now full, nigh to bursting. Semblances most smooth to the touch and eye; most accursed nevertheless to body and soul. Semblances, be they of Sham-woven Cloth or of Dilettante Legislation, which are *not* real wool or substance, but Devil's-dust, accursed of God and man! No man has worked, or

---

[17] *Inferno,* XV.55.
[18] "Behold the man who visits hell": said, on rather remote authority, to have been the words of old women in Ravenna when Dante passed them.
[19] *Absalom and Achitophel,* line 163.
[20] Orpheus momentarily rescued his wife, Eurydice, from Tartarus (Hades) by the music of his lyre. Cf. Ovid, *Metamorphoses,* X.1–77.
[21] A burning issue in 1842: should the black gown or white surplice be worn when the clergyman delivers his sermon?

can work, except religiously; not even the poor day-labourer, the weaver of your coat, the sewer of your shoes. All men, if they work not as in a Great Taskmaster's eye,[22] will work wrong, work unhappily for themselves and you.

Industrial work, still under bondage to Mammon, the rational soul of it not yet awakened, is a tragic spectacle. Men in the rapidest motion and self-motion; restless, with convulsive energy, as if driven by Galvanism, as if possessed by a Devil; tearing asunder mountains, — to no purpose, for Mammonism is always Midas-eared! This is sad, on the face of it. Yet courage: the beneficent Destinies, kind in their sternness, are apprising us that this cannot continue. Labour is not a devil, even while encased in Mammonism; Labour is ever an imprisoned god, writhing unconsciously or consciously to escape out of Mammonism! Plugson of Undershot, like Taillefer of Normandy, wants victory; how much happier will even Plugson be to have a Chivalrous victory than a Chactaw one. The unredeemed ugliness is that of a slothful People. Shew me a People energetically busy; heaving, struggling, all shoulders at the wheel; their heart pulsing, every muscle swelling, with man's energy and will; — I shew you a People of whom great good is already predicable; to whom all manner of good is yet certain, if their energy endure. By very working, they will learn; they have, Antæus-like,[23] their foot on Mother Fact: how can they but learn?

The vulgarest Plugson of a Master-Worker, who can command Workers and get work out of them, is already a considerable man. Blessed and thrice-blessed symptoms I discern of Master-Workers who are not vulgar men; who are Nobles, and begin to feel that they must act as such: all speed to these, they are England's hope at present! But in this Plugson himself, conscious of almost no nobleness whatever, how much is there! Not without man's faculty, insight, courage, hard energy, is this rugged figure. His words none of the wisest; but his actings cannot be altogether foolish. Think, how were it, stoodst thou suddenly in his shoes! He has to command a thousand men. And not imaginary commanding; no, it is real, incessantly practical. The evil passions of so many men (with the Devil in them, as in all of us) he has to vanquish; by manifold force of speech and of silence, to repress or evade. What a force of silence, to say nothing of the others, is

[22] Milton's sonnet, "How soon hath time. . . ."
[23] Antaeus was a Titan who lost his strength when lifted from the earth.

in Plugson! For these his thousand men he has to provide raw-material, machinery, arrangement, house-room; and ever at the week's end, wages by due sale. No Civil-List,[24] or Goulburn-Baring Budget[25] has he to fall back upon, for paying of his regiment; he has to pick his supplies from this confused face of the whole Earth and Contemporaneous History, by his dexterity alone. There will be dry eyes if he fail to do it! — He exclaims, at present, 'black in the face,' near strangled with Dilettante Legislation: "Let me have elbow-room, throat-room, and I will not fail! No, I will spin yet, and conquer like a giant: what 'sinews of war' lie in me, untold resources towards the Conquest of this Planet, if instead of hanging me, you husband them, and help me!" — My indomitable friend, it is *true;* and thou shalt and must be helped.

This is not a man I would kill and strangle by Corn-Laws, even if I could! No, I would fling my Corn-Laws and Shotbelts to the Devil; and try to help this man. I would teach him, by noble precept and law-precept, by noble example most of all, that Mammonism was not the essence of his or of my station in God's Universe; but the adscititious excrescence of it; the gross, terrene, godless embodiment of it; which would have to become, more or less, a godlike one. By noble *real* legislation, by true *noble's*-work, by unwearied, valiant, and were it wageless effort, in my Parliament and in my Parish, I would aid, constrain, encourage him to effect more or less this blessed change. I should know that it would have to be effected; that unless it were in some measure effected, he and I and all of us, I first and soonest of all, were doomed to perdition! — Effected it will be; unless it were a Demon that made this Universe; which I, for my own part, do at no moment, under no form, in the least believe.

May it please your Serene Highnesses, your Majesties, Lordships and Law-wardships, the proper Epic of this world is not now 'Arms and the Man;'[26] how much less, 'Shirt-frills and the Man:' no, it is now 'Tools and the Man:' that, henceforth to all time is now our Epic; — and you, first of all others, I think, were wise to take note of that!

[24] Annual parliamentary grant to the reigning monarch for personal and household expenses.

[25] Henry Goulburn was chancellor of the exchequer, having succeeded Sir Francis Thornhill Baring in that post in 1841.

[26] From the first line of the *Aeneid.*

CHAPTER XIII

IF the Serene Highnesses and Majesties do not take note of that, then, as I perceive, *that* will take note of itself! The time for levity, insincerity, and idle babble and play-acting, in all kinds, is gone by; it is a serious, grave time. Old long-vexed questions, not yet solved in logical words or parliamentary laws, are fast solving themselves in facts, somewhat unblessed to behold! This largest of questions, this question of Work and Wages, which ought, had we heeded Heaven's voice, to have begun two generations ago or more, cannot be delayed longer without hearing Earth's voice. 'Labour' will verily need to be somewhat 'organised,' as they say, — God knows with what difficulty. Man will actually need to have his debts and earnings a little better paid by man; which, let Parliaments speak of them or be silent of them, are eternally his due from man, and cannot, without penalty and at length not without death-penalty, be withheld. How much ought to cease among us straightway; how much ought to begin straightway, while the hours yet are!

Truly they are strange results to which this of leaving all to 'Cash;' of quietly shutting up the God's Temple, and gradually opening wide-open the Mammon's Temple, with 'Laissez-faire, and Every man for himself,' — have led us in these days! We have Upper, speaking Classes, who indeed do 'speak' as never man spake before; the withered flimsiness, the godless baseness and barrenness of whose Speech might of itself indicate what kind of Doing and practical Governing went on under it! For Speech is the gaseous element out of which most kinds of Practice and Performance, especially all kinds of moral Performance, condense themselves, and take shape; as the one is, so will the other be. Descending, accordingly, into the Dumb Class in its Stockport Cellars and Poor-Law Bastilles, have we not to announce that they also are hitherto unexampled in the History of Adam's Posterity?

Life was never a May-game for men: in all times the lot of the dumb millions born to toil was defaced with manifold sufferings, injustices, heavy burdens, avoidable and unavoidable; not play at all, but hard work that made the sinews sore, and the heart sore. As bond-slaves, *villani, bordarii, sochemanni,* nay indeed as dukes, earls and kings, men were oftentimes made weary of their life; and had to say, in the sweat of their brow and of their soul, Behold it is not sport, it is grim earnest, and our back can bear no more! Who knows not what massacrings and harryings there have been; grinding, long-continuing, unbearable injustices, — till the heart had to rise in madness, and some *"Eu Sachsen, nimith euer sachses,* You Saxons, out with your gully-knives then!"[1] You Saxons, some 'arrestment,' partial 'arrestment of the Knaves and Dastards' has become indispensable! — The page of Dryasdust is heavy with such details.

And yet I will venture to believe that in no time, since the beginnings of Society, was the lot of those same dumb millions of toilers so entirely unbearable as it is even in the days now passing over us. It is not to die, or even to die of hunger, that makes a man wretched; many men have died; all men must die, — the last exit of us all is in a Fire-Chariot of Pain.[2] But it is to live miserable we know not why; to work sore and yet gain nothing; to be heart-worn, weary, yet isolated, unrelated, girt in with a cold universal Laissez-faire: it is to die slowly all our life long, imprisoned in a deaf, dead, Infinite Injustice, as in the accursed iron belly of a Phalaris' Bull![3] This is and remains forever intolerable to all men whom God has made. Do we wonder at French Revolutions, Chartisms, Revolts of Three Days?[4] The times, if we will consider them, are really unexampled.

Never before did I hear of an Irish Widow reduced to 'prove her sisterhood by dying of typhus-fever and infecting seventeen persons,' — saying in such undeniable way, "You *see,* I was your sister!" Sisterhood, brotherhood was often forgotten; but not till the rise of these ultimate Mammon and Shotbelt Gospels, did I ever see it so expressly denied. If no pious Lord or *Law-ward*

---

[1] Carlyle prefixed two words to the reported war cry of Hengist for the sake of an etymological play on words. The name *Saxon* is perhaps derived from the Old Teutonic word *sahso,* meaning "knife" or "short sword." "Gully" means "large."

[2] 2 Kings 2:11.

[3] A brazen bull in which Phalaris, a Sicilian tyrant, burned criminals alive.

[4] The 1830 revolution in France (July 27–29).

would remember it, always some pious Lady (*'Hlaf-dig,'* Bene-
factress, *'Loaf-giveress,'* they say she is, — blessings on her beautiful heart!) was there, with mild mother-voice and hand, to
remember it; some pious thoughtful *Elder,* what we now call
'Prester,' *Presbyter* or 'Priest,' was there to put all men in mind
of it, in the name of the God who had made all.

Not even in Black Dahomey was it ever, I think, forgotten to
the typhus-fever length. Mungo Park, resourceless, had sunk
down to die under the Negro Village-Tree, a horrible White object in the eyes of all.[5] But in the poor Black Woman, and her
daughter who stood aghast at him, whose earthly wealth and
funded capital consisted of one small calabash of rice, there lived
a heart richer than *'Laissez-faire:'* they, with a royal munificence,
boiled their rice for him; they sang all night to him, spinning
assiduous on their cotton distaffs, as he lay to sleep: "Let us pity
the poor white man; no mother has he to fetch him milk, no sister
to grind him corn!" Thou poor black Noble One, — thou *Lady*
too: did not a God make thee too; was there not in thee too
something of a God! —

Gurth born thrall of Cedric the Saxon has been greatly pitied
by Dryasdust and others. Gurth with the brass collar round his
neck, tending Cedric's pigs in the glades of the wood, is not what
I call an exemplar of human felicity: but Gurth, with the sky
above him, with the free air and tinted boscage and umbrage
round him, and in him at least the certainty of supper and social
lodging when he came home; Gurth to me seems happy, in comparison with many a Lancashire and Buckinghamshire man, of
these days, not born thrall of anybody! Gurth's brass collar did
not gall him: Cedric *deserved* to be his Master. The pigs were
Cedric's, but Gurth too would get his parings of them. Gurth
had the inexpressible satisfaction of feeling himself related in-
dissolubly, though in a rude brass-collar way, to his fellow-mortals
in this Earth. He had superiors, inferiors, equals. — Gurth is
now 'emancipated' long since; has what we call 'Liberty.' Liberty,
I am told, is a Divine thing. Liberty when it becomes the 'Liberty
to die by starvation' is not so divine!

Liberty? The true liberty of a man, you would say, consisted
in his finding out, or being forced to find out the right path, and

[5] Park, a famous African explorer, told the story in his *Travels in the
Interior of Africa* (1799).

to walk thereon. To learn, or to be taught, what work he actually was able for; and then, by permission, persuasion, and even compulsion, to set about doing of the same! That is his true blessedness, honour, 'liberty' and maximum of wellbeing: if liberty be not that, I for one have small care about liberty. You do not allow a palpable madman to leap over precipices; you violate his liberty, you that are wise; and keep him, were it in strait-waistcoats, away from the precipices! Every stupid, every cowardly and foolish man is but a less palpable madman: his true liberty were that a wiser man, that any and every wiser man, could, by brass collars, or in whatever milder or sharper way, lay hold of him when he was going wrong, and order and compel him to go a little righter. O if thou really art my *Senior*, Seigneur, my *Elder*, Presbyter or Priest, — if thou art in very deed my *Wiser*, may a beneficent instinct lead and impel thee to 'conquer' me, to command me! If thou do know better than I what is good and right, I conjure thee in the name of God, force me to do it; were it by never such brass collars, whips and handcuffs, leave me not to walk over precipices! That I have been called, by all the Newspapers, a 'free man' will avail me little, if my pilgrimage have ended in death and wreck. O that the Newspapers had called me slave, coward, fool, or what it pleased their sweet voices to name me, and I had attained not death, but life! — Liberty requires new definitions.

A conscious abhorrence and intolerance of Folly, of Baseness, Stupidity, Poltroonery and all that brood of things, dwells deep in some men: still deeper in others an *un*conscious abhorrence and intolerance, clothed moreover by the beneficent Supreme Powers in what stout appetites, energies, egoisms so-called, are suitable to it; — these latter are your Conquerors, Romans, Normans, Russians, Indo-English; Founders of what we call Aristocracies. Which indeed have they not the most 'divine right' to found; — being themselves very truly Ἄριστοι, BRAVEST, BEST; and conquering generally a confused rabble of WORST, or at lowest, clearly enough, of WORSE? I think their divine right, tried, with affirmatory verdict, in the greatest Law-Court known to me, was good! A class of men who are dreadfully exclaimed against by Dryasdust; of whom nevertheless beneficent Nature has oftentimes had need; and may, alas, again have need.

When, across the hundredfold poor scepticisms, trivialisms, and constitutional cobwebberies of Dryasdust, you catch any glimpse of a William the Conqueror, a Tancred of Hauteville[6] or such like, — do you not discern veritably some rude outline of a true God-made King; whom not the Champion of England cased in tin, but all Nature and the Universe were calling to the throne? It is absolutely necessary that he get thither. Nature does not mean her poor Saxon children to perish, of obesity, stupor or other malady, as yet: a stern Ruler and Line of Rulers therefore is called in, — a stern but most beneficent *Perpetual House-Surgeon* is called in, by Nature, and even the appropriate *fees* are provided for him! Dryasdust talks lamentably about Hereward and the Fen Counties; fate of Earl Waltheof; Yorkshire and the North reduced to ashes;[7] all which is undoubtedly lamentable. But even Dryasdust apprises me of one fact: 'A child, in this William's reign, might have carried a purse of gold from end to end of England.' My erudite friend, it is a fact which outweighs a thousand! Sweep away thy constitutional, senti-mental and other cobwebberies; look eye to eye, if thou still have any eye, in the face of this big burly William Bastard: thou wilt see a fellow of most flashing discernment, of most strong lion-heart; — in whom, as it were, within a frame of oak and iron, the gods have planted the soul of 'a man of genius!' Dost thou call that nothing? I call it an immense thing! — Rage enough was in this Willelmus Conquestor, rage enough for his occasions; — and yet the essential element of him, as of all such men, is not scorching *fire*, but shining illuminative *light*. Fire and light are strangely interchangeable; nay, at bottom, I have found them different forms of the same most godlike 'elementary substance' in our world: a thing worth stating in these days. The essential element of this Conquestor is, first of all, the most sun-eyed perception of what *is* really what on this God's-Earth; — which, thou wilt find, does mean at bottom 'Justice,' and 'Virtues' not a few: *Conformity* to what the Maker has seen good to make; that, I suppose, will mean Justice and a Virtue or two? —

Dost thou think Willelmus Conquestor would have tolerated ten years' jargon, one hour's jargon, on the propriety of killing Cotton-manufactures by partridge Corn-Laws? I fancy, this was

[6] A Norman leader of the first crusade.

[7] Allusions to the rebellion against William the Conqueror in 1069–70. Hereward the Wake, a landowner, led the English rebels of the Fen Counties (part of East Anglia); Waltheof supported a similar movement by Danish invaders centering farther north, in Yorkshire; and after putting them down, the king ravaged the latter area.

not the man to knock out of his night's-rest with nothing but a noisy bedlamism in your mouth! "Assist us still better to bush the partridges; strangle Plugson who spins the shirts?" — *"Par la Splendeur de Dieu!"*[8] — — Dost thou think Willelmus Conquestor, in this new time, with Steamengine Captains of Industry on one hand of him, and Joe-Manton Captains of Idleness on the other, would have doubted which *was* really the Best; which did deserve strangling, and which not?

I have a certain indestructible regard for Willelmus Conquestor. A resident House-Surgeon, provided by Nature for her beloved English People, and even furnished with the requisite 'fees,' as I said; for he by no means felt himself doing Nature's work, this Willelmus, but his own work exclusively! And his own work withal it was; informed *'par la Splendeur de Dieu.'* — I say, it is necessary to get the work out of such a man, however harsh that be! When a world, not yet doomed for death, is rushing down to ever-deeper Baseness and Confusion, it is a dire necessity of Nature's to bring in her Aristocracies, her Best, even by forcible methods. When their descendants or representatives cease entirely to *be* the Best, Nature's poor world will very soon rush down again to Baseness; and it becomes a dire necessity of Nature's to cast them out. Hence French Revolutions, Five-point Charters, Democracies, and a mournful list of *Etceteras*, in these our afflicted times.

To what extent Democracy has now reached, how it advances irresistible with ominous, ever-increasing speed, he that will open his eyes on any province of human affairs may discern. Democracy is everywhere the inexorable demand of these ages, swiftly fulfilling itself. From the thunder of Napoleon battles, to the jabbering of Open-vestry in St. Mary Axe,[9] all things announce Democracy. A distinguished man, whom some of my readers will hear again with pleasure, thus writes to me what in these days he notes from the Wahngasse of Weissnichtwo, where our London fashions seem to be in full vogue. Let us hear the Herr Teufelsdröckh[10] again, were it but the smallest word!

'Democracy, which means despair of finding any Heroes to govern you, and contented putting up with the want of them, —

---

[8] One of William the Conqueror's oaths.

[9] A London parish.

[10] Carlyle's *persona* in *Sartor Resartus*, his mailing address being Wahngasse (Dream Street), Weissnichtwo (Nowhere). Note the revival of the clothes-and-tailor symbolism which dominated the earlier work.

alas, thou too, *mein Lieber*, seest well how close it is of kin to
Atheism, and other sad *Isms:* he who discovers no God whatever,
how shall he discover Heroes, the visible Temples of God? —
Strange enough meanwhile it is, to observe with what thought-
lessness, here in our rigidly Conservative Country, men rush into
Democracy with full cry. Beyond doubt, his Excellenz the
Titular-Herr Ritter Kauderwälsch von Pferdefuss-Quacksalber,[11]
he our distinguished Conservative Premier himself, and all but
the thicker-headed of his Party, discern Democracy to be inevitable as death, and are even desperate of delaying it much!

'You cannot walk the streets without beholding Democracy
announce itself: the very Tailor has become, if not properly
Sansculottic, which to him would be ruinous, yet a Tailor unconsciously symbolising, and prophesying with his scissors, the
reign of Equality. What now is our fashionable coat? A thing
of superfinest texture, of deeply meditated cut; with Malines-
lace[12] cuffs; quilted with gold; so that a man can carry, without
difficulty, an estate of land on his back? *Keineswegs*, By no
manner of means! The Sumptuary Laws[13] have fallen into such
a state of desuetude as was never before seen. Our fashionable
coat is an amphibium between barn-sack and drayman's doublet.
The cloth of it is studiously coarse; the colour a speckled soot-
black or rust-brown grey; — the nearest approach to a Peasant's.
And for shape, — thou shouldst see it! The last consummation of
the year now passing over us is definable as Three Bags: a big
bag for the body, two small bags for the arms, and by way of
collar a hem! The first Antique Cheruscan[14] who, of felt-cloth or
bear's-hide, with bone or metal needle, set about making himself
a coat, before Tailors had yet awakened out of Nothing, — did
not he make it even so? A loose wide poke for body, with two
holes to let out the arms; this was his original coat: to which holes
it was soon visible that two small loose pokes, or sleeves, easily
appended, would be an improvement.

'Thus has the Tailor-art, so to speak, overset itself, like most
other things; changed its centre-of-gravity; whirled suddenly
over from zenith to nadir. Your Stulz,[15] with huge somerset, vaults

---

[11] Sir Gibberish Clovenfoot-Quack Doctor.
[12] Named for a Belgian town.
[13] Laws designed to curb extravagance in private life.
[14] Member of a German tribe.
[15] Fashionable tailor (German: *stolz*, "proud," "splendid").

from his high shopboard down to the depths of primal savagery, — carrying much along with him! For I will invite thee to reflect that the Tailor, as topmost ultimate froth of Human Society, is indeed swift-passing, evanescent, slippery to decipher; yet significant of much, nay of all. Topmost evanescent froth, he is churned up from the very lees, and from all intermediate regions of the liquor. The general outcome he, visible to the eye, of what men aimed to do, and were obliged and enabled to do, in this one public department of symbolising themselves to each other by covering of their skins. A smack of all Human Life lies in the Tailor: its wild struggles towards beauty, dignity, freedom, victory; and how, hemmed in by Sedan and Huddersfield,[16] by Nescience, Dulness, Prurience, and other sad necessities and laws of Nature, it has attained just to this: Grey Savagery of Three Sacks with a hem!

'When the very Tailor verges towards Sansculottism, is it not ominous? The last Divinity of poor mankind dethroning himself; sinking *his* taper too, flame downmost, like the Genius of Sleep or of Death;[17] admonitory that Tailor-time shall be no more! — For little as one could advise Sumptuary Laws at the present epoch, yet nothing is clearer than that where ranks do actually exist, strict division of costumes will also be enforced; that if we ever have a new Hierarchy and Aristocracy, acknowledged veritably as such, for which I daily pray Heaven, the Tailor will reawaken; and be, by volunteering and appointment, consciously and unconsciously, a safeguard of that same.' — Certain farther observations, from the same invaluable pen, on our never-ending changes of mode, our 'perpetual nomadic and even ape-like appetite for change and mere change' in all the equipments of our existence, and the 'fatal revolutionary character' thereby manifested, we suppress for the present. It may be admitted that Democracy, in all meanings of the word, is in full career; irresistible by any Ritter Kauderwälsch or other Son of Adam, as times go. 'Liberty' is a thing men are determined to have.

But truly, as I had to remark in the meanwhile, 'the liberty of not being oppressed by your fellow man' is an indispensable, yet one of the most insignificant fractional parts of Human Liberty. No man oppresses thee, can bid thee fetch or carry, come or go,

[16] Cloth manufacturing centers.
[17] Twin brothers in classical mythology.

without reason shewn. True; from all men thou art emancipated: but from Thyself and from the Devil — ? No man, wiser, unwiser, can make thee come or go: but thy own futilities, bewilderments, thy false appetites for Money, Windsor Georges[18] and such like? No man oppresses thee, O free and independent Franchiser: but does not this stupid Porter-pot oppress thee? No Son of Adam can bid thee come or go; but this absurd Pot of Heavy-wet, this can and does! Thou art the thrall not of Cedric the Saxon, but of thy own brutal appetites, and this scoured dish of liquor. And thou pratest of thy 'liberty?' Thou entire blockhead!

Heavy-wet and gin: alas, these are not the only kinds of thraldom. Thou who walkest in a vain shew,[19] looking out with ornamental dilettante sniff and serene supremacy at all Life and all Death; and amblest jauntily; perking up thy poor talk into crotchets, thy poor conduct into fatuous somnambulisms; — and *art* as an 'enchanted Ape' under God's sky, where thou mightest have been a man, had proper Schoolmasters and Conquerors, and Constables with cat-o'-nine tails, been vouchsafed thee: dost thou call that 'liberty?' Or your unreposing Mammon-worshipper, again, driven, as if by Galvanisms, by Devils and Fixed-Ideas, who rises early and sits late, chasing the impossible; straining every faculty 'to fill himself with the east wind,'[20] — how merciful were it, could you, by mild persuasion or by the severest tyranny so-called, check him in his mad path, turn him into a wiser one! All painful tyranny, in that case again, were but mild 'surgery;' the pain of it cheap, as health and life, instead of galvanism and fixed-idea, are cheap at any price.

Sure enough, of all paths a man could strike into, there *is*, at any given moment, a *best path* for every man; a thing which, here and now, it were of all things *wisest* for him to do; — which could he be but led or driven to do, he were then doing 'like a man,' as we phrase it; all men and gods agreeing with him, the whole Universe virtually exclaiming Well-done to him! His success, in such case, were complete; his felicity a maximum. This path, to find this path and walk in it, is the one thing needful for him. Whatsoever forwards him in that, let it come to him even in the shape of blows and spurnings, is liberty: whatsoever hinders

[18] Insignia of the Order of the Garter, of which St. George is the patron and St. George's Chapel, Windsor Castle, the seat.
[19] Psalms 39:6.
[20] Job 15:2.

him, were it wardmotes,[21] open-vestries, pollbooths, tremendous cheers, rivers of heavy-wet, is slavery.

The notion that a man's liberty consists in giving his vote at election-hustings, and saying, "Behold now I too have my twenty-thousandth part of a Talker in our National Palaver;[22] will not all the gods be good to me?" — is one of the pleasantest! Nature nevertheless is kind at present; and puts it into the heads of many, almost of all. The liberty especially which has to purchase itself by social isolation, and each man standing separate from the other, having 'no business with him' but a cash-account: this is such a liberty as the Earth seldom saw; — as the Earth will not long put up with, recommend it how you may. This liberty turns out, before it have long continued in action, with all men flinging up their caps round it, to be, for the Working Millions a liberty to die by want of food; for the Idle Thousands and Units, alas, a still more fatal liberty to live in want of work; to have no earnest duty to do in this God's-World any more. What becomes of a man in such predicament? Earth's Laws are silent; and Heaven's speak in a voice which is not heard. No work, and the ineradicable need of work, give rise to new very wondrous life-philosophies, new very wondrous life-practices! Dilettantism, Pococurantism, Beau-Brummelism,[23] with perhaps an occasional, half-mad, protesting burst of Byronism, establish themselves: at the end of a certain period, — if you go back to 'the Dead Sea,' there is, say our Moslem friends, a very strange 'Sabbath-day' transacting itself there! — Brethren, we know but imperfectly yet, after ages of Constitutional Government, what Liberty is and Slavery is.

Democracy, the chase of Liberty in that direction, shall go its full course; unrestrainable by him of Pferdefuss-Quacksalber, or any of *his* household. The Toiling Millions of Mankind, in most vital need and passionate instinctive desire of Guidance, shall cast away False-Guidance; and hope, for an hour, that No-Guidance will suffice them: but it can be for an hour only. The smallest item of human Slavery is the oppression of man by his Mock-Superiors; the palpablest, but I say at bottom the smallest. Let him shake off such oppression, trample it indignantly under his feet; I blame him not, I pity and commend him. But oppression by your Mock-Superiors well shaken off, the grand problem yet

[21] Meetings of wards (divisions of boroughs).
[22] Parliament.
[23] George Bryan Brummell (d. 1840) was the dictator of Regency fashion.

remains to solve: That of finding government by your Real-Superiors! Alas, how shall we ever learn the solution of that, benighted, bewildered, sniffing, sneering, godforgetting unfortunates as we are? It is a work for centuries; to be taught us by tribulations, confusions, insurrections, obstructions; who knows if not by conflagration and despair! It is a lesson inclusive of all other lessons; the hardest of all lessons to learn.

One thing I do know: Those Apes chattering on the branches by the Dead Sea never got it learned; but chatter there to this day. To them no Moses need come a second time; a thousand Moseses would be but so many painted Phantasms, interesting Fellow-Apes of new strange aspect, — whom they would 'invite to dinner,' be glad to meet with in lion-soirées.[24] To them the voice of Prophecy, of heavenly monition, is quite ended. They chatter there, all Heaven shut to them, to the end of the world. The unfortunates! O, what is dying of hunger, with honest tools in your hand, with a manful purpose in your heart, and much real labour lying round you done, in comparison? You honestly quit your tools; quit a most muddy confused coil of sore work, short rations, of sorrows, dispiritments and contradictions, having now honestly done with it all; — and await, not entirely in a distracted manner, what the Supreme Powers, and the Silences and the Eternities may have to say to you.

A second thing I know: This lesson will have to be learned, — under penalties! England will either learn it, or England also will cease to exist among Nations. England will either learn to reverence its Heroes, and discriminate them from its Sham-Heroes and Valets and gaslighted Histrios; and to prize them as the audible God's-voice, amid all inane jargons and temporary market-cries, and say to them with heart-loyalty, "Be ye King and Priest, and Gospel and Guidance for us:" or else England will continue to worship new and ever-new forms of Quackhood, — and so, with what resiliences and reboundings matters little, go down to the Father of Quacks! Can I dread such things of England? Wretched, thick-eyed, gross-hearted mortals, why will ye worship lies, and 'Stuffed Clothes-suits, created by the ninth-parts of men!'[25] It is not your purses that suffer; your farm-rents, your commerces, your mill-revenues, loud as ye lament over these; no, it is not these alone, but a far deeper than these: it is your

[24] Receptions for celebrities.
[25] "Nine tailors make a man." (Old proverb.)

Souls that lie dead, crushed down under despicable Nightmares, Atheisms, Brain-fumes; and are not Souls at all, but mere succedanea[26] for *salt* to keep your bodies and their appetites from putrefying! Your cotton-spinning and thrice-miraculous mechanism, what is this too, by itself, but a larger kind of Animalism? Spiders can spin, Beavers can build and shew contrivance; the Ant lays up accumulation of capital, and has, for aught I know, a Bank of Antland. If there is no soul in man higher than all that, did it reach to sailing on the cloud-rack and spinning sea-sand; then I say, man is but an animal, a more cunning kind of brute: he has no soul, but only a succedaneum for salt. Whereupon, seeing himself to be truly of the beasts that perish, he ought to admit it, I think; — and also straightway universally kill himself; and so, in a manlike manner, at least, *end,* and wave these brute-worlds *his* dignified farewell! —

[26] Substitutes.

CHAPTER XIV

SIR JABESH WINDBAG

O LIVER CROMWELL, whose body they hung on their Tyburn Gallows because he had found the Christian Religion inexecutable in this country, remains to me by far the remarkablest Governor we have had here for the last five centuries or so. For the last five centuries, there has been no Governor among us with anything like similar talent; and for the last two centuries, no Governor, we may say, with the possibility of similar talent, — with an idea in the heart of him capable of inspiring similar talent, capable of coexisting therewith. When you consider that Oliver believed in a God, the difference between Oliver's position and that of any subsequent Governor of this Country becomes, the more you reflect on it, the more immeasurable!

Oliver, no volunteer in Public Life, but plainly a ballotted soldier strictly ordered thither, enters upon Public Life; comports himself there like a man who carried his own life itself in his hand; like a man whose Great Commander's eye was always on him. Not without results. Oliver, well-advanced in years, finds now, by Destiny and his own Deservings, or as he himself better phrased it, by wondrous successive 'Births of Providence,' the Government of England put into his hands. In senate-house and battle-field, in counsel and in action, in private and in public, this man has proved himself a man: England and the voice of God, through waste awful whirlwinds and environments, speaking to his great heart, summon him to assert formally, in the way of solemn Public Fact and as a new piece of English Law, what informally and by Nature's eternal Law needed no asserting, That he, Oliver, was the Ablest-Man of England, the King of England; that he, Oliver, would undertake governing England. His way of making this same 'assertion,' the one way he had of making it, has given rise to immense criticism: but the assertion itself in what way soever 'made,' is it not somewhat of a solemn one, somewhat of a tremendous one!

And now do but contrast this Oliver with my right honourable friend Sir Jabesh Windbag, Mr. Facing-both-ways,[1] Viscount Mealymouth, Earl of Windlestraw, or what other Cagliostro,[2] Cagliostrino, Cagliostraccio, the course of Fortune and Parliamentary Majorities has constitutionally guided to that dignity, any time during these last sorrowful hundred-and-fifty years! Windbag, weak in the faith of a God, which he believes only at Church on Sundays, if even then; strong only in the faith that Paragraphs and Plausibilities bring votes; that Force of Public Opinion, as he calls it, is the primal Necessity of Things, and highest God we have: — Windbag, if we will consider him, has a problem set before him which may be ranged in the impossible class. He is a Columbus minded to sail to the indistinct country of Nowhere, to the indistinct country of Whitherward, by the *friendship* of those same waste-tumbling Water-Alps and howling waltz of All the Winds; not by conquest of them and in spite of them, but by friendship of them, when once *they* have made up their mind! He is the most original Columbus I ever saw. Nay, his problem is not an impossible one: he will infallibly *arrive* at that same country of Nowhere; his indistinct Whitherward will be a *Thither*ward! In the Ocean Abysses and Locker of Davy Jones, there certainly enough do he and *his* ship's company, and all their cargo and navigatings, at last find lodgement.

Oliver knew that his America lay There, Westward Ho; — and it was not entirely by *friendship* of the Water-Alps, and yeasty insane Froth-Oceans, that he meant to get thither! He sailed accordingly; had compass-card, and Rules of Navigation, — older and greater than these Froth-Oceans, old as the Eternal God! Or again, do but think of this. Windbag in these his probable five years of office has to prosper and get Paragraphs: the Paragraphs of these five years must be his salvation, or he is a lost man; redemption nowhere in the Worlds or in the Times discoverable for him. Oliver too would like his Paragraphs; successes, popularities in these five years are not undesirable to him: but mark, I say, this enormous circumstance: *after* these five years are gone and done, comes an Eternity for Oliver! Oliver has to appear before the Most High Judge: the utmost flow of Paragraphs, the utmost ebb of them, is now, in strictest arithmetic, verily no matter at all; its exact value *zero;* an account altogether erased! Enormous; — which a man, in these days, hardly fancies with an effort! Oliver's Paragraphs are all done, his battles, division-lists,

[1] In *The Pilgrim's Progress.*
[2] A late eighteenth-century Italian prince of adventurers, charlatans, and impostors: see Carlyle's essays on him and on "The Diamond Necklace."

successes all summed: and now in that awful unerring Court of Review, the real question first rises, Whether he has succeeded at all; whether he has not been defeated miserably forevermore? Let him come with world-wide *Io-Pæans*,[3] these avail him not. Let him come covered over with the world's execrations, gashed with ignominious death-wounds, the gallows-rope about his neck: what avails that? The word is, Come thou brave and faithful; the word is, Depart thou quack and accursed!

O Windbag, my right honourable friend, in very truth I pity thee. I say, these Paragraphs, and low or loud votings of thy poor fellow-blockheads of mankind, will never guide thee in any enterprise at all. Govern a country on such guidance? Thou canst not make a pair of shoes, sell a pennyworth of tape, on such. No, thy shoes are vamped up falsely to meet the market; behold, the leather only *seemed* to be tanned; thy shoes melt under me to rubbishy pulp, and are not veritable mud-defying shoes, but plausible vendible similitudes of shoes, — thou unfortunate, and I! O my right honourable friend, when the Paragraphs flowed in, who was like Sir Jabesh? On the swelling tide he mounted; higher, higher, triumphant, heaven-high. But the Paragraphs again ebbed out, as unwise Paragraphs needs must: Sir Jabesh lies stranded, sunk and forever sinking in ignominious ooze; the Mud-nymphs, and ever-deepening bottomless Oblivion, his portion to eternal time. 'Posterity?' Thou appealest to Posterity, thou? My right honourable friend, what will Posterity do for thee! The voting of Posterity, were it continued through centuries in thy favour, will be quite inaudible, extra-forensic, without any effect whatever. Posterity can do simply nothing for a man; nor even seem to do much, if the man be not brainsick. Besides, to tell thee truth, the bets are a thousand to one, Posterity will not hear of thee, my right honourable friend! Posterity, I have found, has generally his own Windbags sufficiently trumpeted in all market-places, and no leisure to attend to ours. Posterity, which has made of Norse Odin a similitude, and of Norman William a brute monster, what will or can it make of English Jabesh? O Heavens, 'Posterity!' —

"These poor persecuted Scotch Covenanters," said I to my inquiring Frenchman, in such stinted French as stood at command, "*ils s'en appelaient à*" — "A *la Postérité*," interrupted he, helping me out. — "*Ah, Monsieur, non, mille fois non!* They appealed to the Eternal God; not to Posterity at all! *C'était différent.*"

[3] Solemn songs.

CHAPTER XV

NEVERTHELESS, O Advanced Liberal, one cannot promise thee any 'New Religion,' for some time; to say truth, I do not think we have the smallest chance of any! Will the candid reader, by way of closing this Book Third, listen to a few transient remarks on that subject?

Candid readers have not lately met with any man who had less notion to interfere with their Thirty-Nine, or other Church-Articles; wherewith, very helplessly as is like, they may have struggled to form for themselves some not inconceivable hypothesis about this Universe, and their own Existence there. Superstition, my friend, is far from me; Fanaticism, for any *Fanum*[1] likely to arise soon on this Earth, is far. A man's Church-Articles are surely articles of price to him; and in these times one has to be tolerant of many strange 'Articles,' and of many still stranger 'No-articles,' which go about placarding themselves in a very distracted manner, — the numerous long placard-poles, and questionable infirm paste-pots, interfering with one's peaceable thoroughfare sometimes!

Fancy a man, moreover, recommending his fellow men to believe in God, that so Chartism might abate, and the Manchester Operatives be got to spin peaceably! The idea is more distracted than any placard-pole seen hitherto in a public thoroughfare of men! My friend, if thou ever do come to believe in God, thou wilt find all Chartism, Manchester riot, Parliamentary incompetence, Ministries of Windbag, and the wildest Social Dissolutions, and the burning up of this entire Planet, a most small matter in comparison. Brother, this Planet, I find, is but an inconsiderable sandgrain in the continents of Being: this Planet's poor temporary interests, thy interests and my interests there, when I look fixedly into that eternal Light-Sea and Flame-Sea with *its* eternal interests, dwindle literally into Nothing; my speech of it is — silence for the while. I will as soon think of making Galaxies and Star-

[1] Shrine, temple.

Systems to guide little herring-vessels by, as of preaching Religion that the Constable may continue possible.[2] O my Advanced-Liberal friend, this new second progress, of proceeding 'to invent God,'[3] is a very strange one! Jacobinism unfolded into Saint-Simonism[4] bodes innumerable blessed things; but the thing itself might draw tears from a Stoic! — As for me, some twelve or thirteen New Religions, heavy Packets, most of them unfranked, having arrived here from various parts of the world, in a space of six calendar months, I have instructed my invaluable friend the Stamped Postman to introduce no more of them, if the charge exceed one penny.[5]

Henry of Essex, duelling in that Thames Island, 'near to Reading Abbey,' had a religion. But was it in virtue of his seeing armed Phantasms of St. Edmund 'on the rim of the horizon,' looking minatory on him? Had that, intrinsically, anything to do with his religion at all? Henry of Essex's religion was the Inner Light or Moral Conscience of his own soul; such as is vouchsafed still to all souls of men; — which Inner Light shone here 'through such intellectual and other media' as there were; producing 'Phantasms,' Kircherean Visual-Spectra,[6] according to circumstances! It is so with all men. The clearer my Inner Light may shine, through the *less* turbid media; the *fewer* Phantasms it may produce, — the gladder surely shall I be, and not the sorrier! Hast thou reflected, O serious reader, Advanced-Liberal or other, that the one end, essence, use of all religion past, present and to come, was this only: To keep that same Moral Conscience or Inner Light of ours alive and shining — which certainly the 'Phantasms' and the 'turbid media' were not essential for! All religion was here to remind us, better or worse, of what we already know better or worse, of the quite *infinite* difference there is between a Good man and a Bad; to bid us love infinitely the one, abhor and avoid

[2] "Religion, being a great sanction to civil morality, is of use for keeping society in order, at least the lower classes, who have not the feeling of Honor in due force; and therefore, as a considerable help to the Constable and Hangman, *ought* decidedly to be kept up." (Carlyle's essay on Goethe.)

[3] "If there were no God, it would be necessary to invent him." (Voltaire)

[4] A school of Christian socialist thought some of whose ideas, set forth in a series of works (1817–25) by the Comte de Saint-Simon, are echoed in this concluding book of *Past and Present*.

[5] Prepaid penny postage had been introduced in 1840.

[6] Athanasius Kircher was the seventeenth-century inventor of the magic lantern.

infinitely the other, — strive infinitely to *be* the one, and not to be the other. 'All religion issues in due Practical Hero-worship.' He that has a soul unasphyxied will never want a religion; he that has a soul asphyxied, reduced to a succedaneum for salt, will never find any religion, though you rose from the dead to preach him one.[7]

But indeed, when men and reformers ask for 'a religion,' it is analogous to their asking, 'What would you have us to do?' and such like. They fancy that their religion too shall be a kind of Morrison's Pill, which they have only to swallow once, and all will be well. Resolutely once gulp down your Religion, your Morrison's Pill, you have it all plain sailing now; you can follow your affairs, your no-affairs, go along money-hunting, pleasure-hunting, dilettanteing, dangling, and miming and chattering like a Dead-Sea Ape: your Morrison will do your business for you. Men's notions are very strange! — Brother, I say there is not, was not, nor will ever be, in the wide circle of Nature, any Pill or Religion of that character. Man cannot afford thee such; for the very gods it is impossible. I advise thee to renounce Morrison; once for all, quit hope of the Universal Pill. For body, for soul, for individual or society, there has not any such article been made. *Non extat.* In Created Nature it is not, was not, will not be. In the void imbroglios of Chaos only, and realms of Bedlam, does some shadow of it hover, to bewilder and bemock the poor inhabitants *there.*

Rituals, Liturgies, Creeds, Hierarchies: all this is not religion; all this, were it dead as Odinism, as Fetishism,[8] does not kill religion at all! It is Stupidity alone, with never so many rituals, that kills religion. Is not this still a World? Spinning Cotton under Arkwright and Adam Smith; founding Cities by the Fountain of Juturna, on the Janiculum Mount;[9] tilling Canaan under Prophet Samuel and Psalmist David, man is ever man; the missionary of Unseen Powers; and great and victorious, while he continues true to his mission; mean, miserable, foiled, and at last annihilated and trodden out of sight and memory, when he proves untrue. Brother, thou art a Man, I think; thou are not a mere building Beaver, or two-legged Cotton-Spider; thou hast verily

[7] Luke 16:31.
[8] Worship of inanimate objects, found especially among West African tribes.
[9] A site in Rome.

a Soul in thee, asphyxied or otherwise! Sooty Manchester, — it too is built on the infinite Abysses; overspanned by the skyey Firmaments; and there is birth in it, and death in it; — and it is every whit as wonderful, as fearful, unimaginable, as the oldest Salem[10] or Prophetic City. Go or stand, in what time, in what place we will, are there not Immensities, Eternities over us, around us, in us:

> Solemn before us,
> Veiled, the dark Portal,
> Goal of all mortal: —
> Stars silent rest o'er us,
> Graves under us silent![11]

Between *these* two great Silences, the hum of all our spinning cylinders, Trades-Unions, Anti-Corn-Law Leagues and Carlton Clubs[12] goes on. Stupidity itself ought to pause a little, and consider that. I tell thee, through all thy Ledgers, Supply-and-demand Philosophies, and daily most modern melancholy Business and Cant, there does shine the presence of a Primeval Unspeakable; and thou wert wise to recognise, not with lips only, that same!

The Maker's Laws, whether they are promulgated in Sinai Thunder, to the ear or imagination, or quite otherwise promulgated, are the Laws of God; transcendant, everlasting, imperatively demanding obedience from all men. This, without any thunder, or with never so much thunder, thou, if there be any soul left in thee, canst know of a truth. The Universe, I say, is made by Law; the great Soul of the World is just and not unjust. Look thou, if thou have eyes or soul left, into this great shoreless Incomprehensible: in the heart of its tumultuous Appearances, Embroilments, and mad Time-vortexes, is there not, silent, eternal, an All-just, an All-beautiful; sole Reality and ultimate controlling Power of the whole? This is not a figure of speech; this is a fact. The fact of Gravitation known to all animals, is not surer than this inner Fact, which may be known to all men. He who knows this, it will sink, silent, awful, unspeakable, into

---

[10] Jerusalem.
[11] Goethe, "Symbolum."
[12] The Carlton was a fashionable London club for Conservatives, founded ten years earlier.

his heart. He will say with Faust: "Who *dare* name HIM?"[13] Most rituals or 'namings' he will fall in with at present, are like to be 'namings' — which shall be nameless! In silence, in the Eternal Temple, let him worship, if there be no fit word. Such knowledge, the crown of his whole spiritual being, the life of his life, let him keep and sacredly walk by. He has a religion. Hourly and daily, for himself and for the whole world, a faithful, unspoken, but not ineffectual prayer rises, "Thy will be done." His whole work on Earth is an emblematic spoken or acted prayer, Be the will of God done on Earth, — not the Devil's will, or any of the Devil's servants' wills! He has a religion, this man; an everlasting Loadstar that beams the brighter in the Heavens, the darker here on Earth grows the night around him. Thou, if thou know not this, what are all rituals, liturgies, mythologies, mass-chantings, turnings of the rotatory calabash? They are as nothing; in a good many respects they are as *less.* Divorced from this, getting half-divorced from this, they are a thing to fill one with a kind of horror; with a sacred inexpressible pity and fear. The most tragical thing a human eye can look on. It was said to the Prophet, "Behold, I will shew thee worse things than these: women weeping to Thammuz."[14] That was the acme of the Prophet's vision, — then as now.

Rituals, Liturgies, Credos, Sinai Thunder: I know more or less the history of these; the rise, progress, decline and fall of these. Can thunder from all the thirty-two azimuths,[15] repeated daily for centuries of years, make God's Laws more godlike to me? Brother, No. Perhaps I am grown to be a man now; and do not need the thunder and the terror any longer! Perhaps I am above being frightened; perhaps it is not Fear, but Reverence alone, that shall now lead me! — Revelations, Inspirations? Yes: and thy own god-created Soul; dost thou not call that a 'revelation?' Who made THEE? Where didst Thou come from? The Voice of Eternity, if thou be not a blasphemer and poor asphyxied mute, speaks with that tongue of thine! *Thou* art the latest Birth of Nature; it is 'the Inspiration of the Almighty'[16] that giveth *thee* understanding! My brother, my brother! —

Under baleful Atheisms, Mammonisms, Joe-Manton Dilettant-

---

[13] *Faust,* I.xvi.
[14] Ezekiel 8:14.
[15] Used in the more general sense of points of the compass.
[16] Job 32:8.

isms, with their appropriate Cants and Idolisms, and whatsoever scandalous rubbish obscures and all but extinguishes the soul of man, — religion now is; its Laws, written if not on stone tables, yet on the Azure of Infinitude, in the inner heart of God's Creation, certain as Life, certain as Death! I say the Laws are there, and thou shalt not disobey them. It were better for thee not. Better a hundred deaths than yes. Terrible 'penalties' withal, if thou still need 'penalties,' are there for disobeying. Dost thou observe, O redtape Politician, that fiery infernal Phenomenon, which men name FRENCH REVOLUTION, sailing, unlooked-for, unbidden; through thy inane Protocol Dominion: — far-seen, with splendour not of Heaven? Ten centuries will see it. There were Tanneries at Meudon for human skins. And Hell, very truly Hell, had power over God's upper Earth for a season. The cruelest Portent that has risen into created Space these ten centuries: let us hail it, with awestruck repentant hearts, as the voice once more of a God, though of one in wrath. Blessed be the God's-voice; for *it* is true, and Falsehoods have to cease before it! But for that same preternatural quasi-infernal Portent, one could not know what to make of this wretched world, in these days, at all. The deplorablest quack-ridden, and now hunger-ridden, downtrodden Despicability and *Flebile Ludibrium*,[17] of redtape Protocols, rotatory Calabashes, Poor-Law Bastilles: who is there that could think of *its* being fated to continue? —

Penalties enough, my brother! This penalty inclusive of all: Eternal Death to thy own hapless Self, if thou heed no other. Eternal Death, I say, — with many meanings old and new, of which let this single one suffice us here: The eternal impossibility for thee to *be* aught but a Chimera, and swift-vanishing deceptive Phantasm, in God's Creation; — swift-vanishing, never to reappear: why should *it* reappear! Thou hadst one chance, thou wilt never have another. Everlasting ages will roll on, and no other be given thee. The foolishest articulate-speaking soul now extant, may not he say to himself: "A whole Eternity I waited to be born; and now I have a whole Eternity waiting to see what I will do when born!" This is not Theology, this is Arithmetic. And thou but half-discernest this; thou but half-believest it? Alas, on the shores of the Dead Sea on Sabbath, there goes on a Tragedy! —

But we will leave this of 'Religion;' of which, to say truth, it

17 Lamentable mockery.

is chiefly profitable in these unspeakable days to keep silence.
Thou needest no 'New Religion;' nor art thou like to get any.
Thou hast already more 'religion' than thou makest use of. This
day, thou knowest ten commanded duties, seest in thy mind ten
things which should be done, for one that thou doest! *Do* one
of them; this of itself will shew thee ten others which can and
shall be done. "But my future fate?" Yes, thy future fate, indeed?
Thy future fate, while thou makest *it* the chief question, seems to
me — extremely questionable! I do not think it can be good.
Norse Odin, immemorial centuries ago, did not he, though a
poor Heathen, in the dawn of Time, teach us that, for the Dastard
there was and could be no good fate; no harbour anywhere, save
down with Hela,[18] in the pool of Night! Dastards, Knaves, are
they that lust for Pleasure, that tremble at Pain. For this world
and for the next, Dastards are a class of creatures made to be
'arrested;' they are good for nothing else, can look for nothing
else. A greater than Odin has been here. A greater than Odin
has taught us — not a greater Dastardism, I hope! My brother,
thou must pray for a *soul;* struggle, as with life-and-death energy,
to get back thy soul! Know that 'religion' is no Morrison's Pill
from without, but a reawakening of thy own Self from within: —
and, above all, leave me alone of thy 'religions' and 'new religions'
here and elsewhere! I am weary of this sick croaking for a
Morrison's-Pill religion; for any and for every such. I want none
such; and discern all such to be impossible. The resuscitation of
old liturgies fallen dead; much more, the manufacture of new
liturgies that will never be alive: how hopeless! Stylitisms,[19]
eremite fanaticisms and fakeerisms; spasmodic agonistic posture-
makings, and narrow, cramped, morbid, if forever noble wres-
tlings: all this is not a thing desirable to me. It is a thing the
world *has* done once, — when its beard was not grown as now!

And yet there is, at worst, one Liturgy which does remain forever unexceptionable: that of *Praying* (as the old Monks did
withal) *by Working.* And indeed the Prayer which accomplished
itself in special chapels at stated hours, and went not with a
man, rising up from all his Work and Action, at all moments sanc-
tifying the same, — what was it ever good for? 'Work is Worship:'

[18] The Norse goddess of death.
[19] St. Simeon Stylites lived atop a pillar in the desert, 423–459. After him
came an order of Stylites who practiced the same extreme asceticism.

yes, in a highly considerable sense, — which, in the present state
of all 'worship,' who is there that can unfold! He that understands
it well, understands the Prophecy of the whole Future; the last
Evangel, which has included all others. *Its* cathedral the Dome
of Immensity, — hast thou seen it? coped with the star-galaxies;
paved with the green mosaic of land and ocean; and for altar,
verily, the Star-throne of the Eternal! Its litany and psalmody
the noble acts, the heroic work and suffering, and true Heart-
utterance of all the Valiant of the Sons of Men. Its choir-music
the ancient Winds and Oceans, and deep-toned, inarticulate, but
most speaking voices of Destiny and History, — supernal ever as
of old. Between two great Silences:

> Stars silent rest o'er us,
> Graves under us silent.

Between which two great Silences, do not, as we said, all human
Noises, in the naturalest times, most *preter*naturally march and
roll? —

I will insert this also, in a lower strain, from Sauerteig's *Æsthe-
tische Springwürzel.*[20] 'Worship?' says he: 'Before that inane
tumult of Hearsay filled men's heads, while the world lay yet
silent, and the heart true and open, many things were Worship!
To the primeval man whatsoever good came, descended on him
(as, in mere fact, it ever does) direct from God; whatsoever duty
lay visible for him, this a Supreme God had prescribed. To the
present hour I ask thee, Who else? For the primeval man, in
whom dwelt Thought, this Universe was all a Temple; Life
everywhere a Worship.

'What Worship, for example, is there not in mere Washing!
Perhaps one of the most moral things a man, in common cases,
has it in his power to do. Strip thyself, go into the bath, or were
it into the limpid pool and running brook, and there wash and
be clean; thou wilt step out again a purer and a better man.
This consciousness of perfect outer pureness, that to thy skin
there now adheres no foreign speck of imperfection, how it
radiates in on thee, with cunning symbolic influences, to thy
very soul! Thou hast an increase of tendency towards all good
things whatsoever. The oldest Eastern Sages, with joy and holy
gratitude, had felt it so, — and that it was the Maker's gift and
will. Whose else *is* it? It remains a religious duty, from oldest

[20] *Grand Key to Esthetics.*

times, in the East. — Nor could Herr Professor Strauss,[21] when
I put the question, deny that for us at present it is still such here
in the West! To that dingy fuliginous[22] Operative, emerging from
his soot-mill, what is the first duty I will prescribe, and offer help
towards? That he clean the skin of him. *Can* he pray, by any
ascertained method? One knows not entirely: — but with soap
and a sufficiency of water, he can wash. Even the dull English
feel something of this; they have a saying, "Cleanliness is near
of kin to Godliness:" — yet never, in any country, saw I operative
men worse washed, and, in a climate drenched with the softest
cloud-water, such a scarcity of baths!' — Alas, Sauerteig, our
'operative men' are at present short even of potatoes: what 'duty'
can you prescribe to them!

Or let us give a glance at China. Our new friend, the Emperor
there,[23] is Pontiff of three hundred million men; who do all live
and work, these many centuries now; authentically patronised
by Heaven so far; and therefore must have some 'religion' of a
kind. This Emperor-Pontiff has, in fact, a religious belief of
certain Laws of Heaven; observes, with a religious rigour, his
'three thousand punctualities,' given out by men of insight, some
sixty generations since, as a legible transcript of the same, — the
Heavens do seem to say, not totally an incorrect one. He has not
much of a ritual, this Pontiff-Emperor; believes, it is likest, with
the old Monks, that 'Labour is Worship.' His most public Act of
Worship, it appears, is the drawing solemnly at a certain day, on
the green bosom of our Mother Earth, when the Heavens, after
dead black winter, have again with their vernal radiances
awakened her, a distinct red Furrow with the Plough, — signal
that all the Ploughs of China are to begin ploughing and worshipping! It is notable enough. He, in sight of the Seen and
Unseen Powers, draws his distinct red Furrow there; saying, and
praying, in mute symbolism, so many most eloquent things!

If you ask this Pontiff, "Who made him? What is to become of
him and us?" he maintains a dignified reserve; waves his hand

[21] David Friedrich Strauss was the leader of the school of Biblical "higher
criticism" which sought to prove that portions of Scripture were collections
of myths.

[22] Sooty.

[23] The Emperor was a "new friend" willy-nilly: his friendship was enforced by his losing the Opium War of 1840–42. The details in the ensuing
passage may be derived from recent books on China, such as Samuel Kidd's
(1841).

and pontiff-eyes over the unfathomable deep of Heaven, the 'Tsien,' the azure kingdoms of Infinitude; as if asking, "Is it doubtful that we are right *well* made? Can aught that is *wrong* become of us?" — He and his three hundred millions (it is their chief 'punctuality') visit yearly the Tombs of their Fathers; each man the Tomb of his Father and his Mother: alone there, in silence, with what of 'worship' or of other thought there may be, pauses solemnly each man; the divine Skies all silent over him; the divine Graves, and this divinest Grave, all silent under him; the pulsings of his own soul, if he have any soul, alone audible. Truly it may be a kind of worship! Truly, if a man cannot get some glimpse into the Eternities, looking through this portal, — through what other need he try it?

Our friend the Pontiff-Emperor permits cheerfully, though with contempt, all manner of Buddhists, Bonzes, Talapoins[24] and such like, to build brick Temples, on the voluntary principle; to worship with what of chantings, paper-lanterns and tumultuous brayings, pleases them; and make night hideous, since they find some comfort in so doing. Cheerfully, though with contempt. He is a wiser Pontiff than many persons think! He is as yet the one Chief Potentate or Priest in this Earth who has made a distinct systematic attempt at what we call the ultimate result of all religion, 'Practical Hero-worship:' he does incessantly, with true anxiety, in such way as he can, search and sift (it would appear) his whole enormous population for the Wisest born among them; by which Wisest, as by born Kings, these three hundred million men are governed. The Heavens, to a certain extent, do appear to countenance him. These three hundred millions actually make porcelain, souchong tea, with innumerable other things; and fight, under Heaven's flag, against Necessity; — and have fewer Seven-Years Wars, Thirty-Years Wars, French-Revolution Wars, and infernal fightings with each other, than certain millions elsewhere have!

Nay, in our poor distracted Europe itself, in these newest times, have there not religious voices risen, —with a religion new and yet the oldest; entirely indisputable to all hearts of men? Some I do know, who did not call or think themselves 'Prophets,' far enough from that; but who were, in very truth, melodious Voices from the eternal Heart of Nature once again; souls forever

[24] Both words mean Buddhist monks.

venerable to all that have a soul. A French Revolution is one
phenomenon; as complement and spiritual exponent thereof, a
Poet Goethe and German Literature is to me another. The old
Secular or Practical World, so to speak, having gone up in fire,
is not here the prophecy and dawn of a new Spiritual World,
parent of far nobler, wider, new Practical Worlds? A Life of
Antique devoutness, Antique veracity and heroism, has again
become possible, is again *seen* actual there, for the most modern
man. A phenomenon, as quiet as it is, comparable for greatness
to no other! 'The great event for the world is, now as always,
the arrival in it of a new Wise Man.' Touches there are, be the
Heavens ever thanked, of new Sphere-melody; audible once more,
in the infinite jargoning discords and poor scrannel-pipings[25] of
the thing called Literature; — priceless there, as the voice of
new Heavenly Psalms! Literature, like the old Prayer-Collections
of the first centuries, were it 'well selected from and burnt,' contains precious things. For Literature, with all its printing-presses,
puffing-engines[26] and shoreless deafening triviality, *is* yet 'the
Thought of Thinking Souls.'[27] A sacred 'religion,' if you like the
name, does live in the heart of that strange froth-ocean, not
wholly froth, which we call Literature; and will more and more
disclose itself therefrom; — not now as scorching Fire: the red
smoky scorching Fire has purified itself into white sunny Light.
Is not Light grander than Fire? It is the same element in a state
of purity.

My candid readers, we will march out of this Third Book with
a rhythmic word of Goethe's on our tongue; a word which perhaps has already sung itself, in dark hours and in bright, through
many a heart. To me, finding it devout yet wholly credible and
veritable, full of piety yet free of cant; to me joyfully finding much
in it, and joyfully missing so much in it, this little snatch of music,
by the greatest German Man, sounds like a stanza in the grand
Road-Song and *Marching-Song* of our great Teutonic Kindred,
wending, wending, valiant and victorious, through the undiscovered Deeps of Time! He calls it *Mason-Lodge*,[28] — not Psalm or
Hymn:

[25] *Scrannel:* thin. Cf. Milton, "Lycidas," line 124.
[26] A pun: the secondary meaning of *puff* is "extravagantly laudatory advertising," as of books. It is so used above, p. 144.
[27] Carlyle in his essay on Scott.
[28] Also known as "Symbolum."

The Mason's ways are
A type of Existence,
And his persistance
Is as the days are
Of men in this world.

The Future hides in it
Good hap and sorrow;
We press still thorow,
Nought that abides in it
Daunting us, — onward.

And solemn before us,
Veiled, the dark Portal,
Goal of all mortal: —
Stars silent rest o'er us,
Graves under us silent.

But heard are the Voices,
Voice of the Sages,
The Worlds and the Ages:
"Choose well, your choice is
Brief and yet endless;

Here eyes do regard you,
In Eternity's stilness;
Here is all fulness,
Ye brave, to reward you;
Work, and despair not."

BOOK IV

Horoscope

CHAPTER I

To predict the Future, to manage the Present, would not be so impossible, had not the Past been so sacrilegiously mishandled; effaced, and what is worse, defaced! The Past cannot be seen; the Past, looked at through the medium of 'Philosophical History' in these times, cannot even be *not* seen: it is misseen; affirmed to have existed, — and to have been a godless Impossibility. Your Norman Conquerors, true royal souls, crowned kings as such, were vulturous irrational tyrants: your Becket was a noisy egoist and hypocrite; getting his brains spilt on the floor of Canterbury Cathedral, to secure the main chance, — somewhat uncertain how! "Enthusiasm," and even "honest Enthusiasm," — yes, of course:

> The Dog, to gain his private ends,
> *Went* mad, and bit the Man! — [1]

For in truth, the eye sees in all things 'what it brought with it the means of seeing.' A godless century, looking back on centuries that were godly, produces portraitures more miraculous than any other. All was inane discord in the Past; brute Force bore rule everywhere; Stupidity, savage Unreason, fitter for Bedlam than for a human World! Whereby indeed it becomes sufficiently natural that the like qualities, in new sleeker habiliments, should continue in our time to rule. Millions enchanted in Bastille Workhouses; Irish Widows proving their relationship by typhus-fever: what would you have? It was ever so, or worse. Man's History, was it not always even this: The cookery and eating up of imbecile Dupedom by successful Quackhood; the battle, with various weapons, of vulturous Quack and Tyrant against vulturous Tyrant and Quack? No God was in the Past Time; nothing but Mechanisms and Chaotic Brute-gods: — how shall the poor 'Philosophic Historian,' to whom his own century is all godless, see any God in other centuries?

[1] Goldsmith, "Elegy on the Death of a Mad Dog"; inaccurately quoted.

239

Men believe in Bibles, and disbelieve in them: but of all Bibles the frightfulest to disbelieve in is this 'Bible of Universal History.' This is the Eternal Bible and God's-Book, 'which every born man,' till once the soul and eyesight are distinguished in him, 'can and must, with his own eyes, see the God's-Finger writing!' To discredit this, is an *infidelity* like no other. Such infidelity you would punish, if not by fire and faggot, which are difficult to manage in our times, yet by the most peremptory order, To hold its peace till it got something wiser to say. Why should the blessed Silence be broken into noises, to communicate only the like of this? If the Past have no God's-Reason in it, nothing but Devil's-Unreason, let the Past be eternally forgotten: mention *it* no more; — we whose ancestors were all hanged, why should we talk of ropes!

It is, in brief, not true that men ever lived by Delirium, Hypocrisy, Injustice, or any form of Unreason, since they came to inhabit this Planet. It is not true that they ever did, or ever will, live except by the reverse of these. Men will again be taught this. Their acted History will then again be a Heroism; their written History, what it once was, an Epic. Nay, forever it is either such; or else it virtually is — Nothing. Were it written in a thousand volumes, the Unheroic of such volumes hastens incessantly to be forgotten; the net content of an Alexandrian Library[2] of Unheroics is, and will ultimately shew itself to be, *zero*. What man is interested to remember *it;* have not all men, at all times, the liveliest interest to forget it? — 'Revelations,' if not celestial, then infernal, will teach us that God is; we shall then, if needful, discern without difficulty that He has always been! The Dryasdust Philosophisms and enlightened Scepticisms of the Eighteenth Century, historical and other, will have to survive for a while with the Physiologists, as a memorable *Nightmare-Dream*. All this haggard epoch, with its ghastly Doctrines, and death's-head Philosophies 'teaching by example' or otherwise, will one day have become, what to our Moslem friends their godless ages are, 'the Period of Ignorance.'

If the convulsive struggles of the last Half-Century have taught poor struggling convulsed Europe any truth, it may perhaps be this as the essence of innumerable others: That Europe requires a real Aristocracy, a real Priesthood, or it cannot continue to exist. Huge French Revolutions, Napoleonisms, then Bourbonisms with

[2] Founded about 284 B.C. at Alexandria, Egypt; reputedly the largest collection of books (700,000?) ever assembled before the invention of printing.

their corollary of Three Days, finishing in very unfinal Louis-Philippisms:[3] all this ought to be didactic! All this may have taught us, That False Aristocracies are insupportable; that No-Aristocracies, Liberty-and-Equalities are impossible; that True Aristocracies are at once indispensable and not easily attained.

Aristocracy and Priesthood, a Governing Class and a Teaching Class: these two, sometimes separate, and endeavouring to harmonise themselves, sometimes conjoined as one, and the King a Pontiff-King: — there did no Society exist without these two vital elements, there will none exist. It lies in the very nature of man: you will visit no remotest village in the most republican country of the world, where virtually or actually you do not find these two powers at work. Man, little as he may suppose it, is necessitated to obey superiors. He is a social being in virtue of this necessity; nay he could not be gregarious otherwise. He obeys those whom he esteems better than himself, wiser, braver; and will forever obey such; and even be ready and delighted to do it.

The Wiser, Braver: these, a Virtual Aristocracy everywhere and everywhen, do in all Societies that reach any articulate shape, develop themselves into a ruling class, an Actual Aristocracy, with settled modes of operating, what are called laws and even *private-laws* or privileges, and so forth; very notable to look upon in this world. — Aristocracy and Priesthood, we say, are sometimes united. For indeed the Wiser and the Braver are properly but one class; no wise man but needed first of all to be a brave man, or he never had been wise. The noble Priest was always a noble *Aristos* to begin with, and something more to end with. Your Luther, your Knox,[4] your Anselm, Becket, Abbot Samson, Samuel Johnson, if they had not been brave enough, by what possibility could they ever have been wise? — If, from accident or forethought, this your Actual Aristocracy have got discriminated into Two Classes, there can be no doubt but the Priest Class is the more dignified; supreme over the other, as governing head is over active hand. And yet in practice again, it is likeliest the reverse will be found arranged; — a sign that the arrangement is already vitiated; that a split is introduced into it, which will widen and widen till the whole be rent asunder.

In England, in Europe generally, we may say that these two Virtualities have unfolded themselves into Actualities, in by far

---

[3] Charles X, a Bourbon, was deposed in the three-day revolution of 1830 and succeeded by Louis Philippe.

[4] John Knox, sixteenth-century Scottish church reformer.

the noblest and richest manner any region of the world ever saw. A spiritual Guideship, a practical Governorship, fruit of the grand conscious endeavours, say rather of the immeasurable unconscious instincts and necessities of men, have established themselves; very strange to behold. Everywhere, while so much has been forgotten, you find the King's Palace, and the Viceking's Castle, Mansion, Manorhouse; till there is not an inch of ground from sea to sea but has both its King and Viceking, long due series of Vicekings, its Squire, Earl, Duke or whatever the title of him, — to whom you have given the land that he may govern you in it.

More touching still, there is not a hamlet where poor peasants congregate, but by one means and another a Church-Apparatus has been got together, — roofed edifice, with revenues and belfries; pulpit, reading-desk, with Books and Methods: possibility, in short, and strict prescription, That a man stand there and speak of spiritual things to men. It is beautiful; — even in its great obscuration and decadence, it is among the beautifulest, most touching objects one sees on the Earth. This Speaking Man has indeed, in these times, wandered terribly from the point; has, alas, as it were totally lost sight of the point: yet, at bottom, whom have we to compare with him? Of all public functionaries boarded and lodged on the Industry of Modern Europe, is there one worthier of the board he has? A man even professing, and never so languidly making still some endeavour, to save the souls of men: contrast him with a man professing to do little but shoot the partridges of men! I wish he could find the point again, this Speaking One; and stick to it with tenacity, with deadly energy; for there is need of him yet! The Speaking Function, this of Truth coming to us with a living voice, nay in a living shape, and as a concrete practical exemplar: this, with all our Writing and Printing Functions, has a perennial place. Could he but find the point again, — take the old spectacles off his nose, and looking up discover, almost in contact with him, what the *real* Satanas, and soul-devouring, world-devouring *Devil*, now is! Original Sin and such like are bad enough, I doubt not: but distilled Gin, dark Ignorance, Stupidity, dark Corn-Law, Bastille and Company, what are they! *Will* he discover our new real Satan, whom he has to fight; or go on droning through his old nose-spectacles about old extinct Satans; and never see the real one, till he *feel* him at his own throat and ours? That is a question, for the world! Let us not intermeddle with it here.

Sorrowful, phantasmal as this same Double Aristocracy of Teachers and Governors now looks, it is worth all men's while to know that the purport of it is and remains noble and most real. Dryasdust, looking merely at the surface, is greatly in error as to those ancient Kings. William Conqueror, William Rufus or Redbeard, Stephen Curthose himself, much more Henry Beauclerc and our brave Plantagenet Henry:[5] the life of these men was not a vulturous Fighting; it was a valorous Governing, — to which occasionally Fighting did, and alas must yet, though far seldomer now, superadd itself as an accident, a distressing impedimental adjunct. The fighting too was indispensable, for ascertaining who had the might over whom, the right over whom. By much hard fighting, as we once said, 'the unrealities, beaten into dust, flew gradually off;' and left the plain reality and fact, "Thou stronger than I; thou wiser than I; thou king, and subject I," in a somewhat clearer condition.

Truly we cannot enough admire, in those Abbot-Samson and William-Conqueror times, the arrangement they had made of their Governing Classes. Highly interesting to observe how the sincere insight, on their part, into what did, of primary necessity, behove to be accomplished, had led them to the way of accomplishing it, and in the course of time to get it accomplished! No imaginary Aristocracy would serve their turn; and accordingly they attained a real one. The Bravest men, who, it is ever to be repeated and remembered, are also on the whole the Wisest, Strongest, every way Best, had here, with a respectable degree of accuracy, been got selected; seated each on his piece of territory, which was lent him, then gradually given him, that he might govern it. These Vicekings, each on his portion of the common soil of England, with a Head King over all, were a 'Virtuality perfected into an Actuality' really to an astonishing extent.

For those were rugged stalwart ages; full of earnestness, of a rude God's-truth: — nay, at any rate, their *quilting* was so unspeakably *thinner* than ours; Fact came swiftly on them, if at any time they had yielded to Phantasm! 'The Knaves and Dastards' had to be 'arrested' in some measure; or the world, almost within year and day, found that it could not live. The Knaves and Dastards accordingly were got arrested. Dastards upon the very throne had to be got arrested, and taken off the throne, — by such

[5] All kings of England, 1066–1189: William I, William II, Stephen, Henry I, Henry II.

methods as there were; by the roughest method, if there chanced
to be no smoother one! Doubtless there was much harshness
of operation, much severity; as indeed government and surgery
are often somewhat severe. Gurth born thrall of Cedric, it is like,
got cuffs as often as pork-parings, if he misdemeaned himself;
but Gurth did belong to Cedric: no human creature then went
about connected with nobody; left to go his ways into Bastilles
or worse, under *Laissez-faire;* reduced to prove his relationship
by dying of typhus-fever! — Days come when there is no King in
Israel, but every man is his own king, doing that which is right
in his own eyes;[6] — and tarbarrels are burnt to 'Liberty,' 'Tenpound Franchise' and the like, with considerable effect in various
ways! —

That Feudal Aristocracy, I say, was no imaginary one. To a
respectable degree, its *Jarls*, what we now call Earls, were *Strong-
Ones* in fact as well as etymology; its Dukes *Leaders;* its Lords
Law-wards. They did all the Soldiering and Police of the country,
all the Judging, Law-making, even the Church-Extension; whatsoever in the way of Governing, of Guiding and Protecting could
be done. It was a Land Aristocracy; it managed the Governing
of this English People, and had the reaping of the Soil of England
in return. It is, in many senses, the Law of Nature, this same Law
of Feudalism; — no right Aristocracy but a Land one! The
curious are invited to meditate upon it in these days. Soldiering,
Police and Judging, Church-Extension, nay real Government and
Guidance, all this was actually *done* by the Holders of the Land
in return for their Land. How much of it is now done by them;
done by anybody? Good Heavens, "Laissez-faire, Do ye nothing,
eat your wages and sleep," is everywhere the passionate half-wise
cry of this time; and they will not so much as do nothing, but
must do mere Corn-Laws! We raise Fifty-two millions, from the
general mass of us, to get our Governing done, — or, alas, to get
ourselves persuaded that it is done: and the 'peculiar burden of
the Land' is to pay, not all this, but to pay, as I learn, one twenty-
fourth part of all this.[7] Our first Chartist Parliament, or Oliver
Redivivus,[8] you would say, will know where to lay the new
taxes of England! — Or, alas, taxes? If we made the Holders of
the Land pay every shilling still of the expense of Governing the

---

[6] Judges 17:6, 21:25.
[7] In 1841 the tax paid by landowners was approximately one twenty-fourth
of the total governmental revenue of £52,000,000.
[8] Returned from the dead.

Land, what were all that? The Land, by mere hired Governors, cannot be got governed. You cannot hire men to govern the Land: it is by a mission not contracted for in the Stock-Exchange, but felt in their own hearts as coming out of Heaven, that men can govern a Land. The mission of a Land Aristocracy is a *sacred* one, in both the senses of that old word. The footing it stands on, at present, might give rise to thoughts other than of Corn-Laws! —

But truly a 'Splendour of God,' as in William Conqueror's rough oath, did dwell in those old rude veracious ages; did inform, more and more, with a heavenly nobleness, all departments of their work and life. Phantasms could not yet walk abroad in mere Cloth Tailorage; they were at least Phantasms 'on the rim of the horizon,' pencilled there by an eternal Light-beam from within. A most 'practical' Hero-worship went on, unconsciously or half-consciously, everywhere. A Monk Samson, with a maximum of two shillings in his pocket, could, without ballot-box, be made a Viceking of, being seen to be worthy. The difference between a good man and a bad man was as yet felt to be, what it forever is, an immeasurable one. Who *durst* have elected a Pandarus Dog-draught, in those days, to any office, Carlton Club, Senatorship,, or place whatsoever? It was felt that the arch Satanas and no other had a clear right of property in Pandarus; that it were better for you to have no hand in Pandarus, to keep out of Pandarus his neighbourhood! Which is, to this hour, the mere fact; though for the present, alas, the forgotten fact. I think they were comparatively blessed times those, in their way! 'Violence,' 'war,' 'disorder:' well, what is war, and death itself, to such a perpetual life-in-death, and 'peace and peace where there is no peace!'[9] Unless some Hero-worship, in its new appropriate form, can return, this world does not promise to be very habitable long.

Old Anselm, exiled Archbishop of Canterbury, one of the purest-minded 'men of genius,' was travelling to make his appeal to Rome against King Rufus, — a man of rough ways, in whom the 'inner Light-beam' shone very fitfully. It is beautiful to read, in Monk Eadmer, how the Continental populations welcomed and venerated this Anselm, as no French population now venerates Jean-Jacques[10] or giant-killing Voltaire; as not even an American

[9] Jeremiah 6:14.
[10] Jean-Jacques Rousseau, like Voltaire, was among the philosophical begetters of the French Revolution.

population now venerates a Schnüspel the distinguished Novelist! They had, by phantasy and true insight, the intensest conviction that a God's Blessing dwelt in this Anselm, — as is my conviction too. They crowded round, with bent knees and enkindled hearts, to receive his blessing, to hear his voice, to see the light of his face. My blessings on them and on him! — But the notablest was a certain necessitous or covetous Duke of Burgundy, in straitened circumstances we shall hope, — who reflected that in all likelihood this English Archbishop, going towards Rome to appeal, must have taken store of cash with him to bribe the Cardinals. Wherefore he of Burgundy, for his part, decided to lie in wait and rob him. 'In an open space of a wood,' some 'wood' then green and growing, eight centuries ago, in Burgundian Land, — this fierce Duke, with fierce steel followers, shaggy, savage, as the Russian Bear, dashes out on the weak old Anselm; who is riding along there, on his small quiet-going pony; escorted only by Eadmer and another poor Monk on ponies; and, except small modicum of roadmoney, not a gold coin in his possession. The steelclad Russian Bear emerges, glaring: the old white-bearded man starts not, — paces on unmoved, looking into him with those clear old earnest eyes, with that venerable sorrowful time-worn face; of whom no man or thing need be afraid, and who also is afraid of no created man or thing. The fire-eyes of his Burgundian Grace meet these clear eye-glances, convey them swift to his heart: he bethinks him that probably this feeble, fearless, hoary Figure has in it something of the Most High God; that probably he shall be damned if he meddle with it, — that, on the whole, he had better not. He plunges, the rough savage, from his warhorse, down to his knees; embraces the feet of old Anselm: he too begs his blessing; orders men to escort him, guard him from being robbed, and under dread penalties see him safe on his way. *Per os Dei*, as his Majesty was wont to ejaculate!

Neither is this quarrel of Rufus and Anselm, of Henry and Becket, uninstructive to us. It was, at bottom, a great quarrel. For, admitting that Anselm was full of divine blessing, he by no means included in him all forms of divine blessing: — there were far other forms withal, which he little dreamed of; and William Redbeard was unconsciously the representative and spokesman of these. In truth, could your divine Anselm, your divine Pope Gregory have had their way, the results had been very notable. Our Western World had all become a European Thibet, with one

Grand Lama sitting at Rome; our one honourable business that of singing mass, all day and all night. Which would not in the least have suited us! The Supreme Powers willed it not so.

It was as if King Redbeard unconsciously, addressing Anselm, Becket and the others, had said: "Right Reverend, your Theory of the Universe is indisputable by man or devil. To the core of our heart we feel that this divine thing, which you call Mother Church, does fill the whole world hitherto known, and is and shall be all our salvation and all our desire. And yet — and yet — Behold, though it is an unspoken secret, the world is *wider* than any of us think, Right Reverend! Behold, there are yet other immeasurable Sacrednesses in this that you call Heathenism, Secularity! On the whole I, in an obscure but most rooted manner, feel that I cannot comply with you. Western Thibet and perpetual mass-chanting, — No. I am, so to speak, in the family-way; with child, of I know not what, — certainly of something far different from this! I have — *Per os Dei*, I have Manchester Cotton-trades, Bromwicham[11] Iron-trades, American Commonwealths, Indian Empires, Steam Mechanisms and Shakspeare Dramas, in my belly; and cannot do it, Right Reverend!" — So accordingly it was decided: and Saxon Becket spilt his life in Canterbury Cathedral, as Scottish Wallace did on Tower-Hill, and as generally a noble man and martyr has to do, — not for nothing; no, but for a divine something, other than *he* had altogether calculated. We will now quit this of the hard, organic, but limited Feudal Ages; and glance timidly into the immense Industrial Ages, as yet all inorganic, and in a quite pulpy condition, requiring desperately to harden themselves into some organism!

Our Epic having now become *Tools and the Man,* it is more than usually impossible to prophesy the Future. The boundless Future does lie there, predestined, nay already extant though unseen; hiding, in its Continents of Darkness, 'good hap and sorrow:' but the supremest intelligence of man cannot prefigure much of it: — the united intelligence and effort of All Men in all coming generations, this alone will gradually prefigure it, and figure and form it into a seen fact! Straining our eyes hitherto, the utmost effort of intelligence sheds but some most glimmering dawn, a little way into its dark enormous Deeps: only huge outlines loom uncertain on the sight; and the ray of prophecy, at a short

[11] Birmingham.

distance, expires. But may we not say, here as always, Sufficient for the day is the evil thereof! To shape the whole Future is not our problem; but only to shape faithfully a small part of it, according to rules already known. It is perhaps possible for each of us, who will with due earnestness inquire, to ascertain clearly what he, for his own part, ought to do: this let him, with true heart, do, and continue doing. The general issue will, as it has always done, rest well with a Higher Intelligence than ours.

One grand 'outline,' or even two, many earnest readers may perhaps, at this stage of the business, be able to prefigure for themselves, — and draw some guidance from. One prediction, or even two, are already possible. For the Life-tree Igdrasil, in all its new developments, is the selfsame world-old Life-tree: having found an element or elements there, running from the very roots of it in Hela's Realms, in the Well of Mimer[12] and of the Three Nornas or TIMES, up to this present hour of it in our own hearts, we conclude that such will have to continue. A man has, in his own soul, an Eternal; can read something of the Eternal there, if he will look! He already knows what will continue; what cannot, by any means or appliance whatsoever, be made to continue!

One wide and widest 'outline' ought really, in all ways, to be becoming clear to us; this namely: That a 'Splendour of God,' in one form or other, will have to unfold itself from the heart of these our Industrial Ages too; or they will never get themselves 'organised;' but continue chaotic, distressed, distracted evermore, and have to perish in frantic suicidal dissolution. A second 'outline' or prophecy, narrower, but also wide enough, seems not less certain: That there will again *be* a King in Israel; a system of Order and Government; and every man shall, in some measure, see himself constrained to do that which is right in the King's eyes. This too we may call a sure element of the Future; for this too is of the Eternal; — this too is of the Present, though hidden from most; and without it no fibre of the Past ever was. An actual new Sovereignty, Industrial Aristocracy, real not imaginary Aristocracy, is indispensable and indubitable for us.

But what an Aristocracy; on what new, far more complex and cunningly devised conditions than that old Feudal fighting one! For we are to bethink us that the Epic verily is not *Arms and the Man,* but *Tools and the Man,* — an infinitely wider kind of Epic.

[12] A spring flowing from the roots of Igdrasil.

And again we are to bethink us that men cannot now be bound to men by *brass-collars,* — not at all: that this brass-collar method, in all figures of it, has vanished out of Europe forevermore! Huge Democracy, walking the streets everywhere in its Sack Coat, has asserted so much; irrevocably, brooking no reply! True enough, man *is* forever the 'born thrall' of certain men, born master of certain other men, born equal of certain others, let him acknowledge the fact or not. It is unblessed for him when he cannot acknowledge this fact; he is in the chaotic state, ready to perish, till he do get the fact acknowledged. But no man is, or can henceforth be, the brass-collar thrall of any man; you will have to bind him by other, far nobler and cunninger methods. Once for all, he is to be loose of the brass-collar, to have a scope *as* wide as his faculties now are: — will he not be all the usefuler to you, in that new state? Let him go abroad as a trusted one, as a free one; and return home to you with rich earnings at night! Gurth could only tend pigs; this one will build cities, conquer waste worlds. — How, in conjunction with inevitable Democracy, indispensable Sovereignty is to exist: certainly it is the hugest question ever heretofore propounded to Mankind! The solution of which is work for long years and centuries. Years and centuries, of one knows not what complexion; — blessed or unblessed, according as they shall, with earnest valiant effort, make progress therein, or, in slothful unveracity and dilettantism, only talk of making progress. For either progress therein, or swift and ever swifter progress towards dissolution, is henceforth a necessity.

It is of importance that this grand reformation were begun; that Corn-Law Debatings and other jargon, little less than delirious in such a time, had fled far away, and left us room to begin! For the evil has grown practical, extremely conspicuous; if it be not seen and provided for, the blindest fool will have to feel it ere long. There is much that can wait; but there is something also that cannot wait. With millions of eager Working Men imprisoned in 'Impossibility' and Poor-Law Bastilles, it is time that some means of dealing with them were trying to become 'possible!' Of the Government of England, of all articulate-speaking function- aries, real and imaginary Aristocracies, of me and of thee, it is imperatively demanded, "How do you mean to manage these men? Where are they to find a supportable existence? What is to become of them, — and of you!"

CHAPTER II

BRIBERY COMMITTEE

IN the case of the late Bribery Committee,[1] it seemed to be the conclusion of the soundest practical minds that Bribery could not be put down; that Pure Election was a thing we had seen the last of, and must now go on without, as we best could. A conclusion not a little startling; to which it requires a practical mind of some seasoning to reconcile yourself at once! It seems, then, we are henceforth to get ourselves constituted Legislators not according to what merit we may have, or even what merit we may seem to have, but according to the length of our purse, and our frankness, impudence and dexterity in laying out the contents of the same. Our theory, written down in all books and law-books, spouted forth from all barrel-heads, is perfect purity of Tenpound Franchise, absolute sincerity of question put and answer given; — and our practice is irremediable bribery; irremediable, unpunishable, which you will do more harm than good by attempting to punish! Once more, a very startling conclusion indeed; which, whatever the soundest practical minds in Parliament may think of it, invites all British men to meditations of various kinds.

A Parliament, one would say, which proclaims itself elected and eligible by bribery, tells the Nation that is governed by it a piece of singular news. Bribery: have we reflected what bribery is? Bribery means not only length of purse, which is neither qualification nor the contrary for legislating well; but it means dishonesty, and even impudent dishonesty; — brazen insensibility to lying and to making others lie; total oblivion, and flinging overboard, for the nonce, of any real thing you can call veracity, morality; with dexterous putting on the cast-clothes of that real thing, and strutting about in them! What Legislating can you get out of a man in that fatal situation? None that will profit much, one would think! A Legislator who has left his veracity lying on the door-

[1] A committee of Commons appointed in 1842 to investigate charges of bribery against members from several constituencies.

threshold, he, why verily *he* — ought to be sent out to seek it again!

Heavens, what an improvement, were there once fairly, in Downing-street, an Election-Office opened, with a Tariff of Boroughs! Such and such a population, amount of property-tax, ground-rental, extent of trade; returns two Members, returns one Member, for so much money down: Ipswich so many thousands, Nottingham so many, — as they happened, one by one, to fall into this new Downing-street Schedule A! An incalculable improvement, in comparison: for now at least you have it fairly by length of purse, and leave the dishonesty, the impudence, the unveracity all handsomely aside. Length of purse and desire to be a Legislator ought to get a man into Parliament, not *with*, but if possible *without* the unveracity, the impudence and the dishonesty! Length of purse and desire, these are, as intrinsic qualifications, correctly equal to zero; but they are not yet *less* than zero, — as the smallest addition of that latter sort will make them!

And is it come to this? And does our venerable Parliament announce itself elected and eligible in this manner? Surely such a Parliament promulgates strange horoscopes of itself. What is to become of a Parliament elected or eligible in this manner? Unless Belial and Beelzebub[2] have got possession of the throne of this Universe, such Parliament is preparing itself for new Reform-bills. We shall have to try it by Chartism, or any conceivable *ism*, rather than put up with this! There is already in England 'religion' enough to get six hundred and fifty-eight Consulting Men[3] brought together who do *not* begin work with a lie in their mouth. Our poor old Parliament, thousands of years old, is still good for something, for several things; — though many are beginning to ask, with ominous anxiety, in these days: For what thing? But for whatever thing and things Parliament be good, indisputably it must start with other than a lie in its mouth! On the whole, a Parliament working with a lie in its mouth, will have to take itself away. To no Parliament or thing, that one has heard of, did this Universe ever long yield harbour on that footing. At all hours of the day and night, some Chartism is advancing, some armed Cromwell is advancing, to apprise such

---

[2] Two of the fallen angels in *Paradise Lost*. Elsewhere both names are used for Satan.

[3] The membership of Commons in 1842.

Parliament: "Ye are no Parliament. In the name of God, — go!"[4]

In sad truth, once more, how is our whole existence, in these present days, built on Cant, Speciosity, Falsehood, Dilettantism; with this one serious Veracity in it: Mammonism! Dig down where you will, through the Parliament-floor or elsewhere, how infallibly do you, at spade's depth below the surface, come upon this universal *Liars*-rock substratum! Much else is ornamental; true on barrel-heads, in pulpits, hustings, Parliamentary benches; but this is forever true and truest: "Money does bring money's worth; Put money in your purse."[5] Here, if nowhere else, is the human soul still in thorough earnest; sincere with a prophet's sincerity: and 'the Hell of the English,' as Sauerteig said, 'is the infinite terror of Not getting on, especially of Not making money.' With results!

To many persons the horoscope of Parliament is more interesting than to me: but surely all men with souls must admit that sending members to Parliament by bribery is an infamous solecism; an act entirely immoral, which no man can have to do with, more or less, but he will soil his fingers more or less. No Carlton Clubs, Reform Clubs,[6] nor any sort of clubs or creatures, or of accredited opinions or practices, can make a Lie Truth, can make Bribery a Propriety. The Parliament should really either punish and put away Bribery, or legalise it by some Office in Downing-street. As I read the Apocalypses,[7] a Parliament that can do neither of these things is not in a good way. — And yet, alas, what of Parliaments and their Elections? Parliamentary Elections are but the topmost ultimate outcome of an electioneering which goes on at all hours, in all places, in every meeting of two or more men. It is *we* that vote wrong, and teach the poor ragged Freemen of Boroughs to vote wrong. We pay respect to those worthy of no respect.

Is not Pandarus Dogdraught a member of select clubs, and admitted into the drawingrooms of men? Visibly to all persons he is of the offal of Creation; but he carries money in his purse, due lacker on his dog-visage, and it is believed will not steal spoons. The human species does not with one voice, like the

---

[4] Cromwell's reported words as he dissolved the Long Parliament, 1653.
[5] *Othello*, I.iii.345–360 passim.
[6] The Reform Club was established by liberal members of Parliament to help push the Reform Bill.
[7] Prophetic revelations.

Hebrew Psalmist, 'shun to sit'[8] with Dogdraught, refuse totally to dine with Dogdraught; men called of honour are willing enough to dine with him, his talk being lively, and his champagne excellent. We say to ourselves, "The man is in good society," — others have already voted for him; why should not I? We *forget* the indefeasible right of property that Satan has in Dogdraught, — we are not afraid to be near Dogdraught! It is we that vote wrong; blindly, nay with falsity prepense! It is we that no longer know the difference between Human Worth and Human Unworth; or feel that the one is admirable and alone admirable, the other detestable, damnable! How shall *we* find out a Hero and Viceking Samson with a maximum of two shillings in his pocket? We have no chance to do such a thing. We have got out of the Ages of Heroism, deep into the Ages of Flunkeyism, — and must return or die. What a noble set of mortals are we, who, because there is no Saint Edmund threatening us at the rim of the horizon, are not afraid to be whatever, for the day and hour, is smoothest for us!

And now, in good sooth, why should an indigent discerning Freeman give his vote without bribes? Let us rather honour the poor man that he does discern clearly wherein lies, for him, the true kernel of the matter. What is it to the ragged grimy Freeman of a Tenpound-Franchise Borough, whether Aristides Rigmarole Esq. of the Destructive, or the Hon. Alcides Dolittle of the Conservative Party be sent to Parliament; — much more, whether the two-thousandth part of them be sent, for that is the amount of his faculty in it? Destructive or Conservative, what will either of them destroy or conserve of vital moment to this Freeman? Has he found either of them care, at bottom, a sixpence for him or his interests, or those of his class or of his cause, or of any class or cause that is of much value to God or to man? Rigmarole and Dolittle have alike cared for themselves hitherto; and for their own clique, and self-conceited crotchets, — their greasy dishonest interests of pudding, or windy dishonest interests of praise; and not very perceptibly for any other interest whatever. Neither Rigmarole nor Dolittle will accomplish any good or any evil for this grimy Freeman, like giving him a five-pound note, or refusing to give it him. It will be smoothest to vote according to value received. That is the veritable fact; and he indigent, like others that are not indigent, acts conformably thereto.

Why, reader, truly, if they asked thee or me, Which way we

[8] Psalms 26:5.

meant to vote? — were it not our likeliest answer: Neither way! I, as a Tenpound Franchiser, will receive no bribe; but also I will not vote for either of these men. Neither Rigmarole nor Dolittle shall, by furtherance of mine, go and make laws for this country. I will have no hand in such a mission. How dare I! If other men cannot be got in England, a totally other sort of men, different as light is from dark, as star-fire is from street-mud, what is the use of votings, or of Parliaments in England? England ought to resign herself; there is no hope or possibility for England. If England cannot get her Knaves and Dastards 'arrested,' in some degree, but only get them 'elected,' what is to become of England?

I conclude, with all confidence, that England will verily have to put an end to briberies on her Election Hustings and elsewhere, at what cost soever; — and likewise that we, Electors and Eligibles, one and all of us, for our own behoof and hers, cannot too soon begin, at what cost soever, to put an end to *bribeabilities* in ourselves. The death-leprosy, attacked in this manner, by purifying lotions from without, and by rallying of the vital energies and purities from within, will probably abate somewhat! It has otherwise no chance to abate.

CHAPTER III

W HAT our Government can do in this grand Problem of the Working Classes of England? Yes, supposing the insane Corn-Laws totally abolished, all speech of them ended, and 'from ten to twenty years of new possibility to live and find wages' conceded us in consequence: What the English Government might be expected to accomplish or attempt towards rendering the existence of our Labouring Millions somewhat less anomalous, somewhat less impossible, in the years that are to follow those 'ten or twenty,' if either 'ten' or 'twenty' there be?

It is the most momentous question. For all this of the Corn-Law Abrogation, and what can follow therefrom, is but as the shadow on King Hezekiah's Dial:[1] the shadow has gone back twenty years; but will again, in spite of Free-Trades and Abrogations, travel forward its old fated way. With our present system of individual Mammonism, and Government by Laissez-faire, this Nation cannot live. And if, in the priceless interim, some new life and healing be not found, there is no second respite to be counted on. The shadow on the Dial advances thenceforth without pausing. What Government can do? This that they call 'Organising of Labour' is, if well understood, the Problem of the whole Future, for all who will in future pretend to govern men. But our first preliminary stage of it, How to deal with the Actual Labouring Millions of England? this is the imperatively pressing Problem of the Present, pressing with a truly fearful intensity and imminence in these very years and days. No Government can longer neglect it: once more, what can our Government do in it?

Governments are of various degrees of activity: some, altogether Lazy Governments, in 'free countries' as they are called, seem in these times almost to profess to do, if not nothing, one knows not at first what. To debate in Parliament, and gain

---

[1] 2 Kings 20:8–11.

majorities; and ascertain who shall be, with a toil hardly second
to Ixion's,[2] the Prime Speaker and Spoke-holder, and keep the
Ixion's-Wheel going, if not forward, yet round? Not altogether
so: — much, to the experienced eye, is not what it seems! Chancery and certain other Law-Courts seem nothing; yet in fact they
are, the worst of them, something: chimneys for the devilry and
contention of men to escape by; — a very considerable something!
Parliament too has its tasks, if thou wilt look; fit to wear out the
lives of toughest men. The celebrated Kilkenny Cats, through
their tumultuous congress, cleaving the ear of Night, could they
be said to do nothing? Hadst thou been of them, thou hadst
seen! The feline heart laboured, as with steam up — to the
bursting point; and death-doing energy nerved every muscle:
they had a work there; and did it! On the morrow, two tails
were found left, and peaceable annihilation; a neighbourhood
delivered from despair.[3]

Again, are not Spinning-Dervishes an eloquent emblem, significant of much? Hast thou noticed him, that solemn-visaged
Turk, the eyes shut; dingy wool mantle circularly hiding his
figure; — bell-shaped; like a dingy bell set spinning on the *tongue*
of it? By centrifugal force the dingy wool mantle heaves itself;
spreads more and more, like upturned cup widening into upturned saucer: thus spins he, to the praise of Allah and advantage
of mankind, fast and faster, till collapse ensue, and sometimes
death! —

A Government such as ours, consisting of from seven to eight
hundred Parliamentary Talkers, with their escort of Able Editors
and Public Opinion; and for head, certain Lords and Servants of
the Treasury, and Chief Secretaries and others, who find themselves at once Chiefs and No-Chiefs, and often commanded rather
than commanding, — is doubtless a most complicate entity, and
none of the alertest for getting on with business! Clearly enough,
if the Chiefs be not self-motive and what we call men, but mere
patient lay-figures without self-motive principle, the Government will not move anywhither; it will tumble disastrously, and
jumble, round its own axis, as for many years past we have seen
it do. — And yet a self-motive man who is not a lay-figure, place

[2] Ixion was bound to a fiery wheel in perpetuity for attempting to seduce
Hera.

[3] For an explanation of this striking instance of mutual annihilation, see
the *Oxford Companion to English Literature*.

him in the heart of what entity you may, will make it move more or less! The absurdest in Nature he will make a little *less* absurd; he. The unwieldiest he will make to move; — that is the use of his existing there. He will at least have the manfulness to depart out of it, if not; to say: "I cannot move in thee, and be a man; like a wretched drift-log dressed in man's clothes and minister's clothes, doomed to a lot baser than belongs to man, I will not continue with thee, tumbling aimless on the Mother of Dead Dogs here: — Adieu!"

For, on the whole, it is the lot of Chiefs everywhere, this same. No Chief in the most despotic country but was a Servant withal; at once an absolute commanding General, and a poor Orderly-Sergeant, ordered by the very men in the ranks, — obliged to collect the vote of the ranks too, in some articulate or inarticulate shape, and weigh well the same. The proper name of all Kings is Minister, Servant. In no conceivable Government can a lay-figure get forward! *This* Worker, surely he above all others has to 'spread out his Gideon's Fleece,' and collect the monitions of Immensity; the poor Localities, as we said, and parishes of Palace-yard[4] or elsewhere, having no due monition in them. A Prime Minister, even here in England, who shall dare believe the heavenly omens, and address himself like a man and hero to the great dumb-struggling heart of England; and speak out for it, and act out for it, the God's-Justice it is writhing to get uttered and perishing for want of, — yes, he too will see awaken round him, in passionate burning all-defiant loyalty, the heart of England, and such a 'support' as no Division-List or Parliamentary Majority was ever yet known to yield a man! Here as there, now as then, he who can and dare trust the heavenly Immensities, all earthly Localities are subject to him. We will pray for such a Man and First-Lord; — yes, and far better, we will strive and incessantly make ready, each of us, to be worthy to serve and second such a First-Lord! We shall then be as good as sure of his arriving; sure of many things, let him arrive or not.

Who can despair of Governments that passes a Soldiers' Guardhouse, or meets a redcoated man on the streets! That a body of men could be got together to kill other men when you bade them:

[4] The Westminster scene of a meeting of the London Working Men's Association, September, 1838: an important milestone in the history of Chartism.

this, *a priori,* does it not seem one of the impossiblest things? Yet look, behold it: in the stolidest of Donothing Governments, that impossibility is a thing done. See it there, with buff-belts, red coats on its back; walking sentry at guardhouses, brushing white breeches in barracks; an indisputable palpable fact. Out of grey Antiquity, amid all finance-difficulties, *scaccarium*-tallies, ship-monies, coat-and-conduct monies, and vicissitudes of Chance and Time, there, down to the present blessed hour, it is.

Often, in these painfully decadent and painfully nascent Times, with their distresses, inarticulate gaspings and 'impossibilities;' meeting a tall Lifeguardsman[5] in his snow-white trousers, or seeing those two statuesque Lifeguardsmen in their frowning bear-skins, pipe-clayed buckskins, on their coal-black sleek-fiery quad-rupeds, riding sentry at the Horse-Guards,[6] — it strikes one with a kind of mournful interest, how, in such universal down-rushing and wrecked impotence of almost all old institutions, this oldest Fighting Institution is still so young! Fresh-complexioned, firm-limbed, six feet by the standard, this fighting-man has verily been got up, and can fight. While so much has not yet got into being; while so much has gone gradually out of it, and become an empty Semblance or Clothes-suit; and highest king's-cloaks, mere chi-meras parading under them so long, are getting unsightly to the earnest eye, unsightly, almost offensive, like a costlier kind of scarecrow's-blanket, — here still is a reality!

The man in horsehair wig advances, promising that he will get me 'justice:' he takes me into Chancery Law-Courts, into decades, half-centuries of hubbub, of distracted jargon; and does *get* me — disappointment, almost desperation; and one refuge: that of dismissing him and his 'justice' altogether out of my head. For I have work to do; I cannot spend my decades in mere argu-ing with other men about the exact wages of my work: I will work cheerfully with no wages, sooner than with a ten-years gangrene or Chancery Lawsuit in my heart! He of the horsehair wig is a sort of failure; no substance, but a fond imagination of the mind. He of the shovel-hat, again, who comes forward professing that he will save my soul — O ye Eternities, of him in this place be absolute silence! — But he of the red coat, I say, is a success and no failure! He will veritably, if he get orders, draw out a long

[5] A member of the top-ranking corps of the British Army, whose peace-time assignment is to guard the sovereign.
[6] Headquarters of the London Military District in Whitehall.

sword and kill me. No mistake there. He is a fact and not a
shadow. Alive in this Year Forty-three, able and willing to do
his work. In dim old centuries, with William Rufus, William of
Ipres,[7] or far earlier, he began; and has come down safe so far.
Catapult has given place to cannon, pike has given place to mus-
ket, iron mail-shirt to coat of red cloth, saltpetre ropematch to
percussion cap; equipments, circumstances have all changed, and
again changed: but the human battle-engine, in the inside of
any or of each of these, ready still to do battle, stands there, six
feet in standard size. There are Pay-Offices, Woolwich Arsenals,
there is a Horse-Guards, War-Office, Captain-General; persuasive
Sergeants, with tap of drum, recruit in market-towns and villages;
— and, on the whole, I say, here is your actual drilled fighting-
man; here are your actual Ninety-thousand of such, ready to go
into any quarter of the world and fight!

Strange, interesting, and yet most mournful to reflect on. Was
this, then, of all the things mankind had some talent for, the
one thing important to learn well, and bring to perfection; this of
successfully killing one another? Truly you have learned it well,
and carried the business to a high perfection. It is incalculable
what, by arranging, commanding and regimenting, you can make
of men. These thousand straight-standing firm-set individuals,
who shoulder arms, who march, wheel, advance, retreat; and are,
for your behoof, a magazine charged with fiery death, in the most
perfect condition of potential activity: few months ago, till the
persuasive sergeant came, what were they? Multiform ragged
losels,[8] runaway apprentices, starved weavers, thievish valets; an
entirely broken population, fast tending towards the treadmill.
But the persuasive sergeant came; by tap of drum enlisted, or
formed lists of them, took heartily to drilling them; — and he and
you have made them this! Most potent, effectual for all work
whatsoever, is wise planning, firm combining and commanding
among men. Let no man despair of Governments who looks on
these two sentries at the Horse-Guards, and our United-Service
Clubs![9] I could conceive an Emigration Service, a Teaching Service, considerable varieties of United and Separate Services, of
the due thousands strong, all effective as this Fighting Service

[7] Commander of a Flemish mercenary force hired by King Stephen, 1135.
[8] Ne'er-do-wells.
[9] The United Service was a London social club for officers of the armed
forces.

is; all doing *their* work, like it; — which work, much more than
fighting, is henceforth the necessity of these New Ages we are
got into! Much lies among us, convulsively, nigh desperately
struggling to be born.

But mean Governments, as mean-limited individuals do, have
stood by the physically indispensable; have realised that and
nothing more. The Soldier is perhaps one of the most difficult
things to realise; but Governments, had they not realised him,
could not have existed: accordingly he is here. O Heavens, if
we saw an army ninety-thousand strong, maintained and fully
equipt, in continual real action and battle against Human Starvation, against Chaos, Necessity, Stupidity, and our real 'natural
enemies,' what a business were it! Fighting and molesting not
'the French,' who, poor men, have a hard enough battle of their
own in the like kind, and need no additional molesting from us;
but fighting and incessantly spearing down and destroying Falsehood, Nescience, Delusion, Disorder, and the Devil and his
Angels! Thou thyself, cultivated reader, hast done something
in that alone true warfare; but, alas, under what circumstances
was it? Thee no beneficent drill-sergeant, with any effectiveness,
would rank in line beside thy fellows; train, like a true didactic
artist, by the wit of all past experience, to do thy soldiering; encourage thee when right, punish thee when wrong, and everywhere with wise word-of-command say, Forward on this hand,
Forward on that! Ah, no: thou hadst to learn thy small-sword and
platoon exercise where and how thou couldst; to all mortals but
thyself it was indifferent whether thou shouldst ever learn it. And
the rations, and shilling a day, were they provided thee, — reduced as I have known brave Jean-Pauls,[10] learning their exercise,
to live on 'water *without* the bread?' The rations; or any furtherance of promotion to corporalship, lance-corporalship, or due cat-
o'-nine tails, with the slightest reference to thy deserts, were not
provided. Forethought, even as of a pipe-clayed drill-sergeant,
did not preside over thee. To corporalship, lance-corporalship,
thou didst attain; alas, also to the halberts and cat: but thy re-
warder and punisher seemed blind as the Deluge: neither lance-
corporalship, nor even drummer's cat, because both appeared
delirious, brought thee due profit.

It was well, all this, we know; — and yet it was not well! Forty

[10] Jean Paul Richter, early nineteenth-century German humorist, was
much admired and publicized by Carlyle.

soldiers, I am told, will disperse the largest Spitalfields mob:[11] forty to ten-thousand, that is the proportion between drilled and undrilled. Much there is which cannot yet be organised in this world; but somewhat also which can, somewhat also which must. When one thinks, for example, what Books are becoming for us, what Operative Lancashires are become; what a Fourth Estate,[12] and innumerable Virtualities not yet got to be Actualities are become and becoming, — one sees Organisms enough in the dim huge Future; and 'United Services' quite other than the redcoat one; and much, even in these years, struggling to be born!

Of Time-Bill, Factory-Bill[13] and other such Bills the present Editor has no authority to speak. He knows not, it is for others than he to know, in what specific ways it may be feasible to interfere, with Legislation, between the Workers and the Master-Workers; — knows only and sees, what all men are beginning to see, that Legislative interference, and interferences not a few are indispensable; that as a lawless anarchy of supply-and-demand, on market-wages alone, this province of things cannot longer be left. Nay interference has begun: there are already Factory Inspectors, — who seem to have no *lack* of work. Perhaps there might be Mine-Inspectors too: — might there not be Furrowfield Inspectors withal, and ascertain for us how on seven and sixpence a week a human family does live! Interference has begun; it must continue, must extensively enlarge itself, deepen and sharpen itself. Such things cannot longer be idly lapped in darkness, and suffered to go on unseen: the Heavens do see them; the curse, not the blessing of the Heavens is on an Earth that refuses to see them.

Again, are not Sanitary Regulations[14] possible for a Legislature? The old Romans had their Ædiles;[15] who would, I think, in direct contravention to supply-and-demand, have rigorously seen rammed up into total abolition many a foul cellar in our South-

[11] The silk weavers of Spitalfields, in northeastern London, were especially hard hit by the spread of machinery and often rioted.

[12] The press.

[13] Bills to limit the working day and regulate working and safety conditions in factories.

[14] To improve the water supply and sewage disposal arrangements, both of which were foul and responsible for frequent epidemics in London and the factory cities.

[15] Sanitary inspectors.

warks, Saint-Gileses,[16] and dark poison-lanes; saying sternly, "Shall a Roman man dwell there?" The Legislature, at whatever cost of consequences, would have had to answer, "God forbid!" — The Legislature, even as it now is, could order all dingy Manufacturing Towns to cease from their soot and darkness; to let in the blessed sunlight, the blue of Heaven, and become clear and clean; to burn their coal-smoke, namely, and make flame of it. Baths, free air, a wholesome temperature, ceilings twenty feet high, might be ordained, by Act of Parliament, in all establishments licensed as Mills. There are such Mills already extant; — honour to the builders of them! The Legislature can say to others: Go ye and do likewise;[17] better if you can.

Every toiling Manchester, its smoke and soot all burnt, ought it not, among so many world-wide conquests, to have a hundred acres or so of free greenfield, with trees on it, conquered, for its little children to disport in; for its all-conquering workers to take a breath of twilight air in? You would say so! A willing Legislature could say so with effect. A willing Legislature could say very many things! And to whatsoever 'vested interest,' or such like, stood up, gainsaying merely, "I shall lose profits," — the willing Legislature would answer, "Yes, but my sons and daughters will gain health, and life, and a soul." — "What is to become of our Cotton-trade?" cried certain Spinners, when the Factory-Bill was proposed; "What is to become of our invaluable Cotton-trade?" The Humanity of England answered steadfastly: "Deliver me these rickety perishing souls of infants, and let your Cotton-trade take its chance. God Himself commands the one thing; not God especially the other thing. We cannot have prosperous Cotton-trades at the expense of keeping the Devil a partner in them!" —

Bills enough, were the Corn-Law Abrogation Bill once passed, and a Legislature willing! Nay this one Bill, which lies yet unenacted, a right Education Bill,[18] is not this of itself the sure parent of innumerable wise Bills, — wise regulations, practical methods and proposals, gradually ripening towards the state of Bills? To irradiate with intelligence, that is to say, with order,

[16] Two particularly dreadful London slums.
[17] Luke 10:37.
[18] At the moment Carlyle was writing, Parliament was considering Sir James Graham's Factory Bill, certain clauses of which proposed to provide a modicum of education for factory children. Fierce opposition on religious grounds eventually forced the government to withdraw the clauses.

arrangement and all blessedness, the Chaotic, Unintelligent: how, except by educating, *can* you accomplish this? That thought, reflection, articulate utterance and understanding be awakened in these individual million heads, which are the atoms of your Chaos: there is no other way of illuminating any Chaos! The sum-total of intelligence that is found in it, determines the extent of order that is possible for your Chaos, — the feasibility and rationality of what your Chaos will dimly demand from you, and will gladly obey when proposed by you! It is an exact equation; the one accurately measures the other. — If the whole English People, during these 'twenty years of respite,' be not educated, with at least schoolmaster's educating, a tremendous responsibility, before God and men, will rest somewhere! How dare any man, especially a man calling himself minister of God, stand up in any Parliament or place, under any pretext or delusion, and for a day or an hour forbid God's Light to come into the world, and bid the Devil's Darkness continue in it one hour more! For all light and science, under all shapes, in all degrees of perfection, is of God; all darkness, nescience, is of the Enemy of God. 'The schoolmaster's creed is somewhat awry?' Yes, I have found few creeds entirely correct; few light-beams shining *white*, pure of admixture: but of all creeds and religions now or ever before known, was not that of thoughtless thriftless Animalism, of Distilled Gin, and Stupor and Despair, unspeakably the least orthodox? We will exchange *it* even with Paganism, with Fetishism; and, on the whole, must exchange it with something.

An effective 'Teaching Service' I do consider that there must be; some Education Secretary, Captain-General of Teachers, who will actually contrive to get us *taught*. Then again, why should there not be an 'Emigration Service,' and Secretary, with adjuncts, with funds, forces, idle Navy-ships, and ever-increasing apparatus; in fine an *effective system* of Emigration; so that, at length, before our twenty years of respite ended, every honest willing Workman who found England too strait, and the 'Organisation of Labour' not yet sufficiently advanced, might find likewise a bridge built to carry him into new Western Lands, there to 'organise' with more elbow-room some labour for himself? There to be a real blessing, raising new corn for us, purchasing new webs and hatchets from us; leaving us at least in peace; — instead of staying here to be a Physical-Force Chartist, unblessed and no blessing! Is it not scandalous to consider that a Prime

Minister could raise within the year, as I have seen it done, a
Hundred and Twenty Millions Sterling to shoot the French;[19]
and we are stopt short for want of the hundredth part of that
to keep the English living? The bodies of the English living; and
the souls of the English living: — these two 'Services,' an Education Service and an Emigration Service, these with others will
actually have to be organised!

A free bridge for Emigrants: why, we should then be on a par
with America itself, the most favoured of all lands that have no
government; and we should have, besides, so many traditions and
mementos of priceless things which America has cast away. We
could proceed deliberately to 'organise Labour,' not doomed to
perish unless we effected it within year and day; — every willing
Worker that proved superfluous, finding a bridge ready for him.
This verily will have to be done; the Time is big with this. Our
little Isle is grown too narrow for us; but the world is wide
enough yet for another Six Thousand Years. England's sure
markets will be among new Colonies of Englishmen in all quarters
of the Globe. All men trade with all men, when mutually convenient; and are even bound to do it by the Maker of men. Our
friends of China, who guiltily refused to trade, in these circumstances, — had we not to argue with them, in cannon-shot at
last, and convince them that they ought to trade![20] 'Hostile
Tariffs' will arise, to shut us out; and then again will fall, to let us
in: but the Sons of England, speakers of the English language
were it nothing more, will in all times have the ineradicable pre-
disposition to trade with England. Mycale was the *Pan-Ionian*,[21]
rendezvous of all the Tribes of Ion, for old Greece: why should
not London long continue the *All-Saxon-home*, rendezvous of all
the 'Children of the Harz-Rock,'[22] arriving, in select samples,
from the Antipodes and elsewhere, by steam and otherwise, to
the 'season' here! — What a Future; wide as the world, if we have
the heart and heroism for it, — which, by Heaven's blessing, we
shall:

[19] Carlyle seems to exaggerate. The largest annual revenue during the
Napoleonic Wars was collected in 1814; it amounted to £105,600,000
from all sources. The war expenditure in that year was £71,700,000.

[20] The Treaty of Nanking (1842) opened five Chinese ports to English
merchants.

[21] Festival of the twelve Ionian cities, held on Mt. Mycale.

[22] Carlyle implies, erroneously, that the Anglo-Saxon race came from the
Harz Mountain region of Germany.

Keep not standing fixed and rooted,
Briskly venture, briskly roam;
Head and hand, where'er thou foot it,
And stout heart are still at home.

In what land the sun does visit,
Brisk are we, whate'er betide:
To give space for wandering is it
That the world was made so wide.[23]

Fourteen hundred years ago, it was by a considerable 'Emigration Service,' never doubt it, by much enlistment, discussion and apparatus, that we ourselves arrived in this remarkable Island, — and got into our present difficulties among others!

It is true the English Legislature, like the English People, is of slow temper; essentially conservative. In our wildest periods of reform, in the Long Parliament itself,[24] you notice always the invincible instinct to hold fast by the Old; to admit the *minimum* of New; to expand, if it be possible, some old habit or method, already found fruitful, into new growth for the new need. It is an instinct worthy of all honour; akin to all strength and all wisdom. The Future hereby is not dissevered from the Past, but based continuously on it; grows with all the vitalities of the Past, and is rooted down deep into the beginnings of us. The English Legislature is entirely repugnant to believe in 'new epochs.' The English Legislature does not occupy itself with epochs; has, indeed, other business to do than looking at the Time-Horologe and hearing it tick! Nevertheless new epochs do actually come; and with them new imperious peremptory necessities; so that even an English Legislature has to look up, and admit, though with reluctance, that the hour has struck. The hour having struck, let us not say 'impossible:' — it will have to be possible! 'Contrary to the habits of Parliament, the habits of Government?' Yes: but did any Parliament or Government ever sit in a Year Forty-three before? One of the most original, unexampled years and epochs; in several important respects, totally unlike any other! For Time, all-edacious and all-feracious, does run on: and the Seven Sleepers, awakening hungry after a hun-

[23] Goethe, *Wilhelm Meister.* (C.)
[24] It sat from 1640 to 1653.

dred years,[25] find that it is not their old nurses who can now give them suck!

For the rest, let not any Parliament, Aristocracy, Millocracy, or Member of the Governing Class, condemn with much triumph this small specimen of 'remedial measures;' or ask again, with the least anger, of this Editor,[26] What is to be done, How that alarming problem of the Working Classes is to be managed? Editors are not here, foremost of all, to say How. A certain Editor thanks the gods that nobody pays him three hundred thousand pounds a year, two hundred thousand, twenty thousand, or any similar sum of cash for saying How; — that his wages are very different, his work somewhat fitter for him. An Editor's stipulated work is to apprise *thee* that it must be done. The 'way to do it,' is to try it, knowing that thou shalt die if it be not done. There is the bare back, there is the web of cloth; thou shalt cut me a coat to cover the bare back, thou whose trade it is. 'Impossible?' Hapless Fraction, dost thou discern Fate there, half unveiling herself in the gloom of the future, with her gibbet-cords, her steel-whips, and very authentic Tailor's Hell; waiting to see whether it is 'possible?' Out with thy scissors, and cut that cloth or thy own windpipe!

[25] Legend says that seven persecuted third-century Christians, walled into a cave by the tyrant Decius, slept two hundred years and awoke in the reign of Theodosius II.
[26] Carlyle.

CHAPTER IV

IF I believed that Mammonism with its adjuncts was to continue henceforth the one serious principle of our existence, I should reckon it idle to solicit remedial measures from any Government, the disease being insusceptible of remedy. Government can do much, but it can in no wise do all. Government, as the most conspicuous object in Society, is called upon to give signal of what shall be done; and, in many ways, to preside over, further, and command the doing of it. But the Government cannot do, by all its signalling and commanding, what the Society is radically indisposed to do. In the long-run every Government is the exact symbol of its People, with their wisdom and unwisdom; we have to say, Like People like Government. — The main substance of this immense Problem of Organising Labour, and first of all of Managing the Working Classes, will, it is very clear, have to be solved by those who stand practically in the middle of it; by those who themselves work and preside over work. Of all that can be enacted by any Parliament in regard to it, the germs must already lie potentially extant in those two Classes, who are to obey such enactment. A Human Chaos *in* which there is no light, you vainly attempt to irradiate by light shed *on* it: order never can arise there.

But it is my firm conviction that the 'Hell of England' will *cease* to be that of 'not making money;' that we shall get a nobler Hell and a nobler Heaven! I anticipate light *in* the Human Chaos, glimmering, shining more and more; under manifold true signals from without That light shall shine. Our deity no longer being Mammon, — O Heavens, each man will then say to himself: "Why such deadly haste to make money? I shall not go to Hell, even if I do not make money! There is another Hell, I am told!" Competition, at railway-speed, in all branches of commerce and work will then abate: — good felt-hats for the head, in every sense, instead of seven-feet lath-and-plaster hats on wheels, will then be discoverable! Bubble-periods,[1] with their panics and commercial crises, will again become infrequent; steady modest industry will take the place of gambling speculation. To be a noble Master, among noble Workers, will again be the first ambition with some few; to be a rich Master only the second. How the Inventive Genius of England, with the whirr of its bobbins and billy-rollers shoved somewhat into the backgrounds of the brain, will contrive and devise, not cheaper produce exclusively, but fairer distribution of the produce at its present cheapness! By degrees, we shall again have a Society with something of Heroism in it, something of Heaven's Blessing on it; we shall again have, as my German friend asserts, 'instead of Mammon-Feudalism with unsold cotton-shirts and Preservation of the Game, noble just Industrialism and Government by the Wisest!'

It is with the hope of awakening here and there a British man to know himself for a man and divine soul, that a few words of parting admonition, to all persons to whom the Heavenly Powers have lent power of any kind in this land, may now be addressed. And first to those same Master-Workers, Leaders of Industry; who stand nearest, and in fact powerfulest, though not most prominent, being as yet in too many senses a Virtuality rather than an Actuality.

The Leaders of Industry, if Industry is ever to be led, are virtually the Captains of the World; if there be no nobleness in them, there will never be an Aristocracy more. But let the Captains of Industry consider: once again, are they born of other clay than the old Captains of Slaughter; doomed forever to be no Chivalry, but a mere gold-plated *Doggery,* — what the French well name *Canaille,* 'Doggery' with more or less gold carrion at its disposal? Captains of Industry are the true Fighters, henceforth recognisable as the only true ones: Fighters against Chaos, Necessity and the Devils and Jötuns; and lead on Mankind in that great, and alone true, and universal warfare; the stars in their courses fighting for them,[2] and all Heaven and all Earth saying audibly, Well-done! Let the Captains of Industry retire into their own hearts, and ask solemnly, If there is nothing but vulturous hunger, for fine wines, valet reputation and gilt carriages, discoverable there? Of hearts made by the Almighty God

---

[1] Periods of mania for financial speculation; a reference to the "South Sea bubble" which burst, ruinously, in 1720.
[2] Judges 5:20.

I will not believe such a thing. Deep-hidden under wretchedest godforgetting Cants, Epicurisms, Dead-Sea Apisms; forgotten as under foulest fat Lethe mud and weeds, there is yet, in all hearts born into this God's-World, a spark of the Godlike slumbering. Awake, O nightmare sleepers; awake, arise, or be forever fallen! This is not playhouse poetry; it is sober fact. Our England, our world cannot live as it is. It will connect itself with a God again, or go down with nameless throes and fire-consummation to the Devils. Thou who feelest aught of such a Godlike stirring in thee, any faintest intimation of it as through heavy-laden dreams, follow *it*, I conjure thee. Arise, save thyself, be one of those that save thy country.

Bucaniers, Chactaw Indians, whose supreme aim in fighting is that they may get the scalps, the money, that they may amass scalps and money: out of such came no Chivalry, and never will! Out of such came only gore and wreck, infernal rage and misery; desperation quenched in annihilation. Behold it, I bid thee, behold there, and consider! What is it that thou have a hundred thousand-pound bills laid up in thy strong-room, a hundred scalps hung up in thy wigwam? I value not them or thee. Thy scalps and thy thousand-pound bills are as yet nothing, if no nobleness from within irradiate them; if no Chivalry, in action, or in embryo ever struggling towards birth and action, be there.

Love of men cannot be bought by cash-payment; and without love, men cannot endure to be together. You cannot lead a Fighting World without having it regimented, chivalried: the thing, in a day, becomes impossible; all men in it, the highest at first, the very lowest at last, discern consciously, or by a noble instinct, this necessity. And can you any more continue to lead a Working World unregimented, anarchic? I answer, and the Heavens and Earth are now answering, No! The thing becomes not 'in a day' impossible; but in some two generations it does. Yes, when fathers and mothers, in Stockport hunger-cellars, begin to eat their children, and Irish widows have to prove their relationship by dying of typhus-fever; and amid Governing 'Corporations of the Best and Bravest,'[3] busy to preserve their game by 'bushing,' dark millions of God's human creatures start up in mad Chartisms, impracticable Sacred-Months,[4] and Manchester Insurrections; —

[3] "What is an Aristocracy? A corporation of the Best, of the Bravest." (*Chartism*, Ch. vi.)

[4] The name, reminiscent of the French revolutionary calendar, used by the Chartists in urging a month-long general strike.

and there is a virtual Industrial Aristocracy as yet only half-alive, spellbound amid money-bags and ledgers; and an actual Idle Aristocracy seemingly near dead in somnolent delusions, in trespasses and double-barrels; 'sliding,' as on inclined-planes, which every new year they *soap* with new Hansard's-jargon under God's sky, and so are 'sliding' ever faster, towards a 'scale' and balance-scale whereon is written *Thou art found Wanting:*[5] — in such days, after a generation or two, I say, it does become, even to the low and simple, very palpably impossible! No Working World, any more than a Fighting World, can be led on without a noble Chivalry of Work, and laws and fixed rules which follow out of that, — far nobler than any Chivalry of Fighting was. As an anarchic multitude on mere Supply-and-demand, it is becoming inevitable that we dwindle in horrid suicidal convulsion, and self-abrasion, frightful to the imagination, into *Chactaw* Workers. With wigwam and scalps, — with palaces and thousand-pound bills; with savagery, depopulation, chaotic desolation! Good Heavens, will not one French Revolution and Reign of Terror suffice us, but must there be two? There will be two if needed; there will be twenty if needed; there will be precisely as many as are needed. The Laws of Nature will have themselves fulfilled. That is a thing certain to me.

Your gallant battle-hosts and work-hosts, as the others did, will need to be made loyally yours; they must and will be regulated, methodically secured in their just share of conquest under you; — joined with you in veritable brotherhood, sonhood, by quite other and deeper ties than those of temporary day's wages! How would mere redcoated regiments, to say nothing of chivalries, fight for you, if you could discharge them on the evening of the battle, on payment of the stipulated shillings, — and they discharge you on the morning of it! Chelsea Hospitals,[6] pensions, promotions, rigorous lasting covenant on the one side and on the other, are indispensable even for a hired fighter. The Feudal Baron, much more, — how could he subsist with mere temporary mercenaries round him, at sixpence a day; ready to go over to the other side, if sevenpence were offered? He could not have subsisted; — and his noble instinct saved him from the necessity of even trying! The Feudal Baron had a Man's Soul in him; to

---

[5] Daniel 5:27.

[6] Chelsea Hospital was founded by Charles II as a home for aged or disabled soldiers.

which anarchy, mutiny, and the other fruits of temporary mercenaries, were intolerable: he had never been a Baron otherwise,
but had continued a Chactaw and Bucanier. He felt it precious,
and at last it became habitual, and his fruitful enlarged existence
included it as a necessity, to have men round him who in heart
loved him; whose life he watched over with rigour yet with love;
who were prepared to give their life for him, if need came. It
was beautiful; it was human! Man lives not otherwise, nor can
live contented, anywhere or anywhen. Isolation is the sum-total
of wretchedness to man. To be cut off, to be left solitary: to have
a world alien, not your world; all a hostile camp for you; not a
home at all, of hearts and faces who are yours, whose you are!
It is the frightfulest enchantment; too truly a work of the Evil
One. To have neither superior, nor inferior, nor equal, united
manlike to you. Without father, without child, without brother.
Man knows no sadder destiny. 'How is each of us,' exclaims Jean
Paul, 'so lonely, in the wide bosom of the All!'[7] Encased each as
in his transparent 'ice-palace;'[8] our brother visible in his, making
signals and gesticulations to us; — visible, but forever unattainable: on his bosom we shall never rest, nor he on ours. It was not
a God that did this; no![9]

Awake, ye noble Workers, warriors in the one true war: all
this must be remedied. It is you who are already half-alive, whom
I will welcome into life; whom I will conjure in God's name to
shake off your enchanted sleep, and live wholly! Cease to count
scalps, gold-purses; not in these lies your or our salvation. Even
these, if you count only these, will not long be left. Let bucaniering be put far from you; alter, speedily abrogate all laws of the
bucaniers, if you would gain any victory that shall endure. Let
God's justice, let pity, nobleness and manly valour, with more
gold-purses or with fewer, testify themselves in this your brief
Life-transit to all the Eternities, the Gods and Silences. It is to
you I call; for ye are not dead, ye are already half-alive: there
is in you a sleepless dauntless energy, the prime-matter of all
nobleness in man. Honour to you in your kind. It is to you I
call: ye know at least this, That the mandate of God to His

[7] Richter's *Siebenkäs,* quoted in Carlyle's second essay on him.

[8] The Empress Anna of Russia caused such a palace to be built on the
Neva during the severe winter of 1740.

[9] Contrast Matthew Arnold on the same theme of the isolation of men:
"A god, a god, their severance rul'd!" ("Yes, in the sea of life enisled":
one of the "Marguerite" poems.)

creature man is: Work! The future Epic of the World rests not with those that are near dead, but with those that are alive, and those that are coming into life.

Look around you. Your world-hosts are all in mutiny, in confusion, destitution; on the eve of fiery wreck and madness! They will not march farther for you, on the sixpence a day and supply-and-demand principle: they will not; nor ought they, nor can they. Ye shall reduce them to order, begin reducing them. To order, to just subordination; noble loyalty in return for noble guidance. Their souls are driven nigh mad; let yours be sane and ever saner. Not as a bewildered bewildering mob; but as a firm regimented mass, with real captains over them, will these men march any more. All human interests, combined human endeavours, and social growths in this world, have, at a certain stage of their development, required organising: and Work, the grandest of human interests, does now require it.

God knows, the task will be hard: but no noble task was ever easy. This task will wear away your lives, and the lives of your sons and grandsons: but for what purpose, if not for tasks like this, were lives given to men? Ye shall cease to count your thousand-pound scalps, the noble of you shall cease! Nay the very scalps, as I say, will not long be left if you count only these. Ye shall cease wholly to be barbarous vulturous Chactaws, and become noble European Nineteenth-Century Men. Ye shall know that Mammon, in never such gigs and flunky 'respectabilities,'[10] is not the alone God; that of himself he is but a Devil, and even a Brute-god.

Difficult? Yes, it will be difficult. The short-fibre cotton; that too was difficult. The waste cotton-shrub, long useless, disobedient, as the thistle by the wayside, — have ye not conquered it; made it into beautiful bandana webs; white woven shirts for men; bright-tinted air-garments wherein flit goddesses? Ye have

---

[10] Carlyle was bemused by, and repeatedly alluded to, a supposed exchange during the trial of Thurtell, the murderer, in 1824: Q. "What sort of person was Mr. Weare?" A. "Mr. Weare was respectable." Q. "What do you mean by respectability?" A. "He kept a gig." A gig (a light two-wheeled, one-horse carriage) became Carlyle's abiding symbol of fatuous middle-class status-consciousness. Actually, the reports of the trial contain no such dialogue. Carlyle's source, a writer in the *Quarterly Review* (XXXVII [1828], 15n.), who admitted he was quoting from memory, may have been thinking of a sentence in the *Morning Chronicle*'s coverage of the trial: "He always maintained an appearance of respectability and kept a gig."

shivered mountains asunder, made the hard iron pliant to you as soft putty: the Forest-giants, Marsh-jötuns bear sheaves of golden grain; Ægir the Sea-demon[11] himself stretches his back for a sleek highway to you, and on Firehorses and Windhorses ye career.[12] Ye are most strong. Thor red-bearded, with his blue sun-eyes, with his cheery heart and strong thunder-hammer, he and you have prevailed. Ye are most strong, ye Sons of the icy North, of the far East, — far marching from your rugged Eastern Wildernesses, hitherward from the grey Dawn of Time! Ye are Sons of the *Jötun*-land; the land of Difficulties Conquered. Difficult? You must try this thing. Once try it with the understanding that it will and shall have to be done. Try it as ye try the paltrier thing, making of money! I will bet on you once more, against all Jötuns, Tailor-gods, Double-barrelled Law-wards, and Denizens of Chaos whatsoever!

[11] In Norse mythology, an amiable giant.
[12] 2 Kings 2:11.

CHAPTER V

STANDING on the threshold, nay as yet outside the threshold, of a 'Chivalry of Labour,' and an immeasurable Future which it is to fill with fruitfulness and verdant shade; where so much has not yet come even to the rudimental state, and all speech of positive enactments were hasardous in those who know this business only by the eye, — let us here hint at simply one widest universal principle, as the basis from which all organisation hitherto has grown up among men, and all henceforth will have to grow: The principle of Permanent Contract instead of Temporary.

Permanent not Temporary: — you do not hire the mere red-coated fighter by the day, but by the score of years! Permanence, persistance is the first condition of all fruitfulness in the ways of men. The 'tendency to persevere,' to persist in spite of hindrances, discouragements and 'impossibilities:' it is this that in all things distinguishes the strong soul from the weak; the civilised burgher from the nomadic savage, — the Species Man from the Genus Ape! The Nomad has his very house set on wheels; the Nomad, and in a still higher degree the Ape, are all for 'liberty;' the privilege to flit continually is indispensable for them. Alas, in how many ways, does our humour, in this swift-rolling self-abrading Time, shew itself nomadic, apelike; mournful enough to him that looks on it with eyes! This humour will have to abate; it is the first element of all fertility in human things, that such 'liberty' of apes and nomads do by freewill or constraint abridge itself, give place to a better. The civilised man lives not in wheeled houses. He builds stone castles, plants lands, makes lifelong marriage-contracts; — has long-dated hundred-fold possessions, not to be valued in the money-market; has pedigrees, libraries, law-codes; has memories and hopes, even for this Earth, that reach over thousands of years. Life-long marriage-contracts: how much preferable were year-long or month-long — to the nomad or ape!

Month-long contracts please me little, in any province where there can by possibility be found virtue enough for more. Month-long contracts do not answer well even with your house-servants; the liberty on both sides to change every month is growing very apelike, nomadic; — and I hear philosophers predict that it will alter, or that strange results will follow: that wise men, pestered with nomads, with unattached ever-shifting spies and enemies rather than friends and servants, will gradually, weighing sub-stance against semblance, with indignation, dismiss such, down almost to the very shoeblack, and say, "Begone; I will serve myself rather, and have peace!" Gurth was hired for life to Cedric, and Cedric to Gurth. O Anti-Slavery Convention, loud-sounding long-eared Exeter-Hall[1] — But in thee too is a kind of instinct towards justice, and I will complain of nothing. Only, black Quashee[2] over the seas being once sufficiently attended to, wilt thou not perhaps open thy dull sodden eyes to the 'sixty-thousand valets in London itself who are yearly dismissed to the streets, to be what they can, when the season ends;' — or to the hungerstricken, pallid, *yellow*-coloured 'Free Labourers' in Lancashire, Yorkshire, Buckinghamshire, and all other shires! These Yellow-coloured, for the present, absorb all my sympathies: if I had a Twenty Millions, with Model-Farms and Niger Expeditions, it is to these that I would give it! Quashee has already victuals, clothing; Quashee is not dying of such despair as the yellow-coloured pale man's. Quashee, it must be owned, is hitherto a kind of block-head. The Haiti Duke of Marmalade,[3] educated now for almost half a century, seems to have next to no sense in him. Why, in one of those Lancashire Weavers, dying of hunger, there is more thought and heart, a greater arithmetical amount of misery and desperation, than in whole gangs of Quashees. It must be owned, thy eyes are of the sodden sort; and with thy emancipations, and thy twenty-millionings and long-eared clamourings, thou, like Robespierre with his pasteboard *Etre Suprême,* threatenest to become a bore to us, *Avec ton Etre Suprême tu commences m'embêter!*[4] —

[1] A London auditorium used for mass meetings of religious and charitable societies.

[2] General name for a Negro.

[3] Carlyle's derogatory invention.

[4] Under Robespierre, the French revolutionary convention affirmed the existence of a supreme being. Later, on the "Feast of the Supreme Being" (1794), pasteboard figures of "Atheism," "Anarchy," and similar enemies of the state — at that moment — were burned. Cf. *The French Revolution,* XIX.iv.

In a Printed Sheet of the assiduous, much-abused, and truly useful Mr. Chadwick's,[5] containing queries and responses from far and near, as to this great question, 'What is the effect of Education on workingmen, in respect of their value as mere workers?' the present Editor, reading with satisfaction a decisive unanimous verdict as to Education, reads with inexpressible interest this special remark, put in by way of marginal incidental note, from a practical manufacturing Quaker, whom, as he is anonymous, we will call Friend Prudence. Prudence keeps a thousand workmen; has striven in all ways to attach them to him; has provided conversational soirées; playgrounds, bands of music for the young ones; went even 'the length of buying them a drum:' all which has turned out to be an excellent investment. For a certain person, marked here by a black stroke, whom we shall name Blank, living over the way, — he also keeps somewhere about a thousand men; but has done none of these things for them, nor any other thing, except due payment of the wages by supply-and-demand. Blank's workers are perpetually getting into mutiny, into broils and coils: every six months, we suppose, Blank has a strike; every one month, every day and every hour, they are fretting and obstructing the shortsighted Blank; pilfering from him, wasting and idling for him, omitting and committing for him. "I would not," says Friend Prudence, "exchange my workers for his *with seven thousand pounds to boot.*"[6]

Right, O honourable Prudence; thou art wholly in the right: Seven thousand pounds even as a matter of profit for this world, nay for the mere cash-market of this world! And as a matter of profit not for this world only, but for the other world and all worlds, it outweighs the Bank of England! — Can the sagacious reader descry here, as it were the outmost inconsiderable rock-ledge of a universal rock-foundation, deep once more as the Centre of the World, emerging so, in the experience of this good Quaker, through the Stygian mud-vortexes and general Mother of Dead Dogs, whereon, for the present, all swags and insecurely hovers, as if ready to be swallowed?

Some Permanence of Contract is already almost possible; the principle of Permanence, year by year, better seen into and elaborated, may enlarge itself, expand gradually on every side into a

[5] Edwin Chadwick, leader in the Victorian campaign to improve public health in the towns.
[6] Report on the Training of Pauper Children (1841), p. 18. (C.)

system. This once secured, the basis of all good results were laid. Once permanent, you do not quarrel with the first difficulty on your path, and quit it in weak disgust; you reflect that it cannot be quitted, that it must be conquered, a wise arrangement fallen on with regard to it. Ye foolish Wedded Two, who have quarrelled, between whom the Evil Spirit has stirred up transient strife and bitterness, so that 'incompatibility' seems almost nigh, ye are nevertheless the Two who, by long habit, were it by nothing more, do best of all others suit each other: it is expedient for your own two foolish selves, to say nothing of the infants, pedigrees and public in general, that ye agree again; that ye put away the Evil Spirit, and wisely on both hands struggle for the guidance of a Good Spirit!

The very horse that is permanent, how much kindlier do his rider and he work, than the temporary one, hired on any hack principle yet known! I am for permanence in all things, at the earliest possible moment, and to the latest possible. Blessed is he that continueth where he is. Here let us rest, and lay out seed-fields; here let us learn to dwell. Here, even here, the orchards that we plant will yield us fruit; the acorns will be wood and pleasant umbrage, if we wait. How much grows everywhere, if we do but wait! Through the swamps we will shape causeways, force purifying drains; we will learn to thread the rocky inaccessibilities; and beaten tracks, worn smooth by mere travelling of human feet, will form themselves. Not a difficulty but can transfigure itself into a triumph; not even a deformity but, if our own soul have imprinted worth on it, will grow dear to us. The sunny plains and deep indigo transparent skies of Italy are all indifferent to the great sick heart of a Sir Walter Scott: on the back of the Apennines, in wild spring weather, the sight of bleak Scotch firs, and snow-spotted heath and desolation, brings tears into his eyes.[7]

O unwise mortals that forever change and shift, and say, Yonder, not Here! Wealth richer than both the Indies lies everywhere for man, if he will endure. Not his oaks only and his fruit-trees, his very heart roots itself wherever he will abide; — roots itself, draws nourishment from the deep fountains of Universal Being! Vagrant Sam-Slicks,[8] who rove over the Earth doing 'strokes of trade,' what wealth have they? Horseloads, shiploads

---

[7] Lockhart's *Life of Scott*. (C.)

[8] Sam Slick was a shrewd Yankee peddler in T. C. Haliburton's *The Sayings and Doings of Sam Slick of Slicksville* (1837–40).

of white or yellow metal: in very sooth, what *are* these? Slick rests nowhere, he is homeless. He can build stone or marble houses; but to continue in them is denied him. The wealth of a man is the number of things which he loves and blesses, which he is loved and blessed by! The herdsman in his poor clay shealing,[9] where his very cow and dog are friends to him, and not a cataract but carries memories for him, and not a mountain-top but nods old recognition: his life, all encircled as in blessed mother's-arms, is it poorer than Slick's with the ass-loads of yellow metal on his back? Unhappy Slick! Alas, there has so much grown nomadic, apelike, with us: so much will have, with whatever pain, repugnance and 'impossibility,' to alter itself, to fix itself again, — in some wise way, in any not delirious way!

A question arises here: Whether, in some ulterior, perhaps some not far-distant stage of this 'Chivalry of Labour,' your Master-Worker may not find it possible, and needful, to grant his Workers permanent *interest* in his enterprise and theirs? So that it become, in practical result, what in essential fact and justice it ever is, a joint enterprise; all men, from the Chief Master down to the lowest Overseer and Operative, economically as well as loyally concerned for it? — Which question I do not answer. The answer, near or else far, is perhaps, Yes; — and yet one knows the difficulties. Despotism is essential in most enterprises; I am told, they do not tolerate 'freedom of debate' on board a Seventy-four![10] Republican senate and *plebiscita* would not answer well in Cotton-Mills. And yet observe there too: Freedom, not nomad's or ape's Freedom, but man's Freedom; this is indispensable. We must have it, and will have it! To reconcile Despotism with Freedom: — well, is that such a mystery? Do you not already know the way? It is to make your Despotism *just*. Rigorous as Destiny; but just too, as Destiny and its Laws. The Laws of God: all men obey these, and have no 'Freedom' at all but in obeying them. The way is already known, part of the way; — and courage and some qualities are needed for walking on it!

[9] Hut.
[10] A warship mounting seventy-four guns.

CHAPTER VI

A MAN with fifty, with five hundred, with a thousand pounds a day, given him freely, without condition at all, — on condition, as it now runs, that he will sit with his hands in his pockets and do no mischief, pass no Corn-Laws or the like, — he too, you would say, is or might be a rather strong Worker! He is a Worker with such tools as no man in this world ever before had. But in practice, very astonishing, very ominous to look at, he proves not a strong Worker; — you are too happy if he will prove but a No-worker, do nothing, and not be a Wrong-worker.

You ask him, at the year's end: "Where is your three-hundred thousand pound; what have you realised to us with that?" He answers, in indignant surprise: "Done with it? Who are you that ask? I have eaten it; I and my flunkeys, and parasites, and slaves two-footed and four-footed, in an ornamental manner; and I am here alive by it; *I* am realised by it to you!" — It is, as we have often said, such an answer as was never before given under this Sun. An answer that fills me with boding apprehension, with foreshadows of despair. O stolid Use-and-wont of an atheistic Half-century, O Ignavia,[1] Tailor-godhood, soul-killing Cant, to what passes art thou bringing us! — Out of the loud-piping whirl-wind, audibly to him that has ears, the Highest God is again announcing in these days: "Idleness shall not be." God has said it, man cannot gainsay.

Ah, how happy were it, if he this Aristocrat Worker would, in like manner, see *his* work and do it! It is frightful seeking another to do it for him. Guillotines, Meudon Tanneries, and half-a-million men shot dead, have already been expended in that business; and it is yet far from done. This man too is something; nay he is a great thing. Look on him there: a man of manful aspect; something of the 'cheerfulness of pride' still lingering in him. A free air of graceful stoicism, of easy silent dignity sits well on him; in his heart, could we reach it, lie elements of generosity,

---

[1] Idleness.

self-sacrificing justice, true human valour. Why should he, with such appliances, stand an incumbrance in the Present; perish disastrously out of the Future! From no section of the Future would we lose these noble courtesies, impalpable yet all-controlling; these dignified reticences, these kingly simplicities; — lose aught of what the fruitful Past still gives us token of, memento of, in this man. Can we not save him: — can he not help us to save him! A brave man he too; had not undivine Ignavia, Hearsay, Speech without meaning, — had not Cant, thousandfold Cant within him and around him, enveloping him like choke-damp, like thick Egyptian darkness, thrown his soul into asphyxia, as it were extinguished his soul; so that he sees not, hears not, and Moses and all the Prophets address him in vain.[2]

Will he awaken, be alive again, and have a soul; or is this death-fit very death? It is a question of questions, for himself and for us all! Alas, is there no noble work for this man too? Has he not thick-headed ignorant boors; lazy, enslaved farmers; weedy lands? Lands! Has he not weary heavy-laden ploughers of land; immortal souls of men, ploughing, ditching, day-drudging; bare of back, empty of stomach, nigh desperate of heart; and none peaceably to help them but he, under Heaven? Does he find, with his three hundred thousand pounds, no noble thing trodden down in the thoroughfares, which it were godlike to help up? Can he do nothing for his Burns but make a Gauger of him; lionise him, bedinner him, for a foolish while; then whistle him down the wind, to desperation and bitter death? — His work too is difficult, in these modern, far-dislocated ages. But it may be done; it may be tried; — it must be done.

A modern Duke of Weimar, not a god he either, but a human duke, levied, as I reckon, in rents and taxes and all incomings whatsoever, less than several of our English Dukes do in rent alone. The Duke of Weimar, with these incomings, had to govern, judge, defend, every way administer *his* Dukedom. He does all this as few others did: and he improves lands besides all this, makes river-embankments, maintains not soldiers only but Universities and Institutions; — and in his Court were these four men: Wieland, Herder, Schiller, Goethe.[3] Not as parasites, which was impossible; not as table-wits and poetic Katerfeltoes;[4] but as

---

[2] Luke 16:29.

[3] These four celebrated men of letters were patronized by Karl August, Duke of Weimar.

[4] Gustavus Katerfelto was a late eighteenth-century quack and conjuror.

noble Spiritual Men working under a noble Practical Man. Shielded by him from many miseries; perhaps from many short-comings, destructive aberrations. Heaven had sent, once more, heavenly Light into the world; and this man's honour was that he gave it welcome. A new noble kind of Clergy, under an old but still noble kind of King! I reckon that this one Duke of Weimar did more for the Culture of his Nation than all the English Dukes and *Duces* now extant, or that were extant since Henry the Eighth gave them the Church Lands to eat, have done for theirs! — I am ashamed, I am alarmed for my English Dukes: what word have I to say?

If our Actual Aristocracy, appointed 'Best-and-Bravest,' will be wise, how inexpressibly happy for us! If not, — the voice of God from the whirlwind is very audible to me. Nay, I will thank the Great God, that He has said, in whatever fearful ways, and just wrath against us, "Idleness shall be no more!" Idleness? The awakened soul of man, all but the asphyxied soul of man, turns from it as from worse than death. It is the life-in-death of Poet Coleridge.[5] That fable of the Dead-Sea Apes ceases to be a fable. The poor Worker starved to death is not the saddest of sights. He lies there, dead on his shield; fallen down into the bosom of his old Mother; with haggard pale face, sorrow-worn, but stilled now into divine peace, silently appeals to the Eternal God and all the Universe, — the most silent, the most eloquent of men.

Exceptions, — ah yes, thank Heaven, we know there are exceptions. Our case were too hard, were there not exceptions, and partial exceptions not a few, whom we know, and whom we do not know. Honour to the name of Ashley,[6] — honour to this and the other valiant Abdiel,[7] found faithful still; who would fain, by work and by word, admonish their Order not to rush upon destruction! These are they who will, if not save their Order, postpone the wreck of it; — by whom, under blessing of the Upper Powers, 'a quiet euthanasia spread over generations, in-stead of a swift torture-death concentred into years,' may be brought about for many things. All honour and success to these. The noble man can still strive nobly to save and serve his Order;

[5] Most of Coleridge's mature years were spent in non-productivity, despite his great philosophical intellect.

[6] Lord Ashley, later the Earl of Shaftesbury, who ceaselessly worked to improve, by legislation and other means, the condition of the factory slaves.

[7] Cf. *Paradise Lost*, V.896. Carlyle may be referring to Sir James Graham, then Peel's home secretary, whose Factory Bill (see above, p. 262, n.18) reflected Ashley's humanitarian purposes.

— at lowest, he can remember the precept of the Prophet: "Come out of her, my people; come out of her!"[8]

To sit idle aloft, like living statues, like absurd Epicurus'-gods,[9] in pampered isolation, in exclusion from the glorious fateful battlefield of this God's-World: it is a poor life for a man, when all Upholsterers and French-Cooks have done their utmost for it! — Nay, what a shallow delusion is this we have all got into. That any man should or can keep himself apart from men, have 'no business' with them, except a cash-account 'business!' It is the silliest tale a distressed generation of men ever took to telling one another. Men cannot live isolated: we *are* all bound together, for mutual good or else for mutual misery, as living nerves in the same body. No highest man can disunite himself from any lowest. Consider it. Your poor 'Werter blowing out his distracted existence because Charlotte will not have the keeping thereof:'[10] this is no peculiar phasis; it is simply the highest expression of a phasis traceable wherever one human creature meets another! Let the meanest crookbacked Thersites teach the supremest Agamemnon that he actually does not reverence him, the supremest Agamemnon's eyes flash fire responsive; a real pain, and partial insanity, has seized Agamemnon.[11] Strange enough: a many-counselled Ulysses is set in motion by a scoundrel-blockhead; plays tunes, like a barrel-organ, at the scoundrel-blockhead's touch, — has to snatch, namely, his sceptre cudgel, and weal the crooked back with bumps and thumps! Let a chief of men reflect well on it. Not in having 'no business' with men, but in having no unjust business with them, and in *having* all manner of true and just business, can either his or their blessedness be found possible, and this waste world become, for both parties, a home and peopled garden.

Men do reverence men. Men do worship in that 'one temple of the world,' as Novalis calls it, the Presence of a Man! Hero-worship, true and blessed, or else mistaken, false and accursed, goes on everywhere and everywhen. In this world there is one godlike thing, the essence of all that was or ever will be of godlike in this world: the veneration done to Human Worth by the hearts

[8] Jeremiah 51:45.

[9] According to Epicurus, the gods could not concern themselves with mortal affairs.

[10] Cf. Goethe, *The Sorrows of Young Werther.*

[11] Cf. *Iliad*, II.212 ff.

of men. Hero-worship, in the souls of the heroic, of the clear and wise, — it is the perpetual presence of Heaven in our poor Earth: when it is not there, Heaven is veiled from us; and all is under Heaven's ban and interdict, and there is no worship, or worth-ship, or worth or blessedness in the Earth any more! —

Independence, 'lord of the lion-heart and eagle-eye,'[12] — alas, yes, he is a lord we have got acquainted with in these late times: a very indispensable lord, for spurning off with due energy in-numerable sham-superiors, Tailor-made: honour to him, entire success to him! Entire success is sure to him. But he must not stop there, at that small success, with his eagle-eye. He has now a second far greater success to gain: to seek out his real superiors, whom not the Tailor but the Almighty God has made superior to him, and see a little what he will do with these! Rebel against these also? Pass by with minatory eagle-glance, with calm-snif-fing mockery, or even without any mockery or sniff, when these present themselves? The lion-hearted will never dream of such a thing. Forever far be it from him! His minatory eagle-glance will veil itself in softness of the dove: his lion-heart will become a lamb's; all is just indignation changed into just reverence, dis-solved in blessed floods of noble humble love, how much heaven-lier than any pride, nay, if you will, how much prouder! I know him, this lion-hearted, eagle-eyed one; have met him, rushing on, 'with bosom bare,' in a very distracted dishevelled manner, the times being hard; — and can say, and guarantee on my life, That in him is no rebellion; that in him is the reverse of rebellion, the needful preparation for obedience. For if you do mean to obey God-made superiors, your first step is to sweep out the Tailor-made ones; order them, under penalties, to vanish, to make ready for vanishing!

Nay, what is best of all, he cannot rebel, if he would. Superiors whom God has made for us we cannot order to withdraw! Not in the least. No Grand-Turk himself,[13] thickest-quilted tailor-made Brother of the Sun and Moon can do it: but an Arab Man, in cloak of his own clouting; with black beaming eyes, with flaming sovereign-heart direct from the centre of the Universe; and also, I am told, with terrible 'horse-shoe vein' of swelling wrath in his brow, and lightning (if you will not have it as light) tingling

[12] Smollett, "Ode to Independence."
[13] The Ottoman Sultan.

through every vein of him, — he rises; says authoritatively: "Thickest-quilted Grand-Turk, tailor-made Brother of the Sun and Moon, No: — *I* withdraw not; thou shalt obey me or withdraw!" And so accordingly it is: thickest-quilted Grand-Turks and all their progeny, to this hour, obey that man in the remarkablest manner; preferring *not* to withdraw.

O brother, it is an endless consolation to me, in this disorganic, as yet so quack-ridden, what you may well call hag-ridden and hell-ridden world, to find that disobedience to the Heavens, when they send any messenger whatever, is and remains impossible. It cannot be done; no Turk grand or small can do it. 'Shew the dullest clodpole,' says my invaluable German friend, 'shew the haughtiest featherhead, that a soul higher than himself is here; were his knees stiffened into brass, he must down and worship.'

CHAPTER VII

THE GIFTED

Yes, in what tumultuous huge anarchy soever a Noble human Principle may dwell and strive, such tumult is in the way of being calmed into a fruitful sovereignty. It is inevitable. No Chaos can continue chaotic with a soul in it. Besouled with earnest human Nobleness, did not slaughter, violence and fire-eyed fury, grow into a Chivalry; into a blessed Loyalty of Governor and Governed? And in Work, which is of itself noble, and the only true fighting, there shall be no such possibility? Believe it not; it is incredible; the whole Universe contradicts it. Here too the Chactaw Principle will be subordinated; the Man Principle will, by degrees, become superior, become supreme.

I know Mammon too; Banks-of-England, Credit-Systems, world-wide possibilities of work and traffic; and applaud and admire them. Mammon is like Fire; the usefulest of all servants, if the frightfulest of all masters! The Cliffords, Fitzadelms[1] and Chivalry Fighters 'wished to gain victory,' never doubt it: but victory, unless gained in a certain spirit, was no victory; defeat, sustained in a certain spirit, was itself victory. I say again and again, had they counted the scalps alone, they had continued Chactaws, and no Chivalry or lasting victory had been. And in Industrial Fighters and Captains is there no nobleness discoverable? To them, alone of men, there shall forever be no blessedness but in swollen coffers? To see beauty, order, gratitude, loyal human hearts around them, shall be of no moment; to see fuliginous deformity, mutiny, hatred and despair, with the addition of half a million guineas, shall be better? Heaven's blessedness not there; Hell's cursedness, and your half-million bits of metal, a substitute for that! Is there no profit in diffusing Heaven's blessedness, but only in gaining gold? — If so, I apprise the Mill-owner and Millionaire, that he too must prepare for vanishing; that neither is *he*

---

[1] The Cliffords were a great family on the Scottish border in medieval and Elizabethan times. "Fitzadelms" has been taken to refer to William Fitzald-helm, steward of Henry II and governor of Ireland.

born to be of the sovereigns of this world; that he will have to be
trampled and chained down in whatever terrible ways, and brass-
collared safe, among the born thralls of this world! We cannot
have *Canailles* and Doggeries that will not make some Chivalry of
themselves: our noble Planet is impatient of such; in the end,
totally intolerant of such!

For the Heavens, unwearying in their bounty, do send other
souls into this world, to whom yet, as to their forerunners, in Old
Roman, in Old Hebrew and all noble times, the omnipotent
guinea is, on the whole, an impotent guinea. Has your half-dead
avaricious Corn-Law Lord, your half-alive avaricious Cotton-Law
Lord, never seen one such? Such are, not one, but several; are,
and will be, unless the gods have doomed this world to swift dire
ruin. These are they, the elect of the world; the born champions,
strong men, and liberatory Samsons of this poor world: whom the
poor Delilah-world will not always shear of their strength and
eyesight, and set to grind in darkness at *its* poor gin-wheel![2] Such
souls are, in these days, getting somewhat out of humour with the
world. Your very Byron, in these days, is at least driven mad;
flatly refuses fealty to the world. The world with its injustices,
its golden brutalities, and dull yellow guineas, is a disgust to such
souls: the ray of Heaven that is in them does at least pre-doom
them to be very miserable here. Yes: — and yet all misery is
faculty misdirected, strength that has not yet found its way. The
black whirlwind is mother of the lightning. No *smoke*, in any
sense, but can become flame and radiance! Such soul, once
graduated in Heaven's stern University, steps out superior to your
guinea.

Dost thou know, O sumptuous Corn-Lord, Cotton-Lord, O mutinous Trades-Unionist, gin-vanquished, undeliverable; O much-
enslaved World, — this man is not a slave with thee! None of
thy promotions is necessary for him. His place is with the stars
of Heaven: to thee it may be momentous, to him it is indifferent,
whether thou place him in the lowest hut, or forty feet higher at
the top of thy stupendous high tower, while here on Earth. The
joys of Earth that are precious, they depend not on thee and thy
promotions. Food and raiment, and, round a social hearth, souls
who love him, whom he loves: these are already his. He wants
none of thy rewards; behold also, he fears none of thy penalties.
Thou canst not answer even by killing him: the case of Anax-

2 Judges 16.

archus[3] thou canst kill; but the self of Anaxarchus, the word or act of Anaxarchus, in no wise whatever. To this man death is not a bugbear; to this man life is already as earnest and awful, and beautiful and terrible, as death.

Not a May-game is this man's life; but a battle and a march, a warfare with principalities and powers. No idle promenade through fragrant orange-groves and green flowery spaces, waited on by the choral Muses and the rosy Hours:[4] it is a stern pilgrimage through burning sandy solitudes, through regions of thick-ribbed ice. He walks among men; loves men, with inexpressible soft pity, — as they *cannot* love him: but his soul dwells in solitude, in the uttermost parts of Creation. In green oases by the palm-tree wells, he rests a space; but anon he has to journey forward, escorted by the Terrors and the Splendours, the Archdemons and Archangels. All Heaven, all Pandemonium are his escort. The stars keen-glancing, from the Immensities, send tidings to him; the graves, silent with their dead, from the Eternities. Deep calls for him unto Deep.[5]

Thou, O World, how wilt thou secure thyself against this man? Thou canst not hire him by thy guineas; nor by thy gibbets and law-penalties restrain him. He eludes thee like a Spirit. Thou canst not forward him, thou canst not hinder him. Thy penalties, thy poverties, neglects, contumelies: behold, all these are good for him. Come to him as an enemy; turn from him as an unfriend; only do not this one thing, — infect him not with thy own delusion: the benign Genius, were it by very death, shall guard him against this! — What wilt thou do with him? He is above thee, like a god. Thou, in thy stupendous three-inch pattens,[6] art under him. He is thy born king, thy conqueror and supreme lawgiver: not all the guineas and cannons, and leather and prunella,[7] under the sky can save thee from him. Hardest thickskinned Mammonworld, ruggedest Caliban shall obey him, or become not Caliban but a cramp.[8] Oh, if in this man, whose eyes can flash Heaven's lightning, and make all Calibans into a cramp, there dwelt not, as the essence of his very being, a God's Justice, human Nobleness,

[3] A Greek philosopher whom the tyrant of Cyprus caused to be put to death by pounding in a mortar.

[4] The Horae, Greek goddesses of the seasons and hours.

[5] Psalms 42:7.

[6] Elevated wooden shoes, to keep the feet from the mud.

[7] A heavy silk or woollen material.

[8] Cf. *The Tempest*, I.ii.325, V.i.286.

Veracity and Mercy, — I should tremble for the world. But his strength, let us rejoice to understand, is even this: The quantity of Justice, of Valour and Pity that is in him. To hypocrites and tailored quacks in high places, his eyes are lightning; but they melt in dewy pity softer than a mother's to the downpressed, maltreated; in his heart, in his great thought, is a sanctuary for all the wretched. This world's improvement is forever sure.

'Man of Genius?' Thou hast small notion, meseems, O Mecænas[9] Twiddledee, of what a Man of Genius is! Read in thy New Testament and elsewhere, — if, with floods of mealymouthed inanity, with miserable froth-vortices of Cant now several centuries old, thy New Testament is not all bedimmed for thee. *Canst* thou read in thy New Testament at all? The Highest Man of Genius, knowest thou him; Godlike and a God to this hour? His crown a Crown of Thorns? Thou fool, with *thy* empty Godhoods, Apotheoses *edgegilt;* the Crown of Thorns made into a poor jewel-room crown, fit for the head of blockheads; the bearing of the Cross changed to a riding in the Long-Acre Gig! Pause in thy mass-chantings, in thy litanyings, and Calmuck prayings by machinery; and pray, if noisily, at least in a more human manner. How with thy rubrics and dalmatics,[10] and clothwebs and cobwebs, and with thy stupidities and grovelling baseheartedness, hast thou hidden the Holiest into all but invisibility! —

'Man of Genius:' O Mecænas Twiddledee, hast thou any notion what a Man of Genius is? Genius is 'the inspired gift of God.' It is the clearer presence of God Most High in a man. Dim, potential in all men; in this man it has become clear, actual. So says John Milton,[11] who ought to be a judge; so answer him the Voices of all Ages and all Worlds. Wouldst thou commune with such a one, — *be* his real peer then: does that lie in thee? Know thyself and thy real and thy apparent place, and know him and his real and his apparent place, and act in some noble conformity therewith. What! The star-fire of the Empyrean shall eclipse itself, and illuminate magic-lanterns to amuse grown children? He, the god-inspired, is to twang harps for thee, and blow through scrannel-pipes; soothe thy sated soul with visions of new, still wider Eldorados, Houri[12] Paradises, richer Lands of Cockaigne?[13]

---

[9] The patron of Horace and Virgil.
[10] Gowns worn by deacons and bishops.
[11] In *The Reason of Church Government,* Book II.
[12] Beautiful girls who adorn the Muslim Paradise.
[13] Lands of idle bliss.

Brother, this is not he; this is a counterfeit, this twangling, jangling, vain, acrid, scrannel-piping man. Thou dost well to say with sick Saul, "It is naught, such harping!" — and in sudden rage grasp thy spear, and try if thou canst pin such a one to the wall.[14] King Saul was mistaken in his man, but thou art right in thine. It is the due of such a one: nail him to the wall, and leave him there. So ought copper shillings to be nailed on counters; copper geniuses on walls, and left there for a sign! —

I conclude that the Men of Letters too may become a 'Chivalry,' an actual instead of a virtual Priesthood, with result immeasurable, — so soon as there is nobleness in themselves for that. And, to a certainty, not sooner! Of intrinsic Valetisms you cannot, with whole Parliaments to help you, make a Heroism. Doggeries never so gold-plated, Doggeries never so escutcheoned, Doggeries never so diplomaed, bepuffed, gas-lighted, continue Doggeries, and must take the fate of such.

[14] Saul did not say this; but see 1 Samuel 18:10–11.

CHAPTER VIII

THE DIDACTIC

CERTAINLY it were a fond imagination to expect that any preaching of mine could abate Mammonism; that Bobus of Houndsditch will love his guineas less, or his poor soul more, for any preaching of mine! But there is one Preacher who does preach with effect, and gradually persuade all persons: his name is Destiny, is Divine Providence, and his Sermon the inflexible Course of Things. Experience does take dreadfully high school-wages; but he teaches like no other!

I revert to Friend Prudence the good Quaker's refusal of 'seven thousand pounds to boot.' Friend Prudence's practical conclusion will, by degrees, become that of all rational practical men what-sover. On the present scheme and principle, Work cannot continue. Trades' Strikes, Trades' Unions, Chartisms; mutiny, squalor, rage and desperate revolt, growing ever more desperate, will go on their way. As dark misery settles down on us, and our refuges of lies fall in pieces one after one, the hearts of men, now at last serious, will turn to refuges of truth. The eternal stars shine out again, so soon as it is dark *enough*.

Begirt with desperate Trades' Unionism and Anarchic Mutiny, many an Industrial *Law-ward*, by and by, who has neglected to make laws and keep them, will be heard saying to himself: "Why have I realised five hundred thousand pounds? I rose early and sat late, I toiled and moiled, and in the sweat of my brow and of my soul I strove to gain this money, that I might become conspicuous, and have some honour among my fellow-creatures. I wanted them to honour me, to love me. The money is here, earned with my best lifeblood: but the honour? I am encircled with squalor, with hunger, rage, and sooty desperation. Not honoured, hardly even envied; only fools and the flunkey-species so much as envy me. I am conspicuous, — as a mark for curses and brickbats. What good is it? My five hundred scalps hang here in my wigwam: would to Heaven I had sought something else than the scalps; would to Heaven I had been a Christian

Fighter, not a Chactaw one! To have ruled and fought not in a
Mammonish but in a Godlike spirit; to have had the hearts of the
people bless me, as a true ruler and captain of my people; to
have felt my own heart bless me, and that God above instead of
Mammon below was blessing me, — this had been something.
Out of my sight, ye beggarly five hundred scalps of banker's-
thousands: I will try for something other, or account my life a
tragical futility!"

Friend Prudence's 'rock-ledge,' as we called it, will gradually
disclose itself to many a man; to all men. Gradually, assaulted
from beneath and from above, the Stygian mud-deluge of Laissez-
faire, Supply-and-demand, Cash-payment the one Duty, will
abate on all hands; and the everlasting mountain-tops, and secure
rock-foundations that reach to the centre of the world, and rest on
Nature's self, will again emerge, to found on, and to build on.
When Mammon-worshippers here and there begin to be God-
worshippers, and bipeds-of-prey become men, and there is a Soul
felt once more in the huge-pulsing elephantine mechanic Animalism of this Earth, it will be again a blessed Earth.

"Men cease to regard money?" cries Bobus of Houndsditch:
"What else do all men strive for? The very Bishop informs me
that Christianity cannot get on without a minimum of Four thousand five hundred in its pocket. Cease to regard money? That
will be at Doomsday in the afternoon!" — O Bobus, my opinion
is somewhat different. My opinion is, that the Upper Powers
have not yet determined on destroying this Lower World. A
respectable, ever-increasing minority, who do strive for something
higher than money, I with confidence anticipate; ever-increasing,
till there be a sprinkling of them found in all quarters, as salt of
the Earth[1] once more. The Christianity that cannot get on without
a minimum of Four thousand five hundred, will give place to
something better that can. Thou wilt not join our small minority,
thou? Not till Doomsday in the afternoon? Well; then, at least,
thou wilt join it, thou and the majority in mass!

But truly it is beautiful to see the brutish empire of Mammon
cracking everywhere; giving sure promise of dying, or of being
changed. A strange, chill, almost ghastly dayspring strikes up in
Yankeeland itself: my Transcendental friends announce there, in
a distinct, though somewhat lankhaired, ungainly manner, that
the Demiurgus Dollar is dethroned; that new unheard-of De-

[1] Matthew 5:13.

miurgusships, Priesthoods, Aristocracies, Growths and Destruc-
tions, are already visible in the grey of coming Time.[2] Chronos[3]
is dethroned by Jove; Odin by St. Olaf:[4] the Dollar cannot rule
in Heaven forever. No; I reckon, not. Socinian Preachers quit
their pulpits in Yankeeland, saying, "Friends, this is all gone to a
coloured cobweb, we regret to say!" — and retire into the fields to
cultivate onion-beds, and live frugally on vegetables.[5] It is very
notable. Old godlike Calvinism declares that its old body is now
fallen to tatters, and done; and its mournful ghost, disembodied,
seeking new embodiment, pipes again in the winds; — a ghost
and spirit as yet, but heralding new Spirit-worlds, and better
Dynasties than the Dollar one.

Yes, here as there, light is coming into the world; men love not
darkness, they do love light. A deep feeling of the eternal nature
of Justice looks out among us everywhere, — even through the
dull eyes of Exeter Hall; an unspeakable religiousness struggles,
in the most helpless manner, to speak itself, in Puseyisms and the
like. Of our Cant, all condemnable, how much is not condemnable without pity; we had almost said, without respect!
The *in*articulate worth and truth that is in England goes down
yet to the Foundations.

Some 'Chivalry of Labour,' some noble Humanity and practical
Divineness of Labour, will yet be realised on this Earth. Or why
will; why do we pray to Heaven, without setting our own shoulder
to the wheel? The Present, if it will have the Future accomplish,
shall itself commence. Thou who prophesiest, who believest,
begin thou to fulfil. Here or nowhere, now equally as at any
time! That outcast help-needing thing or person, trampled down
under vulgar feet or hoofs, no help 'possible' for it, no prize
offered for the saving of it, — canst not thou save it, then, without
prize? Put forth thy hand, in God's name; know that 'impossible,'
where Truth and Mercy and the everlasting Voice of Nature
order, has no place in the brave man's dictionary. That when all
men have said "Impossible," and tumbled noisily elsewhither, and
thou alone art left, then first thy time and possibility have come.
It is for thee now: do thou that, and ask no man's counsel, but thy

[2] Carlyle kept up with American developments through his "Transcendental friend" Emerson (who, incidentally, wrote a review of this book in
the *Dial* for July, 1843).
[3] The head of the older dynasty of Greek gods. Correct spelling: *Cronus.*
[4] A Viking converted to Christianity, early eleventh century.
[5] The Brook Farm experiment had begun in 1841.

own only and God's. Brother, thou hast possibility in thee for much: the possibility of writing on the eternal skies the record of a heroic life. That noble downfallen or yet unborn 'Impossibility,' thou canst lift it up, thou canst, by thy soul's travail, bring it into clear being. That loud inane Actuality, with millions in its pocket, too 'possible' that, which rolls along there, with quilted trumpeters blaring round it, and all the world escorting it as mute or vocal flunkey, — escort it not thou; say to it, either nothing, or else deeply in thy heart: "Loud-blaring Nonentity, no force of trumpets, cash, Long-Acre art, or universal flunkeyhood of men, makes thee an Entity; thou art a *Non*entity, and deceptive Simulacrum, more accursed than thou seemest. Pass on in the Devil's name, unworshipped by at least one man, and leave the thoroughfare clear!"

Not on Ilion's or Latium's[6] plains; on far other plains and places henceforth can noble deeds be now done. Not on Ilion's plains; how much less in Mayfair's drawingrooms! Not in victory over poor brother French or Phrygians;[7] but in victory over Frost-jötuns, Marsh-giants, over demons of Discord, Idleness, Injustice, Unreason, and Chaos come again.[8] None of the old Epics is longer possible. The Epic of French and Phrygians was comparatively a small Epic: but that of Flirts and Fribbles, what is that? A thing that vanishes at cock-crowing, — that already begins to scent the morning air![9] Game-preserving Aristocracies, let them 'bush' never so effectually, cannot escape the Subtle Fowler.[10] Game seasons will be excellent, and again will be indifferent, and by and by they will not be at all. The Last Partridge of England, of an England where millions of men can get no corn to eat, will be shot and ended. Aristocracies with beards on their chins will find other work to do than amuse themselves with trundling-hoops.

But it is to you, ye Workers, who do already work, and are as grown men, noble and honourable in a sort, that the whole world calls for new work and nobleness. Subdue mutiny, discord, wide-spread despair, by manfulness, justice, mercy and wisdom. Chaos is dark, deep as Hell; let light be, and there is instead a green

---

[6] Troy's or Rome's.
[7] Ancient race of Asia Minor.
[8] *Othello*, III.iii.92.
[9] *Hamlet*, I.v.58.
[10] Proverbs 6:5, Psalms 91:3, and elsewhere.

flowery World. O, it is great, and there is no other greatness. To make some nook of God's Creation a little fruitfuler, better, more worthy of God; to make some human hearts a little wiser, manfuler, happier, — more blessed, less accursed! It is work for a God. Sooty Hell of mutiny and savagery and despair can, by man's energy, be made a kind of Heaven; cleared of its soot, of its mutiny, of its need to mutiny; the everlasting arch of Heaven's azure overspanning *it* too, and its cunning mechanisms and tall chimney-steeples, as a birth of Heaven; God and all men looking on it well pleased.

Unstained by wasteful deformities, by wasted tears or heart's-blood of men, or any defacement of the Pit, noble fruitful Labour, growing ever nobler, will come forth, — the grand sole miracle of Man; whereby Man has risen from the low places of this Earth, very literally, into divine Heavens. Ploughers, Spinners, Builders; Prophets, Poets, Kings; Brindleys and Goethes, Odins and Arkwrights; all martyrs, and noble men, and gods are of one grand Host: immeasurable; marching ever forward since the Beginnings of the World. The enormous, all-conquering, flame-crowned Host, noble every soldier in it; sacred, and alone noble. Let him who is not of it hide himself; let him tremble for himself. Stars at every button cannot make him noble; sheaves of Bath-garters,[11] nor bushels of Georges; nor any other contrivance but manfully enlisting in it, valiantly taking place and step in it. O Heavens, will he not bethink himself; he too is so needed in the Host! It were so blessed, thrice-blessed, for himself and for us all! In hope of the Last Partridge, and some Duke of Weimar among our English Dukes, we will be patient yet a while.

> The Future hides in it.
> Good hap and sorrow;
> We press still thorow,
> Nought that abides in it
> Daunting us, — onward.

THE END

[11] For the sake of the symbol, Carlyle combines two separate royal orders.